For Reference

Not to be taken from this room

Who's Who
IN LESBIAN AND
GAY WRITING

THE ROUTLEDGE WHO'S WHO SERIES

Accessible, authoritative and enlightening, these are the definitive
biographical guides to a diverse range of subjects drawn from literature
and the arts, history and politics, religion and mythology.

Who's Who in Ancient Egypt
Michael Rice

Who's Who in the Ancient Near East
Gwendolyn Leick

Who's Who in Christianity
Lavinia Cohn-Sherbok

Who's Who in Classical Mythology
Michael Grant and John Hazel

*Who's Who in Contemporary Gay
and Lesbian History*
Edited by Robert Aldrich and
Garry Wotherspoon

*Who's Who in Contemporary Women's
Writing*
Edited by Jane Eldridge Miller

*Who's Who in Contemporary
World Theatre*
Edited by Daniel Meyer-Dinkegräfe

Who's Who in Dickens
Donald Hawes

Who's Who in Europe 1450–1750
Henry Kamen

Who's Who in Gay and Lesbian History
Edited by Robert Aldrich and
Garry Wotherspoon

Who's Who in the Greek World
John Hazel

Who's Who in Jewish History
Joan Comay, new edition revised by Lavinia
Cohn-Sherbok

Who's Who in Military History
John Keegan and Andrew Wheatcroft

Who's Who in Modern History
Alan Palmer

Who's Who in Nazi Germany
Robert S. Wistrich

Who's Who in the New Testament
Ronald Brownrigg

Who's Who in Non-Classical Mythology
Egerton Sykes, new edition revised
by Alan Kendall

Who's Who in the Old Testament
Joan Comay

Who's Who in the Roman World
John Hazel

Who's Who in Russia since 1900
Martin McCauley

Who's Who in Shakespeare
Peter Quennell and Hamish Johnson

*Who's Who of Twentieth-Century
Novelists*
Tim Woods

Who's Who in Twentieth-Century Warfare
Spencer Tucker

*Who's Who in Twentieth-Century
World Poetry*
Edited by Mark Willhardt and
Alan Michael Parker

Who's Who in World War One
John Bourne

Who's Who in World War Two
Edited by John Keegan

Who's Who
IN LESBIAN AND
GAY WRITING

Gabriele Griffin

London and New York

First published 2002
by Routledge
11 New Fetter Lane, London EC4P 4EE

Simultaneously published in the USA and Canada
by Routledge
29 West 35th Street, New York, NY 10001

Routledge is an imprint of the Taylor & Francis Group

Typeset in Sabon by Taylor & Francis Books Ltd
Printed and bound in Great Britain by MPG Books Ltd, Bodmin

British Library Cataloguing in Publication Data
A catalogue record for this book is available from the British Library

Library of Congress Cataloging in Publication Data
A catalog record for this book has been requested

ISBN 0–415–15984–9   8-28-03 doo

Contents

Introduction

The last forty years have seen an explosion in the scholarship on lesbian and gay writing. Changes in attitudes towards homosexuality and in relevant legislation, especially in many Anglophone, Northern, and Western countries, have promoted a much greater knowledge of lesbian and gay cultural production. This has resulted in the increasing documentation of that production through the publication and translation of many primary texts, images, etc., the construction of reference works, and the gradual building up of a body of scholarship and research on lesbian and gay culture. There is thus by now, in many countries, a well-established sense of a lesbian and gay literary history, tradition, heritage, even canon; in many countries, but not in all. The uneven distribution of that knowledge was brought home to me when I asked an Italian friend, a lesbian literary scholar, about lesbian and gay writing in Italy. She did not know of any and stated that in Italy lesbians and gays are still very much closeted, and that writers would not, for example, disclose their sexual preferences. Similarly, a lesbian friend from Belgium who runs a documentation centre sent me, when I asked for information about lesbian and gay writing, a list of four writers, which began with Radclyffe Hall and had no Belgian names included. The point is that the establishment of a lesbian and gay literary or cultural history is in a state of uneven development across different countries and, furthermore, that even within one country potential lesbian and gay readers may not know of the lesbian and gay work produced in their own country, among other things because of small print runs, limited outlets for distribution, an absence of the 'mainstreaming' of lesbian and gay writing or any public debates about lesbian and gay culture, and many other reasons. However, what is also very clear is that there is, and has been, much lesbian and gay work 'out there' that remains unacknowledged and unrecorded.

Lesbian and gay writing – what does this phrase mean and how is it used in this volume? At the beginning of the twenty-first century identity and sexuality are both terms that have become extensively problematized through the arrivals of both postmodern and queer theory. Identity and sexuality are no longer regarded as fixed, stable entities; instead it has become increasingly clear that categories such as 'lesbian' and 'gay' are subject to change. Indeed, some of the most interesting research in the area of lesbian and gay studies has been concerned with questions of the historical specificity and therefore changeability of how 'lesbian' and 'gay' are used. It is not just these specific terms, but also other words for lesbians and gays that were employed prior to those terms becoming fashionable. The shifts in meaning in the terms have become increasingly dated as researchers have begun to understand how lesbians and gays were described in the seventeenth century, for instance, even as the words 'lesbian' and 'gay' were not yet themselves being used. Part of the research on lesbian and gay history, then, has been the uncovering and recovery of lesbian and gay identities from times when those terms themselves were not in use.

In this volume 'lesbian' and 'gay' refer to female and male same-sex love respectively. During the 1980s and 1990s there were extensive debates among lesbians about the kind of love one might be talking about here; was it sexual or 'merely' romantic, that is not involving sex, or...? These debates themselves have long prior histories in theories attempting to explain same-sex love, to determine its origins and its manifestations, its rootedness or otherwise in the biological (a position generally more popular amongst gay men than among lesbians) or in the socio-cultural, the issue of its being a phase in an individual's life, or an immutable condition, etc. These debates have been fuelled and contained through the arrival of postmodernism and of queer, in which contexts the acceptance of a certain degree of pluralism and mutability in identity and sexuality, or identi*ties* and sexuali*ties*, has led to a more nuanced understanding of the terms 'lesbian' and 'gay' than might otherwise be the case. It is now understood that, for many lesbians and gays, identity is directly related to its sexual expression, that it is frequently permanent, and that it is differentiable in all sorts of ways from heterosexuality. Similarly, it is also understood that people may identify as lesbian or gay without that identification finding sexual expression through same-sex sexual activity. Lastly, and importantly, since the 1990s the question about the relationship between morphological make-up (i.e. the bodily self), gender as the enactment of a morphological and socio-cultural identity, and sexuality understood as sexual activity (whether lived out or not, as in the case of celibates) has come more and more to the fore as the seeming certainty of morphology has given way to more complex understandings of the relationship between body, identity, and sexual activity. Both 'queer' and developments in biotechnologies, as well as gene mapping, have contributed to this change. The change itself underwrites the notion of the acculturation and provisionality of identity at the same time as (and paradoxically perhaps) especially among some gay men there has been a continuing and indeed increasing insistence on the notion that sexual identity is 'in the genes' rather than a socio-cultural matter. In this volume I have included entries on some writers such as Kate Bornstein who have played an important role in broadening the debates around sexual/gender identity. However, the majority of entries concern writers whose main textual preoccupation is not 'gender bending', or playing with gender. Many writers, to this day, do not project uncertainty about the identities the lesbian and gay figures they portray inhabit. Rather, ambiguities about the characters' identities, if voiced, frequently need to be viewed in the context of the homophobic environments they inhabit. So, when we talk of who's who in lesbian and gay writing, what are we talking about?

I took *lesbian and gay writing* to refer to two categories of texts:

1 texts with a lesbian and/or gay content;
2 texts written by writers who identify publicly as lesbian and gay, or who are known to be lesbian or gay.

Under the first category one might find texts both by lesbian and gay, and by heterosexual authors. What the texts have in common is that they have some lesbian and/or gay content such as the depiction of homosexual characters or of same-sex attachments or attractions, or the representation of certain kinds of sensibility or milieux. Lesbian and/or gay content in a text can take many forms. Minimally, it may take the form of a narrator expressing admiration for the body of someone of the same sex, i.e. the same morphology. Or it may take the form of playing with gender on a linguistic level so that heterosexual norms and expectations are confounded as, for instance, the gender and/or sexual identity of characters are obscured through the use of invented pronouns, or through the absence of pronouns indicating gender. At the other end of the spectrum one may have the extended description of a same-sex sexual encounter. There may thus be semantic or formal reasons why texts and therefore their authors, are included, irrespective of the authors' personal (sexual) identities. It is, of course, also the case that one cannot always know the (sexual) identity of an author. The quality of the lesbian- or gayness in a text, if one might term it as such, is in part a function of the expression of same-sex affinity. One could, of course, argue that such an affinity may be textually articulated in relation to familial and other bonds that lesbians and gays might not at all recognize as reflecting their own emotional and sexual attachment structures. However, there is a qualitative difference in the kind of same-sex affinity expressed in what I would describe as lesbian and gay writing from the kinds of same-sex affinity that might be presented in any heterosexual novel. Radclyffe Hall's *The Unlit Lamp*, a work undeservedly much less known than her *The Well of Loneliness*, deals precisely with the juxtaposition of different kinds of same-sex affinities, in this instance lesbian. In *The Unlit Lamp* the key female-to-female relationships are all sexualized, invested simultaneously with erotic attraction and with emotional attachment. The novel is ruled by the triangular relation between the central character Joan, her mother, and Joan's governess Elizabeth. Joan's mother desires her daughter erotically, to act as a romantic male who will fulfil her emotionally and erotically (the latter through kisses, strokes and hugs) but without the penetrative sex associated with biological males and so unappealingly enacted by Joan's father. The mother's overt erotic demands on her daughter are greeted with dismay by Joan who becomes increasingly trapped in her mother's erotically charged affective demands. Joan's mother is juxtaposed in the novel with Elizabeth, Joan's 'symbolic mother' as Italian feminists would describe her.

Elizabeth, a lesbian, too develops an erotic attraction to Joan but they are ultimately not able to live as a lesbian couple as Joan is unable to resist her mother. The point of briefly discussing this novel is not to suggest either that all mother–daughter relationships are of necessity erotically charged (though some would have it thus) or that lesbianism is about mother–daughter relationships. Instead I want to highlight that in lesbian and gay writing same-sex affinities, as I have described them, are frequently erotically charged, often overtly, in ways that they are not as a matter of course in what one might term heterosexual writing.

Lesbian and gay characters are constructed both by lesbian and gay, and by heterosexual writers. There is no necessary relation between the (sexual) identity of the writer and that of her/his characters, or indeed between the writer's identity and her/his ability to portray lesbian or gay characters. Lesbian and gay writers may be better able to rely on their knowledge of lesbian and gay milieux to present lesbian and gay experiences but many lesbian and gay writers, especially in previous periods, did not necessarily participate in a wider lesbian and gay culture, or write about it. There is thus no clear correlation between a writer's personal identity and lifestyle and those depicted in her/his works, and a number of heterosexual writers have produced important and interesting portraits of lesbian and gay characters, and lives. Their work is included in this volume.

The second category of entries refers to authors who are known to be lesbian or gay. Again, identities are not clear-cut and not in all cases is it possible to ascertain the (sexual) identity of a writer. However, for each entry it should be completely clear why it has been included. If it is there because a writer is known to be lesbian or gay that does not necessarily mean that she//he has produced writing with a lesbian or gay content. Many lesbian and gay writers have created a limited number of texts or, indeed, none at all with such content. However, it is important to include these writers in a work of this kind because one of the abiding areas of concern in lesbian and gay scholarship is the question of the impact of identity on production. Does my identity make a difference to how I write and if so in what ways and why? Not writing in a way that foregrounds lesbian or gay identity may tell us much about prevailing attitudes towards homosexuality and mores, about censorship, about individual lifestyles, and about perceptions of the meaning of identity. The same is true for texts that overtly portray a lesbian and gay content.

Although the reference so far has been as much to texts as to authors, the *Who's Who* is organized primarily by author name. That is why it is titled *Who's Who*. Even then, the writers, both lesbian and gay, and heterosexual, who have produced texts with lesbian and gay content, are by now too numerous to be contained within one volume. This is not least because, on the one hand, work still remains to be done on many such writers who have yet to be re- or indeed dis-covered for lesbian and gay literary history, and, on the other, the very productivity of such writers since the 1970s when lesbian and gay publishing houses began to proliferate, particularly in the Anglophone world, has made such an undertaking impossible. However, this is a cause for celebration rather than concern. It reflects the explosive growth in lesbian and gay culture, especially writing, of the last three decades of the twentieth century, and bespeaks the visibilization of that culture to the extent that today many mainstream bookshops have whole sections devoted to lesbian and gay literature – a thing unheard of in the 1960s.

A word – or several – about 'texts': on the whole lesbian and gay *writing* in this volume refers to literary texts, whether these be novels, essays, short stories, plays, poems, (auto)biographies, or other such literary texts. In addition the *Who's Who* lists some of the key theorists who have significantly changed our understanding of lesbian and gay identities. I have resisted a distinction between 'high' and 'popular' culture, not least because those distinctions have themselves become the objects of much contemporary critique and interrogation. Additionally, it is also the case that the popular has been extremely important in lesbian and gay communities and culture; it has, one might argue, significantly shaped and represented lesbian and gay identities. Where would we be without certain kinds of pulp fiction, school fiction, without Hollywood movies, without.... For many lesbians and gays, it is the popular bit of culture that has been their touchstone for their sense of self, and while some research on this has already been undertaken, much more needs to be done to analyse the inter-relationship between certain kinds of popular culture and the shaping of collective and individual lesbian and gay identities in and through those cultural instances.

This volume encompasses information about authors and texts that might be described as 'high cultural' as well as examples from popular culture. There are many reasons for this. 'High cultural' writing is much better documented and the object of more extended critical debates than many popular texts are. Witness the Oscar Wilde industry, for example. In consequence, and in general, information about both authors and texts regarded as part of 'high culture' is much more readily available than information about popular cultural texts, many of which remain entirely undocumented. However, as texts by writers such as Ann Bannon testify, popular culture, too, can survive in critical memory and, as the whole notion of what constitutes 'culture' whether 'high' or 'low' has come under debate, popular cultural works have begun to gain some visibility. The sheer number of popular cultural lesbian and gay texts in circulation both historically and now prohibits any comprehensive listing, and I have therefore included writers and texts that are well known among lesbian and gay readers as exemplars of that popular cultural production. They function as such since many popular cultural texts are produced to be ephemeral, that is on poor paper and with a specific circulation, so that many such texts, especially older ones, are lost to contemporary readers. Additionally, since the commodity produced in popular cultural texts is frequently the text itself as part of a certain (sub)genre rather than the author, it can be very difficult to establish information about the author. Thus for some female contemporary writers of lesbian popular fiction included in this volume, for example, no birth dates are included. However, it is nonetheless important to document the work in question, in part as a means of preserving knowledge of that writing for future readers and researchers. The US Naiad Press in Tallahassee have done a wonderful job in finding, resurrecting, and re-issuing some of the popular pulp lesbian fiction from the 1950s, 1960s, and 1970s, and even much earlier times. There are other presses doing similar work. However, the texts, and information about the authors, can be hard to find. There is an interesting project, yet to be undertaken, of tracing the various kinds of popular lesbian and gay texts that have been important for lesbian and gay communities during the second half of the twentieth century and beyond.

Every reader will have her or his own list of favourite authors and texts, and they may not all be included here. For, on one level, this volume represents decades of my own personal reading and that of friends. It therefore of necessity contains specific slants. The emphasis is predominantly on work from the twentieth century when lesbian and gay writing became much more visible and began to articulate lesbian and gay experiences in ways that are recognizable as such for contemporary readers. Particularly the *fin de siècle* of the nineteenth century and the modernist period have become associated with the proliferation of lesbian and gay writing, as have, for the post-Second World War period, the 1950s and 1960s for popular lesbian and gay culture, and later decades for the open celebration of lesbian and gay identities. These periods are well represented in this *Who's Who*, particularly as regards Anglophone writing. The accessibility of these texts needs to be juxtaposed with the production of lesbian and gay writing in other languages. Though much of that material remains untranslated, writers from a range of countries have been included in this volume, especially where their work is accessible for English-speaking readers. This volume, then, constitutes a celebration of the range and diversity of what might be termed lesbian and gay writing that is available not only in the Anglophone world but also more widely.

Note on the text

The *Who's Who in Lesbian and Gay Writing* is organized by author. Where reference is made to another author who also has an entry in the volume, that name appears in capital letters. It was not possible in all cases to ascertain dates of birth and death.

Acknowledgements

Many people have been involved directly and indirectly in the making of this volume. They include Kieran Corless who, whilst still at Routledge, originally suggested the project; Roger Thorp who took over as editor from Kieran; and Milon Nagi who saw the book through its final stages. My thanks to them all. I would also like to thank Kingston University, which awarded me a university sabbatical, enabling me to complete the *Who's Who in Lesbian and Gay Writing*. In addition, many individuals provided information and stimulating conversations that informed my writing. Among them I would like to thank in particular Martha Franken, Chris Zwaenepoel, Christine Michel, Michaela Witz, Ulla Wischermann, the Knitting Circle, Simon Gunn, Liz Stanley, Greg Woods, Stevi Jackson, Sasha Roseneil, Clair Roberts, Lieve Spaas, Rosi Braidotti, and Liana Borghi. Special thanks are also due to David Garnes who provided some of the entries on Christopher Bram, Michael Cunningham, Jaime Manrique, Helman Melville, and Frank Sargeson as indicated in the text.

A

Ackerley, Joe Randolph (1896–1967). British writer who edited *The Listener*, the BBC's literature and arts journal, from 1935 until 1959. He wrote one play, *The Prisoners of War* (1923), which dealt with his own experiences as a German prisoner of war, offering a critique of the British officer class and discussing homosexuality within that context. Ackerley also wrote *Hindoo Holiday* (1932), a diaristic account of his time in India as a private secretary to a maharaja. Two books on dogs (*My Dog Tulip*, 1956; *We Think the World of You*, 1960) and some poems of his were published during his lifetime but the most significant from a gay perspective is his posthumously published autobiography *My Father and Myself* (1968), which is his coming-out story. In it he describes homosexuality within the British public school system, his interest in working-class and uniformed men, gay life in the 1920s and 1930s, and his difficult relationship with his father. Ackerley's father himself may have had a homosexual relationship with Count James Francis de Gallatin when in the Household Cavalry. He also had a secret 'other' family in the form of a mistress and three daughters.

Ackland, Valentine (1906–68). British writer born in London into a well-to-do family who had an unsettled and unhappy early life, including a marriage at nineteen that remained unconsummated and was annulled. Ackland is mainly known for her relationship with Sylvia TOWNSEND WARNER whom she met through T.F. Powys and with whom she lived from 1930 until her death. Together with Townsend Warner she published a collection of poetry, *Whether a Dove or a Seagull* (1934), and in 1973 her poetry collection *The Nature of the Moment* was published posthumously. Her autobiographical essay, *For Sylvia: An Honest Account* (1985), details her relationship with Townsend Warner as well as her other relationships with both women and men, and her coming to terms with her lesbianism.

Acosta, Mercedes de (1893–1968). US lesbian playwright and poet who grew up in the USA and in France. She was an active suffragette who published poetry, plays and a memoir, *Here Lies the Heart* (1960). In 1920 she married the painter Abraham Poole, apparently to pacify her mother. She also met Eva Le Gallienne with whom she had a relationship until 1925 when Eva began an affair with another woman, Gladys E. Calthrop. Acosta wrote two plays in that period, *Jeanne d'Arc* (1925) and one about Simonetta Vespucci, the lover of Sandro Botticelli. Neither was very successful. Acosta had a number of high-profile love affairs with women, among them with the famous Hollywood actress Greta Garbo, whom she persuaded to wear trousers. In 1935 Acosta divorced her husband. She made many trips to Europe and towards the end of the Second World War had an extended affair with Claire Charles-Roux. The last major love of her life was Poppy Kirk (Maria Annunziata Sartori) who had grown up in England and France, and whom she met apparently after seeing her in a dream. They had a flat in Paris and a house in Normandy where they entertained a large circle of lesbian friends.

Acton, Harold (1904–94). Gay British writer Harold Mario Mitchell Acton was born on the family estate Villa La Pietra in Florence, Italy. He was the son of the heiress to a US banking fortune, Hortense Mitchell, and of Arthur Mario Acton, a artist and art collector. Acton, an aesthete, was educated at Eton between 1918 and 1922 where he exerted a certain influence through his promotion of dandyism and aestheticism. He and his fellow pupil Brian Howard founded the Eton Society of the Arts and published the *Eton Candle*, a literary magazine. After Eton Acton went to Christ Church College, Oxford, where he founded the literary magazine *Oxford Broom*. He had two volumes of poetry published, *Aquarium* (1923) and *An Indian Ass* (1925). Among the fellow students with whom Acton had an affair was Evelyn WAUGH, who dedicated his first novel *Decline and Fall* (1929) to Acton, and who recreated Acton as dandyish character Anthony Blanche in his later novel *Brideshead Revisited* (1944). In 1930 Acton published his poetry collection *This Chaos*. He then spent much of the 1930s living and travelling in China. His novel *Peonies and Ponies* (1941) is set in Peking. During his time in China, Acton had an affair with an Englishman, Desmond Parsons, who had to return to England due to illness and who died of Hodgkin's disease. Acton served in the Royal Air Force during the Second World War and afterwards settled on the family estate in Florence. He wrote

and lectured on historical and art historical subjects including *The Last Medici* (1932) and *The Bourbons of Naples* (1957). He published two volumes of autobiography, *Memoirs of an Aesthete* (1948) and *More Memoirs* (1970). Some of his importance for a gay literary history lies in the continuity he gave to the aesthetic and dandyish tradition, which has been an influential strand for the notion of a gay aesthetic.

Al Berto (1948–97). Pseudonym of Alberto Pidwell Tavares, a gay Portuguese poet, who was born in Coimbra but spent most of his life, except for the period 1967–75 when he was in Belgium, in Sines and Lisbon. Al Berto initially wanted to become a painter and attended art school in Lisbon as well as in Belgium. From 1971 he turned to writing and, once returned to Portugal, he published a number of volumes of poetry as well as one novel, *Lunário* (1988; *Lunar Calendar*), which was influenced by his time in Belgium. Al Berto was always open about his homosexuality, and this openness surfaced in his poetry from the 1980s, a period that established him as one of the important poets of the late twentieth century in Portugal. His collected poems were published as *O Medo* (1986; *Fear*), with further editions including some of his later poetry too. Among his other volumes of poetry are *Trabalhos do Olhar* (1982; *Works of Gazing*), *Salsugem* (1984; *Saltiness*), *A Secreta Vida das Imagens* (1991; *The Secret Life of Images*), and *Horto de Incêndio* (1997; *Garden of Fire*). He died of AIDS-related complications.

Albee, Edward (1928–). US playwright whose work includes representations of gay lovers and domestic scenarios that have been attacked by critics as representing the gay world of drag rather than heterosexual marriage. This was one criticism levelled at Albee's one major Broadway hit, *Who's Afraid of Virginia Woolf?* (1963). Albee's work never lived up to his early Off-Broadway successes with one-act plays such as *The Zoo Story* (1958), *The American Dream* (1960) and *The Death of Bessie Smith* (1961). His later plays included adaptations of novels such as Carson MCCULLERS's *The Ballad of the Sad Café* (1964) and James Purdy's *Malcolm* (1966). His plays *The Lady from Dubuque* (1980), *Lolita* (1981) and *The Man Who Had Three Arms* (1983) did not succeed on Broadway. It was mainly in his early plays that Albee addressed homosexuality and homoeroticism. Thus in *The Zoo Story* he portrayed a confrontation between Peter, an ineffectual wealthy man, and Jerry, a figure with counter-cultural associations who tells his life story. The play conjoins sex and violence in a manner typical of Albee's work with the American dream featuring as a beautiful, gay, male, heartless hustler. *Tiny Alice* (1964) features a cardinal and a lawyer who are ex-lovers. Albee saw himself as a critic of the US way of life rather than as a figure representing the gay community.

Aldrich, Ann. Contemporary US writer of lesbian literature who produced a series of works from the mid-1950s to the mid-1960s on lesbian life. As the titles of her works show, she offered a rather depressed and depressing image of lesbians as inhabiting a lonely, beset world. Such a portrayal was of course not uncommon – indeed, the lesbian classic *The Well of Loneliness* might be said to be its precursor. In the repressive atmosphere of 1950s USA the pessimistic tone of Aldrich's work is not surprising. Her writings include *We Walk Alone through Lesbos' Lonely Groves* (1955), *We, too, Must Love* (1958), *We Two Won't Last* (1963) and the collection of short stories *Carol in a Thousand Cities* (1960).

Aldridge, Sarah. Contemporary US writer of lesbian popular fiction, much of it published by the lesbian Naiad Press. Her many volumes that have an explicit lesbian

content include *The Latecomer* (1974), *Tottie: A Tale of the Sixties* (1975), *Cytherea's Breath* (1976), *All True Lovers* (1978), *The Nesting Place* (1982), *Madame Aurora* (1983), *Misfortune's Friend* (1985), *Magdalena* (1987), *Keep to Me Stranger* (1989), *A Flight of Angels* (1992) and *Michaela* (1994).

Aleramo, Sibilla (1876–1960). Italian writer whose real name was Rina Faccio. Born in Alessandria, Aleramo was raped by one of her father's employees when she was sixteen and, as was common for the time and the place, she was forced to marry this man for reasons of family honour. She stayed in the marriage, which produced a son, for nine years because outside of the marriage she had no legal right to her son. However, even in the face of this she finally left the marriage, depicting her experiences in the novel *Una donna* (1906). Once she had left her husband she went to Rome where she lived with the poet Giovanni Cena, began to travel Europe widely, and, together with Cena, was involved in an adult literacy scheme. In 1908 at a women's congress she met Cordula (Lina) Poletti, a student who was nine years younger than Aleramo and who fell in love with her. A year later they began a relationship that lasted for about a year and which came to an end in part because Aleramo rejected Poletti's masculinization of herself, exhorting her instead to live her love for women as a woman. Poletti entered a marriage of convenience in 1910, separating soon afterwards from her husband. Aleramo described their relationship in her novel *Il passagio* (1919; *The Crossing*). In 1913 Aleramo went to Paris where she was a visitor to the salon of Natalie Clifford BARNEY. In *Andando e stando* (1921; *Moving and Being*) she depicted Paris lesbian life through portraits of figures such as Barney and COLETTE. Aleramo led quite a nomadic life travelling around Europe, being active as a communist in post-war Europe, and teaching people from working-class backgrounds and rural communities as part of her vision for a better life. Her many other works include a number of volumes of poetry such as *Momenti* (1921; *Moments*), *Poesie* (1929; *Poems*), *Si alla terra* (1934; *Yes to the Earth*), *Selva d'amore* (1947; *Forest of Love*), *Aiutatemi a dire* (1951; *Help Me to Speak*), and *Luci della mia sera* (1956; *Light of My Evening*). Her prose works include *Transfigurazione* (1922; *Transfiguration*), *Gioie d'occasione* (1930; *Occasional Pleasures*), *Il frustino* (1932; *The Whip*), *Orsa minore* (1938; *Ursa Minor*), *Diario e lettere: dal mio diario* (1945; *Diary of a Woman*), *Gioie d'occasione e altre ancora* (1954; *More Occasional Pleasures*), *Endimione* (1923; *Endymion*, a play), and her *Lettere* (1958; *Letters*). A number of her letters to Poletti survive.

Aletrino, Arnold (1858–1918). Dutch writer and doctor who supported the notion of uranianism, and promoted homosexuality as a natural form of sexual self-expression. This led to outcries from the then prime minister, encouraging Aletrino to become more reticent about his engagement with homosexuality in public fora. When Jacob Israël DE HAAN, a friend of Aletrino, published his first novel *Pijpelijntjes* in 1904, which featured Aletrino as one of the two homosexual protagonists and which had a dedication to Aletrino, the latter tried to buy up as many copies as he could of the novel in order to safeguard his reputation. Aletrino's ambivalence about his sexuality, and his desire not to be ostracized by bourgeois society led to two unhappy marriages and severe morphine addiction. He was a member of the Dutch chapter of the Wissenschaftlich-humanitäres Komitee but not an active member within it.

Allen, Paula Gunn (1939–). Born of a Laguna-Sioux-Scottish mother and a Lebanese-US father, Paula Gunn Allen is a representative of the hyphenated US identity that has become a matter of sustained debate in discussions on postmodern subjectivities and the US condition. She received a BA in English from the University of Oregon in 1966 and an MFA in creative writing in 1968. During the same period she married, had a child, and divorced. In 1975 she received a PhD, having focused on Native American Studies. By the early 1980s Allen had become established as a Native American poet. In the introduction to *The Sacred Hoop: Recovering the Feminine in American Indian Traditions* (1986) she came out as a lesbian. Allen has been central for the redefinition of sexuality within the Native American cultural tradition. Her novel *The Woman Who Owned the Shadows* (1983) deals with the sexual, spiritual, and cultural fragmentation of those disconnected from their roots. Interested in the incorporation of cosmic feminine life forces and spirituality in her work, Allen has produced her own mythos system in *Grandmothers of the Light* (1991). She has been a key figure in the development of Native American Studies in the USA.

Allison, Dorothy E. (1949–). US lesbian writer whose works focus on the life of poor Southern 'white trash', and the violence, poverty, and abuse that accompanies the conditions under which such working-class and under-class people live. In that respect, as well as in terms of her interest in lesbian relationships that relate to butch–femme aesthetics, she has much in common with Joan NESTLE and Pat CALIFIA. Califia dedicated her collection of erotic fiction, *Macho Sluts*, to Allison with the words, 'For Dorothy Allison Who gets the Redneck Trash Encouragement Editorial Award and who may be so completely sick of this book that she will never see this dedication. One more thing: Wait until it's *your* turn.' Allison's own background in Greenville, South Carolina, functions as the backdrop for her first collection of short stories, *Trash* (1988), and for her much acclaimed novel

Bastard out of Carolina (1992). *Trash* won two Lambda Literary Awards, for Best Small Press Book and Best Lesbian Book, in 1989. *Bastard out of Carolina* was a finalist in the National Book Award round of 1992. *The Women Who Hate Me*, a collection of poems, appeared in 1983, and was republished as *The Women Who Hate Me: Poetry 1980–1990* in 1991. Allison has been heralded as one of a new generation of queer writers whose work engages with growing up queer under conditions of deprivation. Her collection of essays *Skin* (1993) testifies to that. In 1998 she published *Cavedweller*, a novel focused on life in the US South. She has also published *Two or Three Things I Know for Sure* (1995), an intimate portrait of her extended family, complete with photos.

Alther, Lisa (1944–). US writer who had a privileged upbringing and went to Wellesley College during the 1960s where she experienced the events fictionalized in her most famous novel, *Kinflicks* (1976). In this novel the heroine Ginny Babacock, meets a radical lesbian, Eddie, while at an elite women's college. Together they move to a lesbian communal farm in Vermont where they live until Ginny moves on, first to marry, then to return to the South to look after her dying mother. As in others of Alther's novels, lesbianism is portrayed as one of several possible versions of how one might live one's life. Alther's heroines tend not to have a single sexual identity but move from lesbian relationships to heterosexual ones, or vice versa. This is as true of *Original Sins* (1981), which focuses on a woman coming to recognize her lesbianism in the context of the women's and civil rights' movements, as it is of *Other Women* (1984) and of *Bedrock* (1990). She has also written *Five Minutes in Heaven* (1995).

Anderson, Margaret (1886–1973). Lesbian writer and editor, born in Indianapo-

lis, who grew up in a well-to-do household where she learnt languages and to play the piano. Anderson left her parental home to move to Chicago where, in 1914, she founded one of modernism's most famous magazines, *The Little Review*. This magazine published work by many of the foremost high modernist writers, including perhaps most famously James Joyce's *Ulysses*, which the magazine began to serialize in 1918. The publication was the object of an obscenity trial in 1920. Shortly after founding *The Little Review* Anderson met Jane HEAP with whom she embarked on a love affair and who became the co-editor of *The Little Review*. Having spent a winter with Jane Heap in California, the two moved to New York in 1918. Anderson had many friendships with lesbian writers such as Amy LOWELL, Solita SOLANO, Janet FLANNER, and Djuna BARNES, and was well established in the lesbian circles of first New York and then Paris, where Heap and Anderson moved in 1922. Heap returned to New York in 1924. By then Anderson had already met and fallen in love with the singer Georgette Leblanc, with whom she lived, and whom she accompanied on the piano during recitals, until Leblanc's death in 1941 in Le Cannet in the south of France, where the two had established their lives together. Anderson and Leblanc spent much of the 1930s in Italy, seemingly unperturbed by the rising fascism in that country. Following Leblanc's death Anderson returned to the USA. On the return journey she met Enrico Caruso's widow, Dorothy Caruso, with whom she was to live in New York and the south of France until Caruso's death in 1955. From 1955 until her death in 1961, Anderson took care of a former friend of Leblanc's, Monique Serrure. In her final years Anderson maintained contact only with Janet Flanner and Solita Solano. She died in Cannes in 1973 and was buried beside Georgette Leblanc. Apart from *The Little Review* Anderson published *My Thirty Years' War* (1930),

The Fiery Mountains (1951), *The Little Review Anthology*, (1953), which she edited, and *The Strange Necessity* (1970).

Anzaldúa, Gloria (1942–). Born and brought up in a south Texas ranching environment, Anzaldúa was educated at the Pan American University, the University of Texas, and the University of California, Santa Cruz. In 1981 together with Cherríe MORAGA she co-edited *This Bridge Called My Back: Writings by Radical Women of Color*, which became a key text in Women's Studies as the first collection to bring together the voices of feminists of colour challenging racism and classism, and fully engaging with lesbian perspectives at a time when their position in Women's Studies was much contested. This was followed by *Making Face, Making Soul/Haciendo Caras: Creative and Critical Perspectives by Women of Color* (1990). Anzaldúa has also become famous for her book *Borderlands: La Frontera: The New Mestiza* (1987). The concept of the mestiza as a liminal figure has subsequently been picked up in a variety of writings on race and on sexual identity.

Arenas, Reinaldo (1943–90). Cuban-born gay writer Arenas was brought up in the impoverished Cuban countryside where, as his first novel *Celestino antes del alba* (1967; *Singing from the Well*) indicates, his imagination became his defence against the deprivations of that existence. It won the Prix Medici in France for best foreign novel in 1969. Against Cuban public cultural policy, his writings supported the individual's right of self-expression, and this stance, together with his homosexuality, made him deeply unpopular with the Cuban government who repeatedly confiscated and burnt his work. In 1980 he managed to escape from the island, leaving with thousands of others from Mariel port, and settling in New York where he continued to write prolifically and across a range of genres, from journalistic pieces, to poetry, prose, and

drama. Arenas was an outspoken critic of the Castro regime and his work reflected that criticism. In virtually all his writings homosexuals are portrayed but they are most explicitly presented in *Otra vez el mar* (1982; *Farewell to the Sea*), *Arturo, la estrella más brilliante* (1984; 'The Brightest Star'), *Viaje a La Habana* (1990; *Trip to Havana*), *El color del verano* (1991; *The Color of Summer*), and *Antes que anchoezca* (1992; *Before Night Falls*; released as a film in 2001). The last text was Arenas's autobiography, mixing fact and fiction in an extraordinary testimony to the life of homosexuals in the repressive Cuba of the 1960s and describing frankly his homosexual encounters. In December 1990 when he was suffering from an AIDS-related illness and unable to continue to write, Arenas took his own life. He sent a moving farewell letter to the Miami Spanish newspaper *Diario las Américas* in which he made clear that he did not want his suicide to be seen as a sign of defeat.

Arnold, June (1926–82). Lesbian US writer and publisher who, together with her partner Parke Bowman, co-founded Daughters Inc., in Vermont. This was the first press specialising in (lesbian) women's writing, and in particular in novels. It ceased to exist in 1978. Arnold's first novel *Applesauce* was published in 1967. It is for her second novel, *The Cook and the Carpenter* (1973), that she was most acclaimed. An experimental work, *The Cook and the Carpenter* played with the gender identity of its characters by substituting personal pronouns like 'she' and 'he' with 'na', a genderless word that draws the reader into an interactive relation to the novel as she tries to figure out what gender the characters are. *Sister Gin* (1977), June Arnold's third novel was published in 1977, to be followed by her final work, *Baby Houston*, which appeared posthumously in 1987, five years after she had died from brain cancer. In the introduction to the 1993 edition of her novel *Lover* (1976, repeatedly reprinted), the US lesbian writer Bertha HARRIS gives an interesting, if probably controversial account of June Arnold and Parke Bowman's life together and of their work at Daughters Inc.

Aron, Jean-Paul (1925–88). Born into a middle-class Jewish family in Strasbourg, France, Aron studied philosophy and psychology before beginning a career as a teacher, scholar, journalist, and author. In 1978 he published *Le Pénis et la démoralization de l'Occident* (*The Penis and the Demoralization of the West*), which he had co-written with Roger Kempf and which analysed nineteenth-century attitudes in France regarding masturbation and homosexuality. *Les Modernes* (*The Moderns*), a further collection of essays, appeared in 1984. When he was diagnosed by his brother, a doctor, as suffering from AIDS in 1986, he decided to come out about his illness in an interview in *Le Nouvel Observateur*. The first writer in France to admit to suffering from AIDS he became a celebrated figure, a fact which he did not relish since he was a rather private man and reticent about his sexuality.

Arrowsmith, Pat (1930–). Contemporary British writer and peace activist who was educated at Cheltenham Ladies' College, and has, according to her preface in *Somewhere Like This* (1970), been in prison eleven times for a total of more than two years for offences such as opposing nuclear weapons, objecting to the deployment of British troops in Northern Ireland, and protesting against the Vietnam War. *Somewhere Like This* is a novel about life in an all-female prison during the late 1960s. The novel is based on Arrowsmith's experiences in Holloway prison in London in which, during the same period, the butch–femme divide was apparently the order of the day. Its central character is Lorry, a butch dyke, and her experiences with other female inmates.

Arrowsmith herself wrote a couple of other texts while she was in prison: *To Asia in Peace* (1972), a book about a non-violent mission to South-east Asia, and the novel *Jericho* (1983). In 1982 she published *The Prisoner* and, together with the lesbian writer and critic Alison Hennegan, Arrowsmith published her memoir, *I Should Have Been a Hornby Train*, in 1995. Other works by her include *Many Are Called* (1998) and *Drawing to Extinction* (2000).

Ashbery, John (1927–). One of the best-known contemporary US poets, Ashbery's work is renowned for its experimental style and postmodern appeal rather than for a specifically gay content. His own gayness is known through his association with other gay artists such as the poet Frank O'HARA and the photographer Robert Mapplethorpe. Interested in visual culture as much as in word-smithing, Ashbery is regarded as a cerebral rather than a sensual writer. His many collections of poetry and other writings include *Turandot and Other Poems* (1953), *The Tennis Court Oath* (1962), *A Nest of Ninnies* (1969, with James Schuyler), *Three Poems* (1972), *The Double Dream of Spring* (1976), *Self-Portrait in the Convex Mirror* (1977), *As We Know* (1979), *Shadow Train* (1981), *April Galleons* (1987), *Three Plays* (1988), *Ice Storm* (1991), *Flow Chart* (1991), *Reported Sightings: Art Chronicles 1957–1987* (1991), *Hotel Lautreamont* (1992), *And the Stars Are Shining* (1994), *Mapplethorpe Pistils* (1996; images of flowers, with Robert Mapplethorpe), *Red Grooms: A Retrospective* (1998, with Judith E. Stein and Jan Cutler), *Wakefulness* (1998), *A Wave* (1998), *Selected Poems* (1998), *Houseboat Days* (1999), *Girls on the Run* (2000), *Your Name Here* (2000), and *Other Traditions* (2000).

Auden, W.H. (1907–73). Born in York as the youngest son of a doctor and a nurse, the gay poet and writer Wystan Hugh Auden grew up in Birmingham. Educated at Gresham's School, Holt, he went to Christ Church, Oxford, where he was a contemporary of Stephen SPENDER. He gained a BA in 1928 and then spent a year in Berlin with his friend Christopher ISHERWOOD. Both men moved in the homosexual circles that were a key feature of Berlin metropolitan culture from the late nineteenth century until the early 1930s, when that scene fell victim to the rise of the Nazi regime. Between 1930 and 1935 Auden taught in private schools in England and in Scotland. In 1935 he married Thomas MANN's lesbian daughter, Erika MANN, in order to enable her to get a British passport and escape from the Nazis. Auden continued to visit Isherwood in Berlin but in 1939 both men decided to emigrate to the USA where they settled in New York City. Auden became a US citizen in 1946. In New York Auden met Chester Kallman, an 18-year-old from Brooklyn, with whom he maintained a life-long relationship. Although Kallman in particular had other relationships and affairs, he and Auden shared a flat in New York and holiday homes in Ischia and in Austria. Auden is one of the major poets of the twentieth century. In 1930 T.S. ELIOT accepted his first volume of poems, *Poems*, for Faber and Faber. Auden then published *The Orators* (1932) and *Look Stranger!* (1936). Like Stephen Spender, Auden wrote drama as well as poetry. In 1932 he began an association with Rupert Doone's Group Theatre, which produced several of his plays. They included *The Dance of Death* (1933), *The Dog Beneath the Skin* (1935; which he co-wrote with Christopher Isherwood), *The Ascent of F6* (1936), and *On the Frontier* (1938). These plays have some affinity with Bertolt BRECHT's early expressionist plays. Auden also became friendly with the gay English composer Benjamin Britten who set some of his poems to music and used Auden's text for his opera *Paul Bunyan*. When Auden went to Iceland with Louis MacNeice in 1936, they co-wrote the *Letters from*

Iceland (1937). In 1939 Auden and Isherwood went to China, resulting in *Journey to a War* (1939). Auden's collection of poems *Another Time* (1940) includes many of his best-known poems such as 'September 1939' and 'Lullaby'. *The Double Man* (1941) was followed by *For the Time Being: A Christmas Oratorio* (1944), which Auden dedicated to his mother who had died in 1941. He simultaneously published *The Sea and the Mirror*, a collection based on William SHAKESPEARE's *The Tempest*. In 1948 *The Age of Anxiety: A Baroque Eclogue* appeared. In 1956 Auden was elected professor of poetry at Oxford, and he spent much of his later life there. He edited many anthologies of poetry as well as essays, and continued to publish collections of poems. Among these are *Nones* (1951), *The Shield of Achilles* (1955), *Homage to Clio* (1960), and *About the House* (1965). Inspired by Kallman, who was very interested in opera, Auden also wrote several librettos including for Stravinsky's *The Rake's Progress* (1951). In 1973 Auden died suddenly while in Vienna.

Augiéras, François (1925–71). French writer who was born in the USA, the son of a French mother of Polish descent and of a French father, whom he never knew as he died shortly before Augiéras was born. His parents had emigrated to the USA in 1922; following her husband's death and the birth of her son, Augiéras's mother went back to France where they initially lived in Paris and then in Périgueux in the Dordogne. Augiéras started to lead a nomadic life during the Second World War. He wanted to join his uncle, a retired colonel who lived in an oasis in the Sahara desert in a former fortress. Augiéras managed to get to this place, which became one of the sources for his writing. In *Le Vieillard et l'enfant* (1949; *The Old Man and the Child*) he described his sexual relationship with his uncle. A gay man who disliked women, he had an unhappy marriage that was not reflected in his writings in which few women figure. *Le Voyage des morts* (1959; *Voyage of the Dead*) described his nomadic life in the Maghreb. Subsequent writings also centred on travel and countries and regions he had visited such as Greece and North Africa. They include *L'Apprenti Sorcier* (1964; *The Apprentice Sorcerer*), *Une Adolescence au temps du maréchal, et de multiples adventures* (1968; *An Adolescence at the Time of the Marshal, and of Other Adventures*), *Un Voyage au Mont Athos* (1970; *Voyage to Mount Athos*), *Domme, ou l'essai d'occupation* (1981), and *Les Barbares d'occident* (1991; *The Barbarians of the West*). Augiéras died in the Dordogne at a local hospital.

B

Baldwin, James (1924–87). Born to a poor unmarried woman, Emma Berdis Jones, at Harlem Hospital in New York City, James Arthur Baldwin had a traumatic early childhood during which he was treated very badly by his abusive father and taunted by other children because of his small stature and effeminate mannerisms. In his adolescence he became involved with the Church and from the age of fourteen acted as a minister, preaching in a variety of evangelical churches in and around Harlem. He then had a number of different jobs before leaving, in 1948, for France where he settled for most of the rest of his life and where he died. In France he became a professional writer of poetry, drama, and prose. His early essays, collected in *Notes of a Native Son* (1955) and *Nobody Knows My Name* (1961) offered trenchant critiques of race relations in the USA. This continued in *The Fire Next Time* (1963), *Blues for Mister Charlie* (1964), and *The Evidence of Things not Seen* (1985). Baldwin's status as a major contributor to gay literary history rests on several novels in which the theme of homosexuality is explicitly and extensively addressed, often within the framework of a critique of the racist and homophobic attitudes prevalent in the USA. In *Go Tell It to the Mountain* (1953), the 14-year-old protagonist strug-

gles with his adolescent gay consciousness. *Giovanni's Room* (1956) tells the story of David, an American in Paris who falls in love with an Italian man but is unable to come to terms with his homosexuality, leading Giovanni, the man he falls for, to seek solace in the Paris sexual underworld. Giovanni eventually murders his abusive employer, is caught, and is condemned to death for this crime. As in his previous novels Baldwin here thematizes the problematic of reconciling being brought up in a repressive heterosexual environment with the private experience of homosexual desire. The same topic is the focus of *Another Country* (1962), which represents a microcosm of the USA of people of diverse racial backgrounds and sexual identities living in a pre-Stonewall USA where racism and homophobia are rife. As in his subsequent novel, *Tell Me How Long the Train's Been Gone* (1968), the homosexual figure Eric is cast in a redemptive role. Whereas *If Beale Street Could Talk* (1974) did not dwell on homosexuality in any way, Baldwin's last novel, *Just above My Head* (1979), focused again on a gay character, Arthur Montana, whose life is recalled by his brother. As an openly gay black writer, Baldwin occupied a key role in fictionalizing gay life in a racialized society, and presenting it not, as was frequently the case in pre-Stonewall days, as a desperate existence of suffering individuals but as an identity to be embraced and celebrated.

Balzac, Honoré de (1799–1850). French writer, some of whose novels and short stories contain representations of lesbian and gay relationships, though the extent to which he himself had homosexual tendencies remains uncertain. The memoirs of one contemporary, Philarète Chasles, suggest that Balzac had homosexual leanings, and his letters register strong feelings for some of the young men who were his protégés and whose careers he sought to further in his later life. After completing his legal studies in 1819 Balzac turned to writing fiction, which became his career. He wrote prodigiously, producing more than ninety novels, which revealed him to be an acute observer of French society. In 1834 Balzac organized his novels systematically, publishing them between 1842 and 1848 under the collective title *La Comédie humaine* (*The Human Comedy*). Balzac's representation of the life of Jacques Collin (alias Vautrin, alias Abbé Carlos Herrera) spans *Le Père Goriot* (1834–5; *Father Goriot*), *Illusions Perdues* (1837–43; *Lost Illusions*), and *Splendeurs et misères de courtisanes* (1838–47; *Highs and Lows of Harlots*). This sequence portrays homosexuality in Paris prisons. In *La Fille aux yeux d'or* (1834–5; *The Girl with the Golden Eyes*), the lesbian relationship between Paquita Valdès and the Marquise de San-Réal turns tragic when Paquita introduces the Marquise's half-brother into the relationship. Balzac's novella *Sarrasine* (1830), the story of a castrato, was picked up by Roland BARTHES in his famous volume *S/Z* (1974) in which Barthes presents his system of semiology, and was also brought to life in a spectacular performance by the British theatre company Gloria under the direction of Neil BARTLETT.

Bannon, Ann (1932–). Ann Bannon is the pseudonym of Ann Thayer who wrote a series of lesbian pulp fictions in the 1950s and 1960s, only claiming her authorship in 1980 when the lesbian Naiad Press republished her novels. Bannon produced a series of novels around the butch character of Beebo Brinker, detailing lesbian life in Greenwich Village during the 1950s and 1960s. *Beebo Brinker* (1962) was the last of the novels to be written but is the one that introduces Beebo who comes to New York from the Midwest to claim her independence as an out lesbian woman. This novel is not unlike Rita Mae BROWN's *Rubyfruit Jungle* and other similar coming-out stories in which the lesbian protagonist leaves repressive small-town living behind in order to find her sexual identity in urban contexts. *Odd Girl Out* (1957) features the lesbian relationship of two college students Laura and Beth. Ambivalent in its depiction of lesbianism, and fully aware of the social price exacted for a lesbian life in pre-Stonewall days, one of the protagonists, Beth, flees into marriage by the end of the novel. *I Am a Woman* (1959) portrays Laura's move after college into both a career within a heterosexual environment and lesbian bar life where she meets Beebo. In *Woman in the Shadows* (1959) the relationship between Laura and Beebo is constructed as deteriorating due to Beebo's alcoholism and general antagonism. By the end of the novel Laura has married a gay man, Jack, and has had artificial insemination. *Journey to a Woman* (1960), the last volume in the series, picks up Beth's story again. She leaves her husband to search for Laura and, eventually, sets up in a new relationship with Beebo. Bannon's depiction of lesbian life in the 1950s and 1960s is conventionally constructed in terms of pulp romance fiction and contains sustained representations of the difficult choices women faced in making sexual choices in a sexually repressive era. Harking back to the much older tradition of representations of lesbians as portrayed in, for example, Radclyffe HALL's *The Well of Loneliness*,

Bannon's novels contain butch women whose sexual identity is unwavering and femme lesbians who negotiate uneasily between their lesbian desires and the pressures a heterosexual world exerts on them.

Barker, Pat (1943–). English novelist whose early novels *Union Street* (1982), *Blow Your House Down* (1984), *The Century's Daughter* (1986; republished as *Liza's England*), and *The Man Who Wasn't There* (1989) centred on English northern working-class life and issues of poverty and deprivation. Her *Regeneration* trilogy, comprising *Regeneration* (1991), *The Eye in the Door* (1993; for which she won the *Guardian* Fiction Prize), and *The Ghost Road* (1995; for which she was awarded the Booker Prize), centres on how soldiers during the First World War were affected by the traumas and stresses of their experiences in the trenches. These novels deal with the interrogation of ideas of masculinity and sexual identity in times of war through featuring a bisexual working-class man, Billy Prior, as well as several gay men, who are sent to Craiglockhart to be treated by a psychiatrist so that they can learn to cope with the traumas of their war-time experiences. The trilogy is based on the experiences of the war poets Wilfred OWEN and Siegfried SASSOON. Barker's subsequent novel, *Another World* (1998), continues the theme of exploring the experiences of men who fought in the First World War. In 2001 Barker published *Border Crossing*, a novel centring on the relationship between a psychologist and a man who as a child was convicted of killing an old woman.

Barnes, Djuna (1892–1982). Lesbian US writer who grew up in poverty-stricken conditions in New York and was sexually abused by her alcoholic father. She began writing and painting at an early age. After the First World War she moved to Greenwich Village where she had an affair with

Mary Pyne, and met and lived for a time with the sculptress Berenice Abbott. In 1915 her *Book of Repulsive Women* appeared. Subsequently she met the publishers of the *Little Review*, Margaret ANDERSON and Jane HEAP, and had an affair with the latter. In 1919 Barnes moved to Paris where she met and lived with the sculptress Thelma Wood for ten years. Both developed an alcohol problem. Barnes was friends with many other women of the left bank, including Mina Loy, Janet FLANNER, Sylvia BEACH, and Adrienne MONNIER. Her *Ladies Almanack* (1928) is a satire of the lesbian artistic scene in Paris. It was published by Robert McAlmon who was married to BRYHER, a US lesbian millionairess, who provided the money to publish many of the lesbian writers in Paris during the 1920s and 1930s. After Thelma Wood's return to the USA in 1930 and Barnes's final decision to leave her in 1931, Barnes travelled widely. She had many affairs including some heterosexual ones. She became pregnant at 41 and had an abortion. Her best-known work, *Nightwood* (1936), can be read as a literary reworking of her relationship with Thelma Wood. It details a society of marginalized people, adrift in the metropoles of Europe, in search of a history of their own. In 1937 Djuna Barnes moved to England for a period of time and then returned to New York for good. There she lived a withdrawn life, keeping in touch only with a few friends like Peggy Guggenheim, who supported her financially during the last decades of her life when she had ceased to write. In the early 1970s Barnes sold her manuscripts to the University of Maryland. About her lesbianism she is supposed to have said: 'I'm not a lesbian, I just loved Thelma.'

Barney, Natalie Clifford (1876–1972). Born in Ohio, Barney enjoyed the privilege of being the child of a man who had inherited a railway fortune. Aged twenty-four she moved permanently to Europe and settled in Paris where she inhabited the house at 20 Rue Jacob for more than fifty years. Famous for her love affairs with lesbians like the poet Renée VIVIEN and the painter Romaine Brooks, Barney's life was the source of a number of literary portraits including those of Flossie in Liane de Pougy's *Idylle Sapphique* (1901; *Sapphic Idyll*), Miss Flossie in COLETTE's *Claudine s'en va* (1903; *Claudine and Annie*), Valerie Seymour in Radclyffe HALL's *The Well of Loneliness* (1928), and Laurette in Lucie DELARUE-MARDRUS's *L'Ange et les pervers* (1930; *The Angel and the Perverts*). Barney's first collection of poetry, *Quelques portraits-sonnets de femmes* (1900), celebrated her lovers. Her memoirs and portraits such as *Aventures de l'esprit* (1929; *Adventures of the Mind*) and *Souvenirs Indiscrets* (1960; *Indiscreet Memoirs*) describe the lesbians and gay men who frequented her literary salon including Oscar WILDE, Gertrude STEIN, Djuna BARNES, Marcel PROUST, COLETTE, and Lucie Delarue-Mardrus. René de Gourmont, a French writer and literary critic, was a close friend of Barney's. He published two collections of letters he wrote to her, *Lettres à l'amazone* (1914) and *Lettres Intimes à l'amazone* (1926). These volumes established the description of Barney as 'the amazon'. Barney published three volumes of epigrams, *Eparpillements* (1930; *Scatterings*), *Pensées d'une amazone* (1920; *Thoughts of an Amazon*), and *Nouvelles Pensées d'une amazone* (1939; *More Thoughts of an Amazon*), which established her literary reputation.

Barnfield, Richard (1574–1627). Born in Staffordshire, the English poet Barnfield took a degree at Oxford in 1591, then lived in London for a few years before settling near Darlaston. Between 1594 and 1598 he published four volumes of poetry after which he stopped publishing such work. He married, and had at least one son and a granddaughter. Barnfield has a reputation of being a homoerotic

poet, in particular because of his two volumes of poetry, *The Affectionate Shepherd* (1594) and *Cynthia, with Certaine Sonnets* (1595). Both sets of poems include homoerotic verse. In the former collection, the title poem details the love of the shepherd Daphnis for a boy, Ganymede. His love is, however, not returned. It has been suggested that Daphnis is modelled on Barnfield and Ganymede on Sir Charles Blount whom Barnfield may have met at Oxford. Barnfield's verse has been considered part of a tradition of homoerotic pastoral verse; the representation in sonnet form of a love not answered going back to Petrarch.

Barrington, Judith (1944–). Contemporary lesbian writer who grew up in England but moved to Oregon in 1976. She has published two collections of poetry, *Trying to Be an Honest Woman* (1975) and *History and Geography* (1989). She was the founder of *The Flight of Mind*, a residential writing workshop for women. Her libretto for the oratorio *Mother of Us All* with music by David York was performed by the Concord Choir in 1991. In the same year her anthology *An Intimate Wilderness: Lesbian Writers on Sexuality* appeared. She has also published *Writing the Memoir: From Truth to Art* (1996) and *Lifesaving: A Memoir* (2000).

Barry, James Miranda (1795?–1865). English army surgeon and Inspector-General of Hospitals who, upon his death, was discovered to have been a woman who had had a child when very young. Her date of birth is uncertain and she gave different dates at different points in her life. The story of James Miranda Barry, who in the guise of a man took a medical degree at Edinburgh University in 1809 at a time when only men were allowed to study medicine, and subsequently joined the army to become an army surgeon, travelling for extended periods of time in this capacity in Africa, has intrigued many since its discovery and first report in the *Manchester Guardian* on 21 August 1865. It is clear that Barry enjoyed the protection of various aristocratic men including General Miranda and the Earl of Buchan. Barry's story inspired two novels, *A Modern Sphinx* by Colonel Rogers, and *Dr James Barry: Her Secret Story* by Olga Racster and Jessica Grove (1932), before Isobel Rae published her biography – containing, as Rae put it, 'no fiction' – in 1958 under the title *The Strange Story of Dr. James Barry.* Interest in Barry was revived in the 1980s when issues of cross-dressing, transsexualism, and transvestism became part of a more general cultural debate within lesbian and gay, and also wider, Western culture. Most recently, Patricia DUNCKER has published a fictional account of Barry's life.

Barthes, Roland (1915–80). Gay French theorist and semiotician whose extensive work on the notion of the text and engagement with cultural signs as sign systems gained him a significant following among cultural and queer theoreticians, in particular from the late 1970s and early 1980s onwards when he was elected to a chair in the Collège de France and when his work was translated into English. A Protestant in a predominantly Catholic country, Barthes for a long time occupied a rather marginal place in French culture. As a consumptive he spent several years in sanatoria before teaching French at universities in Romania and Egypt, eventually joining the Centre National de la Recherche Scientifique to do research in sociology and lexicology. Among his many publications are *Le Degré zéro de l'écriture* (1953; *Writing Degree Zero*), *Mythologies* (1957), *Eléments de sémiologie* (1964; *Elements of Semiology*), *S/Z, L'Empire de signes 1970; SZ), Sade, Fourier, Loyola* (1971), *Fragments d'un discours amoureux* (1977; *A Lover's Discourse), Images – Music-Text* (1977), *La Chambre claire* (1980; *Camera Lucida*),

and *Le Bruissement de la langue (1984; The Rustle of Language).*

Bartlett, Neil (1958–). Born in Chichester, Bartlett is a theatre producer and novelist whose work has been associated with the recuperation of gay history within the celebration in the 1990s of 'queer'. His direction of the theatre company Gloria resulted in some of the most interesting theatre work of the 1980s, including a celebrated adaptation of Honoré de BALZAC's novella *Sarrasine*. In 1988 he published *Who Was that Man?*, a novel about Oscar Wilde that was voted Capital Gay Book of the Year. This was followed in 1990 by *Ready to Catch Him Should He Fall*, an account of the relationship between an older and a younger gay man, Boy, and their courtship and lives within the community of The Bar, a gay venue ruled by Mother who supports their relationship, in a past/present in which gay men are isolated from other communities and are the objects of violent attacks. *Mr Clive and Mr Page* (1996), too, is concerned with the past and with living a gay life in the 1950s. It explores issues of class and a certain kind of 'Englishness' within the context of the highly regulated life of a male sales assistant in London's West End. In the 1990s Bartlett became artistic director of the Lyric Theatre, Hammersmith, in London. Under his direction the theatre has done much to promote work by and for gay men.

Bates, Katharine Lee (1859–1929). US poet and academic who was an ardent feminist and author of the song 'America the Beautiful'. Bates was educated at Wellesley College where she subsequently taught until her retirement in 1925, by which time she was chair of the English Department. While on the staff at Wellesley she met Katharine Coman who also taught there, eventually rising to the chair in Economics and the position of Dean of the college. The two women enjoyed a romantic friendship of an intense nature, captured in many of Bates's poems. When Coman was diagnosed as suffering from cancer, Bates nursed her until the former's death in 1915. Bates remained at Wellesley after Coman's death. Bates's volumes include *Yellow Clover: A Book of Remembrance* (1922) and *Selected Poems*, published posthumously in 1930.

Baudelaire, Charles (1821–67). French poet, art critic, and translator of Edgar Allan POE's work, introducing that writer to the French public. Baudelaire wrote two collections of poetry, *Les Fleurs du mal* (1867; *Flowers of Evil*) and *Le Speen de Paris* (1869; *Paris Spleen*), which became highly influential. *Les Fleurs du mal* shows Baudelaire's fascination with lesbianism. In his poetry lesbians are constructed as beautiful and condemned souls.

Beach, Sylvia (1887–1962). Lesbian US book dealer and writer, born Nancy Beach in Baltimore, Maryland, to Eleanor and Sylvester Beach. Sylvia Beach was the middle daughter of three children all of whom changed their first names. The eldest daughter Hollingsworth shortened her name to Holly, Nancy became Sylvia, a variation of her father's name, and the youngest daughter Eleanor, like Sylvia a lesbian, changed her first name to Cyprian when she became an actress. Sylvia Beach first came to Europe in 1902 when her father was made a pastor at the American Church of Paris. The parents' marriage was very unhappy. Beach's mother Eleanor who was much more liberal than her father Sylvester spent her time with her three daughters either in Europe or in California to escape her unhappy marriage and veered between dependency on her daughters and the desire for freedom. Beach herself had only a limited and sporadic formal education but following a period of two years in Spain she finally settled in Paris in 1917. In 1917 Beach met her lover Adrienne MONNIER, also a book dealer and writer,

for the first time when she went to Monnier's shop looking for a copy of Paul Fort's review *Vers et prose*. Her idea to open a bookshop for English and US authors proved very successful, in part because the Paris of the 1920s was full of émigrés from the USA and from England, all seeking to escape the restrictions of their backgrounds. Beach became famous for her publication of James Joyce's *Ulysses* and for the ways in which her shop attracted modernist avant-garde writers of her day. With the financial help of her mother who provided her with $3000 Beach opened her bookshop, 'Shakespeare and Company', in November 1919. It functioned mainly as a lending library with many readings and exhibitions taking place there. Beach got to know many of the lesbians living in Paris through her shop, including Natalie BARNEY, Gertrude STEIN, and Alice B. TOKLAS, as well as BRYHER who became a lifelong friend. Under Monnier's tutelage, Beach also published books. In 1921 she was asked by James Joyce to publish his *Ulysses*, an undertaking that would prove to be financially ruinous for Beach since Joyce asked constantly for loans and advances that amounted to much more than the publication and translations of his book brought in. Eventually, in 1932, she relinquished all publishing claims to Joyce's work. In 1941 Beach closed her shop when a German officer tried to buy her only copy of *Finnegan's Wake*, displayed in the window of the shop, which Beach refused to sell. In 1942 the Germans interned Beach for a lengthy period in a camp south of Paris. From there she returned to the rue de l'Odéon but did not re-open her bookshop. She continued her friendships with many of the lesbian women. After Monnier's death through suicide in 1955 Beach developed a new relationship with Camilla Steinbrugge. Beach remains an important figure in the literary history of modernism. She published *Les Années vingt: les écrivains américains à Paris, 1920–1930* (1959;

The Twenties: American Writers in Paris 1920–1930) and her memoirs, *Shakespeare and Company* (1960). In these she did not discuss the lesbian nature of her relationship with Monnier.

Beauvoir, Simone de (1908–86). Born into a bourgeois family in Paris, de Beauvoir was sent to the Cours Adeline Desir, an educational establishment for young girls in 1913 where she met Elisabeth Le Coin, called Zaza by de Beauvoir, who entered the school in 1918. Zaza was by all accounts de Beauvoir's first great love, and one of a number of women with whom she was involved during her lifetime. In 1925 de Beauvoir decided to become a *lycée* teacher. She went to the Sorbonne to study, and subsequently, until 1943, earned her living as a school teacher, first in Marseilles and then in Rouen and Paris. In 1929, while a student, she met the philosopher Jean-Paul Sartre with whom she developed the philosophy of existentialism, and with whom she was engaged in a life-long and often uneasy relationship. While teaching at Rouen, de Beauvoir became involved with one of the pupils, Olga Kosakiewitch. At de Beauvoir's behest, the relationship also included Sartre. Gradually de Beauvoir found this triangular relationship more and more difficult. In 1936 de Beauvoir obtained a teaching post in Paris where, in 1939, she embarked on a brief affair with her pupil Bianca Bienenfeld whose great love she was. At the beginning of the Second World War she then had an affair with another of her pupils, Nathalie Sorokine, who was madly attracted to de Beauvoir, a feeling not entirely reciprocated by the latter. In the course of the Second World War de Beauvoir decided to give up her teaching post and focus on her writing. Her much acclaimed first novel, *L'Invitée* (*She Came to Stay*), which details the problematic of a triangular relationship between two women and a man, appeared in 1943. In

1945 de Beauvoir was the object of Violette LEDUC's violent passion but de Beauvoir felt unable to reciprocate except at the level of literary mentor. From 1946 de Beauvoir was co-editor of the journal *Temps Modernes*. Together with Sartre she undertook many journeys and political speaking engagements. At this stage she did not have the reputation as a key feminist of the twentieth century, which she has come to enjoy since and which rests in part on her text *Le Deuxième Sexe* (*The Second Sex*) that appeared in 1949, in which she famously asserted that one was not born but made a woman. This notion has since been taken up by many feminist theorists, who argue that 'woman' as a concept is a patriarchal or man-made construct. In 1954 de Beauvoir was awarded the Prix Goncourt for her novel *Les Mandarins* (*The Mandarins*). From 1958 de Beauvoir began to produce her five-volume autobiography. *Mémoires d'une jeune fille rangée* (*Memoirs of a Dutiful Daughter*) was the first volume; in 1960 it was followed by *La Force de l'âge* (*The Prime of Life*), and in 1963 *La Force de choses* (*Force of Circumstance*) was published. During this period, the early 1960s, de Beauvoir met the 18-year-old philosophy student Sylvie Le Bon with whom she embarked on a relationship that was to last until the end of de Beauvoir's life, and which culminated in her adoption of Sylvie in 1980. This allowed them to share the same surname. During the 1960s de Beauvoir was also very much politically active, speaking out both against the French war in Algeria and against the Vietnam War. In 1968 *La Femme rompue* (*Woman Destroyed*) was published, receiving much critical attention. In 1970 *La Vieillesse* (*Old Age*) came out, followed by *Tout compte fait* (*When All Is Said and Done*). From 1970 de Beauvoir became increasingly involved with feminist politics. Following Sartre's death de Beauvoir published his letters. Her own correspondence was published, after her death, by Sylvie Le Bon. This correspondence documents, *inter alia*, de Beauvoir's love of women.

Becker, Robin (1951–). Contemporary lesbian US poet who lives and works in Cambridge, Massachusetts, teaching creative writing at the Massachusetts Institute of Technology. She has been Poetry Editor of the *Women's Review of Books*, and her own work has been anthologized in a number of collections and in magazines and journals such as *The Antioch Review* and *Harvard Magazine*. Her poetry is not always explicitly lesbian in content but it tends to focus on issues of social fit, and the difficulties of dealing with emotionally loaded moments and experiences. Her first volume of poetry, *Backtalk*, came out in 1982. In 1985–6 she held a Fellowship in Poetry from the Massachusetts Artists Foundation. Other collections of poetry by her include *Giacometti's Dog* (1990), *All-American Girl* (1996), and *The Horse Fair* (2000).

Beckford, William (1760–1844). English writer, renowned for his one Gothic novel, *Vathek* (1786), who was educated at home and developed an attachment to his cousin William Courtenay, known as 'Kitty' to his friends and family. Beckford's letters to Courtenay fell into the hands of Courtenay's uncle, Lord Loughborough, a chief justice who advertized the scandal in the morning newspapers from October through to December 1784. This ruined Beckford's reputation who was never received in polite society again, and forced him to live as an exile on his own estate, Fonthill. He also travelled the Continent and had a series of friendships with men throughout his life.

Benedict, Ruth (1887–1948). US anthropologist and writer who was born and died in New York. Following her father's early death from heart disease (Ruth, too, had a weak heart and was to die of it prematurely), Ruth and her younger sister were brought up predominantly by her mother's parents. Following her studies at Vassar College she married Stanley Benedict, the brother of her friends Agnes and Florence. After the First World War she began to study anthropology under Franz Boas at Columbia University. Finding her marriage more and more of a constraint, and embarking on a career in anthropology, Benedict and her husband separated in 1930. From 1922 she gave lectures in anthropology but it was only in 1930 that she obtained an academic post. At the beginning of the 1920s Benedict met Margaret MEAD who attended her lectures and who shared a passion for poetry with Benedict. Through Mead, Benedict met a number of women writers including Edna St Vincent MILLAY. In 1924 Mead and Benedict went to visit pueblos in the south-west of the USA; they undertook subsequent research there in 1925 and became lovers. Mead, however, was very aware that known homosexuality would impede her career and though they shared Benedict's flat in New York for a while, their relationship did not last. In 1931 Benedict met Natalie Raymond and began a relationship with her that lasted until 1938. During this relatively happy period Benedict wrote her perhaps best-known work, *Patterns of Culture* (1934). This work was well received and influenced the US psychologist Karen Horney whom Benedict subsequently met. By 1938 Benedict's relationship with Natalie Raymond, who wanted to build a career as a photographer for herself and decided to live in Guatemala for a while, had deteriorated and they separated. In the following year Benedict met the psychologist Ruth Valentine, known as Val, with whom she began a relationship. Together they settled in New York but moved to Washington in 1943 to work for the 'Council of Intercultural Relations'. In 1946 Benedict published *The Chrysanthemum and the Sword*. Together with Margaret Mead, with whom she had remained friends, and Ruth Valentine, Benedict founded the 'Contemporary Cultures Project'. Its concern was to present a feminine and multicultural viewpoint of US society. In 1948 Benedict went on a trip to Europe and returned completely exhausted. She died of heart disease in the same year.

Benson, E.F. (1867–1940). Gay British writer and novelist who had an upper middle-class upbringing as the son of Edward White Benson, Headmaster of Wellington College, later Bishop of Truro, then Archbishop of Canterbury, and of Mary Sidgwick. Edward Frederick Benson grew up in a privileged Victorian household and found writing easy. None of the Benson children married. Three suffered periods of depression. All of them had same-sex relationships at some point in their lives. All wrote voluminously. Arthur Christopher Benson, the eldest, is remembered for his poem 'Land of Hope and Glory' and a 5 million-word diary. Unlike his siblings E.F. Benson did not pursue an academic or theological career. Instead he became a very successful novelist, settling eventually in Rye where he acquired Lamb House, Henry JAMES's former home, and where Benson became a mayor. Benson wrote several volumes of autobiography: *Our Family Affairs* (1920), *As We Were: A Victorian Peepshow* (1930), and *Final Edition* (1940). He also produced series of novels devoted to the same central character. *Dodo* (1983) was followed by *Dodo's Daughter* (1913), *Dodo the Second* (1914), and *Dodo Wanders* (1921). His books on Mrs Emmeline Lucas, also known as La Lucia, gathered a cult following. *Queen Lucia* (1920), *Miss Mapp* (1922), *Lucia in London* (1929), *Mapp and Lucia* (1931), *Lucia's Progress* (1935), and *Troubles for Lucia* (1939) were highly successful as camp, social satire. Benson was very discreet about his homosexuality. The theme of same-sex love emerges mainly in his university novels such as *The Babe, B.A.* (1896), *David Blaize* (1916), *David*

Blaize and the Blue Door (1918), *David of King's* (1924), and in *Raven's Brood* (1934).

Berry, Paul (1919–99). Gay British writer, born in the Midlands as one of ten children. Following his early schooling, he served in the Royal Engineers and Royal Ordnance Corps. During the Second World War he was a bomb disposal soldier in London. In 1942 Berry met Vera BRITTAIN and they became close friends. His life before and during the war provided the material for her last novel, *Born 1925*. Berry pursued various jobs and engaged in socio-political issues through prison visiting and pacifist campaigns. He worked for a number of years as a lecturer in secretarial skills at Kingsway Princeton College, London. In 1956 he co-authored *Daughters of Cain*, a book about nine women who were executed in Britain from 1923 onwards. He also co-authored *By Royal Appointment* (1970), a study of Mary Ann Clarke, an eighteenth-century courtesan and mistress of the Duke of York. Together with Alan Bishop he co-edited *Testament of a Generation: The Journalism of Vera Brittain and Winifred Holtby* (1985). With Mark Bostridge he co-edited *Vera Brittain: A Life* (1995) and, with Marion Shaw, *Remember! Remember!*, a selection of short stories by Winifred Holtby. In his last thirteen years he shared his life with the artist Eric (Lea) Leazell. They lived in west Sussex.

Best, Mireille (1943–). Lesbian French writer of working-class origin who was born in Le Havre and whose writings focus predominantly on often thwarted lesbian relationships. Her works, published by the prestigious French publishing house Gallimard, include a collection of five short stories called *Les Mots de hasard* (1980; *Random Words*) and the novels *Hymne aux murènes* (1986; *Hymn to the Muraena*), *Camille en octobre* (1988; *Camille in October*) and *Il n'y a* *pas d'hommes au paradis* (1995; *There are no Men in Paradise*).

Bishop, Elizabeth (1911–79). Celebrated US lesbian poet whose early years were beset by traumas. Her father's death, when she was only eight months old, caused her mother's breakdown and intermittent hospitalization over a period of five years until she was finally committed to a public sanatorium in 1916, where she stayed until her death in 1934. Bishop was looked after by her mother's parents in Great Village until 1917 when she was taken in by her well-to-do paternal grandparents, who hoped to give her the material and social privileges they themselves enjoyed in Worcester. The move resulted in stress-related illnesses such as eczema, asthma, and bronchitis for Bishop, leading to her being taken in by her mother's sister Maude, who lived in a Boston tenement. After little initial formal schooling due to her repeated moves and illnesses, Bishop attended Walnut Hill boarding school in Natick, Massachusetts, between 1927 and 1930, and then went to Vassar College where she majored in English. At Vassar she met the poet Marianne Moore who became her mentor and close friend. After graduation in 1934 Bishop lived off an inheritance from her father's estate and travelled widely. In 1943 she moved in with one of her travel companions from that period, Marjorie Stevens. Their relationship ended in 1947. Bishop's depression and alcoholism led to her being hospitalized in the summer of 1949. She then moved to Washington, DC, where, through the auspices of a new friend, Robert Lowell, she obtained a position as poetry consultant to the Library of Congress for one year, after which she moved to the Yaddo writers' colony until 1951. In March 1951 she won, on the recommendation of Marianne Moore, a Lucy Martin Donnelly Travelling Fellowship from Bryn Mawr College and embarked on a trip to Rio de Janeiro. Following an allergic reaction to cashew nuts, from which she was nursed back to health by her Brazilian friend Lota de Macedo Soares, she embarked on a long-term relationship with Lota that only ended with Lota's suicide in 1967. They remained, for the most part, in Brazil during this period that, for Bishop, was also professionally very productive. Her first volume of poems, *North and South* (1946), was reissued together with *A Cold Spring* (1955), which contains both her famous landscape poems and some lesbian poems. These won her the Pulitzer Prize in 1956. Bishop also translated *Minha Vida de Menina*, the diary of an adolescent girl who lived in a Brazilian diamond-mining village. This book appeared as *The Diary of 'Helena Morley'* in 1957. A collection of poems entitled *Questions of Travel* (1965) followed and her *Complete Poems* (1969) won her the National Book Award in 1970. After Lota's death Bishop continued to live intermittently in Brazil but found it hard to manage life there. Her alcoholism worsened; a new lover had a nervous breakdown in 1970, and in that year Bishop decided to return permanently to the USA. With her new lover, Alice Methfessel, she travelled extensively. She taught at Harvard and at the Universities of Washington and New York. In 1976 *Geographies III* was published – though containing only nine new poems it won Bishop the Books Abroad/Neustadt International Prize for Literature. Unlike a later generation of lesbian poets like Adrienne RICH who found it possible to discuss their sexuality in their work, Bishop tended to be more guarded about that subject, although marginality and the experience of being on the outside were constant themes in her work.

Blais, Marie-Claire (1939–). Born in Québec into a working-class family, Blais attended a convent before being sent to secretarial college when she was fifteen. Her first novel, *La Belle Bête* (1959; *Mad Shadows*), published when she was only nineteen, was followed by *Tête blanche* (1960), *Le Jour est noir* (1962; *The Day Is Dark*), *Une Saison dans la vie d'Emmanuel* (1965; *A Season in the Life of Emmanuel*), *Les Voyagers sacrés* (1966; *Three Travellers*), *L'Insoumise* (1966; *The Fugitive*), *David Sterne* (1967), and *Manuscrits de Pauline Archange* (1970; *The Manuscripts of Pauline Archange*). Blais's early novels, which centred on tormented young protagonists, caused some controversy and led her to move to Paris and the USA where she lived for fifteen years after having been introduced by Edmund Wilson to the painter Mary Meigs, who became her lover. Blais moved in with Meigs in Wellfleet, Cape Cod, where Meigs lived as a closeted lesbian with her long-term lover Barbara Deming. For a while Blais, Meigs, and Deming were involved in a three-way relationship, which ended when Blais and Meigs moved to Brittany from Cape Cod, there to become involved in yet another three-way relationship with a French woman novelist. Meigs has described the time at Cape Cod in her autobiography *Lily Briscoe: A Self-Portrait*; both Blais in *Une Liaison Parisienne* (1975; *A Literary Affair*) and Meigs in *The Medusa Head* describe their time in Brittany. While most of Blais's work contains homosexual characters, she has published three novels actually centring on lesbian and gay characters: *Le Loup* (1972; *The Wolf*), which centres on a gay pianist Sébastian, *Les Nuits de l'underground* (1978; *Nights of the Underground*), a lyrical coming-out story, and *L'Ange de la solitude* (1989). She has also written plays for the stage, radio, and television, several volumes of poetry, and a number of short prose pieces. She has won many literary prizes and fellowships, and is one of the foremost Canadian lesbian writers of the second half of the twentieth century.

Bogarde, Dirk (1921–99). Gay British actor and writer, born in Hampstead, London, as Derek Jules Gaspard Ulric Niven van den Bogaerde. Bogarde's half-Dutch father Ulric was arts editor at *The Times*; his mother an actress who discontinued her acting career upon marriage. Bogarde was brought up in Sussex by his sister, Elizabeth, and his nanny, Lally. This is described in *A Postillion Struck by Lightning* (1988). Bogarde attended both Allen Glen's School in Glasgow and University College, London. He also studied commercial art at Chelsea Polytechnic and, following a brief career as a scene designer and commercial artist, he began his acting career with the Amersham Repertory Company. In 1940 he joined the Queen's Royal Regiment and became a major, earning seven medals during the war. His war paintings are in the Imperial War Museum in London. Following the war Bogarde had many roles on stage and film, memorably in *Victim* (directed by Basil Dearden, 1961) in which he played a blackmailed homosexual lawyer, Melville Farr. Other key roles within gay cinema history he played include Gustav von Aschenbach, the man who falls in love with a beautiful Italian boy, in *Death in Venice* (directed by Luchino Visconti, 1971), adapted from the novel by the German writer Thomas MANN. Bogarde made many films and was quite a screen idol as the romantic lead in heterosexual romances. In his fifties he began to write, producing eight autobiographies as well as a number of novels. These include *Voices in the Garden* (1981), *West of Sunset* (1984), *Backcloth* (1987), *Snakes & Ladders* (1988), *A Gentle Occupation* (1990), *A Particular Friendship* (1990), *Jericho* (1992), *An Orderly Man* (1992), *Great Meadow* (1993), *A Short Walk to Harrods* (1994), *A Period of Adjustment* (1994), *Cleared for Take-off* (1996), *Closing Ranks* (1998), and *For the Time Being* (1998). Bogarde had a fifty-year relationship with his manager Tony Forwood but never came out of the closet completely. For many years Bogarde and Forwood lived near Grasse in Provence, France. When Forwood became seriously ill in

1983 they returned to London where they lived until Forwood's death from cancer in 1988. Bogarde was made a Chevalier de l'Ordre des Lettres in 1982. He was knighted in 1992. In 1996 he suffered a serious stroke and became partly paralysed. He became active in the Voluntary Euthanasia Society and drew up a living will. He eventually died of a heart attack at his Chelsea flat.

Bornstein, Kate (1948–). US performer and writer, born Albert Herman Bornstein, who grew up in New Jersey and for the first thirty years of her life lived as a man. She then underwent surgery to become a woman but, as she makes clear in her writings, she did not achieve the commonly assumed sense of harmony between body and mind through her surgery. Her transsexual status led her to explore gender identities, and in the 1990s she became an icon of queer performance, partly because unlike many transsexuals she continued to question her gender identity. Bornstein epitomizes the troubling of gender theorized by Judith BUTLER and it is significant that she gained prominence in the 1990s, the decade which inaugurated 'queer' in the lesbian and gay community. The work that gained her international recognition was *Gender Outlaw: On Men, Women and the Rest of Us* (1994), which, written in an experimental style, details not only Bornstein's history, including her surgical history, but also engages much more widely with questions of gender identity and gender performance. The volume contains her play *Hidden: A Gender*, first produced in 1989. Together with Caitlin Sullivan, Bornstein wrote *Nearly Roadkill, an Infobahn Erotic Adventure* (1996). In 1998 she published *My Gender Workbook*, a text designed to encourage readers to engage with questions of gender identity and to understand that gender is an ascribed and acculturated category that is the object of socio-cultural con-

straints, which, however, one does not need to subscribe to.

Bory, Jean-Louis (1919–79). Gay French writer and broadcaster, born in the village of Méréville near Paris to a schoolteacher mother and a pharmacist father, both of whom were accepting of his homosexuality when he recognized it at sixteen years of age. During the Second World War Bory served in the French Army and was a member of the Resistance. In 1945 he took a degree in classical literature and was a teacher of Greek, Latin, and French literature in secondary schools until 1962, when he became a full-time writer and broadcaster. His first novel, *Mon village à l'heure allemande* (*My Village on German Time*), won the prestigious Prix Goncourt in 1945. Bory also acted as a film critic and had a weekly radio show, *Le Masque et la plume*. Bory came out as gay in 1969 on a radio show. In 1973 he published an autobiographical text, *Ma moitié d'orange*, (*My Half of the Orange*). Open about his homosexuality, Bory wanted it to be regarded as ordinary and normal, not something to be the object of crusades. In January 1975 he participated in a television programme shown as part of the *Les Dossiers de l'écran* on homosexuality, wanting homosexuality to be seen as simply a fact. In 1979 he committed suicide.

Bowen, Elizabeth (1899–1973). Born in Dublin, Elizabeth Dorothea Cole Bowen had to deal with the death of her mother during childhood and an emotionally unstable father. Her marriage in 1923 to Alan Cameron provided the material and emotional stability that enabled her writing career. In 1930 she inherited the family home in County Cork. As a novelist and short-story writer she focused on the upper and middle classes, portraying difficult relationships and often including characters whose sexual identities were ambiguous, and whose behaviours suggest a coded homosexuality. Bowen was apparently very attractive to other women, among them May SARTON, who, as she recorded in her *A World of Light*, enjoyed a brief romantic encounter and very long friendship with Bowen. Bowen herself was unjudgmental of other people's sexual identities and relationships. Her many novels include *The Hotel* (1927), which is indebted to the work of Henry JAMES, *The Last September* (1929), *The House in Paris* (1935), *The Death of the Heart* (1938), *The Heat of the Day* (1949), *A World of Love* (1955), *The Little Girls* (1964), and *Eva Trout* (1969). *The Death of the Heart* features the novelist St. Quentin, who may be regarded as a version of the dispassionate urban homosexual male *à la* Henry James. *The Little Girls* is probably the book of Bowen's best known to lesbian readers. It has one girl ask another, Clare, if she is lesbian. The question is never answered but Clare appears to be lesbian.

Bowers, William Edgar (1924–2000). Gay US critic and poet who was born in Rome, Georgia, and died in San Francisco. Bowers went to the University of North Carolina in 1942, but interrupted his studies to join the US army. He was stationed at Berchtesgarden, one of Hitler's key residences, immediately after the Second World War, where he acted as a translator for an intelligence unit. He then completed his undergraduate degree at the University of North Carolina, moving to Stanford in 1947 to write his PhD on T. Sturge Moore. One of his contemporaries there, the poet Thom GUNN, was later to become instrumental in publicising Bowers's poetic works. Following his PhD Bowers taught at several universities before settling at the University of North Carolina at Santa Barbara where he continued to work until his retirement in 1991. Bowers's early writings were characterized by the use of rhyme and traditional poetic forms. He was first anthologized in Thom Gunn and Ted Hughes's collection of *Five American*

Poets (1963). Bowers's poetry after 1965 was less traditional but, unlike Thom Gunn for instance, he rarely engaged with homosexuality as a theme. His works include *The Loss of Form* (1956), *The Astronomers* (1965), *Witnesses* (1981), *Living Together* (1988), *Chaco Canyon* (1988), and *Collected Poems* (1997).

Bowles, Jane Auer (1917–73). Born in New York City, Bowles decided to become a writer when she met the French author Celine on a boat returning from Switzerland. Her first novel, *La Phaeton hypocrite* was privately printed and, though liked by her mother, considered immature as a work by Bowles. No copy of the text survives. Bowles pursued life in the lesbian and gay bars of Greenwich Village, much to the consternation of her family. In 1937 she met the gay novelist and composer Paul BOWLES. After their marriage they both continued to have homosexual relationships. Bowles's novel *Two Serious Ladies* (1943) was regarded as too openly lesbian by her family and by her lover Helvictia Perkins. The novel focuses on two women, Christina Goering and Mrs Copperfield, who seek security in a world that appears to be fragmented and threatening. Mrs Copperfield leaves her husband when she meets Pacifica, a prostitute, who initiates her into lesbian sex. Bowles's play *A Quarrelling Pair* (1945) centres on two sisters sitting in separate rooms and endlessly quarrelling with each other over trivia. Attraction between sisters is also central to some of her short stories such as 'Everything is Nice' and 'East Side: North Africa', which were collected in *My Sister's Hand in Mine: An Expanded Edition of the Collected Works of Elizabeth Bowles*, published posthumously in 1978. Bowles's play *In the Summer House* (1953) was put on in Ann Arbor and then moved to Broadway but was not an outright success. Despite reprints of her work Bowles remains an under-recognized writer and is not as well known as she deserves to be.

Bowles, Paul (1910–). Born in New York, Paul Bowles received little affection from his father. A homosexual uncle of whom Bowles was fond was angered when the boy discovered men dancing intimately in his house while he was staying over, though Bowles apparently did not find the sight itself frightening. However, the problematic relations between a boy child and male adults were subsequently explored by him in his most explicitly homosexual story, 'Pages from Cold Point' (1947), in which a boy tries to seduce his father. Bowles matriculated from the University of Virginia, then went to Paris in 1929, returned to New York, but from 1931 spent most of his life outside the USA. In 1938 he married Jane Auer BOWLES and in 1947 they went to live in Tangier. Bowles's groundbreaking novel *The Sheltering Sky* (1949) has been regarded as an existentialist novel in the manner of the work of Albert Camus and Jean-Paul Sartre. The Bowles's home in Tangier became a meeting point for many US writers and artists who sought to escape the confines of US society, especially members of the beat generation who experimented both with drugs and sex, and included writers such as William S. BURROUGHS, Allen GINSBERG, and Tennessee WILLIAMS. Bowles's many works include major translations of Sartre's writings, in particular *No Exit* (1958), and translations by hitherto unknown Moroccan writers such as Mohammed Mrabet and Mohamed Choukri.

Boyd, Malcolm (1923–). Born in New York, this openly gay US theologian and writer was the only child of wealthy parents who separated when he was nine years old. His mother was awarded custody, and they moved to Colorado Springs and then to Denver. In his teens he was, as he describes it, a 'sissy', and therefore lonely and isolated. Boyd appears to have been a studious child. After school he went to the University of Arizona, Tucson, where he gained a BA in 1944. He then spent some years first learning how to write radio scripts and then being hired in Hollywood to work on radio and TV shows. After a period of intense involvement with Hollywood, including a close friendship with Mary Pickford, Boyd decided that he wanted to enter holy orders. In 1951 he went to a seminary in Berkeley, California, and attended the Church Divinity School of the Pacific for three years, receiving a BD in 1954. He then spent a year at Oxford University, and attended an ecumenical seminary in Geneva and the Union Theological Seminary, New York City, from which he graduated in 1956. Following his early career as a copywriter, scriptwriter, and producer of radio programmes, Boyd held various posts as a chaplain and pastor at different churches. Boyd came out as gay in the second half of the 1970s. His life partner, Mark Thompson, is a senior writer on the US gay journalism scene. Engaged in making the church more accessible as well as in various forms of activism, Boyd maintained an intense programme of writing both on issues of spirituality and on being gay. His early work centred on the Church and his engagement with the Church, and was non-fiction. It included *Crisis in Communication* (1957), *Christ and Celebrity Gods* (1958), *If I Go down to Hell* (1962), *The Hunger, the Thirst* (1964), and *Are You Running with Me, Jesus?* (1964), which became a bestseller. Other non-fiction related to Boyd's religious beliefs and his experiences as a religious person include *As I Live and Breathe: Stages of an Autobiography* (1969), *Human Like Me, Jesus* (1971), *Christian: Its Meanings in the Age of Future Shock* (1975), *Am I Running with You, God?* (1977), and *Take off the Masks* (1977), another bestseller which was revised by Boyd in 1984 and in 1993. This volume inaugurated a phase of writing about being a gay priest including *Look Back in Joy: Celebration of Gay Lovers* (1981), *Half Laughing/Half Crying: Songs for*

Myself (1986), *Gay Priest: An Inner Journey* (1987), and *Edges, Boundaries, and Connections* (1992). Boyd's many writings include several volumes of fiction such as *The Fantasy World of Peter Stone, and Other Fables* (1969), *The Lover* (1972), *The Runner* (1974), and *The Alleluia Affair* (1975). Boyd's plays include *They Aren't Real to Me* (produced in New York in 1962), *The Job* (produced in New York in 1962), *Study in Color* (produced in New York in 1962), *Boy* (produced in New York in 1964), and *The Community* (produced in New York in 1964). Boyd has also edited *On the Battle Lines* (1964), *The Underground Church* (1968), which turned him into a celebrity as 'the priest of the underground', and *Amazing Grace: Stories of Lesbian and Gay Faith* (1991). He has contributed to a variety of newspapers and magazines, and appears, throughout his life, to have had both a certain celebrity status and to have courted celebrities. His autobiographical texts proclaim his attraction to religion, his engagement with celebrities from a variety of walks of life, his coming to gayness, and a kind of go-getting, somewhat Californian, missionizing all-American spirit which does not travel too easily. Sentences such as 'Let communication be an event that involves people, not a charade of puppets. Be yourself. Relate to other selves without inhibition and pretence. Help others to be themselves' from *Take off the Masks*, for example, are both of their period and very 'conversation-pit'.

Boye, Karin (1900–41). Lesbian Swedish writer who was born into a middle-class household in Gothenburg from where her family moved to Stockholm in 1909. There she went to university, followed by a period at the University of Uppsala from which she graduated in 1928. She became a teacher and wrote in her spare time, contributing to many journals and publishing poetry. Her first collection of poetry to be published was *Moln* (1922;

Clouds). This was followed by *Gömda Land* (1924; *Hidden Lands*) and *Härdane* (1927; *The Hearths*), which established her as a writer. A member of the left-wing radical cultural organization Clarté, and deeply opposed to Nazism, Boye was very interested in psychoanalysis and, in 1931, founded the psychoanalytic journal *Spektrum*. In 1932–3 she consulted a psychoanalyst in Berlin and it was here that she met her life partner, Margot Hanel, a German Jewess who went to live with Boye in Stockholm. In the early 1930s Boye began to write prose works, among them the novels *Astarte* (1931), *Merit vakner* (1933; *The Awakening of Merit*), and *För lite* (1933; *Too Little*). Her poetry collection *För trädets skull* (1935; *For the Sake of the Tree*) was much influenced by her interest in psychoanalysis. Boye also produced an autobiographical novel, *Kris* (1934), in which she openly discussed lesbian relationships, and a science fiction novel, *Kallocain* (1940). In 1941 Boye, who had suffered from depression all her life, committed suicide, though the precise reasons for her suicide remain unclear. Her partner Margot Hanel killed herself shortly afterwards.

Bradley, Marion Zimmer (1930–99). US novelist and science fiction and fantasy writer who, in the 1960s and not unlike a number of other writers of lesbian pulp fiction such as Ann BANNON, published a series of lesbian romances under a variety of pseudonyms. They include *I Am a Lesbian* (as Lee Chapman, 1962); *Spare Her Heaven* (as Morgan Ives, 1963); *My Sister, My Love* (as Miriam Gardner, 1963); *Twilight Lovers* (as Miriam Gardner, 1964); *Knives of Desire* (as Morgan Ives, 1966); and *No Adam for Eve* (as John Dexter, 1966). Born in Albany, New York, Zimmer Bradley was educated at the New York State College for Teachers (now State University of New York at Albany) between 1946–8, then at Hardin-Simmons University, Abilene, Texas, from where she graduated with a BA in 1964.

She also undertook graduate study at the University of California, Berkeley. Her fantasy and science fiction writing dominated her career. She edited *Marion Bradley Zimmer's Fantasy Magazine*, and wrote many volumes of fantasy and science fiction as well as gothic fiction. Her most famous genre text may well be *The Mists of Avalon* (1982). Her 'Darkover' series, which was begun with *The Swords of Aldones* and *The Planet Savers* (1962), turned into one of the most prolific series of fantasy fiction produced in the second half of the twentieth century. Together with Gene Damon Zimmer Bradley she published *Checklist: A Complete, Cumulative Checklist of Lesbian, Variant and Homosexual Fiction in English* (1960), and she edited *A Gay Bibliography* (1975).

Bram, Christopher (1952–). Since the publication of his first book, *Surprising Myself*, in 1987, Christopher Bram has achieved an increasingly solid reputation as one of the best contemporary gay novelists. Several of Bram's novels take place in New York and appear to contain autobiographical elements, and all deal with predominantly gay themes and characters. While describing himself as a gay novelist, however, Bram has indicated in several interviews that his intention is to depict gayness as having more similarities with than differences from life in general. Carefully plotted and meticulous in historical detail, Bram's novels offer both an examination of gay life and a mirror of a particular time and place. Following *Surprising Myself*, which explores New York gay political activism in the 1970s, Bram published *Hold Tight* (1988), set in the gay underworld of the New York of the 1940s. *In Memory of Angel Clare* (1989) deals with a group of New Yorkers confronting AIDS. *Almost History* (1992) and *Gossip* (1997) are more expansive in setting, the former involving Vietnam and politics in the Philippines, the latter a skilful story of Washington, DC, intrigue

and machinations in a media-obsessed society. *The Notorious Dr. August* (2000), an ambitious and sprawling historical novel, portrays characters, gay and straight, against the backdrop of the Industrial Age USA and *fin de siècle* Europe. Bram's best-known work thus far, *Father of Frankenstein* (1995), is a fictionalized account of the gay Hollywood director James Whale. Sharp and evocative in its depiction of 1950s Hollywood, the novel offers an unsentimental portrayal of both sexual obsession and the universal need to connect. A highly acclaimed film version of *Father of Frankenstein* appeared in 1998 under the title *Gods and Monsters*.

[David Garnes]

Brant, Beth (1941–). Born in Detroit, of Mohawk descent, Brant is a Canadian-US writer whose work addresses issues of lesbian identity, Native American experience, sexism, and racism. Brant got married when she was seventeen years old and had three daughters within an abusive marriage that finally ended in divorce. Supporting herself and her children through various jobs, Brant began to identify as lesbian from the age of thirty-three, and she began writing in her forties. She has lived much of her life in Michigan. Brant's works include the anthology *A Gathering of Spirit: A Collection of North American Indian Women* (1983), which she edited and which was re-issued in a revised and expanded edition in 1988, the collection of writings *Mohawk Trail* (1985), *Food and Spirit* (1991), *Writing as Witness: Essay and Talk* (1994), and *I'll Sing 'til the Day I Die: Conversations with Tyendinaga Elders* (1995). Her writings, in some respects like those of Paula Gunn ALLEN, explore the relationship between sexual and racial identities, portraying the struggles of Native American lesbian women.

Brantenberg, Gert (1941–). Lesbian Norwegian writer, born in Oslo, who grew up in Frederiksstad and taught History and English in secondary schools while writing. In 1970 she completed a degree in English at the University of Oslo. From early on she was involved in the women's liberation movement of the 1970s. In 1973 she published the novel *Opp alle jordens homofile* (1973; *Arise All Gays of the World*, translated as *What Comes Naturally* in 1986) in which, as in her *Sangen om St Croix* (1979; *The Songs of St Croix*), she discussed the emancipation of the gay community in the form of a coming-out story. However, among lesbian readers in the English-speaking world she probably became most famous with *Egalias døtre* (1977; *Daughters of Egalia*), a feminist science fiction novel that appeared at a time when feminist and lesbian-feminist science fiction, fuelled by the hopes and aspirations of the women's movement, emerged as a genre in which new and often separatist worlds for women might be imagined. For a few years between the mid-1970s and the mid-1980s this fiction enjoyed much popularity. Brantenberg followed that volume with a trilogy featuring Inger, a young woman who explores her lesbian identity. The three novels are the previously mentioned *Sangen om St Croix*, *Ved fergestedet* (1985; *At the Quay*), and *For alle vinder* (1996; *The Four Winds*). In 1983 she also published a novel about the relationship between a married woman and a lesbian, *Favntak* (*Embraces*). She has also written a collection of essays, *Eremitt og entertainer* (1991; *Hermit and Entertainer*), and a co-authored study of love between women in European literature translated into Scandinavian languages, *På sporet av den tapte lyst* (1986; *In Remembrance of Lusts Past*). In 1997 she published a historical novel, *Agusta og Bjørnsterne*. Brantenberg has been very active in the lesbian and gay movements in Scandinavia. She helped found the Lesbian Movement in Denmark (1974) and in Norway (1975). She is a regular contributor to lesbian and gay papers and magazines in Scandinavia.

Brecht, Bertolt (1898–1956). One of the most influential German dramatists of the twentieth century, as well as a notable writer of theatre theory, poetry, and short prose, Brecht portrayed same-sex desire in a number of his plays, especially in his early work. In that work those same-sex relationships are often represented in terms of men of different class and cultural dispositions: one refined and idealising; the other uncouth, driven by his appetites, and often very working class. Thus Brecht's play *Baal*, of which he wrote several versions beginning in 1918, features Baal, the epitome of self-seeking desire, in a friendship with the composer and idealist Ekart, whom he eventually kills in a jealous rage. Homoerotic as well as homosocial relations dominate much of Brecht's work which feminists would regard as misogynistic in its impulses and representations of women. Driven out of Germany during the Nazi era for his communist beliefs, Brecht moved variously to the Netherlands, Denmark, and the USA, only to take up permanent residence in what became East Germany after the Second World War. In East Germany he lived in a privileged situation under what were for others dire circumstances, with a major theatre, the Berliner Ensemble, devoted to the performance of his work in accordance with the *Modellbücher* that were made of each production. During his time in the USA Brecht collaborated with Leon Feuchtwanger on an adaptation of Christopher MARLOWE's play *Edward II*, under the title *Das Leben Eduard des Zweiten* (*The Life of Edward II*). This play, which centres on the relationship between Edward II and his favourite, Gaveston, has been variously adapted, including in film versions by Derek JARMAN and in a feature film starring Ian McKellen, a celebrated British gay actor. The same homoerotic tension that haunts *Baal* is evident in Brecht's play *Im Dickicht der Städte* (*In the Jungle of the Cities*), the central relationship of which is between a timber merchant, Shlink, and an impoverished library clerk, Garga. Brecht himself had a number of complex and problematic relationships including with his lead actress Helene Weigel, much celebrated for her portrayal of several of his key female characters, including in *Mutter Courage* (*Mother Courage*). His intense friendships with various men suggest the possibility of bisexuality.

Brittain, Vera (1893–1970). English novelist, biographer, journalist, and poet who was born into a prosperous family in Newcastle under Lyme and educated at St Monica's School, Surrey, as well as Somerville College, Oxford, the latter against her parents' will. Following the death of her fiancé Roland Leighton in action during the First World War, Brittain left Somerville for a time in 1915 to become a Voluntary Aid Detachment nurse. In 1925 she married the political philosopher George Catlin who spent his time in the USA while Brittain stayed in England with her close friend Winifred Holtby. She is the mother of Shirley Williams, for a time a prominent politician in England and then a professor at Harvard. Brittain detailed her childhood, the influence of Olive SCHREINER, and her wartime experiences in her most famous book, *Testament of Youth* (1933). Its second volume, *Testament of Friendship* (1940), is of more interest to lesbians since it is a tribute to Winifred Holtby who died in 1935. Brittain and Holtby shared political, pacifist, and feminist commitments. Brittain's final volume in this series, *Testament of Experience* (1957), covers the period 1925–50. Brittain wrote a number of other books, and the most notable within a lesbian context was perhaps *Radclyffe Hall: A Case of Obscenity?* (1968), in which she examined the trial for obscenity of Hall's *The Well of Loneliness*. Brittain's novels are in the main autobiographical. They include

The Dark Tide (1923) and *Born 1925* (1948). Her diaries of the period 1913 to 1917 were published as *Chronicle of Youth* (1981). The *Selected Letters of Winifred Holtby and Vera Brittain* were published in 1960.

Brophy, Brigid (1929–95). English novelist who wrote prolifically during the 1950s and 1960s, and whose contribution to lesbian writing is the rather misogynistic satire *The Finishing Touch* (1963). Part of the sub-genre of lesbian boarding-school fictions, of which Olivia's (see STRACHEY BUSSY, DOROTHY) *Olivia* (1949), Rosemary MANNING's *The Chinese Garden* (1962), and Henry Handel RICHARDSON's *The Getting of Wisdom* (1910) are other examples, it presents a narrative of the tragic adoration of a schoolgirl for her capricious and teasing schoolmistress. Brophy herself, the daughter of an archbishop, attended St Paul's Girls' School, London, before going to St Hugh's College, Oxford, in 1947. She was sent down after two years for 'unspecified offences', variously rumoured to be drunkenness in chapel or lesbianism. In 1954 she married Michael Levey, an art historian and the author of *The Case of Walter Pater*. Their unconventional marriage, as well as Brophy's outspoken views in favour of bisexuality and against monogamy, drew the public's attention to them. John Bailey, husband of the novelist Iris MURDOCH, reports that Brophy tried to seduce Murdoch. Brophy has written a number of novels that explore a variety of social and sexual concerns. They include *The King of a Rainy Country* (1956), *Flesh* (1962), and *In Transit* (1969). She has also published several volumes of essays, and biographies of Mozart, Ronald FIRBANK, and the painter Aubrey Beardsley. In her later years she suffered from multiple sclerosis.

Brossard, Nicole (1943–). Canadian radical lesbian writer whose middle-class upbringing, travels in Europe, and education at the Université de Montréal contributed to the experimental, increasingly postmodern style of writing that dominates her work. While still married she met a gym teacher, Germaine, who became her lover in 1973, the same year that her first book of fiction, *Turn of a Pang (Sold-out)* appeared. She also found herself pregnant and had a daughter in 1974. Brossard reinvented herself as a radical lesbian and her writings fully inhabit a radical feminist position. *L'Amèr* (1977; *These Our Mothers or The Exploding Chapter*) followed, as part of a lesbian trilogy that also included *Lovhers (Amantes)* and *Le Sens apparent* (1980; *Surfaces of Sense*). The trilogy critiques phallogocentrism and articulates lesbian desire. *Lovhers* and *Picture Theory* (1982) were written in celebration of Marisa, the love of Brossard's life, whom she met in 1978. In 1987 she published *Le Désert mauve* (*Mauve Desert*), a postmodern text. Her work, including her poetry and essays, continues to explore writing from a feminine and feminist lesbian perspective.

Broumas, Olga (1949–). Born in Greece, Broumas moved to the USA when young and attended the University of Pennsylvania where she gained a BA in architecture in 1970. She then went to the University of Oregon to do creative writing. She has held several fellowships (National Endowment for the Arts 1978; Guggenheim 1981) and taught in a number of universities and colleges. Her first work to be published in North America, *Caritas* (1976), is a collection of five unbound broadsides about one woman's love for another. This has established Broumas firmly within a lesbian literary tradition. Subsequent collections do not focus as clearly on lesbian relationships. She has also translated other poetry from Greek into English.

Brown, Rita Mae (1944–). Born in Hanover, Pennsylvania, to an unmarried mother who turned her over to an orpha-

nage, Rita Mae Brown is one of the USA's best-known lesbian novelists. Brown's fame rests predominantly, though not exclusively, on her first novel *Rubyfruit Jungle* (1973), which was published by the now no longer existing but still legendary Daughters Inc., a lesbian collective publishing house. With this novel she produced a classic of lesbian fiction. Its protagonist, Molly Bolt, belongs to a generation of young out lesbian characters who rebel against their small-town backgrounds and decide to live openly as lesbians. Like Beebo Brinker in Ann BANNON's novels and Jeanette in Jeanette WINTERSON's *Oranges Are Not the Only Fruit*, Molly Bolt is a character who engages the reader's sympathies through her feistiness and assertiveness. Like Winterson would do after her, Brown uses humour to mediate the heroine's plight in a heterosexist world. Molly Bolt is a not always right-on hero/ine who escapes from the small-town background she grew up in to live as a lesbian. Molly's devil-may-care attitude projects a celebratory defiance and rebelliousness that is in complete contrast to the long-suffering attitude of some previous lesbian hero/ines such as Stephen in Radclyffe HALL's classic lesbian novel *The Well of Loneliness*. This resilience and overcoming endeared Molly Bolt and *Rubyfruit Jungle* both to lesbian and mainstream audiences. Some subsequent lesbian novels such as Winterson's *Oranges Are Not the Only Fruit* (1985) have continued the tradition of presenting lesbian coming-out stories of plucky working-class hero/ines as triumphalist narratives of overcoming in the face of small-town prejudice. Brown herself attended the University of Florida but was expelled in 1964 from that institution for her campaigning activities around civil rights and greater racial integration. She moved to Greenwich Village, New York, for a time, living in poverty and continuing her political activities. An early member of the National Organization for Women, she was expelled for demanding greater recognition for its lesbian members. Apart from lesbian poetry and *Rubyfruit Jungle* Brown, who also pursued her academic studies and gained a BA and a PhD, has written a number of novels including *In Her Day* (1976), *Six of One* (1978), *Sudden Death* (1983), *Southern Discomfort* (1982), *High Hearts* (1986), *Bingo* (1988), *Wish You Were Here* (1990), *Rest in Pieces* (1992), and *Venus Envy* (1993). In the late 1970s and early 1980s Brown had a relationship with the openly lesbian tennis star Martina Navratilova with whom she lived between 1979–81.

Bryant, Dorothy (1930–). Contemporary US writer of lesbian fiction. Born in San Francisco, Bryant is the second daughter of immigrants from northern Italy. Having studied and taught music until 1960, she then devoted herself to writing and publishing. Together with her husband she lives in Berkeley, California, where they run the independent publishing house Ata Books, which has published many of Bryant's works. Bryant has written novels, plays (four of which have been produced in the Bay area of San Francisco), and short stories. In *Killing Wonder* (1981) she created a lesbian detective. Other texts by her featuring lesbian characters include *Miss Giardino* (1978), *Garden of Eros* (1979), *Prisoners* (1980), *Day in San Francisco* (1983), *Kin of Ata are Waiting for You* (1983), *Myths to Lie by: Short Pieces* (1984), *Test* (1991), *Anita, Anita: Garibaldi of the New World* (1994), and *Ella Price's Journal* (1997 reprint).

Bryher (1894–1983). Pseudonym, adopted from the name of one of the isles of Scilly, of (Annie) Winifred Ellerman, the lesbian novelist, essayist, poet, and autobiographer who was the close companion of the poet H.D. whom she met in 1918. Through H.D., Bryher met the US writer Robert McAlmon with whom she contracted a marriage of convenience in 1929. The couple moved to Paris where Bryher

began a long friendship with Gertrude STEIN, moving in avant-garde modernist circles. She wrote a study of the poet Amy Lowell (1918) and founded the film journal *Close-up*. In 1929 she published *Film Problems of Soviet Russia*. Bryher helped to establish the *Psychoanalytic Review* in England. Her other writings included historical novels such as *The Coin of Carthage* (1963). She published two volumes of autobiography, *The Heart to Artemis* (1962) and *The Days of Mars 1940–1946* (1972), which details her relationship with H.D.

Bulkin, Elly (1944–). Jewish lesbian US writer whose father and maternal grandparents emigrated from Eastern Europe to the USA where Bulkin grew up in the Bronx, living in New York City for most of her life. She has intermittently earned her living as a teacher of English and of Women's Studies, and worked for five years at the Women's Center of Brooklyn College. Like Elana NACHMAN, she belongs to a generation of Jewish lesbians who emerged on the US literary scene during the 1970s. She has spent much time and effort promoting lesbian writing and her literary work includes many anthologies that she has either edited or co-edited such as *Amazon Poetry: An Anthology of Lesbian Poetry* (1975; with Joan Larkin), *Lesbian Fiction: An Anthology* (1981), *Lesbian Poetry: An Anthology* (1981; with Joan Larkin), and *Yours in Struggle* (1984; with Minnie Bruce Pratt and Barbara Smith). Together with Jan CLAUSEN and Rhima Shore she has edited *Conditions*, a journal of women's writing and in particular lesbian writing that, in its volume 11/12 (1985), contained four poems by Dorothy ALLISON. Bulkin has also contributed to lesbian journals such as *Sinister Wisdom*, and other journals like *College English*, *Radical Teacher*, and the *Women's Studies Newsletter*. She regularly reviews women's poetry.

Burford, Barbara (1946–). Black British woman poet, dramatist, and fiction writer whose best-known work to date is the collection of lesbian short stories, *The Threshing Floor*, which came out in 1986. Her poetry has been published in *A Dangerous Knowing: Four Black Women Poets* (1985). She edited *Dancing the Tightrope: New Love Poems by Women* (1987), and her play *Patterns* was commissioned by Changing Women's Theatre and performed in 1984.

Burns, John Horne (1916–53). Born in Andover, Massachusetts, to a prominent Irish Catholic family where he was one of seven children, the gay writer John Horne Burns spent his life as an author frustrated by the lack of critical recognition of his work. Educated initially at the Sisters of Notre Dame convent and at the Andover Academy, he then went on to Harvard to study literature, graduating in 1937. Following a brief period in teaching, he joined the infantry as a private in 1942, served in military intelligence in Casablanca and Algiers, and, finally, due to his knowledge of Italian, was commissioned as a second lieutenant, censoring prisoner-of-war mail in Africa and Italy. A further year teaching at Loomis School, Windsor, Connecticut, followed after the war. He also began his publishing career at that time, writing travel pieces for *Holiday* to survive. His first novel, *The Gallery*, appeared in 1947. It was followed by *Lucifer with a Book* (1949) and *A Cry of Children* (1953), his last published novel, written after he moved to Italy. He wrote a fourth novel; however, this was not published because he died before being able to make required revisions to the book. None of his novels centre on homosexual characters but all deal with gay and/or lesbian figures in a marginal way. Burns himself remained a dissatisfied figure. When he died of a cerebral haemorrhage it was suggested that he had committed suicide because his literary career had failed to take off

and because of the ending of a relationship with an Italian doctor. Initially buried in Rome, his remains were eventually taken back to Boston and reburied there.

Burroughs, William S. (1914–). Gay US writer who acknowledged his homosexuality in the 1950s and is renowned for the transgressiveness of his writing, which deals with violence and violent sexualities in a quasi-satirical mode, portraying both sexuality and language as sites of conflict. Born to a wealthy family in Missouri, Burroughs studied English, Medicine, and Anthropology at Harvard and the University of Vienna before becoming addicted to narcotics in the mid-1940s. He fled to Mexico after being arrested for possession of drugs. In Mexico he shot his wife, Joan Burroughs, during a drunken imitation of William Tell. An unfinished manuscript of Burroughs, *Queer*, written during the 1950s while he was recovering from heroin addiction but published only in 1985, represented the gay demimonde of that period. Burroughs moved from a naturalistic depiction of outsider culture as portrayed in *Junky* (1953) to a more satirical and surrealist mode in *The Naked Lunch* (1959). This novel was subject to a number of court cases for obscenity. In 1992 it was made into a film by David Cronenberg. Burroughs's trilogy *The Soft Machine* (1961), *The Ticket that Exploded* (1962), and *Nova Express* (1964) centred on the hallucinatory world of addiction. Later novels include *The Wild Boys* (1971), *The Place of Dead Roads* (1983), and *The Western Lands* (1987).

Busi, Aldo (1948). Gay Italian writer who was born in Montichiari in northern Italy near Lake Garda, and initially spent a number of years leading a fairly itinerant life in various European countries and working in jobs such as waitering before becoming a writer. During his travels he learnt French, German, and English, and then worked as a translator for a time. He has translated a number of works into

Italian, including Joe R. ACKERLEY's *My Father and Myself*. His first novel, *Seminario sulla gioventù* (translated as *Seminar on Youth*) was published in 1984. The text is a kind of *Bildungsroman*, or novel of education, centring on the protagonist's journey from the Lombardy countryside to Paris. It was followed by *Vita standard di un venditore provvisorio di collant* (1985; translated as *The Standard of Life of a Temporary Pantyhose Salesman*, 1988). Busi does not want to be viewed as a 'gay writer' and is more interested in overcoming the binarisms of hetero- and homosexuality than in cementing a gay identity. In 1989 he was the object of an obscenity trial in Italy, following the publication of his novel *Sodomie in corpo 11* (1988; translated as *Sodomies at Elevenpoint*, 1992), but was not found guilty. His publications since that time include *Vendita galline km. 2* (1993) and *Cazzi e canguri (pochissimi i canguri)* (1994; translated as *Uses and Abuses*, 1995).

Butler, Judith. Contemporary US theorist and academic whose work during the 1990s became hugely influential in the interrogation of sexual identities, of the dualism of sex and gender, and the binarism of masculinity and femininity that Butler's work puts into question, becoming instrumental in the forging of a new lesbian and gay cultural sensibility, aesthetic, and politic: 'queer'. Butler became interested in the debates about the meaning of gender that occurred during the 1980s. Her first work, *Subjects of Desire: Hegelian Reflections in Twentieth-century France*, had little impact but *Gender Trouble: Feminism and the Subversion of Identity* (1990) became a bestseller, shaping debates about gender throughout the 1990s and catapulting Butler into the celebrity circuit of international star academics. In this volume Butler argued for the notion of gender as performance, as a kind of daily enactment that – by virtue of

its performative nature – allowed for all kinds of different performances that rendered the conventional notions of masculinity and femininity as well as their anchorage in supposedly biological sex and acculturated gender problematic. Butler instantly became the celebrated theorist of 'queer' and while many attacked the seeming implication of the book that anyone could 'play with gender' as they pleased, the book was a landmark text in changing debates about sex and gender. Many lesbian performers began to interrogate gender identities in their work, among them Claire DOWIE and SPLIT BRITCHES, and 'queer' performers such as Kate BORNSTEIN gained new followings. In avant-garde lesbian and gay circles of the 1990s 'queer' became the new self-consciously in-your-face self-assertiveness of communities who felt that their identities and sexual activities had been the objects of censorship for too long. Answering her critics concerning the seemingly ludic and voluntaristic nature of gender play, which many questioned, Butler published *Bodies that Matter* in 1993, a text that argues that gender performance is about the 'compulsory citation of norms', which is much more constrained by socio-cultural and political factors than the original volume seemed to suggest. Butler has since continued to interrogate the relation between power, performance, and gendered identities in books such as *Excitable Speech: A Politics of the Performative* (1997) and *The Psychic Life of Power: Theories in Subjection* (1997). She has also published *Antigone's Claim* (2000). Together with Joan Wallach Scott, one of the foremost lesbian feminist historians in the USA, Butler edited the influential *Feminists Theorize the Political* (1992). With Ernesto Laclau and Slavoj Zizek she has published *Contingency, Hegemony, Universality* (2000). She has taught at several universities in the United States and other countries, and is currently Chancellor's Professor of Rhetoric and Comparative Literature at the University of California, Berkeley.

Butler, Lady Eleanor (1739–1829) and Sarah Ponsonby (1755–1831). Known as the Ladies of Llangollen, a village in Wales to which this lesbian couple went to live in 'delicious Retirement', Lady Eleanor Butler and Sarah Ponsonby came from Anglo-Irish backgrounds and eloped together in 1778. Ponsonby had lost her parents in early childhood and her stepmother when she was thirteen. In the care of her father's cousin Lady Betty Fownes, she was sent to Miss Parke's boarding school in Kilkenny. There she met Lady Eleanor in 1768 who became her mentor and friend. After Ponsonby left the school in 1773, they began a secret correspondence and decided to live together. Their first elopement failed; they were separated by their families but resisted pressures to marry or enter a convent. Eventually, their families relented; the two women went to Wales where they rented a cottage that they named Plas Newydd and where they lived until the end of their lives. Their pastoral retreat drew many prominent visitors and their romantic lives together were the subject of many subsequent texts such as COLETTE's *The Pure and the Impure* (1928), Doris GRUMBACH's *The Ladies* (1984), and Morgan Graham's *These Lovers Fled Away* (1988). There has been some speculation as to whether or not they had a sexual relationship and if they should be described as lesbians or as having a romantic friendship. Anne LISTER, a lesbian contemporary of theirs, was fairly convinced that they were lovers.

Butler, Samuel (1835–1902). Samuel Butler was born into a family of Anglican clergy in Nottinghamshire. He was educated at Shrewsbury School and at St John's College, Cambridge, where he received a degree in 1853. In 1860 he emigrated to New Zealand to become a

sheep farmer but returned to England after four years, together with his companion Charles Paine Pauli whom he had met in New Zealand in 1861. Butler supported Pauli financially for the next thirty years, only to learn on his death that Pauli had amassed a fortune, had cut Butler out of his will, and had also been financially supported by two other men. Butler was apparently also infatuated with another young man, a Swiss named Hans Faesch whose death prompted the poem 'In Memoriam H.R.F.'. Butler wrote a number of novels, essays, and other texts. In *Shakespeare's Sonnets Reconsidered* (1899) he suggests that Shakespeare was infatuated with a younger man who betrayed him. His most famous novel was *The Way of All Flesh* (published posthumously in 1903), which offered a critique of Victorian family and social values. In *The Way of All Flesh* Butler presents intense male friendships and shows their dissolution through the social demands for heterosexual marriage. The text strongly influenced E.M. FORSTER whose novel *The Longest Journey* (1907) expresses similar sentiments. When Butler died in 1902 after a long illness he was attended by his loyal manservant Alfred Catie and by his companion Henry Festing Jones.

Byron, Lord George Gordon (1788–1824). The English poet, dramatist, letter and journal writer, Lord Byron was the son of Captain John Byron, 'Mad Jack', who eloped with and married Lady Carmarthen. Together they had a daughter, Augusta Leigh, Byron's half-sister with whom Byron had an affair and whose daughter, born in 1814, was almost certainly his. Captain Byron's second wife, Catherine Gordon of Gight, was Byron's mother. Byron was born with a club-foot, a fact that did not detract from his general flamboyance and attractiveness to women and men. He was educated in Aberdeen until he was ten years old, and eventually inherited the family title. Sent to Harrow school, it is there that his sexual interest in boys began. Byron's homosexual leanings were not discussed until biographies by G. Wilson Knight and Leslie Marchand in 1957, although the phenomenon of romantic friendships between boys in English private schools was known about. However, scandal attached to homosexuality for such a long time that few dared to be open about their sexual interests. Byron later expressed his feelings for younger boys at Harrow in two collections of poems, *Fugitive Pieces* (1806) and *Poems on Various Occasions* (1807), which he printed privately while at Cambridge. Some of these early friendship poems were reprinted in *Hours of Idleness* (1807), a collection that was strongly attacked in *The Edinburgh Review*. Byron countered that attack with his 1809 satire *English Bards and Scotch Reviewers*. While at Cambridge Byron fell in love with John Edleston, a chorister at Trinity College. His poem 'To Cornelian' records their affair. After Cambridge Byron took his seat in the House of Lords and between 1809 and 1811 travelled around Europe, visiting Portugal where William BECKFORD lived in exile at Cintra following allegations of homosexuality. He also visited Spain, Malta, Greece, and the Levant. Letters to his friends Charles Skinner Matthews and John Cam Hobhouse suggest that he had many homosexual experiences while he was in Greece. He also had an affair with Theresa Macri, the 'Maid of Athens', but his main involvement was with two boys, Eustathius Giorgiu and Nicolo Giraud. Byron made the latter his heir on his return to England. The publication of the first two cantos of *Childe Harold's Pilgrimage* in March 1812 made him an overnight literary success in England. He had a tempestuous love affair with Lady Caroline Lamb, who later threatened to expose his homosexuality, and was deeply involved with his half-sister Augusta. In 1913 he wrote *The Bride of Abydos*,

which hints at incest, *The Corsair* and *The Giaour*. In 1814 he wrote *Lara* in which homosexuality takes the form of a page who turns out to be a girl devoted to a girl called Lara. Eventually, in 1815 he married Annabella Milbanke with whom he had a daughter, Ada. He also wrote *Hebrew Melodies* during that year. However, in the face of mounting debts and rumours about his incestuous relationship with Augusta, his wife sought a separation from him after one year of marriage. Byron left England for good, travelling to Geneva where the poet Percy Bysshe Shelley and Claire Claremont had rented a villa. Claire became his mistress and gave birth to their daughter, Allegra, in 1817. During this period he gradually completed the four cantos of *Childe Harold* as well as writing other poetry. He finally settled in Venice where there was no English colony. He began his satire *Don Juan* which ridiculed English prudery. Byron settled down with Teresa Guiccioli but in 1823, when the London Committee for Greek Independence was formed, he decided to sail to Greece to help that cause. On Cephalonia he became embroiled with Lukas, the 15-year-old son of a Greek widow whom he helped. Lukas appears not to have returned Byron's love, as suggested in his poem 'On This Day I Complete My Thirty Sixth Year'. Byron died of fever at Missolonghi. After his death his friend Hobhouse persuaded Byron's publisher John Murray, and Thomas Moore, to destroy his memoirs. In his own works Byron never expressed his homosexuality very clearly, possibly for fear of the repercussions that such publication entailed. However, within a decade of his death a pseudo-autobiography, entitled *Don Leon, a Poem by Lord Byron* appeared that offered detailed accounts of his affairs. This poem was an attempt to protest against the capital punishment that was still meted out to those found guilty of homosexual acts.

C

Cahun, Claude (1894–1954). Lesbian French Jewish writer and photographer who was born Lucy Schwob into a family of prominent Jewish intellectuals. Her father was the publisher of the newspaper *Le Phare de la Loire*, and her uncle was a founder of the review *Mercure de France* as well as a member of the symbolist movement and friend of Oscar WILDE. Brought up on the island of Jersey, Cahun studied at Oxford in 1907–8. Subsequently she moved to Paris, together with her lover Suzanne Malherbe, who worked as a designer and artist under another male pseudonym, Marcel Moore. Photos of both women show them presenting a boyish image, with very short hair and androgynous faces. In 1914 Cahun published *Vues et visions*, a selection of her poetry. This was followed by *Héroines*, a collection of short stories, in 1925. For her first photographic self-portraits Cahun used the pseudonym Claude Courlis. Cahun published in *L'Amité*, a homosexual magazine. In 1929 *Mercure de France* published Cahun's translation into French of Havelock ELLIS's *Study of Social Psychology*. In 1930 *Aveux non avenus* appeared, an autobiographical text complete with a photo-montage with Suzanne Malherbe. In 1932 Cahun became a member of the Association des Ecrivains et Artistes Révolutionnaires that included André Breton and other surrealists who, a year later, were expelled from the group for their views. In 1934 she published a polemical tract, *Les Paris sont ouverts*, which defended creative expression against the cultural policy of the Communist International. Cahun and her lover Malherbe returned to La Rocquaise on Jersey in 1937. After the German invasion of Jersey in 1940 they became active in the resistance movement but were arrested by the Nazis in 1944 and sentenced to death for inciting Nazi troops to mutiny. They remained imprisoned until 1945 when the island was liberated. Cahun died from the after-effects of her imprisonment.

Califia, Pat. Contemporary queer US writer of S&M/erotica/pornography, Califia's texts focus on lesbian, gay, and queer relationships in sexual scenarios that involve and celebrate power differentials. Califia's work is considered highly controversial within lesbian feminist circles. It harks back to the butch–femme relationships depicted in the work of Joan NESTLE and is associated in particular with pre-Stonewall lesbian circles, on the one hand, and, on the other, it has much in common with Dorothy ALLISON's depiction of violent, poor, white, working-class lives. Califia's writings emerged in the 1980s as part of the new celebration of sexual diversity in lesbian, gay, and queer circles. Her most famous collection of short stories is, without doubt, *Macho Sluts* (1988). She has also published *Melting*

Point (1993) as well as other short stories and collections. A poetry collection, *Diesel Fuel: Passionate Poetry*, appeared in 1997. Califia lives in San Francisco.

Calloway, Kate (1957–). Lesbian US writer of crime fiction who divides her time between Southern California and the Pacific North-west, where the lesbian thrillers for which she is renowned are set. Like Claire MCNAB and Katherine V. FORREST, Calloway has invented a lesbian investigator who features in all her crime fiction, Cassidy James. Works centring on Cassidy James include *First Impressions* (1996), *Second Fiddle* (1997), *Third Degree* (1997), *Fourth Down* (1997), *Fifth Wheel* (1998), *Sixth Sense* (1999), and *Seventh Heaven* (1999). Readers may speculate about the obsession with numerical sequence evident in the titles of Calloway's crime thrillers.

Capote, Truman (1924–84). Born Truman Steckfus Persons in New Orleans, Capote spent his childhood with eccentric relatives in Monroeville, Alabama. His story 'Miriam', published in *Mademoiselle* in 1945, was a great success, as was 'A Tree of Night', which appeared in *Harper's Bazaar* in the same year. His story *In Cold Blood* (1966) came out as a book after being published in the *New Yorker* and constituted the height of his success. Other novels such as *Other Voices, Other Rooms* (1948), *The Grass Harp* (1951), and *A Christmas Memory* (1966) were not as successful. Capote's work, most especially *Breakfast at Tiffany's* (1958), presented a certain homosexual sensibility in an age when homosexuality was still very much closeted. This sensibility included a focus on his southern background, the attention given to older women and the adoration of certain female socialites, an effeminacy of manner, and a certain acerbic wit that in his later years proved to be part of his downfall. Capote never received the critical acclaim he desired. His alcoholism and

bitchiness in later life revealed him as a victim of the homophobia that beset his generation of gay writers. In an unfinished novel, *Answered Prayers*, he turned on friends and foes alike; its publication in *Esquire* proved disastrous for him.

Carpenter, Edward (1844–1929). English poet and theorist whose homosexuality resulted in a number of key texts on homosexuality and women's liberation in the early twentieth century. Carpenter was brought up in a middle-class household with six sisters. He was educated at Oxford and Cambridge, and began to teach at Trinity Hall, Cambridge, in 1868. In his second year there he was elected a clerical fellow, and then ordained a deacon. However, his own liberal background soon found itself in conflict with the Anglican Church and by 1871 he had abandoned his Church roles. During his time at Cambridge Carpenter had a romantic attachment to Andrew Beck but it was broken off when Beck decided to marry and pursue a career as Master of Trinity Hall. Following this break-up Carpenter's poetry became much influenced by the work of Walt WHITMAN, especially his *Calamus*. He also began to embrace a socialist vision that viewed sex and gender relations as effects of capitalism, and which came to be prominent in his later writings. To get away from Cambridge Carpenter joined the University Extension movement, which had been set up in response to women's demands for academic education, and resulted in the establishment of an extension university in Sheffield where Carpenter soon became a leading figure. He bought Millthorpe, a retreat near Sheffield, and began a systematic study of the *Bhagavad-Gita*, an indication of his abiding interest in mysticism and spirituality. In 1881 he completed his initial version of his epic poem cycle, *Towards Democracy* (1883), to which he kept adding poems until 1902. Through his involvement with groups such as the Fellowship of New

Life, the Progressive Association, the Fabian Society, and the Social Democratic Federation, Carpenter met a number of important theorists including Havelock ELLIS, William Morris, and Olive SCHREINER. When William Morris set up the Socialist League, Carpenter joined him. Following travels in the East, Carpenter met George Merill on his return to England in 1891. Prior to that he had been involved in a relationship with George Adams who lived in Millthorpe from 1893 until 1898 together with his wife Lucy. Carpenter's love for Merrill, who had no formal education and convinced Carpenter of the possibility of cross-class relationships, destroyed the friendship between Carpenter and Adams. It is possible that Merill and Carpenter's relationship formed the basis for E.M. FORSTER's representation of the relationship between Maurice and a gamekeeper in *Maurice*. Carpenter's key works are *Love's Coming-of-age* (1896), *The Intermediate Sex* (1906), and *Intermediate Types among Primitive Folks* (1914) in which he campaigned for equality between the sexes, sexual liberation, and recognition of the heightened sensibility of homosexuals.

Catala, Victor (1869–1966). Pseudonym of the Spanish political activist and writer Caterina Albert who was born into a family of rural Catalan gentry. She spent most of her life in the Mediterranean coastal town L'Escala on the Costa Brava, where the house in which she lived and which she gave to her female companion is still kept as a museum. Her early works were mostly poetry and drama. In 1901 she published *Quatre monologues*, intended for the stage. Her novel *Solitud* (1905; *Solitude*) is considered her masterpiece. She also published *Caires vius* (1907; *Living Aspects*). Catala also painted and her work can be seen in her old house in L'Escala. Writing under a male pseudonym, Catala was attacked when her true identity became known. Her lesbian identity, evident in the mu-

seum, has been suppressed in the public acknowledgement of her work.

Cather, Willa (1873–1947). US fiction writer whose talent was initially nurtured by Sarah Orne JEWETT. Born in Virginia, her family moved to Nebraska when she was nine. The prairie world that she thus entered is represented in her novels *O Pioneers!* (1913), which is dedicated to the memory of Jewett, and *My Antonia* (1918). Cather's family was supportive of her and accepted her four-year masquerade as 'William Cather', which lasted from the age of fourteen until after she moved to Lincoln, Nebraska, to study at the university there. Studio photos show her with crew-cuts and wearing men's clothes. The repudiation of femininity implicit in her male impersonation carried forward into her fiction, in which female characters could be very marginalized. After the turn of the century Cather spent a number of years supporting herself financially through journalism, ending up as managing editor of the successful magazine *McClure's*. She established a domestic partnership with Edith Lewis and, on advice from Jewett, left journalism to concentrate on her writing. Her early collection of poetry, *April Twilights* (1903), and her collection of short stories, *The Troll Garden* (1905), were then quickly followed by *Alexander's Bridge* (1912) and *O, Pioneers!* (1913) which established her reputation as a writer. After *The Song of the Lark* (1915) she received the Pulitzer Prize for *One of Ours* (1922), a novel about the First World War. In the 1920s she was very productive, and her novels *A Lost Lady* (1923), *The Professor's House* (1925), *My Mortal Enemy* (1926), and *Death Comes for the Archbishop* (1927) appeared. In the 1930s she suffered a series of personal losses through the deaths of her mother, a brother, and a beloved female friend. She wrote three well-received novels, *Shadows on the Rock* (1931), *Lucy Gayheart* (1935), and *Sapphira and the Slave Girl* (1940), as well as a collection of short stories. Cather was keenly aware of the marginalization of women writers in US culture, and concerned about possible revelations regarding her lesbianism. In an effort to protect her privacy she destroyed all personal letters in her possession, asked friends to do the same, and specified in her testament that publication from any surviving letters was forbidden.

Cavafy, C.P. (1863–1933). The gay Greek poet Constantine P. Cavafy was born into a rich Greek merchant family in Alexandria. In 1872, following his father's death and the financial impoverishment of the family, he was taken to England where he stayed between the ages of nine and sixteen. He eventually settled in Alexandria, making occasional trips to Greece, England, and France. Little is known about Cavafy's personal life. He seems to have had no long-term companion. Between 1889 and 1922 he worked for the Ministry of Irrigation and then retired on a pension and money he had made on the stock market. Cavafy's acclaim as a poet was consolidated after his death from cancer of the throat. The collection of 154 short poems he wanted to be preserved was published in 1935, two years after his death. Cavafy's work falls into three main groups: historical, philosophical, and erotic. His general claim to fame is associated with his historical poems, especially 'The City' (1894), 'Waiting for the Barbarians' (1898), 'The God Abandons Antony' (1910), and 'Ithaka' (1910). Between 1903 and 1915 Cavafy wrote a series of erotic poems that were published privately from 1912 until 1918. They were republished in the first edition of the canonical poems, which was edited by Singopoulos and came out in 1935. These poems often focus on the poet and a desired other who is considerably younger. The homoerotic desire described is mainly unfulfilled.

Cernuda, Luis (1902–63). Gay Spanish poet, born into a well-to-do Andalusian family who, like many of the so-called Generation 27, left Spain after the Civil War, initially for Britain where he taught Spanish at Cambridge University, then for the USA, and settling finally in Mexico. Although he fell in love in Mexico in 1951, and this love inspired his *Poemas para un cuerpo* (*Poems for a Body*), he was generally unhappy in exile and frequently suffered from ill health. His poetry addresses homosexuality in the form of the object of desire that eludes one, admiration for male youths, and a fascination with the male body. Homoeroticism is most evident in his collections *Los placeres ocultos* (1931) and in the *Poems for a Body* mentioned above. His collected poems were published as *La realidad y el deseo* (*Reality and Desire*). His last volume of poetry, *Desolación de la quimera* (1962), reveals Cernuda's difficult final years.

Chambers, Jane (1937–83). Born Carolyn Jane Chambers in Columbia, South Carolina, the lesbian poet and playwright Chambers began her early writing career by producing scripts for local radio stations. In 1954 she enrolled at Rollins College in Winter Park, Florida, intent on becoming a playwright. After a frustrating period there she moved to study acting at California's Pasadena Playhouse in 1956. After one season there she moved on to New York, then to Poland Spring, Maine, and then back to New York. As she wanted to complete her undergraduate degree she then enrolled at Goddard College, Vermont, where she met her lover, manager, and life-long companion Beth Allen. Chambers completed her degree in 1971, receiving the Rosenthal Award for Poetry and a Connecticut Educational Television Award for her play *Christ in a Treehouse*. In 1972 she was given a Eugene O'Neill Fellowship for her play *Tales of the Revolution and Other*

American Fables. During the same period Chambers began to work with the Women's Interart Center in New York City, which produced her play *Random Violence*. Her CBS-TV soap opera *Search for Tomorrow* resulted in her gaining the Writers' Guild of America Award in 1973. Chambers's first play to portray openly lesbian characters was *A Late Snow* which Playwrights Horizons in New York produced in 1974. The play features two lesbians stranded during a snowfall. In 1980 Chambers began working with the Glines, a New York theatre company that focused on plays about lesbians and gays. She wrote *Last Summer at Bluefish Cove* about a woman who is diagnosed as having terminal cancer and the impact this has on her and her lesbian friends who take annual vacations together. The play was written after one of her friends had died from cancer. Chambers herself was diagnosed as suffering from cancer in 1981. She went on to produce *My Blue Heaven* for the Glines Second Gay American Arts Festival and *The Quintessential Image* for the Women's Theatre Conference at Minneapolis. In 1982 Chambers received the Fund for Human Dignity award. After her death from cancer in 1983, her partner published a collection of her poetry. The Women in Theatre Program of the Association for Theatre in Higher Education honoured Chambers by setting up the Jane Chambers Playwriting Award. As one of the first US playwrights to create positive images of lesbians, Chambers is an important figure in lesbian and gay cultural history.

Charke, Charlotte (1713–*c*.1760). English actress and writer, the youngest of twelve children of the former actress Katherine Shore and the actor and dramatist Colley Cibber, Charke manifested unconventional behaviour from her youth onwards, engaging in manly pursuits such as shooting and hunting, and cross-dressing as a man in later life. In today's terms she

might have been described as queer, possibly lesbian. She was educated at Mrs Draper's school in Westminster and at home. Charke married Richard Charke, an actor and musician, when she was seventeen but left him because of his infidelity. She had a daughter, Katherine or Kitty, by him. Subsequent to her marriage to Richard Charke, Charlotte Charke married John Sacheverelle but left him after two months. Charke embarked on a series of careers including as a drawer or barmaid in a pub, a sausage seller, and a valet. She also pursued her acting and writing careers. Initially she worked as an actress playing both men and women. Her first role was in *The Provo'ked Wife* at Drury Lane (1730). She played Harlequin in her own unpublished *The Carneval* (1735). She was thrown out of Drury Lane for scandalous conduct. She satirized her employer in her play *The Art of Management, or Tragedy Expell'd* (1735). For a time she worked with the troupe of the writer and dramatist Henry Fielding, and then embarked on other kinds of work. She began crossdressing and became 'Mr Charles', an itinerant actor and show assistant. For eight years she, Kitty, and Charke's friend 'Mrs Brown' toured the provinces, with Charke appearing as 'Mr Brown'. In 1755 she published *A Narrative of the Life of Mrs Charlotte Charke* in eight instalments. Charke also published the novel *The History of Henry Dumont, Esq.; and Miss Charlotte Evelyn* (1756). This novel, unusually for the period, features a homosexual, albeit in negative terms. Her other works include *The Mercer; or Fatal Extravagance* (1755), *The Lover's Treat; or Unnatural Hatred* (1758), and the undated *The History of Charles and Patty*. Charke died impoverished.

Chatwin, Bruce (1940–89). British novelist and travel writer who was born in Sheffield into a middle-class family. Educated at boarding school and at Marlborough, Chatwin went on to work as a porter for Sotheby's but rapidly rose there, apparently developing a reputation for spotting fakes. While still at Sotheby's he wrote his first novel, *Rotting Fruits*. In 1966 he left Sotheby's and started a university course in Archaeology at Edinburgh but left after two years before completing the course. He was a writer on *The Sunday Times Magazine* for five years. In 1977, his *In Patagonia* was an instant success. It was followed by *The Viceroy of Ouidah* (1980), *On the Black Hill* (1982), *Utz* (1988), and *What Am I doing here?* (1989). In the last work he wrote about his friend of more than twenty years, Howard Hodgkin, who apparently considers the work inaccurate. In his texts Chatwin blends fiction and fact. In his life Chatwin seems to have been a complex and evasive person whom many accused of arrogance and affectation. One of his lovers, Miranda Rothschild, is quoted as saying that 'He's out to seduce everybody, it doesn't matter if you are male, female, an ocelot or a tea cosy.' Chatwin was certainly uneasy about his sexuality and although he had male lovers throughout his life he did not identify as gay. At the age of twenty-five he married Elizabeth Chanler whom he had met at Sotheby's. They separated after fifteen years of marriage but resumed their relationship towards the end of his life. Chatwin developed AIDS but went to considerable lengths to hide this. He died in Nice.

Cheever, John (1912–82). Born in Quincy, Massachusetts, to older parents, Cheever was very close to his older brother Fred but felt neglected by his father and haunted by a story he included in two of his own works of his father having invited an abortionist to dinner during his mother's pregnancy. In 1926 his father lost his job as a salesman and his mother opened a gift shop to help the family survive. Cheever saw his mother as emasculating his father. In 1930 he published his first story, 'Expelled', which is based

on his own experience of being expelled from a prestigious prep school, the Thayer Academy. Cheever and his brother moved to Boston in 1932 where they shared a flat until Cheever moved out as he found the set-up too incestuous. His brother Fred helped him financially even after he had moved to New York in 1934. With the publication of 'Brooklyn Rooming House' in the *New Yorker* in 1934, Cheever began a long association with that magazine. In 1941 he married Mary Winternitz and, despite numerous affairs with people of both sexes, never left her. His first book, *The Way Some People Live*, was published in 1943, the same year that the first of his three children was born. Cheever went on to win many prestigious awards including the National Book Award (1957) in the year that *The Wapshot Chronicle* appeared, the Pulitzer Prize (1978) the year after *Falconer* and *The Stories of John Cheever* had been published, and the National Medal for Literature (1982). He is considered a master of the short story. In his work he treated homosexuality repeatedly, initially in rather stereotypical ways, later more sympathetically, particularly in *Falconer*. In the 1970s and 1980s Cheever appears to have become more accepting of his own bisexuality. He depicts bisexuality in 'The Leaves, the Lion-Fish, and the Bear' (1974) and in *Oh What a Paradise it Seems* (1982). Cheever was an alcoholic for most of his life but was successfully treated for it in 1975.

Chughtai, Ismat (1915–92). Indian dramatist, novelist, and short-story writer and one of the most important feminist voices in the Urdu language. Born into a middle-class family in Badayun, Chughtai was educated at the local municipal school. Later she attended Aligarh University. At the university she met her later husband, Shahid Latif, who became a film director and with whom she had two daughters. While at the university Chughtai attended the first meeting of the Progressive

Writers Movement in Lucknow and became fascinated by Rashid Jahan, a female doctor and writer who struck Chughtai because of her open-mindedness. For some time following her university education (she gained both a BA and a BT) she was principal of the Girls' College in Bareilly. She then moved to Jodhpur and to Bombay. In 1942 she wrote the text that is of particular interest to a lesbian readership, 'Lihaaf' ('The Quilt'), a short story about a frustrated housewife who develops a sexual relationship with her female servant. Told through the eyes of a woman remembering events she observed but could not adequately interpret in her childhood, 'The Quilt' was the object of an obscenity trial in Lahore that went on for two years but was eventually dismissed for lack of evidence. Chughtai wrote many more texts besides this one. She is best known for her novel *Terhi Lakir* (1944; *Crooked Line*). Chughtai was an active campaigner for Indian independence, campaigning for social reform and civil liberties once independence had been achieved.

Clausen, Jan. Contemporary lesbian US writer whose work includes poetry, fiction, and essays. Among her many publications are: *After Touch* (1975); the volume of poetry *Waking at the Bottom of the Dark* (1979); *Mother, Sister, Daughter, Lover* (1980); a collection of stories, *Duration* (1983); *Sinking, Stealing* (1985), a novel about a lesbian on the run with her dead partner's female child; *Illustrated by None: The Prosperine Papers* (1988); *Books and Life* (1989); *Beyond Gay or Straight: Understanding Sexual Orientation* (1996); and *Apples and Oranges: My Journey through Sexual Identity* (1999). Together with Elly BULKIN she has co-edited the journal of women's writing *Conditions*.

Cliff, Michelle (1946–). Born in Jamaica, lesbian writer Cliff moved with her family to New York, where she spent her child-

hood in its Jamaican neighbourhood. She studied at the University of London, and now lives with Adrienne RICH, her partner, in Santa Cruz, California. Cliff is a novelist and short-story writer whose work produces lyrical and haunting evocations of life in poor black communities, of multi-ethnic identities, and of the black diaspora. In 1984 she published her first novel, *Abeng*, which was followed, in 1985, by *the Land of Look Behind*, and *No Telephone to Heaven* (1987). She has also published a collection of short stories, *Bodies of Water* (1990), two collections of poetry, and *Free Enterprise* (1993), a historical novel based on the life of Mary Ellen Pleasant, a nineteenth-century civil rights activist.

Clod, Bente (1946–). Danish lesbian poet who was born into a left-wing family in Copenhagen. After leaving school in her mid-teens Clod worked in various odd jobs before returning to school, where in 1973 she met a married woman called Jeannette with whom she fell in love and had a ten-year relationship. This coincided with the period when Clod was extensively engaged in the women's and lesbian movements in Denmark, and when she became established as one of the most important Scandinavian lesbian writers of that time. In 1975 Clod published *Det Autoriserede danske samleje* (*The Authorized Danish Sexual Intercourse*). Her breakthrough came with *Brud* (1977), which might be translated as *Breaks* or *Bride*. In it she discusses her passionate relationship with Jeannette. The text became a great success, convincing many of its female readers to come out as lesbian. Clod joined the Lesbian Movement, a radical lesbian activist group. Together with several other women she founded Kvindetryk (Women's Press) in 1978. In 1979 she co-founded the Women's Cultural Foundation. Her second novel, a sequel to *Brud*, came out under the title *Syv sind* (*In Two Minds*) in 1980. It focuses on the identity crisis of its female protagonist. In 1979 Clod also attended the Danish Film School, and began writing for stage and for screen. In 1983 she wrote *Vent til du hórer mig le'* (*Wait till You Hear Me Laugh*), a follow-on from *Syv sind*. Her first collection of poetry, which contains an exploration of lesbian love, *Imellem os* (*Between Us*), came out in 1981. It was followed in 1990 by *Gul engel* (*Yellow Angel*). In 1987 Clod became a member of the Association of Lesbian and Gay Writers in Europe. She continues to be a key figure in the Danish lesbian movement.

Cocteau, Jean (1889–1963). Gay French writer and film-maker who was born into a middle-class Parisian family and, having lost his father when he was only ten, was very close to his mother until the end of her life in 1943. He was a gay man who loved the company of women, and was friends with many such as Coco Chanel. At school he was deeply impressed by a fellow pupil, Pierre Dargelos, who represented the wild and untameable to Cocteau and was portrayed by Cocteau in a number of his writings including *The White Paper* (1928), the novel *Children of the Game* (1929), his journal *Opium* (1930), and the film *The Blood of the Poet* (1931). Cocteau immersed himself in the life of the avant-garde in Paris, aided by the actor Edouard de Max who helped him publish his first three volumes of poetry, *Alladin's Lamp* (1909), *The Frivolous Prince* (1910), and *Sophocles' Dance* (1912). In 1913 he published a collection of poems, drawings, and meditations entitled *Potomoc*; and in 1914 he wrote *The Cape of Good Hope* for the famous flyer Roland Garros. Interested in a whole range of cultural forms and their interplay, Cocteau also wrote the scenario for the ballet *Parade* (1917), with sets by Picasso and music by Satie; a book on music entitled *The Rooster and the Harlequin* (1918); a pantomime *Do-Nothing Bar* (1920), performed by two clowns; and the play *The Wedding on the Eiffel*

Tower (1922), which combined dance, acrobatics, mime, drama, and music. In his early years in Paris Cocteau sought the guidance of older men; by the second decade of the twentieth century he became involved with a series of younger lovers with whom he collaborated on a number of projects. Among these was the poet John Le Roy who died in 1918. In 1919 Cocteau met the 15-year-old Raymond Radiguet. While living together they wrote several celebrated novels: Cocteau's *The Great Split* (1923) and *The Imposter* (1923), and Radiguet's *Devil in the Flesh* (1923) and *Count d'Orgel* (1924). Radiguet died of typhoid in 1923. Both Maurice Sachs and Jean Desbordes, with whom Cocteau had subsequent relationships, were killed by the Nazis. Sachs left an account of Cocteau in the posthumously published *Witches' Sabbath* (1946). Desbordes' long love letter to Cocteau, *J'Adore* (1928), contained a preface by Cocteau. In 1929 Cocteau published his novel *The Holy Terrors*. One of Cocteau's major inspirations was Greek myth. This was reflected in his early collection of poems, *Sophocles' Dance*, his great dramas *Antigone* (1922), *Oedipus Rex* (1925), *The Infernal Machine* (1932), and *Bacchus* (1951), and in his films *Orpheus* (1950) and *Testament of Orpheus* (1960). Cocteau continued to work across a range of media throughout his life. Thus he illustrated Jean GENET's *Querelle* (1948) and supported Genet during his many trials. He also started a journal in 1951, *Past/Tense*, in response to the publication of André Gide's journal, which was published during that year and which derided Cocteau. During his lifetime Cocteau received many prizes and honours that celebrated him as a writer. Today he is remembered in particular for his films.

Colette (1873–1954). Born in the Burgundian village of Saint-Saveur-en-Puisaye, Colette's early life seemed a paradise presided over by her mother Sido. The family was forced to leave the village when Colette was seventeen for financial reasons. At twenty she married the famous Paris critic Henri Gauthier-Villars (known as Willy). Due to their financial constraints and under his instruction she began to write the so-called *Claudine* series, featuring a young girl's and woman's life, complete with sexual adventures designed to titillate the audience and generate an income. Willy made Colette acknowledge and entertain his mistresses. She later recorded this in *My Apprenticeships* (1936). Towards the end of the marriage to Willy, Colette was introduced to Natalie Clifford BARNEY's circle and there met Missy. After her separation from Willy in 1906 she then made her living as a dancer and mime. She described this in *The Vagabond* (1911). Together with Missy, Colette at one point acted out a love scene at the Moulin Rouge that involved a passionate kiss between her and Missy, which caused a storm among the audience. After Sido's death in 1912 Colette married Henri de Jouvenel, with whom she had her only child, a daughter. She divorced him in 1924, and eleven years later married Maurice Goudeker who was sixteen years younger than her. The marriage lasted until her death. Lesbian texts and subtexts appear in many of Colette's writings. In the *Claudine* series, there is a lesbian headmistress in *Claudine at School* (1900), and a lesbian affair is featured in *Claudine Married* (1902). These lesbian scenes have generated much discussion because Willy's demands of Colette to produce 'spicy' novels suggest that they were written to heterosexual male order. In *Tendrils of the Vine* (1908) another lesbian encounter is described, and *The Pure and the Impure* contains several chapters devoted to lesbian and gay characters in an exploration of what constitutes impurity, viewed by Colette as sensual excess, and purity, which is about the containment of sensual impulses. In this text Colette wrote, among others,

about the Ladies of Llangollen (see BUTLER, LADY ELEANOR). Colette may have been a bisexual woman. Her work explores life on the margins, and has been considered by many to be 'feminine'. On her death she was given a state funeral, the Church having refused her a religious burial.

Collard, Cyril (1957–93). French author and film-maker, brought up in Versailles, the son of a bourgeois family. Both he and his father shared a passion for sailing and for sports, and their trips together took them to North Africa and the Mediterranean, where Collard developed his taste for the exotic and the other. For a time he read for a Science degree at Lille University but he left without completing his degree. In 1979 he and his father went to Puerto Rico to attend the Panamerican games. Collard stayed on alone, and began to explore his bisexuality. After becoming the object of a gang-bang by Puerto Rican street boys he returned to Paris, and there began both his career in writing and film, and a period of frenetic sexual activity, often taking the form of anonymous sex with multiple partners. In 1987 he published his first novel, *Condamné Amour* (*Love Condemned*). The novel deals with disintegration in the context of a 'divine virus', an indication that Collard already knew that he had contracted the HIV virus. His second novel, *Les Nuits fauves* (1989), is his most famous and abiding work, which he turned into a highly successful film, gaining no less than four Césars in 1993, shortly after his death. Indebted to writers such as Jean GENET and Pier Paolo PASOLINI, the novel and film explore the relationship between eroticism and death.

Compton-Burnett, Ivy (1884–1969). English writer and novelist who was born in Pinner, educated privately, and then went on to Royal Holloway Women's College to read Classics, gaining a BA in 1906. She acted as a governess to her younger siblings following the death of their mother in 1911. The brother to whom she was closest died shortly before she gained her BA; another brother died in the First World War; and her two youngest sisters committed joint suicide in 1918. Compton-Burnett suffered from a long physical and mental breakdown during the early 1920s. She lived her life with the writer, editor, and antiques expert Margaret Jourdain from 1919 until Jourdain's death in 1951 but never articulated anything about this domestic situation in her novels. Compton-Burnett's fiction is inevitably set in the traditional world of the English squirearchy before the First World War. Her earliest novel, *Dolores* (1911), details the passionate friendship of two women, Dolores and Perdita. Compton-Burnett later disowned this novel, apparently because her brother had interfered in its writing. Her subsequent novels are novels-in-dialogue in which characters reveal the secrets of their lives between the lines. Two of her novels contain lesbian and gay characters. *More Women than Men* (1933) focuses on the staff of a girls' school, most of whom are homosexual. However, homosexuality is not constructed as something permanent but as something one grows out of. In *Two Worlds and Their Ways* (1949) Compton-Burnett writes again about public-school life, this time a boys' school, in which a number of homosexual relationships are obliquely referred to. *Brothers and Sisters* (1929) centred on incest. Many of Compton-Burnett's most famous novels centre on parental tyranny and the claustrophobia of genteel households. They include *Brothers and Sisters* (1929), *Men and Wives* (1931), *A House and Its Head* (1935), *Daughters and Sons* (1937), *A Family and a Fortune* (1939), *Parents and Children* (1941), *Elders and Betters* (1944), *Manservant and Maidservant* (1947), *Mother and Son* (1955), which won the James Tait Black Memorial Prize, *A Heritage and Its History* (1959), *A God and His Gifts* (1963), and *The Last and*

the First (1969). Compton-Burnett's other novels are *Pastors and Masters* (1925), *Darkness and Day* (1951), *The Present and the Past* (1953), *A Father and His Fate* (1957), and *The Mighty and Their Fall* (1961). Compton-Burnett received a CBE in 1951 and was made a Dame for her services to literature in 1967.

Cook, Eliza (1818–89). English feminist poet and essayist, born in London, the youngest of eleven children, who then grew up in Horsham, Sussex. Cook never married but was passionately attracted to the actress Charlotte Cushman. Self-educated, Cook began publishing her poems in 1837 with *Lays of a Wild Harp*. That volume was well received and she began contributing poetry to publications such as the *New Monthly Magazine*, the *Weekly Dispatch*, and the *Metropolitan Magazine*. In 1838 her second volume of poetry, *Melaia and Other Poems*, appeared. It was followed by three others: *Poems: Second Series* (1845), *I'm Afloat: Songs* (1850), and *New Echoes, and Other Poems* (1864). The text for which she is probably best known today is *Eliza Cook's Journal*, which she wrote between 1849 and 1854. A feminist collection of writings, it addressed a variety of topics including marriage, work, and the law. *Jottings from My Journal*, a selection of that work, appeared in 1860, and a collection of aphorisms, *Diamond Dust*, was published in 1865.

Corelli, Marie (1855–1924). Born Mary (or Minnie) Mackay in Perth, Scotland, as the 'natural' daughter of Dr Charles Mackay, a Scottish songwriter, and a servant whom Mackay married in 1864, Corelli pursued a brief career as a concert pianist in her twenties and adopted the name Marie Corelli, supposedly descended from the seventeenth-century Venetian composer Arcangelo Corelli. From 1876 until her death Corelli lived with Bertha Vyer who acted as her companion, confidante, housekeeper, and nurse in

Stratford-upon-Avon. Corelli wore a ring Vyer had given her when they were young. The two women appeared arm in arm in public and their entwined initials were carved into the mantelpiece in their home with the inscription *amor vincit*. It is difficult to say if Corelli's relation with Vyer went beyond romantic friendship and included a sexual relationship. Corelli wrote novels that contained the standard theme of heterosexual romance. She was an outspoken enemy of women's suffrage and denounced women with political and professional ambitions. She maintained a close friendship with Henry Labouchère, who was the author of the amendment to the Criminal Law Act of 1885, under which Oscar WILDE was later convicted. Her melodramatic plots and purple prose, which might be described as flamboyant and camp, brought her extensive fame and fortune. She wrote over thirty novels, many of which, such as *The Soul of Lilith* (1892), *Barrabas, a Dream of the World's Tragedy* (1893), were bestsellers and, like *The Sorrows of Satan* (1895), sold unheard of numbers of copies. By the end of her life Corelli had fallen out of public favour.

Corinne, Tee A. (1943–). Lesbian US artist, renowned first and foremost for her photography but also for her erotic writing. Corinne was born and brought up in Florida in a middle-class family marred by alcoholism, a fact which she documented in *Family* (1990). She attended the University of South Florida and the Pratt Institute in Brooklyn, New York, before devoting her time to activism in the lesbian and gay movement, to lesbian art, and to writing on lesbian sexuality and life. Her photographs have appeared in lesbian journals and magazines such as *Sinister Wisdom* and *On Our Backs*. Her art books include *The Cunt Coloring Book* (1975), *Women Who Loved Women* (1984), and *Lesbian Muse: The Women behind the Words* (1989). Her erotic short stories were published as

Dreams of the Woman Who Loved Sex (1987; republished 1999). She has also edited *Intricate Passions* (1989), *Riding Desire: An Anthology of Erotic Writing* (1991), and *The Poetry of Sex: Lesbians Write the Erotic*. In 1991 *The Sparkling Lavender Dust of Lust* came out. Corinne has been active in the lesbian art world for more than thirty years and in 1997 she was awarded the Women's Caucus for Art President's Award for services to women in the arts. In the same year her memoir *Sex Lives of Daffodils: Growing Up as an Artist Who Also Writes* was published.

Coward, Noël (1899–1973). Gay English actor, playwright, and composer, born in Teddington, Middlesex, to a piano salesman and an ambitious mother who encouraged his theatrical aspirations from an early age. His first play was performed in 1917 but he achieved fame with *The Vortex* (1924) in which he played Nicky Lancaster, a young drug addict tormented by his mother's adulteries. Coward's world was that of Edwardian gentility. He always paid homage to the dominant culture and would not permit public discussion of his homosexuality. His plays centre on heterosexual romance, often in very camp fashion, but also on the tedium of bourgeois life and day-to-day responsibilities to others. Best known for his three plays *Private Lives* (1930), *Design for Living* (1933), about a *ménage à trois*, and *Blithe Spirit* (1941), Coward was an entertainer who delighted audiences with his camp, English, upper-crust humour. During the Second World War he entertained the troops, revealing his patriotic side in works like *Cavalcade* (1931), *Brief Encounter* (1944), and *This Happy Breed* (1942). It also manifested itself in his admiration of the Royal Family, detailed in his *The Noël Coward Diaries*, published posthumously in 1982. Coward continued to write prolifically after the Second World War but fell out of favour for a while as his style did not fit into the prevailing mood of the post-war period.

His work experienced a revival from the 1960s. He was knighted in 1970, and died in Jamaica. In 1999 Coward's archive of sixty plays and over 300 popular songs was bequeathed to Birmingham University by his long-time companion Graham Payn.

Crane, Hart (1899–1933). Gay US poet who had a short and rather unhappy life before killing himself. Born in Garrettsville, Ohio, as the only child of Grace Hart Crane and C.A. Crane, Harold Hart Crane, who was later to shorten his name to Hart Crane, had a financially secure but emotionally unstable childhood. His parents' relationship was uneasy until their divorce in 1916. His mother spent time in a sanatorium while he was sent to her parents. His early closeness to his mother was irreparably damaged when she threatened to tell his father of his homosexuality and tried to block an inheritance left to him by his grandparents. Her letters sent him into bouts of alcoholism, and her inability to allow him a life of his own eventually led to an irretrievable break in 1928. From 1916 until 1923 Crane moved between Cleveland where he worked for his father and New York. He had his first affairs with men during this period and wrote many of the poems collected in *White Buildings* (1926). In 1926, a grant from a banker, Otto Kahn, enabled Crane to work on his long poem *The Bridge* for a few months, first in New York, and then at his grandparents' Caribbean plantation on the Isles of Pines. In 1927 he lived as a paid companion to a wealthy invalid in Pasadena. Before his final break with his mother, he spent some months helping her nurse his grandmother through her terminal illness. With his inheritance, following his grandmother's death, he sailed to Europe. He met Harry Crosby, the owner of the Black Sun Press, who encouraged him to finish *The Bridge*, which he finally did in 1929. It was published in 1930. Crane's last few years

were beset by drink problems as well as his inability to find work and to produce poetry. He obtained a Guggenheim Fellowship that enabled him to spend a year in Mexico but his drinking, his grief over his father's sudden death in 1932, and his first heterosexual love affair took their toll and meant that he managed only one poem, 'The Broken Tower', during that time. On his journey back from Mexico on the ship Vera Cruz, Crane was beaten up very badly by sailors whom he had solicited for sex. He returned to the stateroom he shared with his lover at noon, said goodbye to her, went up to the deck, and threw himself overboard. Crane did not hide his homosexuality but was born in an era when it was only just beginning to be possible to articulate that sexuality.

Crisp, Quentin (1908–99). Gay British performer and writer, born Denis Charles Pratt to 'middle-class, middle-brow, middling parents' in Sutton, Surrey, UK, the youngest of four children. Crisp began using his pseudonym from the late 1920s onwards. At the age of fourteen he won a scholarship to the boarding school Denstone College, Staffordshire. Later he began a course in journalism at King's College, London, but dropped out. He took arts courses at Battersea Polytechnic and at High Wycombe, and worked in various jobs before becoming a commercial artist. He worked as a prostitute for a brief time. Exempted from war service during the Second World War due to his homosexuality he took a job as a nude model in a government-funded art school, hence the title of his 1968 autobiography, *The Naked Civil Servant*, which made him an icon in the gay community. This book was made into a film for television in 1975, starring John Hurt as Quentin Crisp. *The Naked Civil Servant* tells the story of Crisp's experiences as a gay man in the England of the 1930s. It turned Crisp into 'one of the stately homos of England' whose flamboyance, effeminacy, aestheticism, and elegant camp style, which aligned him to characters like Oscar WILDE, on the one hand, and contemporary performers like Lilly Savage, on the other, made him a darling of the media. In the autumn of 1977 Crisp travelled to New York where he subsequently went to live in Manhattan. Crisp was one of the few gay men who by going public about his experiences as a homosexual relatively late in life became a celebrity in his old age. Much of his work both on film and in writing postdates the publication of *The Naked Civil Servant*. In 1936 he wrote *Lettering for Brush and Pen* and in 1938 he published *Colour in Display*, a text on window dressing. His later publications include *How to Have a Life-style* (1975), *How to Become a Virgin* (1981), *The Wit and Wisdom of Quentin Crisp* (1984), *Manners from Heaven* (1985), and *Resident Alien: The New York Diaries* (ed. Donald Carroll, 1997), which was turned into a play for stage by Tim Fountain. Crisp starred in a number of films in his later life including as narrator in *The Ballad of Reading Gaol* (1988), *Resident Alien* (1991), and as Elizabeth I in *Orlando* (1993), a film based on Virginia WOOLF's novel *Orlando*. In *Philadelphia* (1993) he acted as one of the party guests. Both *The Divine Mr Crisp* and *Naked in New York* (1994) featured Crisp as himself and centred on his life. Crisp suffered a heart attack at the age of ninety while on tour with his one-man show *An Audience with Quentin Crisp* in the UK, and died in Manchester.

Croft-Cooke, Rupert (1903–79). Extremely prolific gay British writer, born in Kent and educated at the University of Buenos Aires (1923–6). Croft-Cooke served in the British Army in India before returning to Britain to become a writer. He wrote autobiographically about his life as a gay man in Britain and in Morocco, as well as producing biographies of other well-known gay figures. In 1953–4 Croft-Cooke spent six months in prison for 'gross indecencies' following an

incident where two men who had spent a weekend with him and his Indian companion, Joseph Alexander, gave evidence against Croft-Cooke and Alexander to extricate themselves from other charges. He described these experiences in *The Verdict of You All* (1955). Following his release from prison Croft-Cooke and Alexander went to live in Tangier, Morocco, where they stayed until 1968. Croft-Cooke described his life there in *The Tangerine House* (1956) and in *The Caves of Hercules* (1974). His other works include *The Life for Me* (1952), *Bosie: The Story of Lord Alfred Douglas, His Friends and Enemies* (1963), *Feasting with Panthers: A New Consideration of Some Late Victorian Writers* (1967), and *The Unrecorded Life of Oscar Wilde* (1972). Other biographical texts include *Rudyard Kipling* (1948) and *Buffalo Bill* (1952). Croft-Cooke produced a whole range of other writings. His detective novels *Case for Sergeant Beef* (1980 reprint), *Case for three Detectives* (1982 reprint), *Jack on the Gallows Tree* (1983 reprint), and *Such is Death* (1986 reprint) were all published under the pseudonym Leo Bruce and reprinted in the 1980s. Croft-Cooke also wrote about the circus, publishing a number of volumes on the subject entitled *The Sawdust Ring: The Romantic Story of the English Circus, Its Great Showmen and Performers* (with W.S. Meadmore, not dated, *c*.1940), *The Circus Book* (not dated, *c*.1950), *The Circus Has no Home* (not dated, *c*. 1950s), and, with Peter Cotes, *Circus: A World History* (1977). He published books on food including *Sherry* (1956), *English Cooking: A New Approach* (1960), and *Exotic Food* (1971). Other works include *Cosmopolis* (1933), *Escape to the Andes* (1938), *Neck and Neck* (1940), *Miss Allick* (1947), *A Few Gypsies* (1955), *Seven Thunders* (1955), *The Numbers Game* (1963), *The Glittering Pastures* (1962), *Madeira* (1966), *The Purple Streak* (1966), *Wolf from the Door* (1969), *The Sound of*

Revelry (1969), and *Conduct Unbecoming* (1975).

Crow, Christine M. Contemporary British academic and writer who has been an Honorary Research Reader in French Literature at the University of St Andrews in Scotland, in which capacity she has produced several works on the French poet Paul Valéry, the first of which was *Paul Valéry: Consciousness and Nature* (1972). To a lesbian readership she will be better known for her novel *Miss X, or The Wolf Woman* (1990), an experimental novel that belongs to and subverts the genre of boarding school fiction which has been a key narrative format in lesbian writing, including texts such as Rosemary MANNING's *The Chinese Garden*, Antonia WHITE's *Frost in May*, and Olivia's (see STRACHEY BUSSY, DOROTHY) *Olivia*. A self-consciously precocious text, written in the first person, and with a self-conscious take on the construction of narrative as narrative, the novel tells the story of a pupil's infatuation with a teacher, Miss X.

Cullen, Countee (1903–46). An African American poet of the Harlem Renaissance, Cullen's birthplace is assumed to be Louisville, Kentucky. He was brought up by his grandmother, who took him to New York when he was nine years old. He used the name Countee Leroy Porter until 1920, though by 1918 the orphaned Cullen had been adopted by the pastor Frederick A. Cullen of the Salem Methodist Episcopal Church in Harlem. Cullen was educated at the prestigious DeWitt Clinton High School, graduated from New York University in 1925, and received an MA in literature from Harvard in 1926. Cullen wanted to be a poet from his youth; his first volume of poems, *Color*, was published the same year that he graduated. He produced several more volumes of poetry, a novel for adults, edited an African American poetry anthology, and two storybooks for children.

At a time when many homosexuals were closeted, Cullen's sexuality was problematic. He first married W.E.B. DuBois's daughter Yolande, and then, six years before his death, Ida Robertson. He also had a string of male lovers both in France and in the USA. He was a key member of the gay coterie in Harlem. In so far as homosexuality is thematized in his poetry, it is done in coded form. *Copper Sun* (1927) contains poems such as 'Uncle Jim', 'Colors', and 'More than a Fool's Song' that may be read through a gay sensibility. 'The Black Christ' (1929) is a powerful evocation of lynching in which the black man Jim, accused of rape, is a victim of racism and heterosexism. *Medea and Some Poems* (1935) also contains poems with a veiled gay theme.

Cunningham, Michael (1952–). Although openly gay, Michael Cunningham has stated in several interviews that he does not wish to be known exclusively as a 'gay novelist'. With the awarding in 1999 of the Pulitzer Prize to *The Hours*, he has in fact been given the kind of cross-over popular and critical recognition unavailable to most contemporary gay writers. After the publication of several short stories and an early novel, *Golden States* (1984), Cunningham's next book, *A Home at the End of the World* (1991), received wide praise. The novel deals with the interwoven relationships among four people, straight and gay, over an extended period from the 1960s to the 1980s. Complex in its depiction of character and skilful in the delineation of time and place, *A Home at the End of the World*, shortlisted for several book awards, established Cunningham's reputation as a writer to watch. *Flesh and Blood* (1995), an ambitious family saga spanning nearly a hundred years, further explores the complexities of human relationships and sexual identities. Like *A Home at the End of the World*, *Flesh and Blood* masterfully portrays a broad spectrum of US society and, like the earlier novel, invokes the spectre of AIDS. It too was well received, receiving the Whiting Writers' Award. In *The Hours*, which brilliantly pays homage to Virginia WOOLF's *Mrs. Dalloway*, Cunningham tells three separate stories (one of them involving Woolf herself) set in three time frames. By the end of the novel, the plots and characters have connected in a surprising but thoroughly persuasive manner. Throughout, the spirit of both Woolf and her novel inform the book in a manner both stylistically impressive and emotionally moving. *The Hours* appeared on a variety of bestseller lists, and with its success Cunningham achieved celebrity status, in addition to increased critical acclaim. Besides the Pulitzer, *The Hours* was the winner of a host of other prizes, including the PEN/Faulkner award, and the American Library Association's award for gay and lesbian literature.

[David Garnes]

D

Daly, Mary (1928–). US radical lesbian feminist theologian and writer, born in Schenectady, New York. Her work was particularly influential in the 1970s and 1980s both in the USA and in Great Britain as part of the debates about women's difference from men and of divergent, women-centred styles of writing. Daly was educated at the College of St Rose where she gained a BA in 1950. She then attended the Catholic University of America, receiving an MA in 1952, and completed her PhD at St Mary's College, Notre Dame, Indiana in 1954. From 1954 until 1959 she was a teacher of theology and philosophy at Cardinal Cushing College, Massachusetts. Between 1959 and 1966 she taught on the Junior Year Abroad programmes at the University of Fribourg in Switzerland where she also gained an STD in 1963 and a PhD in 1965. Since 1969 she has taught theology at Boston College, Chestnut Hill, Massachusetts. In 1966 Daly published *Natural Knowledge of God in the Philosophy of Jacques Maritrain* but it was her *The Church and the Second Sex* (1968) that in its critique of women's subordinate role within the church led to Daly's dismissal from her teaching post at Boston College. Though she was reinstated following student protests, this book established Daly as a radical feminist theologian. In 1973 she published *Beyond God the Father: Toward a Philosophy of Women's Libera-*

tion. This book struck a chord with many women in the women's movement at that time, partly because it critically addressed a particular form of patriarchy, and such critiques were very much at the heart of the women's movement then. Daly became internationally renowned with *Gyn/Ecology: The Metaethics of Radical Feminism* (1978; revised 1990), which responded to then current preoccupations with discovering divergent styles of language appropriate to women and breaking with traditional academic discourse, but which also called for a female cosmos in which words denoting women are revalued. Similar demands could be found in the lesbian feminist science fiction of the period, for instance in the work of Joanna RUSS. Daly continued her exploration of a female language in her next three volumes of work, *Pure Lust: Elemental Feminist Philosophy* (1984), *Webster's First New Intergalactic Wickedary of the English Language* (1987), which she co-wrote with Jane Caputi, and *Outercourse: The Be-dazzling Voyage* (1993). Subsequently she published *Quintessence... Realizing the Archaic Future. A Radical Elementa* (1998). Daly's work has become less central to lesbian feminist concerns during the 1990s as moves towards the postmodern, queer, and critiques of the notion of gender-specific languages have become more prominent. However, her jubilant embrace of a women-centred universe, exuberantly divergent use of language, and trenchant critique of the role of women within institutionalized religion have made her one of the key lesbian theoreticians and writers of the late twentieth century.

Dane, Clemence (1887–1965). English novelist and dramatist, as well as sculptress, whose real name was Winifred Ashton. She started to work as an actress before her deteriorating health during the First World War encouraged her to take up writing. Of her many novels and plays the one most renowned in lesbian circles is Dane's first novel *Regiment of Women* (1917), which belongs to the girls' boarding-school genre and centres on the passionate relationships between pupils and teachers at that school. Like other novels of the same genre, it is tragic in content: Clare, the cruel protagonist, loses her love Alwynne to a man. In its ending the novel bears strong resemblances to other novels on lesbian relationships from the period, most notably *The Well of Loneliness* by Radclyffe HALL. A prolific writer, Dane also published many plays, among them *A Bill of Discernment* (1921), *Will Shakespeare* (1921), and *Wild Decembers* (1932), a collection of essays entitled *The Women's Side* (1926), and a volume of short stories, *Fate Cries Out* (1935). Her novels include *Legend* (1919), *Broome Stages* (1931), *The Moon is Feminine* (1938), and *The Arrogant History of White Ben* (1939). *Regiment of Women* apart, Dane is largely a forgotten writer today.

Daniel, Herbert (1946–92). Gay Brazilian writer, political activist, and *guerrillero* in whose work politics and autobiography intertwine to raise questions of homosexuality and, in his later writings, of HIV/AIDS in the context of his life experiences and Brazil. Daniel studied medicine at the university in Belo Horizonte. Initially a student activist, he became active in various guerrilla groups as Brazil succumbed to a repressive right-

wing, military dictatorship during the 1960s and 1970. In 1971 he met his long-term partner Cláudio Mesquita. Daniel was under threat from a death sentence and eventually left Brazil to live in Lisbon and Paris before returning home in 1981. On his return he became involved in both left-wing politics and in AIDS activism. He himself was diagnosed as HIV positive in 1989 and died from AIDS-related illnesses in 1992. In 1981 he wrote *Passagem para o próximo sonho* (*Ticket to the Next Dream*) about his life as a *guerrillero* and his exile in Lisbon and Paris. Together with Leila Míccolis he wrote *Jacarés e lobisomens: dois ensaios sobre a homossexualidade*, a work about homosexuality and the impact of HIV/AIDS on the treatment of homosexuals by the media. In 1984 *Meu corpo daria um romance: narrativa desarmada* (*My Body Would Produce a Novel: Unarmed Narrative*) appeared. His 1987 novel *Alegres e irresponsáveis abacaxis americanos* (*Gay and Irresponsible American Pineapples*) also focused on HIV/AIDS as did *Vida antes da morte* (1989; *Life before Death*). Together with Richard Parker he finally wrote *AIDS: a terceira epidemia* (1991; *AIDS: The Third Epidemic*). Some of the essays from this work appeared in a posthumously published collection by him and Richard Parker entitled *Sexuality, Politics and AIDS in Brazil: In Another World?* (1993).

Daniels, Sarah (1957–). British lesbian playwright, born in London, whose work has been performed in some of the most important venues for new playwriting in Britain including the Royal Court Theatre, London, the Crucible Theatre, Sheffield, and the Manchester Royal Exchange. Daniels belongs to the generation of women playwrights such as Caryl Churchill, Pam Gems, and others who made their name during the 1980s and were supported by the Royal Court Theatre. Unlike some of her contemporaries' plays, Daniels's work has been marked by an engagement with current (lesbian) feminist issues that have not always endeared her to mainstream audiences but which have made her one of the greatest playwrights of the lesbian feminist movement. Since Daniels writes issue-based theatre it is often predominantly realist in form. At the same time the endings of her plays frequently explode their realist frame and offer improbable solutions – such as an all-female heaven – to intractable problems such as the persistence of patriarchal attitudes among men, the pervasive abuse women suffer at the hands of men, and women's inability to escape a second-class citizen status. *Ripen Our Darkness* (1981), one of Daniels' first plays, featured a lesbian couple whose all-female household offers an antidote to the heterosexist environment in which the two women's parents live. The play made plain that men's abuse of women is not a class issue – it happens in all social classes – but takes class-specific forms. Following *Ma's Flesh is Grass* (1981) and *Penumbra* (1981), Daniels shot to the limelight with her perhaps most controversial play, *Masterpieces* (1983). That play dealt with the sexploitation of women in the pornography industry, presented as an extension of the disdainful attitude men have towards women. Daniels's play showed – to support from feminists and dismay from many male viewers – that men's abuse of women is so normalized in our culture that an unbridgeable gulf exists between women and men. *Masterpieces* was influenced by Andrea DWORKIN's work, *Pornography – Men Possessing Women*. In Daniels's plays heterosexuality and patriarchy are at the root of social ills, which, the plays often suggest, can only be overcome in all-female environments. In consequence, Daniels celebrates female friendship and the support women give each other, whether in a sexualized or a nonsexual context. *The Devil's Gateway* (1983) shows this very strongly, and highlights one of the hallmarks of Daniels's plays, the representation of friendships

between older women and of older women as key figures in promoting change, leaving their own lives for new ones, helping their daughters escape their unsatisfactory marriages and vengeful partners, and supporting other women through rough times. Daniels's *Neaptide*, for example, which won the 1982 George Devine Award, featured Claire, a lesbian, who – with the help of her mother – runs away to escape having to give up her daughter Poppy to her ex-husband in the wake of their custody case. In *Byrthrite* (1986) Daniels went back to the witch trials of the seventeenth century, linking the issue of women's ability to heal and support other women in childbirth with their persecution. Such historicization of social issues also surfaced in *The Gut Girls* (1988), which arose out of a request to write a play about women who had worked as gut girls on the cattle market in Deptford, London, at the turn of the century. Daniels's other plays, all issue-based, all featuring women supporting each other through crises and resisting patriarchal institutions, include *Beside Herself* (1990), *Head-rot Holiday* (1992), and *The Madness of Esme and Shaz* (1994).

Dauthendey, Elisabeth (1854–1943). German writer, born in St Petersburg, where her father was a court photographer. Dauthendey wrote a series of novellas, novels, and fairytales, exploring the psychology of women. Her book *Vom neuen Weibe und seiner Liebe. Ein Buch für reife Geister* (1900; *Of the New Woman and Her Love-life. A Book for Mature Spirits*) was widely read, and advocated lesbian love as offering women fulfilment beyond 'mere sex'.

Davidson, Michael (1897–1976). Gay British memoirist and journalist, born into an upper middle-class family and educated at Lancing. Davidson went to Cambridge but enlisted when the First World War broke out. He was wounded in 1916 but did not leave the army until

1919. He then became a reporter. A socialist and anti-fascist he sympathized with the Communist Party. He frequented London swimming baths in pursuit of amorous encounters with adolescents and as a result eventually served a prison sentence in Wormwood Scrubs (1936). Upon his release he took up the role of foreign correspondent, which enabled him to live more securely as a homosexual since he was less likely to be persecuted for his sexual inclinations abroad than in England. He had a long career as foreign correspondent with major British newspapers including the *Observer*, the *New York Times*, and the *Christian Science Monitor*. He published two volumes of memoirs in which he addressed his homosexual life frankly, *The World, the Flesh and Myself* (1962) and *Some Boys* (1970).

Davis, Jill (1949–). British lesbian academic working in theatre studies, Davis gained a degree in Drama and French at the University of Hull in 1970. Since 1971 she has taught Theatre Studies, first at the University of Glasgow and then at the University of Kent in Canterbury. Between 1979 and 1983 she was a member of the Arts Council Drama Panel, chairing the New Applications and Projects Committee from 1980 until 1982. Between 1984 and 1986 she was Chair of the South East Arts Drama Panel. Davis was the first British academic to champion the work of lesbian playwrights. Her abiding claim to fame rests on the publication of two key volumes for the history of lesbian playwriting, *Lesbian Plays* (1987) and *Lesbian Plays: 2* (1989), both of which appeared in the Methuen New Theatre Scripts series. The first volume contained *Chiaroscuro* by Jackie KAY, now one of the best-known lesbian British poets and writers. Davis published the volumes in the context of both the AIDS crisis and, later, the debates about the infamous Section 28, which became law in the summer of 1988 and which, among other things, forbade the promotion of homo-

sexuality as a desirable form of relationship in schools. Her pioneering work did much to herald the work of lesbian playwrights, and to document its existence in the UK.

de Haan, Jacob Israël (1881–1924). Dutch writer of Jewish extraction who was born in Smilde in the north of the Netherlands, the son of a rabbi and his wife. De Haan's family eventually moved to Zaandam near Amsterdam where de Haan first studied to become a teacher and then undertook a course in law at the University of Amsterdam. He earned his living through teaching and writing for the children's page of the socialist daily newspaper, *Het Volk* (*The People*). At the University of Amsterdam he became friends with Arnold ALETRINO, who taught Criminal Anthropology there. In 1904 de Haan published his first novel, *Pijpelijntjes*, which centred on the sexual and sadistic relationship between two students called Joop and Sam, the nicknames in real life of de Haan and Aletrino. The novel was dedicated to Aletrino. Its explicit treatment of homosexuality, including sexual activity, caused an outcry that resulted in de Haan losing both his teaching job and his work on the paper. Subsequently de Haan published another novel, *Pathologieën* (1908), which also centred on a gay relationship. De Haan also wrote short stories but after 1910 his writing focused mainly on poetry in which he brought together his Judaism and his gay sensibility. Among his volumes of poetry were *Libertijnsche liederen* (1914; *Libertine Songs*), *Liederen* (1917; *Songs*), and *Kwatrijnen* (1924). Simultaneously de Haan continued with his legal studies, on which he also published. After the Second World War de Haan, who had become a Zionist, went to Palestine, teaching law and writing for British and Dutch papers. He had relationships with Arabs and Jewish boys, and began to dissociate publicly from the Zionist cause. He received death threats and when he was assassinated, it was suggested that he had been killed by Arabs because of his homosexual relationships with Arab boys. De Haan's collected poems were published posthumously in 1952 and his work reissued during the 1980s.

de Wolfe, Elsie (1865–1950). Born in New York, the daughter of Georgina Copeland and Stephen de Wolfe, Elsie de Wolfe started adult life as an actress before becoming famous for her interior designs and, in lesbian circles, for her relationship with the lesbian theatre agent Elizabeth Marbury. Her first theatre appearance was at Proctor's 23rd Street Theater, New York, as Fabienne in *Thermidor*. In 1894 she joined the Empire Company under Charles Frohman with whom she remained until 1904. By this time she had already met Elizabeth Marbury. The two women met in 1886 in the house of the two unmarried sisters Sara and Eleanor Hewitt, who were close friends of Marbury. In 1987 de Wolfe and Marbury set up home together. In 1890 Marbury opened her theatrical agency and became one of the most renowned agents on Broadway. Both de Wolfe and Marbury made many trips to Europe and, in 1907, decided to move into the Villa Trianon in Versailles, which they eventually shared with Anne Morgan, a wealthy US heiress. The three were known as the 'triangle of Versailles' living in a *ménage à trois*, not unlike that of Edy Craig and her companions Christopher St John and Claire Atwood. In 1910 de Wolfe became active in the Woman Suffrage Party but the outbreak of the First World War necessitated a swift return to the USA. De Wolfe, however, was keen to return to Europe and returned, together with Anne Morgan, to work for the Red Cross. De Wolfe's relationship with Marbury gradually began to drift and in 1920 Marbury sold her part in the Villa Trianon. Marbury recorded her relationship with de Wolfe in her autobiography *My*

Crystal Ball (1923) but, as was common for the period, she kept silent about the erotic aspect of their relationship. In 1926 de Wolfe married to become Lady Mendl, a move that alienated her from Marbury. Despite this event, Marbury eventually forgave her, aided by her new relationship with Elizabeth Arden. On Marbury's death in 1933 de Wolfe became her sole heir. In 1935 de Wolfe published her memoir, *After All*, in which she was equally discreet about her relationship with Marbury.

Delany, Samuel R. (1942–). Gay African American science fiction writer, born in Harlem, New York, whose early understanding of his homosexuality led to him becoming the object of therapy in an attempt to make him heterosexual, a fate not uncommon among lesbians and gays in the 1950s and 1960s. In 1962 he published his first science fiction text, *The Jewels of Aptor*. Subsequently, he wrote many further volumes of science fiction including *The Einstein Intersection* (1967), *Nova* (1968), and *Neveryona or: The Tale of Signs and Cities* (1983). *Stars in my Pocket like Grains of Sand* (1984) features a gay male relationship and *Flight from Neveryon* (1987) portrays the effect of an AIDS-like plague on an imaginary community. In 1988 he published his autobiography *The Motion of Light on Water* in which Delany came out as gay. Between 1961 and 1980 Delany was married to the lesbian poet Marilyn HACKER.

Delarue-Mardrus, Lucie (1874–1945). Prolific French writer, the youngest of six girls whose father was a successful and prosperous shipping lawyer, Mardrus spent an idyllic childhood in the family mansion and estate at Honfleur in Normandy. This childhood is described in her novel *Le Roman de six petites filles* (1909). In 1900 she married the translator of the *Arabian Nights*, Joseph-Charles Madrus. He was an eccentric man who dismissed her lesbian inclinations as schoolgirl romances. Unconventionally, he ordered Mardrus to marry him in the bicycling outfit that was fashionable then: breeches, a check overdress, and a straw boater. By the time of her marriage Mardrus had already had the experience of passionate attachments to women, in particular to Impéria de Heredia (wife of the poet José-Maria de Heredia) whom she loved for three years. Mardrus recounted her attraction to women in *L'Acharnée* (1910), and in *Le Beau Baiser* (1929). Her husband introduced Mardrus to French literary society and she began to meet other lesbian writers such as Renée VIVIEN, who admired Mardrus's poetry, and Natalie BARNEY, with whom Mardrus fell in love. Unfortunately for her it was an unrequited passion. Mardrus expressed her love for Barney through a series of poems that Barney published twelve years after Mardrus's death as *Nos secrètes amours* (1957). These poems of the period 1902–3 express both Mardrus's desire and Barney's rejection of her. In later life Mardrus, who divorced her husband some fifteen years after they had got married, became the lover of the Jewish opera singer Germaine de Castro whom Mardrus met in 1932 when she was fifty-eight years old. De Castro was corpulent, in Barney's eyes vulgar, and growing old – a combination that in the eyes of some of Mardrus's friends rendered her an unsuitable love object for Mardrus, who herself was ageing but thin. Mardrus tried to help de Castro revive her flagging career as a singer by organizing musical events and performances. During the 1930s both Mardrus and de Castro were the objects of anti-Semitic persecution by the German occupying forces. Mardrus's books were banned and the publishing house Plon refused to publish her work. As Mardrus began to suffer from impecunity, friends of hers secured her a pension from the Société des Gens de Lettres and generated some money by selling the film rights to her novel *Graine au vent* (1925; filmed in

1943). Mardrus's failing health eventually led to her death just as the Second World War was coming to an end. Her work has largely fallen out of favour though in her time she was a prolific writer producing poems, novels, and biographies at a rapid rate. Among the novels now best known is *L'Ange et les pervers* (1930; republished in a translation by Anna LIVIA as *The Angel and the Perverts* in 1995), a novel that portrays the life of Laurette Wells, a thinly disguised version of Natalie Barney, and her circle of friends. In the novel the 'noble' lives of homosexuals are contrasted with the mercenary nature of bourgeois life. At the centre of the novel is Mario/Marion, a hermaphroditic person whose gender and social identity is fluid due to both a biological and a social ambiguity regarding her/his status. The novel forms part of a whole series of texts from the 1880s onwards that explored ambivalent gender roles and bodily ambiguities. They include RACHILDE's *Monsieur Vénus* (1902) as much as Virginia WOOLF's *Orlando* (1928) and Djuna BARNES's *Nightwood* (1936). Many of Mardrus's novels were serialized in journals before being published as books, and she enjoyed great popularity in the first two decades of the twentieth century. Her many writings include volumes of poetry such as *Occident* (1901), *Ferveur* (1902), *Horizons* (1904), *La Figure de proue* (1908), *Souffles de tempête* (1918), *A Maman* (1920), and *Mort et printemps* (1932). She also wrote the plays *La Prêtresse de Tanit* (1907), and *La quatrième Eve* (1932). Her many novels include *Marie, fille-mère* (1908), *Comme tout le monde* (1910), *Tout l'amour* (1911), *L'Inexperminentée* (1912), *La Monnaie de singe* (1912), *Un Cancre* (1914), *Un Roman civil en 1914* (1916), *Deux amants* (1917), *L'Ame aux trois visages* (1919), *La Mère et le fils* (1924), *Hortensia dégénérée* (1925), *La Petite Fille comme ça* (1927), *Anatole* (1930), *L'Amour à la mer* (1931), *L'Autre Enfant* (1931), *François et la liberté* (1933),

Roberte (1937), *Fleurette* (1938), *La Girl* (1938), *La Perle magique* (1940), and *Le Roi de reflets* (1944). In 1938 Mardrus published her autobiography, *Mes mémoires*, in which she discussed her passionate relations with women. She also published a biography of *Sainte Thérèse de Lisieux* (1926), of Oscar WILDE in *Les Amours d'Oscar Wilde* (1929), and *Eve Lavallière* (1935).

DeLynn, Jane. New York-based contemporary lesbian US writer who has written plays, journalistic pieces, librettos and novels. She made her debut in the UK with *Don Juan in the Village* (1990), which depicts a cruising first-person narrator who describes in unromantic detail her sexual adventures with women, many of them not successful. The novel was viewed as a more 'realistic' portrayal of lesbian sexual relationships than many lesbian romantic novels make them out to be. DeLynn's other writings include *Some Do* (1978), *In Thrall* (1982), *Real Estate* (1988), *Bad Sex is Good* (1998), and *Leash* (2001).

Dickinson, Emily (1830–86). Born to one of Amherst's leading families (her grandfather helped to found the Amherst Academy), the US poet and letter-writer Dickinson herself attended Amherst Academy for seven years, as well as spending a year at Mount Holyoke Female Seminary before returning to Amherst where she lived the rest of her life in an increasingly reclusive fashion. Her withdrawal from direct social intercourse was counterpointed by her intense correspondence with a wide range of people of whom in particular Susan Gilbert Dickinson, her brother Austin's wife, and Helen Hunt Jackson stand out as recipients of Dickinson's passionate correspondence. Dickinson's enigmatic and elusive poetry, influenced by the Puritan context in which she lived, has enabled much speculation regarding her sexual identity. This has been heightened by the contradiction

between her self-confinement, eccentric habits such as always wearing white, and her impassioned writing that appears to have acted as an outlet for her emotions. A very sophisticated and complex poet, Dickinson had few of her poems published during her lifetime and then usually at the unsolicited instigation of her friends. Her ordering and binding of her poems, of which there are over 1,700, made their publication possible after her death. Now recognized as one of the leading US women poets of the nineteenth century, there is still considerable debate over whether or not she can be classified as lesbian. Some of her enigmatic poems allow for readings of lesbian passion; her attachment to Susan Gilbert Dickinson and to Helen Hunt Jackson is unquestionable. However, she also had an emotional attachment to Samuel Bowles, the editor of a prominent local newspaper. In the pantheon of lesbian poets, she is regarded as a forerunner of Adrienne RICH.

Diderot, Denis (1713–84). In an effort to question monastic life Diderot produced a novel, *La Religieuse*, in 1760 (published in 1796), which portrays the attempted seduction of a nun by her Mother Superior. The point of this novel was to condemn vows of celibacy and same-sex incarceration since they might lead to lesbianism.

Dixon, Melvin (1950–92). Born in Stamford, Connecticut, this gay African American writer was educated at Wesleyan University, Middletown, Connecticut where he gained a BA in 1971, and at Brown University, Providence, Rhode Island where he completed first his MA in 1973 and then his PhD in 1975. He then became Assistant Professor of English at Williams College, Williamstown, Massachusetts where he taught between 1976 and 1980 when he moved to Queen's College of the City University of New York, Flushing, where he was a member of the English Department until his premature death from an AIDS-related illness in 1992. His partner, Richard Horovitz, also died. Dixon held a National Endowment of the Arts poetry fellowship in 1984, and a New York Arts Foundation artist fellowship in fiction in 1988. In 1989 he was awarded the Nilon Award. During his short writing career, Dixon produced work in several genres, always to great acclaim. His began with poetry, publishing *Climbing Montmartre* (1974), *Change of Territory* (1983), and *The Collected Poems* (1991). His novel *Trouble in Water* (1989) drew on a number of themes typically found in African American writing: the return home to the South, the notion of education representing progress being shattered, and the idea of the family representing security and constituting a haven being called into question. His second novel *Vanishing Rooms* (1991) dealt explicitly with homophobia and homophobic violence, and the eroticization of race and racial difference in a gay relationship. The novel begins with the homophobically motivated murder of Metro, a white man who has a relationship with the African American Jesse, by a white gang. It then proceeds to follow the lives of Jesse, Ruella, a woman who befriends Jesse after the murder, and one of the members of the murderous gang. At the centre of the novel remains the exploration of the relationship between Metro and Jesse. Dixon translated *Drumbeats, Masks, and Metaphor: Contemporary Afro-American Theatre* (1983) and *The Collected Poems of Léopold Sédar Senghor* (1991). He wrote *Ride Out the Wilderness: Geography and Identity in Afro-American Literature* (1987), and contributed to several volumes including 'Red Leaves' in *Men on Men 2* (1988, ed. George Stambolian), to *Brother on Brother* (1991, ed. Essex Hemphill), and 'I'll be Somewhere Listening for My Name' in *Sojourner: Black Gay Voices in the Age of AIDS* (1993, ed. B. Michael Hunter).

Donne, John (1572–1631). One of the great English metaphysical poets, Donne wrote verse, in some of which images of lesbians and of gay men appeared. He was born into a devout Catholic family. His father, a prominent member of the London Ironmongers' Company, died when he was four. Six months later his mother married a Catholic physician, Dr John Symminges. Donne was educated at home by Catholic tutors, then sent to Hart Hall, Oxford, at the age of eleven. He may later have transferred to Cambridge but could not take a degree because of his religion. Little is known about his adolescence. It seems that when he was eighteen he wrote four poems to 'T.W.', which may have been addressed to Thomas Woodward, the 16-year-old brother of his friend Rowland Woodward. The poems are full of sexual puns and highly charged homoeroticism. Among his other poems 'Sapho to Philaenis' stands out as providing an early positive image of lesbian love. In 'The Jughler' Donne takes a dig at effeminacy. However, such poems apart, Donne seems to have led a heterosexual lifestyle. Together with Essex he sailed to sack Cadiz (1596), and with Raleigh he went to hunt Spanish treasure ships off the Azores (1597). Through one of his comrades-in-arms he became Sir Thomas Egerton's secretary but lost his job and was briefly imprisoned when he secretly married the niece of his employer. Together they had twelve children. Donne eventually took holy orders in the Church of England and rose to the position of Dean of St Paul's Cathedral. His son published most of his poems after his death.

Donoghue, Emma (1969–). Lesbian Irish novelist, playwright, and critic, born as the youngest of eight children into a literary family in Dublin. She thought of herself as lesbian from the age of fourteen but did not come out to her family until she was twenty-one. Her first novel, *Stir Fry* (1994), a coming-out story, gained much critical acclaim. Her second novel, *Hood* (1995), also focuses on lesbian relationships and the coming to terms with the death of a lesbian partner. It won the 1997 American Library Association's Gay, Lesbian and Bisexual Award. Her play, *I Know My Own Heart*, is based on the diaries of Anne LISTER. She has also written a critical volume on *Passion between Friends: British Lesbian Culture, 1668–1801* (1994), based on her PhD research at Cambridge on eighteenth-century literary friendships. Her other work includes the plays *Ladies and Gentlemen* and *Trespasses*, *Poems between Women: Four Centuries of Love, Romantic Friendship and Desire* (1997), *Kissing the Witch* (1998), *Outlines: We Are Michael Field* (1998), *Crow Town* (1999), and *Slammerkin* (2000). Her partner is Chris Roulston of the French Department in London of the University of Western Ontario.

Doolittle, Hilda *see* H.D.

Dorcey, Mary (1950–). Irish lesbian poet, short story writer and journalist who was raised in County Dublin, Ireland, but who has also lived in England, France, the USA, and Japan. Dorcey was co-founder of Irish Women United, a national feminist group in Dublin, and of the Irish Gay Rights Movement. She has worked on the feminist papers *Banshee* and *Wicca*. Her first volume of poetry, *Kindling*, appeared in 1982. A short-story collection, *A Noise from the Woodshed*, came out in 1989. Her work, which has been widely anthologized, focuses on women, and on women's erotic relationships with each other.

Doty, Mark (1953–). Gay US writer who grew up in Tennessee in a religious household. He has taught at various universities in the USA, including at Sarah Lawrence College, Brandeis University and at Vermont College. His poetry addresses

homosexual themes explicitly. His collections of poetry include *Turtle, Swan* (1987), *Bethlehem in Broad Daylight* (1991), *My Alexandria* (1993), for which he received the national Book Critics Circle award and the T.S. Eliot Prize, *Atlantis* (1995), and *Sweet Machine* (1998). In 1996 he published his memoir *Heaven's Coast* for which he won the PEN/Martha Albrand Award for First Nonfiction. This memoir contains a moving account of the death from AIDS-related illnesses of his long-term lover Wally Roberts in 1994. Other works include *An Island Sheaf* (1998), *Firebird: A Memoir* (1999), *Still Life with Oysters and Lemons* (2001), and *Source* (2002).

Douglas, Alfred Lord Bruce (1870–1945). Best known as the love of Oscar WILDE's life, Douglas was also a poet in his own right. Born into an aristocratic English family, son of John Sholto Douglas, the 8th Marquis of Queensbury, Douglas was introduced to Wilde by the poet Lionel Johnson, who arranged a meeting at Oscar Wilde's house at 34 (formerly 16) Tite Street, Chelsea, in the late summer of 1891. Douglas attended the première of *Lady Windermere's Fan* in February 1892. They began their relationship a few days later. At the time of Wilde's trials Douglas went to France to avoid being called as a witness. Douglas's first collection of *Poems*, published anonymously in English in 1899 (it had appeared in France in 1896), was a great success. In 1894 a homosexual undergraduate at Oxford University, John Francis Bloxam, asked Douglas to contribute to a new periodical entitled *The Chameleon*. Douglas contributed two poems that were subsequently cited at Wilde's trial for homosexual offences in April 1895. One of these poems, 'Two Loves', contained the final line, 'the Love that dare not speak its name', a phrase that has since become a commonplace to describe homosexual love. The Wilde affair caused a rift between Douglas and his father, who left his fortune to his other son Percy. Percy lost this fortune to speculation. Douglas and Wilde resumed their friendship in France once Wilde had been released from prison. In 1902 Douglas married his cousin Olive Constance. She deserted him in 1913. Together they had a son, Raymond, who was deranged and spent much of his life in confinement. Douglas was imprisoned for a time in Wormwood Scrubs, having been sentenced to six months' hard labour for alleging that Winston Churchill had taken part in a Jewish-financed conspiracy to have Kitchener murdered in 1916. While in prison he wrote *In Excelsis*, which was published in 1924. In 1935 his *Sonnets and Lyrics* appeared. Douglas continued to be interested in men throughout his life. At the age of fifty-six he fell in love with the 18-year-old Ivor Goring, with whom he had a brief relationship. Among Douglas's other publications are *Autumn Days* (1890), and, importantly, a series of texts devoted to his relationship with Oscar Wilde including *Oscar Wilde and Myself* (1914), *The Autobiography of Lord Alfred Douglas* (1929), *Oscar Wilde: A Summing Up* (1940), and *The Collected Satires of Lord Alfred Douglas*, published posthumously in 1976. Douglas has remained a controversial figure in gay criticism, not least because of his intermittent homophobia and his anti-Semitism.

Douglas, Norman (1868–1952). Born in Thuringen, Vorarlberg, Austria to a Scottish father, the manager of a cotton mill, and a Scottish-German mother, Douglas was educated at Uppingham School (1881–3) and then at Karlsruhe Gymnasium (1883–9). He entered the British Foreign Office for which he worked between 1893 and 1901, and was posted to St Petersburg between 1894 and 1896. He bought a house on Capri, the Mediterranean island about which he wrote eight books and, in 1898, he married his cousin Elizabeth Theobaldino FitzGibbon, with whom he had two sons. The mar-

riage ended in 1904. Douglas became financially impoverished after 1907 and lived in poverty for about two decades with his later companion Guiseppe Orioli in Paris, St Malo, Menton, Florence, Lisbon, and London, before returning to Capri in 1946. Douglas's first published work, which he thought of as contributing to the abolition of child labour, was an official report on *The Pumice Stone Industry of the Lipari Islands* (1895). He became better known for his geographical and topographical works *Siren Land* (1911), *Fountain in the Sand* (1912), and *Old Calabria* (1915). Between 1912 and 1914 Douglas was assistant editor of *The English Review*. He produced a number of other texts including *London Street Games* (1916), *Looking Back* (1933), and *Late Harvest* (1946). His only popular success was the hedonistic *South Wind* (1917).

Dowie, Claire. Contemporary British writer, performer, and pioneer of stand-up comedy who has a cult following in lesbian and gay venues such as the Drill Hall in London, where she regularly performs her one-handers, several of which were published as *Why Is John Lennon Wearing a Skirt? and Other Stand-up Theatre Plays* in 1996. The collection contains five plays, all of which deal with identities in crises, often sexual identities in crisis. The plays take issue with the social construction of masculinity and femininity, showing how individuals under pressure to conform to specific gender roles may vacate or query these through fantasy and role play. *Why Is John Lennon Wearing a Skirt?* deals with a girl who begins life by identifying, against the social grain, with men since they get to have all the fun and action. The social isolation the character experiences as she is repeatedly uncovered as being a girl rather than the boy she plays is alleviated only by meeting a man who hates men and stereotypical gender roles. Dowie might be said to embrace queer in her plays' quest for a liveable identity outside conventional gender roles. Apart from this published collection of her work, Dowie has also written a play entitled *All Over Lovely*, which was performed at the Drill Hall in 1998, and which was published together with another of her plays, *Easy Access (for the Boys)*. The latter explores the issue of father–son incest and the impact that experience has on Michael, one of the characters who works as a rent boy but thinks lovingly of his father, and his mate Gary, who hates his father for what he did. In 1995 Dowie was awarded an Arts Council bursary to write *Easy Access (for the Boys)*, a play with no part for herself, which is unusual since she normally performs (in) her own work. However, the birth of her daughter in the 1990s changed this, and recently she has written new work for other actresses (*Designs for Living*, 2000) as well as performing *The Year of the Monkey* at the Drill Hall in London (2000), a piece originally done by BBC Radio 3 in 1995. Other work includes the funny and sad film *Came Out, it Rained, Went Back In Again* (1992, BBC2, City Shorts season), a coming-out film, and *Kevin* (1994, Central Children's Television).

Dreher, Sarah (1937–). Contemporary US lesbian novelist, playwright, and clinical psychologist who lives in Amherst with her life partner. Dreher's mother was of Welsh descent and instilled in her daughter a love for theatre through regular trips to New York to see shows. In the mid-1950s Dreher attended Wellesley College, studying clinical psychology. It was at college that she began to be aware of her sexual identity, trying to, as she has put it, 'come to grips with being a lesbian in a homophobic world'. At college, as she has described it, the only way to be lesbian meant 'to live – once I had decided to live at all – as a heterosexual woman'. However, she also had the experience of being called to the Dean's office because another woman had accused Dreher and a

friend of being in a lesbian relationship, which they were not. This experience is reflected in Dreher's play *Alumnae Years: The Doris Day Years*, one of the plays in her edited collection *Lesbian Stages: Plays by Sarah Dreher* (1988), which contains five plays with explicitly lesbian content. These plays were all written for a group of women with whom, in 1974, she had done a performance at the local women's centre to celebrate International Women's Week. At the time that *Lesbian Stages* was published, this group of women were performing under the name Theater, Too. Dreher is particularly well known for her lesbian detective novels centring on lesbian butch sleuth Stoner McTavish. She, like Val MCDERMID, Katherine V. FORREST, and Kate CALLOWAY, belongs to a generation of often lesbian women writers who appropriated a traditionally male popular genre, the detective novel, in order to resituate it in a lesbian context. Dreher's Stoner McTavish novels include *Stoner McTavish* (1985), *Something Shady* (1986), *Gray Magic* (1987), *A Captive in Time* (1990), *Otherworld* (1993), *Bad Company* (1995), and *Shaman's Moon* (1998). She has also published the novel *Solitaire and Brahms* (1997).

du Maurier, Angela (1904–?). Born in London, one of three daughters of the then well-known actor-manager Gerald du Maurier, the lesbian writer Angela, less commercially successful than her younger sister Daphne DU MAURIER, tried her hand at acting before deciding to become a writer. All three du Maurier daughters – Jeanne, the youngest, Daphne, and Angela, the oldest – had lesbian relationships, with Jeanne and Angela, in contrast to Daphne, living as lesbians most of their adult lives. Through the theatre Angela du Maurier met women such as Tallulah Bankhead with whom she shared a singing teacher, Olga Lynn, and Audry Carten. Angela du Maurier, like her younger lesbian painter sister Jeanne who lived with the poet Noel Welch, accepted her lesbian identity. She was friendly with Naomi JACOB, who had had to give up the theatre and decided to write for health reasons. In 1930 Angela du Maurier met Angela Halliday, her 'twin' and partner, with whom she shared her first name and the year and date of birth. In the early 1930s Angela du Maurier began to write but her first novel, *The Little Less*, was rejected by publishers due to its lesbian content. In 1939 *The Perplexed Heart* by Angela du Maurier was published and in 1941 *The Little Less* finally appeared. During the war Angela Halliday was an ambulance driver in London while Angela du Maurier and Jeanne ran a market garden in Cornwall. After the war Angela du Maurier remained in Cornwall. Du Maurier published a number of novels including *Treveryan* (1942), *Lawrence Vane* (1946), *The Road to Leenane* (1963), and *Pilgrims by the Way* (1967). In 1951 her autobiography *It's Only the Little Sister* appeared. In it Angela du Maurier praises both Christa WINSLOE's *Girls in Uniform* and the novel *Olivia* by Dorothy STRACHEY BUSSY for describing lesbian relationships as something ordinary. It might be argued that the unhappy fate that meets the lesbian protagonists in both novels makes their lives less ordinary, but clearly Angela du Maurier's approval centred on the notion of focusing on lesbian relationships in a text at all, as opposed to hiding such relationships or not mentioning them. Du Maurier's work is virtually unknown today though she is an important figure for lesbian literary history of the mid-twentieth century.

du Maurier, Daphne (1907–89). English writer, born in London, the second of three daughters of the then well-known actor-manager Gerald du Maurier. While her older sister Angela DU MAURIER, also a writer, and her younger sister, Jeanne, a painter, both lived openly as lesbians, Daphne du Maurier found her intermittent attachments to women difficult to come to terms with and did not write about them. She, like her sisters, was educated privately at home and in Paris but lived most of her life in Cornwall, which forms the setting of many of her best-known works. Today Daphne du Maurier is best known for the romantic historical novels she began to write in the 1930s. Her first novel was *The Loving Spirit* (1931). This was followed by her so-called Cornish novels *Jamaica Inn* (1936), *Rebecca* (1938) (which was made into a highly successful Hollywood film (1940) by Alfred Hitchcock and carries a sub-theme of a passionate attachment of a female housekeeper to her previous mistress, the first Mrs de Winter), *Frenchman's Creek* (1941), and *My Cousin Rachel* (1952). Du Maurier also published two volumes on Cornwall, *Cornwall, Vanishing Cornwall* (1981) and *Enchanted Cornwall: Her Pictorial Memoir* (1989), a biography of Branwell Brontë (1960), a family history of her own family, *The Du Mauriers* (1937), and two autobiographical volumes, *Growing Pains* (1977), and *Myself When Young: The Shaping of a Writer* (1978). Daphne du Maurier's private life was rather unhappy. Her parents had hoped for a boy when she was born and she was aware of their disappointment throughout her life. Her first emotional attachment was to her governess Maud Woddell, called 'Tod', who came into the family when Daphne was eleven years old. Daphne then fell in love with her teacher in Paris, Fernande Yvon. Both this teacher and Edgar Wallace, a friend of the family, encouraged Daphne du Maurier to write. In 1932 Daphne married Tommy Browning with whom she had her first daughter Tessa in 1933. While her husband was stationed in Egypt during the Second World War, Daphne returned to England to give birth to her second daughter Flavia in 1937. Apparently she was disappointed at having another daughter. In 1940 her son Christian was born. He clearly had a happier childhood than his sisters. In 1943 du

Maurier rented Menabilly, a house in Cornwall to which she became very attached. Her marriage deteriorated after the Second World War. In 1947 Daphne du Maurier visited the publishing couple Nelson and Ellen Doubleday, and fell in love with Ellen Doubleday who, however, did not return her affections. Daphne du Maurier then fell in love and had a relationship with Gertrude Lawrence, the actress who played the lead in her *September Tide*. Gertrude Lawrence apparently inspired the novel *My Cousin Rachel*. In 1952 Gertrude Lawrence died, which left Daphne bereft and lonely. Her lease for Menabilly was not renewed in 1968 and she was forced to move to Kilmarth nearby. In 1969 she was made Dame of the British Empire for her services to literature. Her final years were beset by depression and isolation. In 1978 Ellen Doubleday died, another loss for Daphne. She maintained contact with her sisters and their female partners but otherwise lived a retired existence. At the beginning of 1989 Daphne du Maurier began to refuse food, seemingly wanting to die. She died in her sleep in April of that year.

Duffy, Carol Ann (1955–). Born in Glasgow, the poet Duffy grew up in Staffordshire and attended university in Liverpool before moving to London, and then to Manchester. She now lives there with her partner, the poet Jackie KAY, to whom, among others, her collection of poetry entitled *The World's Wife* (1999) is dedicated. Her poetry, which explores the lives of those often marginalized in high culture, has received many prizes and awards. In 1984 she won an Eric Gregory Award. She received the Scottish Arts Council Book Award for her collections *Standing Female Nude* (1985) and *The Other Country* (1990). In 1987 she published the collection *Selling Manhattan*. She won the prestigious Somerset Maugham Award in 1988, and the Dylan Thomas Award in 1989 as well as a

Cholmondeley Award in 1992. In 1993 *Mean Time* appeared, which details an earlier, fraught relationship with a heterosexual lover. Duffy has edited a variety of anthologies of poetry. They include *I Wouldn't Thank You for a Valentine* (1992), *Stopping for Death* (1996), *Anvil New Poets* (1996), and *Time's Tidings* (1999). Duffy's poetry often focuses on people from working- or lower middle-class backgrounds, especially women, who are trapped in loveless marriages, feel empty because they are childless, have suffered domestic violence at the hands of their partners, or abuse from others. Her work's concern is with the social and economic realities that engulf people living under materially strained or emotionally depressed circumstances. Duffy, who is considered one of the most outstanding poets of her generation, hit the news in 1999 when, in the wake of the death of the Poet Laureate Ted Hughes, a replacement was sought. For a time it looked as if she might be a serious contender for this position but her lesbianism was persistently cited in the media as the reason why she was unlikely to be offered the position as, indeed, and to the shame of the establishment, in the end she was not. Her most recent collection, *The World's Wife*, which features the wives of famous males such as Sigmund Freud, King Kong, Aesop, and Quasimodo speaking out about their positions, is a reminder of the ways in which women still come second, have to be 'the wife', in cultural terms.

Duffy, Maureen (1933–). British lesbian writer born in Worthing, Sussex, the daughter of Grace Wright and Cahia Duffy, an Irish labourer who left soon after her birth. Until the outbreak of the Second World War, when she was evacuated to Wiltshire, she was raised in London by her mother's extended family. Duffy was very close to her mother who encouraged her daughter's interest in writing stories and poetry from an early age. In 1956 Duffy received a BA from King's

College, London. In her final year at university she got married, a marriage that ended when she was twenty-eight. Following university Duffy went to Italy to teach English. She then taught in various South London schools for five years, writing plays and poetry at the same time. In 1962 her first, semi-autobiographical novel, *That's How It Was*, was published. This novel centres on the relationship between a mother and her daughter, a theme that would recur in Duffy's fiction as one of the key relationships shaping individuals. *The Love Child* (1971), for example, dealt with a similar topic. From *A Single Eye* (1964) onwards Duffy dealt more openly with homosexuality in her fiction. *The Microcosm* (1966), an experimental novel, details life in London's lesbian bars. Placing lesbians and gay men within broader social contexts, her trilogy about London life, *Wounds* (1969), *Capital* (1975), and *Londoners: An Elegy* (1983) were followed by *Change* (1987) and *Illuminations* (1992). She has written numerous other texts such as the parodic thriller *I Want to Go to Moscow* (1973), and the futuristic tale *Gor Saga* (1981). *The Erotic World of Fairy* (1972) is a Freudian study of erotic themes in literature. In 1990 Duffy published a collection of *Five Plays* by the playwright Aphra Behn about whom she also wrote a critical biography entitled *The Passionate Shepherdess: The Life of Aphra Behn 1640–1689*. Duffy has campaigned much both for animal rights, about which she has written in *Men and Beasts: An Animal Rights Handbook* (1984), and about the rights of authors. Her many publications include plays such as *The Lay Off* (1962), *The Silk Room* (1966), and *A Nightingale in Bloomsbury Square* (1972). Among her other works are *Housespy* (1978), *Occam's Razor* (1993), *Collected Poems 1949–1984* (1985), *Restitution* (1999), *A Fine Target* (1999), and *England: The Making of the Myth from Stonehenge to Albert Square* (2001). Much respected in mainstream literary

circles, she is less well known among lesbian readers than she deserves to be.

Duffy, Stella (1963–). Contemporary lesbian writer, born in the UK, who grew up in New Zealand and presently lives in London with her partner Shelley. In 2000 she wrote movingly about her experience of cancer in the Sunday newspapers in the UK. Duffy works with the comedy company Spontaneous Combustion. Like Val MCDERMID, Katherine V. FORREST, and Sarah DREHER, Duffy is a writer of popular lesbian crime fiction, featuring the lesbian sleuth Saz Martin. Her lesbian crime fiction includes *Calendar Girl* (1994), *Wavewalker* (1996), *Beneath the Blonde* (1997), and *Fresh Flesh* (1999). Duffy has also written the novels *Singling out Couples* (1998), *Eating Cake* (1999), and *Immaculate Conceit* (2000). She wrote a play, *The Hand*, for Gay Sweatshop, the lesbian and gay touring theatre company, and a one-woman show, *The Tedious Predictability of Falling in Love*.

Dufrénoy, Adelaïde (1765–1825). French poet whose writings had a decided homosexual sub-text and who was dubbed the 'French Sappho' for her witty and sometimes erotic work. Born in Nantes, Dufrénoy married at fifteen, leaving France after the Revolution of 1789 since her husband was a member of the royal entourage. She returned to France in 1812. Her first volume of poetry, *Elégies* (1807; *Elegies*) proved very popular and she received the approbation of the Académie Française in 1815. Dufrénoy published in a variety of other genres, including edited collections of literary works for women. Her woman-centredness is apparent in many of the titles of her works. They include *Etrennes à ma fille* (1815; *New Year's Gift to My Daughter*), *La Petite Ménagère* (1816; *The Little Housewife*), *Biographie des jeunes demoiselles* (1816; *Biography of Young Ladies*), *Les Françaises nouvelles* (1818; *The New*

Frenchwomen) and *Le Livre des femmes* (1823; *The Women's Book*).

Duncan, Robert (1919–88). Gay US poet, born in Oakland, California, to Edward and Marguerite Duncan. His mother died during his birth and, since his father felt himself incapable of raising a baby as well as the rest of his family, Duncan was adopted by Edwin and Minnehaha Symmes when he was seven months old. The Symmes belonged to a group called the Hermetic Brotherhood, a variant of theosophy. Duncan was educated at the University of California at Berkeley where he was involved in a homosexual relationship, aged eighteen. From California Duncan moved to New York City to pursue his career as a writer. In 1944 he published 'The Homosexual in Society' in Dwight Macdonald's magazine *Politics*. In this article Duncan acknowledged his own homosexuality and called for openness regarding homosexuality. As a result of this article John Crowe Ransom refused to publish a previously accepted poem of Duncan's in the *Kenyon Review*. Despite this rebuff Duncan continued to write poetry and became a leader of the San Francisco Renaissance as well as of the poets associated with Black Mountain College, where he taught during the 1950s. From 1951 Duncan was in a life-long relationship with the artist Jess Collins. Many of his later poems celebrate his relationship with Collins and their domesticity. In 1958 his *Letters* appeared, followed in 1960 by his collection *Opening the Field*. *Ground Work: Before the War* (1984) includes a cycle of lyrics inspired by his fellow gay poet Thom GUNN. *Ground Work II: In the Dark* (1987) celebrates not just homosexual love but love in general. Duncan was open about his homosexuality and discussed it in his work, despite the negative consequences that such openness sometimes entailed.

Duncker, Patricia. Born in the West Indies, this contemporary writer and academic teaches Literature, Creative Writing, and Feminist Theory at the University of Wales. Her first novel, *Hallucinating Foucault* (1996), might be described as a queer novel. It features a male PhD student's quest for a gay French writer, Paul Michel, on whose work he is writing his thesis. The student's quest is prompted by his girlfriend who, it turns out, is the daughter of a former lover's of Paul Michel, and who herself made a life-long commitment to Paul Michel. Paul Michel, in turn, had mistaken her for a lovely boy when young. *Hallucinating Foucault* won Dillon's First Fiction Award and the McKitterick Prize for the best first novel. Since then Duncker has published a collection of short stories, *Monsieur Shoushana's Lemon Trees* (1997), and *James Miranda Barry* (1999). The latter is a fictional account of a real-life character who was born as a biological woman but lived her life as a man. Various accounts of Barry's life exist but little is known about the person. Barry served as an army doctor between 1813 and 1859, during which time his sexual identity was the object of some speculation although the facts of his biological womanhood were not known until after his death. Duncker's novel belongs to a similar tradition as Jackie KAY's novel *Trumpet* in that it tries to provide an imaginative account of a real-life figure, a biological woman who lived her life as a man.

Durrell, Lawrence (1912–90). British poet, novelist, and travel writer who was born in Julundar, India, of an Irish mother and a British civil engineer father. He returned to England in his late teens, having attended the College of St Joseph in Darjeeling, India, before going to St Edmund's School, Canterbury. He then travelled widely, lived in Paris during part of the 1930s, and then, once his family had moved to Corfu, Greece, spent much of his life in the eastern Mediterranean. From there he regularly visited London and Paris. In 1937 he met Henry Miller after they had had a two-year correspondence. While he was in Paris in 1937 and 1938 Durrell, Miller, and Alfred Perlès set up an avant-garde literary magazine, initially called *Booster*, then renamed *Delta*. Durrell was a heterosexual man who married many times. His writings expressed a libertarian sexual attitude and contained representations of gays and lesbians. His poetry collections include *A Private Country* (1943), *Cities, Plains and People* (1946), *On Seeming to Presume* (1948), and *The Tree of Idleness* (1955). His *Collected Poems* appeared in 1960. *The Black Book* (1938), his first novel to come to public attention, was heavily influenced by Henry Miller. It did not appear in Britain until 1973 and is a pornographic fantasy. It chronicles the lives of the guests of the Hotel Regina, and includes the figures of the homosexual Tarquin and the prostitute Livia. *Livia* (1974), a much later book, contains a brothel scene with a promiscuous lesbian. *Monsieur* (1974) also features a black lesbian. Durrell became renowned for his *Alexandria Quartet*, consisting of *Justine* (1957), *Balthazar* (1958), *Mountolive* (1959), and *Clea* (1960). The style of these novels is ornate and lyrical. Each of the novels has an epigraph from the Marquis de Sade. Influenced by the latter as well as by Miller, from a feminist perspective Durrell might be regarded as a misogynistic writer whose titillating texts are addressed to a voyeuristic male audience. Durrell also translated the poetry of C.P. CAVAFY and wrote several volumes of travel writing including *Prospero's Cell* (1945) about his pre-war years on Corfu, *Reflections on a Marine Venus* (1953) about Rhodes, and *Bitter Lemons* (1957) about Cyprus.

Dworkin, Andrea (1946–). Born in Camden, New Jersey, this radical feminist activist and writer has consistently engaged with the issue of violence of men against women, and her vocal stance against pornography has generated both much admiration and great dissent among other feminists. Educated at Bennington College where she gained a BA in 1968, she became involved in anti-Vietnam demonstrations, which ended with her being sent to gaol for four days during which time she was sexually abused and brutalized by both prison employees and inmates. This experience became one source for her writings against sexual violence. The publication of *Woman Hating: A Radical Look at Sexuality* (1974) catapulted Dworkin to fame. As a result she gave a series of lectures that were published two years later as *Our Blood: Prophecies and Discourses on Sexual Politics* (1976). The volume includes 'Lesbian Pride', a speech delivered at the Lesbian Pride week in Central Park in June 1975. In this speech Dworkin defined her vision of what it means to be a lesbian. In 1976 the San Francisco-based Women against Violence in Pornography and the Media was set up, resulting in major debates about pornography, its status in society, and the role and representation of women within it. Together with the lawyer Catherine MacKinnon, Dworkin set out to change the law concerning pornography by drafting an ordinance that defined pornography as a form of sex discrimination and described those abused through it as having been deprived of their civil rights. This ordinance became the two women's most famous action. It was passed into law in the states of Indianapolis, Indiana, and Minneapolis, Minnesota, before being declared unconstitutional in 1986. The ordinance generated one of the most sustained and heated arguments amongst feminists, and affected many including, for instance, the lesbian playwright Sarah DANIELS whose play *Masterpieces* was directly influenced by Dworkin's work. Dworkin had various jobs including as a waitress, receptionist, secretary, paid political organizer, and teacher, before settling into a life of campaigning and activism. Following on from the pornography debates of the 1970s and 1980s, Dworkin wrote *Pornography: Men Possessing Women* (1981) and contributed to *Take Back the Night: Women on Pornography* (1980, ed. Laura Lederer). Together with Catherine MacKinnon she wrote and edited *The Reasons Why: Essays on the New Civil Rights Law Recognizing Pornography as Sex Discrimination* (1985), *Pornography and Civil Rights: A New Day for Women's Equality* (1988), and *In Harm's Way: The Pornography Civil Rights Hearings* (1997). Her radical sexual politics also formed the basis of *Right-wing Women: The Politics of Domesticated Females* (1983), *Intercourse* (1987), *Letters from a War Zone* (1989), and *Life and Death* (1997). In the last she explored, *inter alia*, questions of anti-Semitism and feminism, which she then picked up on in *Scapegoat: The Jews, Israel and Women's Liberation* (2000). Dworkin has also written two autobiographical novels, *Ice and Fire* (1986) and *Mercy* (1990), and *Four Walls Eight Windows* (1991). A collection of short stories, *The New Woman's Broken Heart*, appeared in 1980. A controversial figure, Dworkin, who lives with John Stoltenberg in New York, has always defended women's rights not to be sexually abused and violated by men.

Dykewomon, Elana (1949–). Lesbian Jewish US poet and writer who was born Elana Nachman in New York City to middle-class Jewish parents. Her father is a lawyer, her mother a librarian. The family moved to Puerto Rico when Dykewomon was eight years old. She studied fine art at Reed College in Portland, Oregon, and received a BFA in Creative Writing from the California Institute of Art. At the age of twenty-one, Dykewomon wrote her first novel, *Riverfinger Women*, published in 1974 by the pioneering women's press, Daughters Inc., which had been co-founded by June ARNOLD. *Riverfinger Women* became a cult novel among lesbians as one of the first texts of the period of the second women's liberation movement to portray lesbian relationships with a happy ending. With the publication of *They Will Know Me by My Teeth* (1976), Elana changed her surname to 'Dykewoman', an expression of her commitment to the lesbian community who would know her as lesbian from her new surname. By 1981, with the publication of *Fragments from Lesbos*, Dykewomon spelt her new surname as it now is in order to avoid etymological connections with men. Such renamings and related creative uses of language were part of a lesbian and feminist recognition of the 1970s and 1980s that language and how we name things matters, and that conventional language use was very male-centred. It led to extensive new scholarship around women's and men's use of language. One of its victories was the introduction of the abbreviation 'Ms' instead of 'Mrs' and 'Miss' to denote independent women, not wanting to be known by their connection to a man ('Mrs') or their seeming virginity and/or unmarriedness ('Miss'). Dykewomon became the editor of *Sinister Wisdom*, a lesbian journal, in 1987. Her work, which has been much anthologized, always places the lesbian as an active character and lesbian relationships centre stage.

E

Eliot, T.S. (1888–1965). Born in St Louis, Missouri, and educated at Harvard, the Sorbonne, and Merton College, Oxford, Thomas Stearns Eliot settled in England on encouragement from Ezra Pound whom he met in 1915. Before that, between 1910 and 1911 while Eliot was studying at the Sorbonne, he had a relationship with the Frenchman Jean Verdenal (1889–1915). Verdenal died in the First World War at the age of twenty-six. A month later Eliot married his first wife Vivien Haigh-Wood. She suffered repeated physical and mental breakdowns; in 1932–3 they were formally separated, and she finally died in 1947. In 1957 he married his second wife, Valerie Fletcher. Eliot, who is one of the great figures of twentieth-century literature, dedicated his *Prufrock and Other Observations* (1917) to Verdenal's memory, over an epigraph from Dante's *Purgatorio* that comes from one of Eliot's two favourite sections of the *Divine Comedy*, both of which he returned to repeatedly throughout his career. These are in *Inferno XV*, in which Dante meets Brunetto Latini among the sodomites, and in *Purgatorio XXVI*, in which he encounters Arnaut Daniel among more sodomites and hermaphrodites. Eliot's love for Verdenal is at the centre of his perhaps most famous poem, *The Waste Land* (1922), which first appeared in the new literary journal *The Criterion*, which Eliot founded. It is possible to identify the so-called Hyacinth girl with the poet's sentimental memory of 'a friend coming across the Luxembourg Gardens in the late afternoon, waving a branch of lilac'. The poem then fuses that figure with death and references to the trenches of the Great War, culminating in the crucial line, 'He who was living is now dead.' *The Waste Land* may be viewed as a funeral elegy but when John Peter wrote an essay in 1952 stating this, Eliot instructed his solicitors to intervene and all traceable copies of that volume of *Essays in Criticism* were destroyed. Peter reissued the essay in amended form after Eliot's death. One of Ezra Pound's self-appointed tasks as editor of the manuscript of *The Waste Land* was to tone down its homoeroticism. Eliot worked for a time at Lloyd's Bank but in 1925 became a director of Faber & Faber, building up one of the great lists of poetry for that publisher. In 1927 he became a British subject and a member of the Anglican Church. He published *Four Quartets* (1935–42), and in that same period also wrote a number of plays including *Sweeney Agonistes* (1932), *Murder in the Cathedral* (1935), and *The Family Reunion* (1939), as well as the comedies *The Cocktail Party* (1950), *The Confidential Clerk* (1954), and *The Elder Statesman* (1959). His book of children's verse, *Old Possum's Book of Practical Cats* (1939), was turned into a successful stage musical, *Cats*, in 1981. Eliot also wrote several volumes of literary criticism. He received the Nobel Prize for Literature in 1947.

Elliott, Sumner Locke (1917–91). Gay Australian writer who was born in Sydney to Helena Sumner Locke, a writer, who died the day after she had given birth to him, and Henry Logan Elliott, a journalist who was dispatched to England with the Australian army only ten days after he had got married. Elliott's father granted two of his wife's sisters guardianship over the child. This resulted in an unhappy and unsettled childhood for Elliott since the sisters could not agree who was to take care of him. He described these experiences in his first novel, *Careful, He Might Hear You* (1963), which won the Miles Franklin Award for best Australian novel. Much of Elliott's writing is autobiographical in content and does not deal with the issue of homosexuality. He wrote stage plays such as *Rusty Bugles* (1948) and then wrote for television before turning novelist in the 1960s. In 1990 he finally came out as gay in *Fairyland*. By that stage he had immigrated to the USA (1948) and had acquired US citizenship (1955). In the late 1970s Elliott met a widower, Whitfield Cooke, with whom he became very friendly. Cook moved into Elliott's house after the latter had suffered a stroke in 1985 and the two men enjoyed a companionship that seems to have eluded Elliott in his earlier life. Elliott's *Radio Days* was published posthumously in 1993. His other works include *Some Doves and Pythons* (1966), *Edens Lost* (1970), *The Man Who Got Away* (1973), *Going* (1975), *Water under the Bridge* (1977), *Signs of Life* (1981), and *Waiting for Childhood* (1987).

Ellis, Edith (1861–1916). Born in Ashton-under-Lyne, the only daughter of Mary Laetitia Bancroft who died soon after Edith's birth, and of Samuel Oldham Lees, a landed proprietor. Edith Mary Oldham Lees Ellis now largely figures as the lesbian wife of the sexologist Havelock ELLIS, who inspired her husband's work on homosexuality and who shared his affections with the writer Olive SCHREINER, with whom Ellis continued to have a passionate correspondence after Schreiner had returned to South Africa. Through her father Edith Lees had a 'bachelor income'. She met her future husband through the 'Fellowship of the New Life' of which she was secretary and from which the Fabian Society originated (1884). Lees and Ellis were interested in James Hinton's ideas about sex. They married in 1891 and lived for the most part in Carbis Bay, Cornwall. Edith Ellis was a writer in her own right whose literary output included sketches, novels, short stories, one successful short play, and essays. In 1910 she published *Three Modern Seers*, a book on James Hinton, Friedrich Nietzsche, and Edward CARPENTER. Her life and work need yet to be fully documented and explored.

Ellis, Havelock (1859–1939). Henry Havelock Ellis, one of the earliest English sexologists, was born in Croydon, South London. He spent some years studying and teaching in Australia before returning to London in 1879 and qualifying as a physician. Passionately interested in literature, he edited the Mermaid Series of Elizabethan dramatists (1887–9) and the Contemporary Science Series. In 1984 he met Olive SCHREINER, who became a close friend. A prolific writer, it was his seven-volume series, *Studies in the Psychology of Sex* (1897–1928), which made him a lasting influence in the history of sexuality in general and homosexuality in particular. Together with John Addington SYMONDS he collaborated on the series' first volume on sexual inversion in which homosexuality was treated neither as sin nor as sickness but as an innate condition. The volume was published as *Sexual Inversion* in 1897, and had a significant influence on ideas about the origins and manifestations of homosexuality. Radclyffe HALL's protagonist Stephen in *The Well of Loneliness*, for instance, represents a version of Ellis's view of homosexuality. Ellis moved in progressive circles, particularly as regards questions of sexuality. His friends included Edward CARPENTER and Arthur Symons. At the age of thirty-two he married Edith Lees (Edith ELLIS), a progressive lesbian. In 1939 Ellis published his autobiography, *My Life*.

Evaristo, Bernardine (1959–). Lesbian writer, born in London of Nigerian and British descent. Evaristo has worked in theatre as a performer, playwright, and drama tutor. One of her quests has been to 'find the root; the direct line to my ancestors'. Both her work for theatre and her poetry explore lesbian relationships and the search for one's cultural origins. Her poems have been published in the anthologies *Beautiful Barbarians: Lesbian Feminist Poetry* (1986; ed. Lilian Mohin) and in *Charting the Journey*, a collection published by Sheba Feminist Publishers. In the 1980s Evaristo worked with the Theatre of Black Women touring theatre company who produced her plays *Tiger Teeth Clenched Not to Bite* (1983), *Silhouette* (1984), and *Pyeyucca* (1985). She co-wrote the latter two with Patricia Hilaire. During the 1990s Evaristo turned to novel writing and published *Island of Abraham* (1994), *Lara* (1997), and *The Emperor's Babe* (2001).

F

Faderman, Lillian (1940–). Lesbian American writer and academic whose work has been of outstanding importance in charting lesbian histories both inside and outside of the mainstream of literary traditions. Born in New York, Faderman was educated at the University of California where she received a BA from Berkeley in 1962 and a PhD from UCLA in 1967. In 1985 she published the book that established her as an international lesbian scholar, *Surpassing the Love of Men: Romantic Friendship and Love between Women from the Renaissance to the Present*. The first extended narrative account of lesbian women's presence in literary history since Jeannette H. FOSTER's account of 1956, *Surpassing the Love of Men* became not only a landmark text in lesbian literary criticism but also formed part of a debate about the 'nature' of lesbian identity, in particular the vexed question of whether or not a relationship between women had to be sexual, rather than simply emotional, in order to qualify as lesbian. Faderman, rather like Adrienne RICH in her famous essay 'Compulsory Heterosexuality', gives credence to the notion of a lesbian continuum along which romantic friendships without a sexual component have as much a place as fully-fledged same-sex sexual relationships. She had previously edited two collections of writings about specific ethnic groups in the USA: *Speaking for Ourselves: American Ethnic Writing* (1969), and *From the Barrio: A Chicano Anthology* (1973). During the early 1980s, however, her work focused increasingly on lesbian histories. In 1980 she published *Lesbian Feminism in Turn-of-the-century Germany*. She then wrote *Scotch Verdict: Miss Pirie and Miss Woods vs. Dame Cumming Gordon* (1983), an account of an early nineteenth-century trial of two school teachers who were accused of having a relationship by one of the girls in their school. This case formed the basis of Lillian HELLMAN's play *The Children's Hour*. Other works by Faderman include *Speaking for Ourselves* (co-written with Barbara Bradshaw, 1969), *Odd Girls Out and Twilight Lovers: A History of Lesbian Life in 20th-Century America* (1991), *Chloe plus Olivia: An Anthology of Lesbian Literature from the 17th Century to the Present* (1994), which Faderman edited, and *To Believe in Women: What Lesbians Have Done for America* (1999).

Fairbanks, Tash (1948–). Contemporary British lesbian playwright, novelist, and performer. Fairbanks was involved in street theatre in Brighton in the late 1970s and, together with Jude Winter and Jane Boston, formed the lesbian theatre company Siren in 1979 for which she wrote and as part of which she performed. The company took on issues of lesbian and gay rights, as well as other socio-political concerns, in their

work, much of which was written by
Tash Fairbanks, deriving from work-
shopped ideas. The plays scripted by Tash
Fairbanks for Siren include *Mama's Gone
a Hunting* (produced 1980–1), *Curfew*
(produced 1982–3), *From the Divine*
(produced 1983–4), *Now Wash Your
Hands Please* (produced 1984–5), *Pulp*
(produced 1985–6), *Hotel Destiny* (produced 1987–8), and *Swamp* (produced
1989). Siren, and Fairbanks's career as a
playwright, were inextricably bound up
with the heyday of feminist and lesbian
theatre in Britain when other lesbian and
gay companies such as Gay Sweatshop, of
which Fairbanks had also been a member,
were funded to produce touring productions, often with an explicitly political
agenda. It was a time that helped promote
the work of British lesbian playwrights
including Bryony LAVERY and Sarah DA-
NIELS, as well as Fairbanks. When Siren
closed in 1989 due to lack of funding, its
members went their separate ways. In
1996 three of Fairbanks's plays appeared
in an edited collection entitled *Pulp and
Other Plays by Tash Fairbanks*. Fairbanks, who has always had an interest in
popular genres and their appropriation
within a lesbian context, has also published a novel, *Fearful Symmetry* (1996),
featuring the lesbian sleuth Sam Carter.

Fanthorpe, U.A. (1929–). British lesbian
poet Ursula Askham Fanthorpe was born
in London, educated at St Anne's College,
Oxford, from 1949 until 1953, and then
until 1954 at the Institute of Education,
University of London, where she gained a
teaching qualification. Initially, she worked
as an assistant English teacher, eventually
becoming head of English at Cheltenham
Ladies' College, Gloucestershire. However, she moved from there to a job as an
admissions clerk at a Bristol hospital and
worked in that capacity until 1983. Just
before she turned fifty she published her
first collection of poems, *Side Effects*
(1978). Between 1983 and 1985 she was
Arts Council Writing Fellow at St Martin's

College, Lancaster. From 1987 until 1988
she was Northern Arts Literary Fellow at
the universities of Newcastle and Durham. In 1999 she, as well as the lesbian
poet Carol Ann DUFFY, were contenders
for the post of Poet Laureate. Fanthorpe's
collections of poetry include *Four Dogs*
(1980), *Standing To* (1982), *Voices Off*
(1984), *A Watching Brief* (1987), *U.A.
Fanthorpe: Selected Poems* (1989), *Neck-
verse* (1992), *Sauce* (1994, with Linda
France), *Safe as Houses* (1995), an audio-
cassette entitled *Double Act* (1997), and
Consequences (2000).

Feinberg, David B. (1956–). Gay US
writer who was born in Lynn, Massachusetts, where he attended the Massachusetts Institute of Technology (MIT) until
1977, before receiving an MA from New
York University in 1981. Since then he
has been the manager of MLACC for the
Modern Language Association of America. He is a regular contributor to various
gay magazines such as *Tribe*, *Advocate*,
Outweek, and *Gay Community News*. He
is an active member of ACT UP (AIDS
Coalition to Unleash Power). In 1977,
following the Gay Pride March in Los
Angeles, Feinberg came out as gay. He
began writing fiction while living in Los
Angeles. His first novel, *Calculus*, remains
unpublished. Feinberg's writings reflect
the impact of HIV/AIDS on the gay
community. He has published two novels,
Eighty-Sixed (1989) which centres on
AIDS, and *Spontaneous Combustion*
(1991). Both narratives share the same
narrator, B.J. Rosenthal. Both novels are
marked by a consciousness of being Jewish and living in the age of HIV/AIDS.
The narrative structure of the novels is
episodic, capturing gay life in New York.
Feinberg has also produced a number of
short stories and essays, frequently revolving around the theme of HIV/AIDS and
the gay community. They include *Queer
and Loathing: Rants and Raves of a
Raging AIDS Clone* (1994).

Feinberg, Leslie. Contemporary US transgender activist and writer, partner and 'beloved lesbian husband' of the US writer Minnie Bruce PRATT. Hir (as Pratt writes it) writings emerged in the 1990s as part of the new engagement with transgender issues and with queer. In that respect she is a contemporary of Kate BORNSTEIN and Sandie Stone. However, unlike the other two, Feinberg has also been extensively involved in the trade union movement and in other fights against oppression. Ze (as it appears on hir website) is an activist who has been a national leader of the Workers' World Party, and has worked extensively in the working-class movement. His non-fiction writings include *Transgender Liberation: A Movement Whose Time Has Come* (1992), *Transgender Warriors: Making History from Joan of Arc to RuPaul* (1996), which won the Firecracker Alternative Book Award for Non-Fiction in 1996, and *Trans Liberation: Beyond Pink or Blue* (1998). Her most famous book, however, is the novel *Stone Butch Blues*, published in 1993, which won the American Library Association Award for Gay and Lesbian Literature and a Lambda Literary Award in 1994.

Fernandez, Dominique (1929–). Gay French writer and academic, born in Neuilly-sur-Seine into a middle-class family, who was educated at the Ecole Normale Supérieure and wrote his doctoral thesis on the gay Italian writer Cesare Pavese. In 1957–8 he taught French at the French Institute in Naples but the scandal resulting from a lecture on eroticism and communism in the work of Vailland forced Fernandez to abandon this post. He married Diane Jacquin de Margerie in 1961, had two children with her, and divorced ten years later to live as a homosexual. Fernandez continued to work in academia as Professor of Italian at the University of Haute-Bretagne, publishing a number of academic works in this capacity. However, he also wrote a number of novels, often biographical,

which addressed homosexuality. He won the Prix Médici with *Porporino ou les mystères de Naples* (1974; *Porporino or the Mysteries of Naples*), a novel about a castrato. In 1978 he published *L'Etoile rose* [*The Pink Star*], a text that combines documentary, autobiography, and fiction engaging with the issue of homosexuality and its depiction in French culture. Fernandez also wrote a series of novels based on historical and contemporary figures whose homosexuality was more or less known. These include *Dans la main de l'ange* (1982; *In the Hand of the Angel*), about Pier Paolo PASOLINI, *L'Amour* (1986; *Love*), about the religious painter Friedrich Overbeck, *Le Dernier de Médicis* (1994; *The Last of the Médicis*), and *Tribunal d'honneur* (1996; *Court of Honour*), about the composer Tchaikovsky. Other writings by Fernandez include *La Gloire du paria* (1987; *The Glory of the Outcast*) and *Le Rapt de Ganymède* (1989; *The Abduction of Ganymede*). Fernandez's depiction of homosexuality as a source of suffering and outsider existence has generated a certain amount of criticism of his work.

Ferro, Robert (1941–88). One of the original members of the Violet Quill, a group of seven gay writers who met in New York City in the permissive post-Stonewall era to read and discuss each other's work. Ferro's novels rely heavily on autobiography. They celebrate gay existence within the structure of the heterosexual family, demanding the unconditional acceptance of gay love within that setting. His novels contrast the machismo of heterosexual Italian men, who find homosexuality difficult to deal with, with the more sympathetic views of mothers and female relatives. Two novels that express this kind of situation most clearly are *The Family of Mark Desir*, which appeared in 1983, and *Second Son*, which came out in 1988. *The Blue Star* (1985) also focuses on American-Italian relationships. Set in Florence it traces the experiences of two gay men, Peter Conrad and Chase Walker, in that town. Peter asserts his homosexuality, which he will not compromise, while Chase is induced to sire an heir for an ancient Florentine family. Ferro's novels, though in the main realist in style, tend to contain somewhat fantastical elements. He died of an AIDS-related illness, only three months after his lover, Michael Grumley, had died of the same illness.

Fichte, Hubert (1935–86). German writer, renowned for his introduction of homosexuality into post-Second World War German literature. Born in Perleberg, Westpriegnitz, his Jewish father fled Germany before his birth, and his unwed Protestant mother brought Fichte up in her parents' home in Hamburg. To avoid Nazi persecution, Fichte's mother hid him in a Catholic orphanage in Upper Bavaria for a year (1942). At the age of eleven Fichte began to work as a child actor at some of Hamburg's well-known theatres. In his teens he met the Hamburg author and hormone researcher Hans Hanny Jahnn who had a strong impact on Fichte's intellectual development and self-awareness. From his mid-teens to his late twenties, Fichte studied French, worked as a shepherd in Provence, directed a shelter for the homeless in Paris, studied agriculture in Northern Germany and in Sweden, and worked in a home for juvenile delinquents. From 1963 he worked as a freelance writer. In his work he was always preoccupied with outsider positions, inspired by his own status of outsider as a half-Jewish man, an illegitimate child, and a bisexual. His first four novels, *Das Waisenhaus* (1965; *Orphanage*), *Die Palette* (1968; *The Palette*), *Detlevs Imitationen* (1971; *Detlev's Imitations*), and *Versuch der Pubertät* (1974; *Attempt at Puberty*), homosexuality only gradually came to the fore. The most successful of these four novels, *The Palette*, focuses on a bar in Hamburg's underworld and features a range of mar-

ginalized figures, including gay men. When Fichte died in Hamburg, he was still working on a nineteen-volume novel cycle entitled *The History of Sensitivity*. These novels were published posthumously and suggested that homosexuality predisposes towards greater sensitivity towards other marginalized figures.

Field, Edward (1924–). Gay US poet whose biography as a gay man is revealed in his poetry, in which he depicts himself as an ageing Jewish gay New York poet who never had enough sex because he repressed his homosexuality when he was younger. Field's poetry is plain in its use of language and easy to understand. It is also often confessional in nature. In his first collection of poetry, *Stand Up Friend with Me* (1963), which won the Lambert Poetry Selection for 1962, there are few explicit references to homosexuality. It contains some poems about Sonny Hugg, a boyhood friend, which have homoerotic undertones. In *Variety Photoplays* (1967) Field uses popular culture as his main source of reference. The only explicitly gay poem is 'Graffiti', while 'Sweet Gwendolyn and the Countess' and 'Nancy' contain lesbian material. In *A Full Heart* (1977) Field came out as a gay poet writing his most explicitly gay work, including his gay manifesto, 'The Two Orders of Love'. His *New and Selected Poems* of 1987 were less focused on homosexuality but in *Counting Myself Lucky* (1992) growing old as a gay man became the primary focus of Field's writing.

Field, Michael. Pseudonym of the English aunt and niece couple Katherine Bradley (1846–1914) and Edith Cooper (1862–1913) who were born into affluent Birmingham merchant families, and decided in 1878, at the University College of Bristol, where they were both supporters of anti-vivisectionist causes and women's rights, to live and work together. In 1893 they published *Underneath the Bough*, a collection of their love lyrics to each other. Katherine was 'Michael' to Edith's 'Henry' within their relationship. Together they wrote a series of dramas set in antiquity such as *Callirrhoe* (1884), *Brutus Ultor* (1886), and *Canute the Great* (1887). The last contains an explicit love scene between two women. Their collection of poetry, *Long Ago* (1889), an imitation of SAPPHO's verse, celebrated lesbian love. During the 1890s the two women were celebrated as writers, attracting the attention of others such as Oscar WILDE. In *The Tragic Mary* (1890) they presented Mary as a politically exploited woman. Other dramas such as *Stephania, a Tragedy* (1892), *Attila, My Attila* (1896), and *A Question of Memory* (1893) followed. In 1907 the two women converted to Catholicism and began writing devotional poetry. Their later poetry is regarded as expressive of their embrace of an anti-rational, anti-bourgeois aesthetic, cloaked in mystical terms, as well as a celebration of women's love for each other. Sturge Moore edited their work in *Works and Days* (1933) and Mary Sturgeon wrote their biography (1922).

Fierstein, Harvey (1954–). Gay US writer and performer Harvey Forbes Fierstein was born in Brooklyn to Irving Fierstein, a handkerchief manufacturer, and Jacqueline Harriet Gilbert Fierstein, a housewife. He went to Brooklyn public schools and received a BFA in Art from the Pratt Institute in 1973. He appeared in drag shows in various New York City clubs and bars during the 1970s, and played an asthmatic lesbian in Andy Warhol's only play *Pork* in 1971. His own earliest, unpublished plays such as *Freaky Pussy, Flatbush and Tosca*, and *Cannibals* were all set in the drag world of New York. He also made a number of film and television appearances, and he provides the voice for the gay male secretary in *The Simpsons*. Of his own work, it is his Broadway plays *Torch Song Trilogy* (1982), which was made into a highly successful film, and *Safe Sex* (1987), his Off-Broadway

show *Spockhouse* (1984), and his book for the award-winning Broadway musical *La Cage aux Folles* (1983) for which he is best known. In his work one of his key achievements has been to portray drag queens sympathetically. He is one of the leading contemporary American gay playwrights.

Findley, Timothy (1930–). Canadian writer born in Toronto into a middle-class family. He pursued careers in the ballet and in acting before settling down in 1962, with his long-term companion William Whithead, in Ontario to live as a writer. His brief marriage had ended some time before then. In his writing Findley tends not to address homosexuality but engages instead with questions of masculinity and the tension of being an outsider. His first novel *The Last of the Crazy People* appeared in 1967. It was followed by *The Butterfly Plague* (1969), *The Wars* (1977), *Famous Last Words* (1981), and several collections of short stories, including *Stones* (1988), *Dinner along the Amazon* (1985), and *Dust to Dust* (1997). Findley does not want to write for a gay audience exclusively though he acknowledges his own homosexuality. His other works include *The Newcomer* (1979; co-edited), *The Telling of Lies: A Mystery* (1986), *Inside the Memory Pages of a Writer's Workbook* (1990), *Headhunter* (1993), *The Piano Man's Daughter* (1995), and *Pilgrim* (1999).

Firbank, Ronald (1886–1926). Born Arthur Annesley Ronald Firbank, this gay English writer whose work is associated with the modernist period, was the son of Sir Thomas Firbank, a Member of Parliament, and the grandson of Joseph Firbank, who had made his fortune as a railway contractor. Ronald's mother was the educated daughter of a clergyman who, together with her husband, became a renowned collector of rare prints and porcelain. Lady Firbank offered steady support to her second son, who did not receive much recognition from the literary establishment since his writings were too overtly concerned with homosexual matters. Firbank was initially educated privately but went to Trinity Hall, Cambridge, for six terms, leaving in 1909 without taking a degree. At Trinity Hall, he met R.H. Benson who received him into the Catholic Church in 1907, a conversion that many lesbian and gay men, such as Michael FIELD, of the early twentieth century underwent. Firbank then went to Rome, apparently to take holy orders, but as he wrote to Lord Berners, 'The Church of Rome wouldn't have me, and so I mock her.' This is indeed what he does in many of his works. Firbank's wealthy background enabled him to travel extensively and to publish his novels at his own expense. Before going to university, in 1905 he had already published a volume of two stories, *Odette d'Antrevernes* (revised version, 1916) and *A Study in Temperament*. During the First World War he showed no interest in participating in the war effort but lived in Oxford, writing novels in rapid succession. All these novels had at their centre female characters. *Vainglory* (1915) focuses on the ambitions of Mrs Shamefoot who wants to achieve immortality by having a stained-glass window commemorating herself installed at St Dorothy's Cathedral. *Inclinations* (1916) is about Miss Geraldine O'Brookomore whose dream of an Arcadian lesbian romance is destroyed when the hostile count Pastorelli marries her companion Miss Mabel Collins. *Caprice* (1917) centres on the adventures of a stage-struck clergyman's daughter. *Valmouth* (1919) is set in an imaginary health resort run by the black masseuse Mrs Yajñavalkya. In 1920 Firbank published his one-act play *The Princess Zoubaroff*, which portrays a pastoral world of homosexual freedom and features Lord Orkish, Firbank's version of Oscar WILDE, to whom his work was indebted. Further novels such as *Santal* (1921), about the religious aspirations of a young Islamic

boy, and *The Flower beneath the Foot* (1924) followed. *Sorrow in Sunlight* (1924), Firbank's only novel to be published by a commercial publisher, follows the lives of the black Mrs Almadou Mouth and her daughters. Set in the West Indies, it describes their social aspirations and adventures. On advice from his friend Carl van Vechten, Firbank had this novel published under the astonishing title of *Prancing Nigger* in the USA, where it enjoyed commercial success. His last finished novel, *Concerning the Eccentricities of the Cardinal Pirelli* (1926), was also his most explicitly homosexual. After his early death from a disease of the lungs in Rome, *The Artificial Princess* (1934), a reworking of Oscar Wilde's tragic play *Salome*, was published, as were *The New Rhythm and Other Pieces* (1962). Firbank was a flamboyant dandy, aesthete, and frequenter of the Café Royal. His style of writing, which involved oblique narratives, fantasy, exotic characters and settings, and an intense concentration on language and image, mark him out as a writer reacting against the realist mode of the nineteenth century and place him with other modernist innovators.

Fitzroy, A.T. (1890–1980). Pseudonym of Rose Laure Allantini who was born in Vienna to a Polish mother and an Italian father, but was brought up in England. She left home to become a writer. Her first book was published by Mills & Boon, the romance publishers, in 1914. In 1921 she married the composer Cyril Scott with whom she had a son and a daughter. During that time she published one novel under her married name, *White Fire* (1933). In 1941 Allantini and Scott separated, and she went to Rye to live there with Melanie Mills. Between 1941 and 1978 Allantini published some thirty novels under the pseudonym Eunice Buckley, one of several she used, as did Melanie Mills, also a writer. Allantini's main claim to fame in the pantheon of lesbian and gay writers rests on her novel

Despised and Rejected (1918), which was published by C.W. Daniel but became the object of an obscenity trial in the same year that it appeared and was then withdrawn from the market until its reprint in 1988. Rose Allantini hardly figured in the trial. The novel features a gay man Dennis and a lesbian Antoinette, trying to love each other but recognizing their homosexuality. Dennis finds Alan but Antoinette is left at the end trapped in her family. One key aspect of the novel, and the issue that became central to its prosecution, was that Dennis gets involved with the pacifist movement and becomes a conscientious objector. The fear that this novel aroused was that young men would refuse to be drafted to help with the war effort. Interestingly, the homosexual component played only a very limited role in the book's ban. Critics assumed A.T. Fitzroy to be the *nom de plume* of a male. *Despised and Rejected* was at one point claimed to be the first openly homosexual British novel. Allantini offered the book to the publishers George Allen & Unwin who had already published a book of hers. However, they turned it down due to its focus on homosexuality.

Flanner, Janet (1892–1978). Lesbian US writer, journalist, and translator who was born in Indianapolis, Indiana, as one of three girl children, but was keen to escape her family. She matriculated at the University of Chicago in 1912 but left after two years, first to work in a girls' reformatory, then to become a drama and art critic for the *Indianapolis Star* in 1916. Towards the end of the First World War she married but by 1922 was divorced again. She moved to New York City where she met Harold Ross, founding editor of the *New Yorker* and his wife Jane Grant. Through them she met the love of her life, Solita SOLANO, who was drama editor for the *New York Tribune*. In New York Flanner got involved with the lesbian and gay community of Greenwich Village. When Solano was given an

assignment in Greece in 1921 Flanner went with her. The two women settled in Paris in 1922 in the Hotel Saint Germain where they stayed until the beginning of the Second World War. Flanner lived in Paris for most of the rest of her life, returning to the USA only for the duration of the Second World War, and again towards the end of her life when she died in New York City. In Paris Flanner was very much involved with the literary expatriate community. She regularly wrote to Jane Grant. Those letters inspired Grant's husband to ask Flanner to write a regular column for the *New Yorker*, which she did as her 'Letter from Paris' from 1925 until 1975. Her first letter went out under the signature Genêt. Flanner did not write directly about her lesbian experiences but she was a prominent member of the Paris lesbian community. She was a regular guest at Natalie Clifford BARNEY's salon and was satirized, together with Solano, by Djuna BARNES in her *Ladies Almanack* (1928) as 'Nip and Tuck', a pair of plucky journalists. In 1931 Flanner fell in love with the singer Noel Haskins Murphy and spent increasing amounts of time with her at her country home in Orgeval, a small town to the west of Paris. Solano had to come to terms with this intrusion into her relationship with Flanner and became a frequent visitor to Orgeval. Flanner wrote one novel, *The Cubical City* (1926), *An American in Paris* (1940), which was a profile of the period between the wars based on her writings for the *New Yorker*, *Pétain: The Old Man of France* (1944), *Men and Monuments* (1957), *Paris Journal: 1944–1965*, which won the National Book Award, *Paris Journal: 1965–71* (1971), *Paris was Yesterday: 1925–1939* (1975), and *Janet Flanner's World: Uncollected Writings 1932–1975* (1979). She translated two novels by her friend COLETTE. She received several honorary awards from US universities including Smith College and Indiana University. Flanner had a number of passionate friendships or lesbian relationships with women such as Natalia Danesi Murray and Monica Stirling. When Flanner became increasingly involved with Murray, Solano met and fell in love with Elizabeth (Lib) Jenks Clark. The two moved first to the USA and then, after the end of the Second World War, to Orgeval in France, close to the home of Flanner's lover, Noel. Some of Flanner's numerous letters to lovers and friends have appeared in print. They reveal Flanner to be a very loyal person, deeply concerned for others, and fully established in the lesbian metropolitan circles of her era.

Forrest, Katherine V. (1939–). Born in Ontario, Canada, Katherine V. Forrest was educated at Wayne State University, Detroit, and at the University of California, Los Angeles. For many years, she worked as fiction editor for the lesbian publishing house Naiad Press. She now lives in San Francisco with her partner Jo Hercus. Forrest is well known for a set of complex lesbian novels written in the first half of the 1980s that include *Curious Wine* (1983), *Daughters of a Coral Dawn* (1984), which is a lesbian feminist sci-fi story, and *An Emergence of Green* (1986). In 1987 she brought out a collection of short stories entitled *Dreams and Swords*. However, she entered the popular lesbian market with a series of detective novels featuring the lesbian sleuth Kate Delafield. They include *Amateur City* (1984), *Murder at the Nightwood Bar* (1987), the reference to 'Nightwood' an obvious allusion to Djuna BARNES's novel by the same title, *The Beverley Malibu* (1989), and *Murder by Tradition* (1991), for which she won the Lambda Literary Award, *Flashpoint* (1994), and *Apparition Alley* (1997). Forrest has also edited a number of short-story volumes for the Naiad Press such as *The Erotic Naiad* (1992) and *The Romantic Naiad* (1993) (both with Barbara Grier).

Forster, E.M. (1879–1970). Born Edward Morgan Forster, the only child of Edward Morgan, an architect, who died during Forster's first year of life, and Alice 'Lily' Whichelo. Forster's early life was spent predominantly with female relatives, including his great-aunt and benefactress Marianne Thornton, whose biography he was later to write and who bequeathed him a trust of £8,000 on her death in 1887. His happiest childhood years were spent at Rooksnest, Stevenage, a house he evokes in *Howard's End* (1910). In 1903 he and his mother moved to Tonbridge where he attended Tonbridge School, very unhappily. In 1897 he went to King's College, Cambridge, where he found a circle of friends and fell in love with a fellow student. His time at Cambridge was followed by a year of travel in Italy with his mother, and a cruise in Greece. On his return he began to write for the new *Independent Review*, launched in 1903 by a group of Cambridge friends. In 1905 he published *Where Angels Fear to Tread*. He then spent some months in Germany as tutor to the children of the Countess von Arnim. In 1906, now in Weybridge with his mother, he became tutor to Syed Ross Masood, a striking Indian Muslim for whom he developed an intense affection. *The Longest Journey* was published in 1907, *A Room with a View* in 1908, and *Howard's End*, which established Forster's reputation as a writer, in 1910. He also published a collection of short stories, *The Celestial Omnibus*, in 1911. In 1912–13 he visited India for several months, meeting Masood in Aligarh and travelling with him. In 1913, he visited Edward CARPENTER and his working-class lover George Merrill in their home in Derbyshire and, inspired by that relationship, wrote *Maurice*. Since homosexuality was illegal in England until 1967, *Maurice* – which juxtaposes the relationship between Maurice and his Cambridge fellow student Clive with Maurice's relationship with Alec, the under-gamekeeper on Clive's estate – was published only posthumously. Forster had a sexual preference for foreign and for working-class men. Like Carpenter he thought that homosexuality could overcome class barriers. He did not have a full homosexual relationship until 1919 when he fell in love with an Egyptian tram conductor in Alexandria, Mohammed el Adl, which ended with the latter's premature death in 1922. While in Alexandria he met the gay Greek poet C.P. CAVAFY, whose work he helped introduce to a British audience. The completion of *A Passage to India* (1922–4) was overshadowed by Adl's death, which occurred while Forster was in India, working for a few months as personal secretary to the maharaja of the native state of Dewas Senior. This was his last novel and while he engaged in a wide range of literary activities, including campaigning against the suppression of Radclyffe HALL's novel *The Well of Loneliness* in 1928, and appearing as a witness in the obscenity trial of D.H. Lawrence's novel *Lady Chatterley's Lover* in 1960, he never published another novel during his lifetime. In 1930 Forster developed a long-lasting relationship with a police constable, Bob Buckingham, which survived Buckingham's marriage in 1932 and lasted until Forster's death at Coventry in the Buckingham's home in 1970. In 1946 King's College, Cambridge, offered him an honorary fellowship and a permanent home. He was awarded the Order of Merit in 1969. Forster's novel *Maurice* was not published until 1971. In 1972 a collection of short stories, *The Life to Come*, was published, which contained many stories with homosexual themes. Forster felt frustrated during his lifetime at not being able to write about homosexual love for publication. After his death he was recognized as a major gay author of the twentieth century. *Maurice* was made into a very successful film, as were a number of his other novels.

Foster, Jeannette H. (1895–1981). Lesbian US academic and writer who worked at the University of Kansas City library in the year that her survey of lesbian writing, *Sex Variant Women in Literature* (1956), was published. This extensive survey of lesbian literature, perhaps the first of its kind, which attempted to cover more than 2,000 years of writing, was prompted, according to the author, by her experiences at a women's university when two fellow students were told that they would be expelled from their college dormitory if they did not alter their habits. These habits had involved locking themselves into their bedroom together. Foster professes not to have understood why the women were thus disciplined but, fired by the experience, she began to read *Studies in the Psychology of Sex* by Havelock ELLIS, and, as she puts it, talking about herself in the third person: 'it enabled her to help in averting more than one minor tragedy and to conduct her own life with some measure of wisdom'. *Sex Variant Women in Literature* is a classic of lesbian literature. In 1974 it was awarded the Third Annual Gay Book Award by the Gay Task Force for the Social Responsibilities Round Table of the American Library Association. The lesbian press Naiad in Tallahassee, Florida, has repeatedly reprinted it. It remained the key source on lesbian writing in the English-speaking world until Lillian FADERMAN's *Surpassing the Love of Men* and has not been bettered.

Foucault, Michel (1926–84). French writer and philosopher, born Paul-Michel Foucault in Poitiers into a well-to-do upper middle-class family. Foucault studied Philosophy in Poitiers and Paris, where he attended the Ecole Normale Supérieure. He graduated in Psychology at the Sorbonne in 1949, completed his teaching certificate, the *agrégation*, in 1951, and finished his doctorate in Philosophy in 1961. Between 1952 and 1955 he taught Psychology at the University of Lille. He then had successive posts as director, first of the Maison de France in Uppsala, Sweden, then of the Centre de Civilisation Française in Warsaw, and finally at the Institut Français in Hamburg, before teaching Psychology and Philosophy at several universities. In 1970 he became Chair in the History of Systems of Thought at the Collège de France, a chair specially created for him. In 1963 Foucault met his life-long companion Daniel Defert. As a gay academic Foucault has been hugely influential in cultural history. His books on *Madness and Civilization* (1961, translated 1965), *The Birth of the Clinic* (1963, translated 1970), *The Order of Things* (1966, translated 1977), *Archaeology of Knowledge* (1969, translated 1972), *Discipline and Punish: The Birth of the Prison* (1975, translated 1977), and the three-volume *History of Sexuality* (1976–84; translated 1978–86) all share a similar preoccupation with the ways in which human beings are constructed through practices and institutional structures that coerce them into reproducing particular subject positions including that of the homosexual. Foucault's work inspired many lesbian and gay theorists of the late twentieth century, in part because he so effectively exposed the institutional machineries of the prison, the clinic, and the Catholic Church, which contributed so much to the oppression and repression of homosexuals. Coming from a society, that of the France of the 1950s and 1960s, which was very repressive towards homosexuals, Foucault enjoyed the gay lifestyle that San Francisco offered when he visited the town and its gay scenes during the mid-1970s as part of a period of lecturing abroad. Foucault suffered from AIDS-related illnesses in the last stages of his life from which he eventually died.

Frederics, Diana (dates unknown). Who this author is remains unknown and it is assumed that the name Diana Frederics is a pseudonym for the writer who published *Diana: A Strange Autobiography* in 1939. The status of the text is complicated by the fact that the book was also published in France in 1946, this time with the title *Diana: roman*, which suggests a fictional as opposed to an autobiographical account. The text details the story of a young girl's coming to terms with her lesbianism. It utilizes sexological language and was prefaced, in its US edition, by sexologist Dr Victor Robinson. In contrast to other texts from this period, this one portrays a woman achieving a lesbian identity and fulfilment within a lesbian relationship rather than relinquishing or sublimating her lesbian desires.

Freeman, Mary Eleanor Wilkins 1853–1930). Woman-centred US writer, born in Randolph, Massachusetts, whose adolescence was marred by the increasing financial difficulties of her family. The family moved from Randolph to Brattleboro, Vermont, where first Freeman's only sibling, her younger sister Nan, then her mother, and finally her father died in quick succession between 1876 and 1883. Freeman found herself alone, with no income, profession, or interests in conventional social activities. She returned to Randolph to live with the family of her life-long friend, Mary Wales. The two Marys lived together during the years of Freeman's greatest literary successes and until she finally, in 1902, married Charles Freeman, a New Jersey physician turned businessman. This marriage had been repeatedly postponed and turned out to be disastrous, in part because of Charles's alcoholism and its associated disorders. The couple separated after a few years. Freeman herself was part of a network of literary women that included Annie Adams Fields, the wife of Henry Fields, the publisher of the *Atlantic Monthly*, and Sarah Orne JEWETT, who had been Freeman's inspiration when she started her career as a writer.

Many of the women in this circle never married and Freeman herself led a woman-centred life until her ill-fated marriage. In 1883 *Harper's Bazaar* published her story 'Two Old Lovers'. This was followed by the publication of more of her stories both in *Harper's Bazaar* and in *Harper's New Monthly Magazine* to the point where, in 1887, Freeman's first collection of stories, *A Humble Romance*, could appear. In 1901 *A New England Nun* followed. Freeman received the Howells Medal of the American Academy of Arts and Letters, and was elected to the National Institute of Arts and Letters in 1926. Her work explores the relationship between necessity and desire in women's lives. Many of her stories such as 'Two Friends' and 'The Long Arm' feature passionate friendships between women, sometimes explicitly lesbian ones. An important practitioner of literary realism, Freeman is also an important part of the lesbian literary heritage of the nineteenth century.

French, Alice (1850–1934). US short-story writer and novelist. Born in Andover, Massachusetts, French and her family moved to Davenport, Iowa, in 1856 where her mother provided strong support for Elizabeth Cady Stanton. French's father became a wealthy manufacturer, which meant that French and her five siblings could enjoy the privileges that such wealth brings. French was very interested in club work and was, at one point, president of the Iowa Society of Colonial Dames. Records suggest that she was a conservative with xenophobic views who helped organize against suffragettes. This seems to contradict some of her fiction, which satirizes snobbery and portrays images of emotionally independent, financially self-sufficient women. She was an important contributor to a number of national literary magazines including *The Century Illustrated Monthly Magazine*. She became known as a regionalist whose representation of local colour in her

stories set in Iowa and Arkansas made her a popular literary success. Her stories were collected in various volumes, including *Knitters in the Sun* (1887), *Stories of a Western Town* (1893), *A Slave to Duty and Other Women* (1906), and *Stories that End Well* (1911). In 1890 French began work on her first novel, *We All*. Her novels *Expiation* (1890) and *The Man of the Hour* (1905) also appeared. French wrote under the androgynous pseudonym Octave Thanet. 'Octave' was a reference to her beloved schoolmate Octavia Putman with whom she had shared a room and double bed during their year at Andover Academy. 'Thanet' was apparently a word she had seen painted on the side of a freight train. During the 1880s French settled into her life-long partnership with Jane Allen Crawford, dividing their time between their home in Davenport, Iowa, and their plantation in Arkansas. The two women lived together throughout their lives with the exception of two periods: Jane's four-year marriage, which ended mysteriously, and a tour of Europe Jane undertook.

Fry, Stephen (1957–). Gay British comedian, actor, and writer, born Stephen John Fry in Hampstead, London. Fry was brought up in Norfolk and studied at Queen's College, Cambridge, appearing in over thirty plays while at the university. Together with Hugh Laurie he was part of the Cambridge Footlights revues. His first play, *Latin! Or Tobacco and Boys* (1980), won the Fringe First award at the Edinburgh Festival that same year. He cowrote *Electric Voodoo* (1980) and *The Cellar Tapes* (1981) for the Cambridge Footlights, and appeared in many TV and radio productions throughout the 1980s and 1990s. In the 1990s he published a variety of volumes including *Paperweight* (1992), *The Liar* (1992), *The Hippopotamus* (1994), *Making History* (1997), and his autobiography *Moab is My Washpot*. In 1995 he hit the headlines when he disappeared from London shortly before he was to act in Simon Gray's play *Cell Mates*. It appeared that he'd suffered some sort of breakdown and decided to travel to Europe to escape media pressure and general stress. On his return to the UK, and after a long period of claiming celibacy, he publicly acknowledged his homosexuality and acquired a boyfriend, seeming happier all round.

Frye, Marilyn (1941–). Born in Tulsa, Oklahoma, lesbian theorist and critic Marilyn Frye was brought up as the younger of two daughters in what she has described as a 'stable, traditional, (but remarkably non-violent), devoutly Christian family'. In 1963 she graduated with a Bachelor's degree from Stanford University and then completed her doctorate in Philosophy at Cornell University in 1969. She has lived in the Midwest, on both US coasts, and in Western Canada, and worked variously in a bookshop, a lesbian centre, and a small press before embarking on a career as an academic. For many years she has taught Philosophy and Women's Studies at Michigan State University. Frye had a great impact on feminist and lesbian thinking with her two volumes of essays, *The Politics of Reality: Essays in Feminist Theory* (1983) and *Willful Virgin: Essays in Feminism* (1992). The latter collection in particular interrogates the relationship between lesbianism and feminism, and in a key essay entitled 'Willful Virgin *or* Do You Have to be a Lesbian to be a Feminist?', Frye, rather like Monique WITTIG, takes what might be described as a radical lesbian position in her assertion that women who refuse heteropatriarchy are 'willful virgins', a term here used not to denote sexual activity but separation from men and a refusal to be oppressed by them. Frye's work, as much as that of Wittig, and that of de Beauvoir, has been extremely useful in exploring women's position in heteropatriarchy and women's relation with each other in structures of male domination. In that respect she also has something in common with the French lesbian feminist critic Luce IRIGARAY who, however, takes a much more psycholinguistically inflected stance than does Frye.

Fullerton, Mary Eliza (1868–1946). Australian poet, born in Victoria and brought up in a Scots-Presbyterian community in Gippsland. During the 1890s she moved to Melbourne and became active in the women's suffrage movement. She published poetry, fiction, and a range of articles in a variety of magazines. In 1909 Fullerton met Mabel Singleton who was also involved in the Women's Political Association. Fullerton became emotionally attached to Singleton and by 1911 Singleton had left her husband. When she left for England with her son in 1921 Fullerton followed, dying in Sussex over twenty years later. Fullerton and Singleton's love appears to have been platonic, based on a passionate but unconsummated attachment.

G

Gale, Patrick (1962–). Prolific gay British comic novelist whose fictions are peopled with lesbian and gay characters, making them everyday rather than exceptional. Born on the Isle of Wight where his father was a prison governor, Gale won a scholarship to Pilgrims, the choir school of Winchester Cathedral and college where he was educated. Subsequently he went to Oxford. Between 1979 and 1985 he worked variously as a waiter, a cook, a singer, a temporary typist, and a bone sorter for an archaeological team. He lives in Cornwall with his partner Aiden Hicks. In 1985 both *Ease* and *The Aerodynamics of Pork* appeared, to be followed in 1987 by *Kansas in August* and *Facing the Tank* in 1988. His other works include *Little Bits of Baby* (1989), *The Cat Sanctuary* (1990), *Secret Lives* (1993), *The Facts of Life* (1996), *Dangerous Pleasures* (1996), *The Scarlet Boy* (1998), *Tree Surgery for Beginners* (1999), *Outlines: Armistead Maupin* (1999), and *Rough Music* (2000).

Galford, Ellen. Lesbian writer of US origin who migrated to the UK in 1971, after a brief marriage in New York. She came out in the mid-1970s. Galford has worked variously as a book editor, copywriter, TV researcher, and freelance writer. She has lived in Glasgow, London, and Edinburgh. Her books include *Moll Cutpurse: Her True Story* (1984), *The Fires of Bride* (1986), *Queendom Come* (1990), and *The Dyke and the Dybbuk* (1993). Her most recent work is *Genealogy* (2001).

Galgóczi, Erszébet (1930–89). Lesbian Hungarian novelist who was born into a very poor family in western Hungary but was educated and rose to prominence under the communist regime. Galgóczi's novels focus on the life of the poor in rural areas, and on *rites de passage* such as her own from poverty to literary fame in Budapest. Besides being a novelist Galgóczi was a journalist, worked in film, and was a member of Parliament until her death from cancer. She won several literary prizes for her works which include *A közös bün* (1976; *Common Sin*); *A törvényen belül* (1980; *Inside the Law*); and *Vidravas* (1984; *Otter Trap*), which caused a scandal in Budapest because of its take on the 1956 uprising.

Garber, Marjorie. Contemporary US academic whose work has been very influential in opening up debates about queer, cross-dressing, and gender identity as culturally encoded. In 1987 she published *Cannibals, Witches, and Divorce: Estranging the Renaissance*, but it was her *Vested Interests: Cross-dressing and Cultural Anxiety* (1992) that made her an international figure on the lesbian, gay, and queer cultural theory scene. She followed this with *Dog Love* (1996), *Vice Versa:*

Bisexuality and the Eroticism of Everyday Life (2000), *Sex and Real Estate: Why We Love Houses* (2000), *Academic Instincts* (2001), and *The Medusa Reader* (2001).

Gautier, Théophile (1811–72). French writer who played a prominent role in the Romantic movement of the 1830s, and who was closely associated with the notion of 'art for art's sake', which he elaborated upon in the preface to in his novel *Mademoiselle de Maupin* (1835), the reason for his inclusion in this book. In this novel Gautier portrays a young poet, d'Albert, who falls in love, as does his mistress, with a young man who turns out to be Mademoiselle de Maupin. The simultaneous representation of gay and lesbian attraction is justified through beauty since the novel suggests that one may fall in love with beauty irrespective of sex. Gautier wrote widely and on a whole range of subjects including travel, the ballet, and the theatre, but it is *Mademoiselle de Maupin* that is of particular interest to lesbian and gay readers.

Gearhart, Sally Miller (1931–). Lesbian US writer and academic, born in Virginia. Gearhart completed an MA in Theatre and Rhetoric in 1953, and a PhD in Theatre in 1956. She has taught at various colleges in Texas, including as Professor of Speech and Communication Studies at San Francisco State University. She has been involved in the animal rights movements, and has sung bass in a lesbian-feminist barbershop quartet. Together with the Reverend William Johnson she published *Loving Women/Loving Men: Gay Liberation and the Church* (1974), and with Susan Rennie she wrote *A Feminist Tarot* (1976). Her abiding claim to fame, however, is perhaps her science fiction novel *The Wanderground: Stories of the Hill Women* (1979), which was published at a time when women were not only reclaiming genres that had conventionally been dominated by men such as the thriller and science fiction, but

were also exploring the possibility of utopian and dystopian separatism and the benefits of all-female environments. Gearhart's novel presents women's relation to nature, and to ponies, in a utopian vision of oneness and peaceful union within an all-female setting in which harmonious co-existence, including physical co-existence with nature, is foregrounded rather than women's sexual relationships with each other. Gearhart's utopic take on women is very different from that of other lesbian writers of the period such as Joanna RUSS, who also produced lesbian-feminist science fiction.

Gems, Pam (1925–). One of Britain's foremost contemporary women playwrights, Pam Gems began to write plays as a child, encouraged by staff at the school which she attended, Priory Church School in Christchurch, Dorset. It was not until she was in her forties, had had a number of different jobs, and brought up four children that she began to find work in fringe theatre. Her work for theatre is characterized by a resolute commitment to women and the creation of women-centred worlds. She has written many plays, some of which produced revisions of famous female figures such as *Queen Christina* (1977), *Piaf* (1978), *Camille* (1984) and *Passionara* (1985). The year 1982 saw the production of her extraordinary play *Aunt Mary*, the gender-bending content of which prefigures 'queer' as it emerged at the turn of the 1980s and into the 1990s. Other plays she has written include *Dusa, Fish, Stas, and Vi* (1976), *Ladybird, Ladybird* (1979), and her own versions of *Uncle Vanya* (1979), *A Doll's House* (1980), and *The Cherry Orchard* (1984). In 1989 she published her first novel, *Mrs Frampton*, followed by its sequel, *Bon Voyage, Mrs Frampton* (1990). She continues to write for theatre, always placing women at the centre of her work.

Genet, Jean (1910–86). Gay French novelist and dramatist who was born illegitimately and abandoned by his mother at birth, brought up by Public Assistance, and sent to live with foster parents when he was seven. He started petty criminal activities early on in his life. By the age of fifteen he was sent to Mettray, a French 'reform' school for boys. His young adulthood was repeatedly spent in prison for offences such as theft and prostitution. He was pronounced an unreformable criminal in 1948 and was nearly incarcerated for life until literary figures such as Jean COCTEAU convinced the authorities that he was an important literary figure who should be spared for that reason. Genet's work was heavily influenced by his early criminal lifestyle and his homosexuality. Rather like the Baal figure in Bertolt BRECHT's eponymous drama, Genet lived and associated with those marginalized by bourgeois society. He had extensive sympathies for other marginalized groups of people and was active in radical politics, supporting the causes of the Black Panthers in the late 1960s, and of the Palestine Liberation Organization (PLO). His work is peopled with figures who are disempowered or marginalized. They contain narratives of violence, betrayal, and erotic desire. His first novel, *Our Lady of the Flowers* (1944), was written in prison over an extended period, and contains the erotic fantasies of a prisoner masturbating under his blanket. The 'hero' of this novel is Louis Culafroy, also known as Divine. He has a number of erotic relationships that are explicitly represented with pimps and brutal killers. *The Thief's Journal* (1949) is one of Genet's more accessible novels, which deals with Genet's journeys through Spain, Germany, Yugoslavia, and Belgium in the 1930s. He explores the relationship of a gay sub-culture with the criminal underworld within an overall framework of the inversion of traditional bourgeois values. That constellation of homosexuality and criminality is one of the chief hallmarks of his work, a problematic configuration since it produces the kind of vision of homosexuality that has

led to the persecution of gay men and to their criminalization. *Miracle of the Rose* (1946) is a novel about gay relationships. His final novel was *Prisoner of Love*, written in the year of his death, after his return from Palestine, which he had visited in the wake of the 1982 massacres in Sara and Shatila. Genet is today best known for his plays, which like his novels feature marginalized characters. Among his most famous plays are *The Maids* (1948), about two servants' relationship to their mistress, *The Blacks* (1958), a play for an all-black cast, consisting of three complex stories all related to the murder of a white woman, *The Balcony* (1956), set in a brothel, and *The Screens*, Genet's response to the Algerian war of 1954–63. His *Querelles de Brest* was made into a film by the bisexual German film-maker Rainer Werner Fassbinder, who was much influenced by Genet.

George, Stefan (1868–1933). German poet and gifted linguist, born in Rüdesheim into a family of wealthy wine merchants. His linguistic ability led to his translating into German works by the French symbolists, by Dante, and by Shakespeare. A cultural elitist, George founded a circle of literary and artistic friends, the Georgekreis (George-Circle). He edited a literary journal, *Blätter für die Kunst (Journal for Art)*, which was distributed only to those who were part of his circle. George was a closeted homosexual but some of his work betrays a homosexual sensibility. Chief among these are *Agabal* (1892) in which a young king builds himself an underground world, the artificiality of which surpasses the natural beauty of the world above. The references to beauty, barrenness, and the embrace of the unnatural in this poem may be read as indices of a homosexual sensibility. Similarly in *Maximin* (1906) such sensibility manifests itself. The poem is dedicated to the Bavarian king Ludwig II, a gay icon from the turn of the century. It mythologizes the memory of the Munich high school student Maximilian Kronberger who died young. The poem suggests that George responded to his physical beauty. Other poems of George's that are about love tend to de-genderize their addressee by using the genderless 'you'. George left Nazi Germany to live in Locarno, Switzerland, where he died.

Ghazali, Mehemmed (d. 1535). Born in Bursa in the second half of the fifteenth century, where he became professor of Sufism, Ghazali joined the court of Crown Prince Qorqud in Manisa near the Aegean coast of Turkey. While at the court, Ghazali produced a pornographic allegorical work entitled *The Repellers of Troubles and the Remover of Anxieties*, which consisted of a mixture of prose and poetry. The topic of this text is sex, with a section of the text devoted to depictions of the battle between boy-lovers and women-lovers in which the boy-lovers win. Praises are also sung for the anus as a source of pleasure. The book was not well received though Ghazali stayed at the court until 1512 when he returned to Bursa. Subsequently he moved to Istanbul where he built a compound containing a mosque, a garden, a convent, and a bathhouse. The last attracted many boys, and city officials finally destroyed the compound. Ghazali resurfaced in Mecca where he rebuilt his compound but little else is known about his later life.

Gide, André (1869–1951). French writer who struggled all his life against his austere Protestant upbringing and with his homosexual desires. Following his father's death in 1880 Gide was surrounded predominantly by women who had a great influence on his attitudes and work. As described in his autobiography, *Si le grain ne meurt* (1921; *If It Die*) Gide considered his childhood confused and unsettling. This was counter-acted by his writing, and the production of a large and diverse *œuvre*, encompassing most literary forms. His early works such as *Les*

Cahiers de André Walter (The Notebooks of André Walter, published anonymously in 1891), *Le Traité de Narcisse* (1891; *Treatise on Narcissus*), and *Le Voyage d'Urien* (1893; *Urien's Voyage*) tended to be impersonal. At the age of twenty-four, Gide travelled to North Africa with his friend, the painter Paul A. Laurens, and had his first homosexual experiences there with an Arab called Ali. In 1895 he returned to North Africa where he had further homosexual adventures with young Arab boys. In the wake of his mother's death he married his cousin Madeleine though the marriage was never consummated. His cousin became an important figure in his writings, however, and in particular in *L'Immoraliste* (1902; *The Immoralist*) and in *La Porte étroite* (1909; *Strait is the Gate*). Much preoccupied with sexual mores, the failure of heterosexual relationships, and the compensations of homosexuality he published *Corydon* in 1924, four Socratic dialogues between the narrator and a doctor who is preparing a text in defence of homosexuality, and *Les Faux-monnayeurs* (*The Counterfeiters*) in 1926. The republication of his autobiography in 1926 caused a scandal because of its frank discussion of his homosexual experiences. Gide also embarked on an affair with Elisabeth Van Rysselberghe, the daughter of longstanding friends, and had his only daughter, Catherine, by her in 1923. In 1947 he received an honorary doctorate from Oxford University. He was awarded the Nobel Prize for Literature in the same year. His last major work was *Thésée* (1946; *Theseus*).

Gidlow, Elsa (1898–1986). Born in Hull, Yorkshire, lesbian Bay poet Gidlow and her parents moved to the French Canadian village Tetreauville in Québec when she was six years old. Gidlow experienced no formal education as a child. Instead she helped her mother in the household while secretly nurturing her ambitions to be a poet. Following a period of working as secretary to her father, who had a variety of jobs and treated his wife appallingly, Gidlow moved with her family to Montréal when she was sixteen. There she took a typing job, attended courses at McGill College (now University), and had her first passionate relationship with a woman. Between 1918 and 1921 she worked as a journalist and editor of in-house industry periodicals. She then was English secretary at the Consulate of Serbians, Croatians, and Slovenians in Montréal. Between 1921 and 1926 she worked as a poetry editor for *Pearson's* in New York City, then had a brief spell as editor of the *Pacific Coast Journal of Nursing* in San Francisco, and, from 1940, was a freelance writer, contributing to various periodicals. She also co-founded and owned the publishing house Druid Heights Books. In 1962 she became co-founder of the Society for Comparative Philosophy. Gidlow lived openly as a lesbian. Her long-term partners were Violet Henry-Anderson and Isabel Quallo. In 1923 she published *On a Grey Thread*, a collection of explicit lesbian poetry, possibly the first openly lesbian poetry published in the USA. This was followed by further poetry collections that continued to be explicitly lesbian. Among these were *California Valley with Girls* (1932), *From Alba Hill* (1933), *Wild Swan Singing* (1954), *Letters from Limbo* (1956), *Moods of Eros* (1970), *Makings for Meditation: A Collection of Parapoems, Reverent and Irreverent* (1973), and *Sapphic Songs: Seventeen to Seventy* (1976), which was revised and reissued as *Sapphic Songs: Eighteen to Eighty – The Love Poetry of Elsa Gidlow* in 1982. Gidlow also wrote a drama in verse, *Wise Man's Gold* (1972). In 1975 she brought out *Ask no Man Pardon: The Philosophical Significance of Being Lesbian*. She regarded herself as having been born lesbian and was adamant, including during very adverse times for lesbians and gays, that there was nothing to be ashamed of. In 1981 Gidlow was awarded the Lesbian

Rights Award by the Southern Californian Women for Understanding who, together with the International Gay and Lesbian Archives, held a reception for her. In 1986 she published her frank autobiography, *Elsa, I Come With My Songs: The Autobiography of Elsa Gidlow*. She died of a heart attack in Marin County, California.

Gilman, Charlotte Perkins (1860–1935). US writer, born Charlotte Anna Perkins in Hartford, Connecticut, who married at the age of twenty-four, had her only daughter, Katherine, the following year, and separated from her husband in 1887. In 1900 she remarried, this time George Houghton Gilman. After he died in 1934, Perkins Gilman, suffering from inoperable cancer, committed suicide in 1935. Her autobiography, *The Living of Charlotte Perkins Gilman*, was published after her death. Perkins Gilman was a defender of women's rights and became famous for her representations of women's economic oppression within patriarchy. She wrote a series of non-fiction texts exploring these issues, among them *Women and Economics* (1898), her most famous non-fiction work, *Concerning Children* (1900), *The Home: Its Work and Influence* (1903), *Human Work* (1904), *Man-made World* (1911), and *His Religion and Hers: A Study of the Faith of Our Fathers and the Work of Our Mothers* (1923). Perkins Gilman also co-edited and contributed to several journals, among them *The Impress* and *The American Fabian*. Between 1909 and 1916 she edited a monthly magazine, *The Forerunner*, in which her four novels were serialized. These were later published separately as *What Diantha Did* (1910), *The Crux* (1911), *Moving the Mountain* (1912), and *Herland* (1979). The last is of particular interest to lesbian readers as it is an early evocation of a separatist community. When Perkins Gilman's writings were rediscovered in the 1970s and 1980s she was heralded, first, for her short story 'The Yellow Wallpaper', which was published originally in

The New England Magazine (1892) and which spoke eloquently to women's imprisonment, literal and figurative, under patriarchy, and, second, for *Herland*, which was regarded as one of the forerunners of the lesbian feminist science fiction that became so popular during the 1970s and 1980s.

Ginsberg, Allen (1926–). Gay US poet whose work and life are associated with the counter-culture that emerged in the post-Second World War Western world and included the hippie movement, the student revolt of 1968, protest movements of various kinds such as the anti-nuclear one, pacifism, the Beat generation of poets, an anti-bourgeois attitude, the celebration of sexual liberation, experimentation with drugs, and an interest in Eastern religions. Ginsberg's first book *Howl and Other Poems* (1956) created much controversy. Its open treatment of homosexuality contributed to the book being confiscated by the San Francisco police and by US customs. Ginsberg's romantic relationships with fellow poets Jack KEROUAC and William S. BURROUGHS, as well as a period in therapy, enabled Ginsberg to draw on his personal experiences in his work, moving away from strict verse forms and creating instead rapidly written, uncensored compositions that draw on the work of Walt WHITMAN as well as on Kerouac's novels. Ginsberg's later poems conjoin a confessional mode with the notion of a public address designed to admonish. His poem 'Kaddish' (1959) details the difficulties of living with a schizophrenic mother. Other poems celebrate his long-term relationship with Peter Orlovsky. He has also written about his Buddhism and his political involvements. His *Gay Sunshine Interview* (1974) records his time as a pre-Stonewall gay spokesperson. His lectures and essays appeared as *Composed on the Tongue* (1980), and his *Collected Poems* were published in 1984.

Gíppius, Zinaida Nikolaevna (1869–1945). Russian writer who began publishing in 1888 but whose career took off with a series of poems of the 1890s such as 'Song' (1893), 'Impotence', and 'Flowers of the Night' (1894) that showed the influence of Western European decadence on her work. Anti-materialist and against moderation Gíppius was an innovative poet whose use of free verse and complex rhythm influenced a number of later writers. Gíppius's work and life highlighted her refusal of conventional biological gender and sexual roles. In her poetry she tended to use masculine or androgynous personae, and her writings explored sexuality including lesbianism, homosexuality, and androgyny. Many of Gíppius's stories such as 'The Ill-fated Girl' (1890), 'Two Hearts', and the novel *The Devil's Doll* (1911) detail relationships between lower-class girls and upper-class cads in which the girls are inevitably betrayed. Her play *The Green Ring* (1914) appeared at the height of her fame in Russia. In 1920 she and her husband moved to Paris where they held a Sunday salon between 1925 and 1940, and founded the literary and philosophical society 'the Green Lamp'. During her emigrant years Gíppius published poetry, her memoir *Living Faces* (1925), and wrote a biography of her husband that appeared in 1951.

Gogol, Nikolai Vasilevich (1809–52). Russian dramatist, novelist, and prose writer who was born in Sorochintsy in the Ukraine, the backdrop for his early writings. Gogol's father was a serf-owning country squire who wrote pseudo-folkloric Ukrainian comedies in verse. His mother, Maria Kosiarowska, instilled in Gogol a morbid religiosity that laid emphasis on retribution rather than on mercy. Gogol was strongly attached to his younger brother Ivan who died when Gogol was ten and left him looking for an ideal companion for the rest of his life. In his teens Gogol attended a single-sex boarding school in

Nezhin. At school he began to write prose and poetry, and was, apparently, a great success in the school's theatrical performances. He became sentimentally attached to a fellow student, Gerasim Vysotsky, who left for St Petersburg two years before Gogol's own graduation. Gogol wrote a series of amorous letters to Vysotsky but found himself rebuffed when reunited with him in St Petersburg in 1828. This was Gogol's first unhappy infatuation with a heterosexual man. In St Petersburg Gogol published at his own expense his book-length narrative poem *Hanz Kuechelgarten* (1829), which was a publishing failure. He then wrote a series of novellas based on his mother's and female relatives' recollections of a fairy-tale-like Ukraine that he published in two volumes as a collection of short stories under the title *Evenings on a Farm near Dikanka* (1831–2). These novellas brought him literary success. The first one, *St John's Eve*, contains one of Gogol's main themes, the notion that love of or marriage to a woman leads to danger for men. Gogol was appointed assistant professor of History at St Petersburg University but was dismissed the following year. His subsequent short-story collections *Mirgorod* (1835) and *Arabesques* (1835) were followed by a play, *The Government Inspector* (1836), which was a satire of provincial Russian town life. The play was very successful and liked by the Tsar but read, as Gogol had apparently not intended, as an indictment of Russian institutions. Gogol who was conservative fled abroad and eventually settled in Rome where he lived until 1848. Between 1835 and 1841 he wrote his St Petersburg tales, 'The Portrait', 'Nevsky Prospect', 'Diary of a Madman', 'The Nose', and 'The Overcoat'. These stories showed St Petersburg as an unreal and fantastic place in which the individual man faces an inhuman metropolitan machine. While in Rome Gogol had an open relationship with Iosif Vielhorsky who died of consumption a year after they

had met. He then fell in love with the poet Nikolai Yazykov who did not respond to Gogol's passionate letters. During his time in Rome Gogol wrote two comedies, *Marriage* (1842), an attack on the institution of marriage, and *The Gamblers* (1943), a play that shows an all-male criminal sub-culture rather like Jean GENET's work. He also worked on his comic epic *Dead Souls* of which the first part was published in 1842 but the second part of which was burnt by Gogol during a spiritual crisis in 1845. In 1847 he published a series of prose writings, *Selected Passages from Correspondence with Friends*, in which he publicized his conservative political views including the need for the preservation of serfdom, the notion that social hierarchies were set in place by God, and similar views. In January 1852 Gogol confessed his homosexual longings to a bigoted priest, Father Matvei Konstantinovsky, who advised him to abstain from literature, food, and sleep to cleanse himself. Gogol died of starvation in February 1852, having burnt the second half of his *Dead Souls*.

Gomez, Jewelle (1948–). Black US lesbian writer and political activist, born in Boston, and educated at Northeastern University, from where she graduated with a BA in 1971, and Columbia School of Journalism, which she left in 1973 after completing her MS. While at university Gomez worked on the Boston-based series *Say Brother* for public television. This was one of the first weekly Black television programmes. She then helped to produce the Children's Television Workshop in New York during the mid 1970s, and had a variety of jobs between 1975 and 1980. She taught Women's Studies and English for a time, including at Hunter College in 1989–90, and was director of the Literature Program of the New York State Council on the Arts between 1989 and 1993. Gomez has published two collections of poetry, *The Lipstick Papers* (1980), and *Flamingoes* *and Bears* (1986). Her novel *The Gilda Stories* (1991) won her Lambda Literary Awards for fiction and science fiction in 1991. Gomez gained international fame with this volume that features the life, over 200 years, of Gilda, an African American lesbian vampire, traversing cultures and history from 1850 to 2050. This novel reflected a preoccupation in the late 1980s and early 1990s with the notion of the lesbian as vampire, a preoccupation that had already found earlier expression in Hollywood movies from the 1930s, for instance, which featured certain kinds of dominant, glam, predatory women. However, it was in the early 1990s that this phenomenon began to be critically investigated and analysed. Gomez's novel thus captures a certain moment in lesbian literary critical history. She followed this novel with *Forty-three Septembers* (1993), *Oral Tradition: Selected Poems Old and New* (1995), and *Don't Explain* (1998). Gomez is now established as one of the key African American lesbian writers, sharing this platform with other lesbian writers such as Audre LORDE and Michelle CLIFF. Gomez has also held a Ford Foundation fellowship (1973); and has won the Beards Fund award for fiction in 1985, and the Barbara Deming/Money for Women Award in fiction in 1990. Her essay on 'A Celebration of Butch-Femme Identities in the Lesbian Community' appeared in Joan NESTLE's *The Persistent Desire: A Butch-Femme Reader* (1992). Gomez has been politically active in the defence of lesbian and gay rights for many years, contributing to organizations such as the Gay and Lesbian Alliance Against Defamation (GLAAD), and the Feminist Anti-Censorship Taskforce (FACT).

Goytisolo Gay, Juan (1931–). Spanish novelist born in Barcelona whose mother, Julia Gay, was a Catalan, and whose father's family background was Basque. During the Spanish Civil War his family lived in the mountains in Catalonia but Goytisolo's mother was killed during a visit to

Barcelona when he was seven years old. His father was a supporter of Franco who was imprisoned by the Republicans for a period. At the age of eight Goytisolo was sexually molested by his maternal grandfather. Following an education with Jesuit priests he studied Law in Madrid and Barcelona. *Juegos de manos* (1954; translated as *The Young Assassins* in 1959), his first novel, was a great success and established Goytisolo as a writer. Goytisolo was very anti-bourgeois in his attitudes including in his views of sexuality, which in a Catholic country was the object of serious repression under a veneer of respectability. Goytisolo was bisexual and during the 1950s appears to have had sex both with female prostitutes and with men of his own class. He published *Duelo el paraiso* (1955; translated as *Children of Chaos* in 1958). In 1956 he moved to Paris and in 1958 took a job as a reader for the prestigious French publishing house Gallimard. There he met a number of other Spanish writers including Manuel PUIG. Goytisolo also wrote for various French and Spanish papers including *El País*, *L'Express*, and *L'Observateur.* In 1959 he supported the Cuban revolution about which the Cuban writer Reinaldo ARENAS has written with such bitterness as a period of terrible persecution for gay men. Goytisolo met Monique Lange, the woman he married in 1978 after she had had a health scare, at a translation agency in Paris. Initially, they entered a long-term relationship and had affairs. Goytisolo eventually wrote to her in 1965 that he was irrevocably homosexual, which she accepted. Through Lange, Goytisolo met Jean GENET who became a mentor to him. In the early 1960s Goytisolo began to have sexual relations with Arab men whose relation to homosexuality he regarded as more natural than that of the repressed Western world. In 1966 he published the autobiographical *Señas de identidad* (translated as *Marks of Identity* in 1969), which addressed his new-found sexual openness.

His subsequent books were all banned in Spain as mocking Spanish Catholic society. They were published in Argentina and Mexico instead. In 1996 Lange died and Goytisolo went to live in Marrakesh. His many other works include *Reivindicaticación del conde Don Julian* (1970; translated as *Count Julian* in 1974), *Juan sin tierra* (1975; translated as *John the Landless* in 1977), *Colera De Aquines* (1979), *Makbara* (1980; translated 1993), *Landscapes after the Battle* (1982), *Crónicas Sarracinas* (1982; translated as *Saracen Chronicles*), *Coto vedado* (1985; translated as *Forbidden Territory*), *Realms of Strife* (1986), an autobiography, *Las virtudes del pájaro solitario* (1988; translated as *The Virtues of the Solitary Bird*), *Quarantine* (1991), *The Marx Family Saga* (1993), *The Garden of Secrets* (1997, translated 2000), and *Carajicomedia* (translated as *Cock-eyed Comedy* in 2000).

Grahn, Judy (1940–). Lesbian writer and gay rights activist who was born in Chicago but who grew up in a New Mexico town, the daughter of a photographer's assistant and a cook. Grahn put herself through trade school while working nights and then worked as a medical secretary, attending night school. In 1984 she received a BA from San Francisco State. Grahn became seriously ill when she was twenty-five and fell into a coma. Following this experience she decided to dedicate her life to writing. Her first work, 'The Psychoanalysis of Edward the Dyke' (1964), an indictment of the attempt to 'cure' homosexuality through medical and psychiatric treatment, was considered unpublishable. Together with Wendy Cadden, Grahn founded the Women's Press Collective in 1969 in order to publish work by women nobody else would touch. Grahn was also part of the first lesbian feminist collective, the Gay Women's Liberation Group, and one of the founders of 'A Woman's Place', the first US women's bookstore. All of Grahn's writings engage with her politics

and her lesbianism. She has published a number of collections of poems and prose writings including *The Common Woman* (1969), *She Who* (1971–2), *The Queen of Wands* (1982), *The Queen of Swords* (1987), *Another Mother Tongue: Gay Words, Gay Worlds* (1984), *The Highest Apple: Sappho and the Lesbian Poetic Tradition* (1985), *Really Reading Gertrude Stein* (1989), and *Blood, Bread, and Roses: How Menstruation Created the World* (1993). In all her work Grahn is concerned with the importance of language for identity, a positive revisioning of lesbian identity, the need for women to support each other, and to fashion their own identities.

Gray, John Henry (1866–1934). British poet, born into a working-class Nonconformist family in Bethnal Green, London, who sublimated his early 'decadent' years by becoming a priest in the Catholic Church in later life. Gray initially worked as a metal turner at the Woolwich Arsenal but then moved into office posts in the British civil service and in the Foreign Office. His good looks aided his upward mobility. He began publishing in 1889, and met Oscar WILDE, with whom he enjoyed a close friendship for several years. His surname served as the surname of Dorian Gray, Wilde's central character in his novel *The Picture of Dorian Gray*. Wilde paid for the publication of Gray's first collection of poetry, *Silverpoints* (1893), which was illustrated by the artist Charles Ricketts and appeared in a limited edition. This collection contained translations of poems by VERLAINE and Mallarmé. When Wilde moved his affections from Gray to Lord Alfred DOUGLAS, their friendship broke up, the final rift occurring in 1893. Gray then established a friendship with Marc-André RAFFALOVICH and both men eventually entered the Roman Catholic Church. In 1890 Gray was received into the Church. In 1897 he moved to Edinburgh and in 1901 he was ordained as a priest, following a period of study at the Scots College in Rome. Gray then served as a priest both in St Andrews and in Edinburgh where he became rector of St Peter's, the building of which was partly paid for by Raffalovich. Among Gray's other works are a surreal novel, *Park: A Fantastic Story* (1932), which is set in the future, and various volumes of poetry and of devotional verse. His best-known poem is 'The Flying Fish', which appeared in *The Dial* in 1896 and was republished in *The Long Road* in 1926. He died shortly after Raffalovich.

Gray, Thomas (1716–71). Born in London to a scrivener and a milliner, Gray was a lonely child whose life improved only when two of his uncles who were masters at Eton arranged for him to be matriculated there. At Eton, where he went in 1725, he met Horace WALPOLE, Richard West, and Thomas Ashton. Together they formed the Quadruple Alliance, sharing an interest in poetry and writing. Gray developed sentimental attachments to both Walpole and West. When West died in 1742 Gray was left bereft. He expressed his feelings of melancholy and abandonment in a variety of elegies and sonnets. After a spell at Peterhouse, Cambridge, Gray accompanied Walpole on a tour of France and Italy during 1739–41 but they quarrelled and returned separately. In 1741 Gray's father died, leaving the family financially insecure. Gray moved to Cambridge in 1742 where he lived for the rest of his life, first at Peterhouse, then from 1756 at Pembroke. He began to write in English rather than in Latin. He was reconciled with Walpole in 1745 and encouraged by the latter in his work. Walpole published the most famous of Gray's poems, 'Elegy Written in a Country Churchyard' (1751). That poem as well as 'Sonnet on the Death of Richard West' (1742) and 'Ode on a Distant Prospect of Eton College' (1742) are memorials to the love Gray felt for other young men. When Gray was in his early fifties he fell in love

with a young man, Charles-Victor de Bonstettin, who had come to Cambridge from Switzerland to study with Gray. Bonstettin did not respond to Gray's attachment. In 1754 Gray completed his Pindaric ode on *The Progress of Poesy*. It was followed by a second Pindaric ode, *The Bard* (1757). Owing to his 'Elegy', Gray's work was so popular that he was offered the Poet Laureateship on the death of Cibber (1757) but he declined. His final years were devoted to botanical and antiquarian studies. His *Journal* (1775), kept for Dr Thomas Wharton, was an account of a trip to the Lakes he was supposed to have taken together with Wharton. Gray's letters have also been published.

Grimké, Angelina Weld (1880–1958). US writer, born in Boston, the only daughter of Sarah Stanley, who came from a white abolitionist background, and of Archibald Grimké, who was the son of a white man and a black slave. Angelina Weld Grimké was named after her great aunt Angelina Grimké Weld, who was a famous abolitionist and women's rights advocate. Grimké was educated at the Boston Normal School for Gymnastics from which she received a degree in Physical Education in 1902. She then worked as a gym teacher before turning to teaching English in 1907, which she continued until her retirement in 1926. While teaching Grimké wrote poetry, fiction, reviews, biographical sketches, and a play, *Rachel*, her only work to appear in a book. The play centres on an African American woman who refuses marriage and motherhood so as not to produce children that will be the objects of racial discrimination. Grimké's journal and letters provide an indication of her lesbian identity as do her poems, many of which remain unpublished. Some deal with issues of racism but the majority focus on Grimké's love for women such as 'Rosabel', 'You', 'To Her of the Cruel Lips', and 'My Shrine'.

These poems reveal her lesbian longings. Her work needs yet to be fully explored.

Grumbach, Doris (1918–). US writer and broadcaster who was born in New York City, educated at Washington Square College of New York University, and holds a master's degree in English from Cornell University (1940). In 1941 she married Leonard Grumbach. They divorced in 1972. She has four daughters. Grumbach lived with her life partner Sybil Pike first in Washington, DC, and now in Sargentville, Maine. Following her first two novels, *The Spoil of the Flowers* (1962) and *The Short Throat, the Tender Mouth* (1964), Grumbach wrote a biography of Mary McCarthy, *The Company She Kept* (1967), which generated much controversy because of the inclusion of personal material from McCarthy that the latter had not wanted to be published. In the late 1970s Grumbach wrote four novels based on actual people: *Chamber Music* (1979), which focuses extensively on both gay and lesbian relationships; *The Missing Person* (1981); *The Ladies* (1984), a portrait of Eleanor Butler and Sarah Ponsonby, one of the famous lesbian couples whose history has been recorded; and *The Magician's Girl* (1987), which also features a lesbian relationship. In 1991 Grumbach published a memoir, *Coming into the End Zone*, inspired by the death from AIDS of many gay friends and concerned with ageing. This was followed in 1993 by *Extra Innings*, a second memoir.

Gunn, Thom (1929–). A major gay poet of the twentieth century, Thomson William Gunn was born in Gravesend, Kent, and educated at University College School, Bedales, and, after National Service, read English at Trinity College, Cambridge. His first volume of poetry, *Fighting Terms* (1954), was published while he was an undergraduate. That collection as well as *The Sense of Movement* (1956) established him as a poet associated with rebellious leather boys whose assertive masculinity is a reaction against the boredom of conformity. Gunn took up a fellowship at Stanford University, California, in 1954, and settled permanently in San Francisco in 1960. Subsequent collections of poems include *My Sad Captains* (1961), *Positives* (1966), which contains poems by Thom Gunn and photographs by Ander Gunn, *Touch* (1967), *Moly* (1971), *Jack Straw's Castle* (1976), *The Passages of Joy* (1982), and *The Man with the Night Sweats* (1992), which addresses the issue of AIDS. Gunn's *Collected Poems* appeared in 1993.

Gypsy Rose Lee (1914–70). Born Rose Luise Hovick, a US lesbian actress, dancer, and writer whose early career as a dancer and stripper was superseded by the end of the 1930s with a career as a writer of crime fiction. One of her novels, *The G-string Murders*, was made into a film entitled *Lady of Burlesque* in 1943. Her autobiography *Gypsy* became the source for a Broadway musical and later a Hollywood film. In 1940 she shared a house with Carson MCCULLERS.

H

H.D. (1886–1961). H.D. was the pseudonym of Hilda Doolittle, US poet, novelist, short-story writer, and essayist, whose work was preoccupied with questions of female sexuality. In 1911 she followed the poet Ezra Pound, who was a friend and with whom she had an affair, to Europe. She toured Europe with her friend Frances Clegg. In 1913 she married the English writer Richard Aldington to whom she was introduced by Pound and with whom she worked on the magazine *The Egoist*. She also had passionate friendships with men such as the writer D.H. Lawrence and Cecil Gray. The latter is the father of her daughter Perdita, born in 1919. Her long-term relationship with BRYHER (the pseudonym for Winifred Ellerman) stabilized her life. Her novel *Her* (1928) centres on a lesbian relationship and the ultimate need of the heroine to sever her relations to her background in order to find her identity as a writer, culminating in her leaving her lesbian lover and moving to Europe. A central theme in this novel is the notion of masculinity and femininity as embodied in the protagonist's parents, as actual and as symbolic power figures. This issue returns in other writings by H.D., including her childhood memoir *The Gift* (1969), her autobiographical *roman-à-clef Bid Me to Live* (1960), and in her *Tribute to Freud* (1965). Her other novels were *Palimpsest* (1926) and *Hedylus* (1928). H.D. published eleven volumes of poetry.

Hacker, Marilyn (1942–). Lesbian US poet whose work, sometimes explicitly lesbian in content, reveals the poet's versatility in using traditional poetic forms such as the sonnet and the rondeau, and adapting them to her own ends. Her poetry collections include *Presentation Piece* (1974), which won the National Book Award for poetry in 1975, *Separations* (1976), *Taking Notice* (1980), *Assumptions* (1995), *The Hang-glider's Daughter: New and Selected Poems* (1990), *Going Back to the River* (1990), and *Winter Numbers* (1994), both of which won a Lambda Literary Award, and *Selected Poems 1965–1990* (1994). Her best-known collection is possibly *Love, Death, and the Changing of the Seasons* (1986) that, in sonnet form, charts a lesbian relationship from beginning to end. This sequence has affinities with Adrienne RICH's 'Twenty-one Love Poems'. Together with Claire Malroux, Hacker has co-edited *Edge – Contemporary French Poetry in Translation* (1996), and *A Long-gone Sun* (2000). Her *Squares and Courtyards: Poems* also appeared in 2000. Between 1961 and 1980 Hacker was married to the gay Afro-American science fiction writer Samuel R. DELANY.

Hall, Radclyffe (1880–1943). The English lesbian novelist and poet Marguerite Radclyffe Hall was the daughter of Marie Diehl, a US widow, and Radclyffe Radclyffe Hall, grandson of a wealthy and knighted Lancashire physician. Her parents' marriage was unhappy and brief, and her mother, whom her father had left some months before Hall was born, brought up Hall. As a woman of independent means due to her inheritance at the age of twenty-one, Hall was able to pay for the publication of her first volume of poetry, *'Twixst Earth and Stars*, in 1906. A second volume, *A Sheaf of Verses*, was published in 1908 when she had begun to live with Mabel Veronica Batten ('Ladye'). This volume inaugurated her thematization of lesbianism. Hall produced three further volumes of poetry. From 1915 she had a relationship with Una Vincent TROUBRIDGE who became her companion and lover after Mabel's death in 1916. Hall's first novel, *The Unlit Lamp* (1924), explored the problematic of a daughter freeing herself from the intense bond to her mother in favour of a lesbian relationship with another woman. The following novels, *The Forge* (1924) and *A Saturday Life* (1925), centred on married life, although *The Forge* provides a portrait of the US artist Romaine Brooks, Natalie BARNEY's long-time lover. *Adam's Breed* (1926) with its focus on a religious awakening was awarded the James Tait Memorial Prize and the Prix Femina. Hall's best-known lesbian classic novel, *The Well of Loneliness*, became famous for the obscenity trial that followed its publication in 1928. It is in some respects a coming-out narrative detailing the desire and despair of its lesbian (then known as invert) protagonist. Hall was prosecuted for obscenity and the book suppressed even though writers such as Virginia WOOLF and Vera BRITTAIN supported it. The novel centres on Stephen Gordon, a 'mannish lesbian' or invert (i.e. a person supposedly trapped in a body with the sexual characteristics of the opposite sex). In line with early twentieth-century thinking about lesbians and gays (see CARPENTER, EDWARD), this character is constructed as a sensitive, noble, artistic being who – in quasi-Christian fashion – renounces her love for the feminine Mary so that the latter might engage in a heterosexual marriage rather than being a social outcast in the lesbian demimonde of Paris to which Stephen Gordon finds herself exiled. Hall's interest in religion and the institution of the Catholic Church found expression in the novel *The Master of the House* (1932). Her novel *The Sixth Beatitude* (1936) also did not centre on a lesbian character but *Miss Ogilvy Finds Herself* (1934), a collection of short stories, featured lesbian protagonists in search of their identity. In 1934 Hall, also known as 'John', met Evguenia Souline, a 30-year-old White Russian *émigrée* without citizenship. She and Evguenia became lovers, and a troubled triangular relationship between John, Evguenia, and Una began that stifled John's creativity. Having first decided to live permanently in Florence, Italy, the Second World War necessitated a return to England where the women retired to Devon. Hall developed cancer of the stomach and died in London. She is buried with Ladye in Highgate Cemetery, London. After her death Una Troubridge published the biography *The Life and Death of Radclyffe Hall* (1945).

Hall, Richard (1926–92). Born Richard Hirshfeld in New York City, his family moved to White Plains in 1934 where his mother became involved with the Episcopal Church and he and his sister were baptized. An anti-Semitic incident prompted the name change in 1938. Hall went to Harvard. During the 1950s Hall underwent Freudian analysis in an effort to change his sexual orientation but stopped the analysis when he fell in love with Dan Allen, whom he described as a great influence on his life. He worked in advertizing and publishing before becoming acting director of the University Press at the Inter American University in San Juan, Puerto Rico, in 1970. During the 1970s he began a long-term relationship with Arthur Marceau who died of AIDS in 1989. In this period he also began to write and contributed to the gay magazine *The Advocate*. His writings focused on gay subject matter. He wrote a popular mystery, *The Butterscotch Prince* (1975), an autobiographical novel, *Family Fictions* (1991), and a number of plays. He also published three collections of short fiction: *Couplings* (1981); *Letters from a Great Uncle* (1985); and *Fidelities* (1992). Hall died of an AIDS-related illness in 1992.

Hall, Sandi. New Zealand writer of science fiction whose two novels, *The Godmothers* (1983) and *The Wingwomen of Hera* (1987), are utopian and radical. They centre on lesbians, and challenge conventional heterosexual social roles in much the same way that a great deal of feminist science fiction of the 1970s and 1980s did.

Halliday, Caroline. Contemporary British lesbian poet, with a daughter born in 1980 whom she co-parents. Halliday's writings are informed by her position as a lesbian feminist. Her poetry has appeared in a collection edited by Lilian MOHIN entitled *One Foot on the Mountain* (1979), in *Hard Words and Why Lesbians Have to Say Them* (1982), *Dancing the Tightrope* (1987), in *New British Poetry 1968–1988* (1988), and in *Naming the Waves* (1988), edited by Christian MCEWEN. Her own collection of poetry, *Some Truth, Some Change* appeared in 1983. In it she describes life as a lesbian feminist mother.

Hampton, Christopher (1948–). British playwright, born Christopher James Hampton in the Azores where his father was stationed as an engineer. The first few years of his life were spent in a variety of locations, dependent on his father's post-

ings, which included Aden and Egypt. Hampton was sent back to England to attend boarding school, initially a prep school in Reigate, then Lancing College, where he had his first sexual experiences, which were mostly homosexual. This is not uncommon in the public boarding-school system, especially for Hampton's generation when most boarding schools were still single-sex. Hampton began both writing and acting while he was at Lancing (1959–63), but he had his break-through when he went to Oxford (1964–8) where he studied French and German. There he wrote *When Did You Last See My Mother?*, a play about the anxieties that can be part of adolescent homosexuality. The play was produced by the Oxford University Dramatic Society at their annual festival. Hampton also sent it to Peggy Ramsey, a legendary London agent, who took it and him on, and 'sold' the play to the Royal Court Theatre where it was produced on their Upstairs stage. Hampton was heralded as a *Wunderkind*, and followed his first success with *Total Eclipse* (1968), his second and last play to date with a homosexual theme. *Total Eclipse* centres on the destructive relationship between the poets RIMBAUD and VERLAINE. In 1971 Hampton married Laura d'Holesch with whom he has two daughters. Since his early engagement with homosexuality, he has become a mainstream, 'straight' play-wright, initially writing predominantly for the stage but increasingly producing film scripts and translations of plays for the stage. His other plays for the stage include *The Philanthropist* (1970), *Savages* (1973), *Treats* (1976), *Tales from Hollywood* (1982), and *Les Liaisons Dangereuses* (1985), which was success-fully adapted for screen and for which he won many awards including the London Theatre Critics Best Play Award (1985), the Laurence Olivier Play of the Year Award (1986), the New York Critics' Circle Best Foreign Play Award (1987), and an Oscar for the screen version in

1989. He also wrote the autobiographical play for the stage, *White Chameleon* (1991). His film credits include *The Quiet American* (2001), *Carrington,* (1995) about the painter Dora Carrington who was the companion of Lytton STRACHEY, *Tales from Hollywood* (1992), *Dangerous Liaisons* (1988), *The Good Father* (1987), *Hotel du Lac* (1986), *The Honorary Consul* (1983), and *The History Man* (1981).

Hansberry, Lorraine (1930–65). US playwright, journalist, and essayist who was born into a middle-class African American family in Chicago, Illinois. Hansberry studied at Roosevelt College, University of Wisconsin, and at the School of Art Institute of Chicago. In 1950 she went to New York and attended the New School. She then joined the staff of *Freedom*, a radical African American journal. This brought her into contact with a number of leading black intellectuals such as Langston Hughes and W.E.B. DuBois. She was an associate editor from 1952. In 1953 she married Robert Nemiroff but her continued political engagement with radical race and gender politics led her to feminism and, by 1957, she and Nemiroff, with whom she remained on very good terms until her death from cancer in 1965, had separated quietly and she had begun to come out as a lesbian. In August 1957 she wrote two letters to the new lesbian journal *The Ladder*, supporting the emerging US lesbian liberation movement and connecting homophobia and anti-feminism. Hansberry's first play, *A Raisin in the Sun* (1959), won the New York Drama Critics' Circle Award. It marked the first time that a black US woman's work had been produced on Broadway. Her second play, *The Sign in Sidney Brustein's Window* (1964), focused on a Jewish intellectual and challenged the notion that African Americans should write about 'black' subjects only. Hansberry was committed to fighting racism

and sexism, and challenging social inequalities until her all too early death.

Hanscombe, Gillian (1945–). Born and brought up in Melbourne, Hanscombe, a lesbian academic and writer, and long-term partner of the writer Suniti NAMJOSHI, read English and History of Music at the University of Melbourne and at Monash University. In 1969 she moved to Britain where she completed a DPhil on the modernist writer Dorothy Richardson at the University of Oxford. This thesis formed the basis of her first book, *Art for Life: Dorothy Richardson and the Development of Feminist Consciousness* (1982). She also wrote *Between Friends* (1982). In 1987, together with Virgina Smyers, she published the highly influential *Writing for Their Lives: The Modernist Women 1910–1940*, which appeared at the time of the revisioning of the modernist canon to include works by women from the period beyond Virginia WOOLF, many of whom were lesbian such as H.D., Djuna BARNES, and Gertrude STEIN. Hanscombe has also published a variety of other texts and written in a number of different genres. Together with Suniti Namjoshi she published *Flesh and Paper* (1986) and *Kaliyug, or Circles of Paradise* (1993). *Sybil: The Glide of Her Tongue* came out in 1992, and in 1996 she published *Figments of a Murder*.

Hansen, Joseph (1923–). US writer who is well known for his Dave Brandstetter mystery series, Hansen was born in South Dakota but has lived in southern California ever since his family moved there in 1936. In 1943 he married Jane Bancroft. They have a daughter. Hansen's writings focus on homosexual characters and themes. He published under the pseudonym James Colton in the 1960s. Early novels like *Lost on Twilight Road* (1964) and *Strange Marriage* (1965) belong to the genre of pre-Stonewall gay pulp fiction, portraying the homophobia of the period and its internalization by gay characters as they attempt to live hetero-normative lives. During the 1980s Hansen wrote mainstream novels such as *A Smile in His Lifetime* (1981) and *Job's Year* (1983) in which the main gay characters continued to suffer from loneliness and loss. In the 1990s Hansen set out to chronicle gay life on the West Coast of the USA during the 1940s and 1950s. His *Living Upstairs* (1993), set during the Second World War, is not merely concerned with the problems of being gay in a repressive era but also with the fulfilment gay relationships can bring.

Harris, Bertha (1937–). Born in Fayetteville, North Carolina, and educated at the University of North Carolina at Greensboro, US lesbian Harris is considered one of the great innovators of lesbian fiction, comparable in her experiments with style to Djuna BARNES, or, more contemporarily, with Jeanette WINTERSON. Though rooted in the South of the USA, she went to New York and, during the period of social unrest of the 1960s, briefly married and had a daughter. While at the University of North Carolina she wrote her first novel, *Catching Saradove* (1969), as part of her degree requirement. *Catching Saradove* is Harris's perhaps most conventional novel, semi-autobiographically focused on the central character's attempts to transcend her upbringing. Following her second novel, *Confessions of a Cherubino* (1972), Harris wrote *Lover* (1976) 'in order to seduce Louise Fishman. It worked' according to Harris's introduction to the 1993 New York University Press edition of the novel. In that edition Harris also provides an extended introduction to her publishing history that offers a detailed account of her relationship with the writer and publisher June ARNOLD and Arnold's lover Parke Patricia Bowman. Harris has also worked with Emily Sisley on *The Joy of Lesbian Sex* (1977), a guide to the methods and politics of lesbian lovemaking.

Heap, Jane (1887–1964). US lesbian editor and curator whose main claim to fame is her co-editorship, together with her one-time lover Margaret Anderson, of *The Little Review* (1914–29). *The Little Review* proved to be one of the most important magazines of the high modernist period. Anderson started it in Chicago but it, and Heap and Anderson, moved to Paris in 1922. In 1924 Jane Heap, by now estranged from Anderson, went back to New York but returned to Paris in 1927, only to close *The Little Review* in 1929. In its heyday *The Little Review* published the work of some of the most important figures of high modernism including Emma Goldman, Richard Aldington, Djuna BARNES, Hart CRANE, H.D., and James Joyce's *Ulysses*. The last was serialized from 1918 and became the object of an obscenity trial in 1920. Jane Heap was an active member of the lesbian circles of Paris and New York during the 1920s. She is supposed to have had an affair with Djuna Barnes. Between 1924 and 1927 she lived in New York where she had a gallery on Fifth Avenue. In 1926 she organized an international theatre exhibition that included, for the first time, scenery paintings from Russia. In 1927 she opened an exhibition on art in the age of its mechanical reproduction. In her later life she led a rather withdrawn existence. Little is known about her final years.

Hellman, Lillian (1906–84). US dramatist and screenwriter, born in New Orleans to Jewish parents, and much influenced by her African American nurse Sophronia. Hellman went to New York University but in 1925 she left university to marry Arthur Kober. She then worked as a play reader and as a scenario reader for Hollywood. In 1932 she and Kober divorced and she began living with the detective fiction writer Dashiell Hammett. Since the pair and many of their friends were involved in left-wing politics, the House of Un-American Activities Committee blacklisted them during the 1950s. Hell-man was quite a prolific writer, taking up moral and socio-political issues in her work. Her play *The Children's Hour* (1934), later made into a successful film, is a lesbian boarding-school fiction in which a pupil accuses her two female teachers, the owners of the boarding school, of having a lesbian affair, thus ruining not only their livelihoods but also their lives. Like other texts in this genre, Hellman's play ends unhappily, and les-bianism is depicted as a tragedy when uncovered. The play was based on a real-life early nineteenth-century story, re-searched and retold by the lesbian aca-demic Lillian FADERMAN in *Scotch Verdict* (1983). In that story the two teachers embarked on a court case to clear their names. The court case lasted decades and was never resolved, in part because the judges could not believe that women could have a sexual relationship. Hell-man's other writings include *Days to Come* (1936), *The Little Foxes* (1939), *Watch on the Rhine* (1941), *The North Star: A Motion Picture about Some Rus-sian People* (1943), *The Searching Wind: A Play in Two Acts* (1944), *Another Part of the Forest: A Play in Three Acts* (1947), *Montserrat: Play in Two Acts* (1950), *The Autumn Garden* (1951), *The Lark* (1956), *Toys in the Attic* (1960), *Collected Plays* (1972), and *Maybe* (1980). Her memoirs include *An Unfinished Wo-man* (1969), *Pentimento* (1973), and *Scoun-drel Time* (1976).

Herbst, Josephine (1892–1969). American writer born in Sioux City, Iowa. A poli-tical and social activist, Herbst acted as a special news correspondent during the 1930s, investigating political dissent in the USA, Germany, Spain, and Cuba. Herbst's novels did not engage with her sexual identity or thematize homosexual-ity. Instead they attacked the values of the US middle classes. Her characters in novels like *Nothing is Sacred* (1928) and *Money for Love* (1929) were depicted as

victims of capitalism and materialism. This subject also dominates her trilogy *Pity is not Enough* (1933), *The Execu-tioner Waits* (1934), and *Rope of Gold* (1939). Herbst's other works include *Sa-tan's Sergeants* (1941), *Somewhere the Tempest Fell* (1947), and *New Green World* (1954). Herbst tried to keep her sexuality separate from her public life. In that she was not unlike many lesbians and gays in the first half of the twentieth century who remained closeted for fear that their sexuality might make them the objects of public persecution and denun-ciation. After her death, however, letters by her to the radical muralist Marion Greenwood and to other women were discovered revealing her lesbian relation-ships. In 1984 Elinor Lange wrote a biography of Herbst entitled *Josephine Herbst: The Story She Could Never Tell* in which Lange discussed these relation-ships.

Highsmith, Patricia (1921–95). Born in Texas, part German and part British, Highsmith lived her life in Europe, mainly in Switzerland, and in the USA. Known predominantly for her crime writing, her first novel, *Strangers on a Train* (1949), was made into a film by Alfred Hitch-cock. Like other novels of hers, this one centred on the psychological imprison-ment between two people and portrayed an explicitly homoerotic obsession be-tween two murderers. Many works of crime fiction followed. *The Talented Mr Ripley* (1955) was awarded the Edgar Allen Poe Scroll by the Mystery Writers of America. In 1952 Highsmith published *The Price of Salt*, her only explicitly lesbian novel, which appeared under the pseudonym Claire Morgan. Not until its reissue under the title *Carol* in 1991 did Patricia Highsmith reveal herself to be the writer of this work, a fact that received much publicity at the time.

Hine, Daryl (1936–). Gay poet, born in British Columbia, Canada, who attended

McGill University in Montreal before moving to the USA in 1967 where he has lived ever since. Hine travelled widely in Europe before going to the University of Chicago in 1967. His first two volumes of poetry, *Five Poems* (1955) and *The Carnal and the Crane* (1957), were highly praised. He went on to write a novel, *The Prince of Darkness & Co*, (1961) and a travel account, *Polish Subtitles* (1962). He also published further volumes of poetry, *The Wooden Horse* (1965) and *Minutes* (1968). He taught Classics at the University of Chicago for several years, and both classics and Catholicism helped him deal with his sexuality. In 1975 he brought out an autobiography of his early years in verse, *In & Out*, which articulated his homosexuality and the difficulties he had in dealing with that. Since 1975 his poetry has dealt more explicitly with the issue of growing up gay in the 1940s and 1950s.

Hirschfeld, Magnus (1868–1935). German sexologist and sexual rights activist whose own homosexuality and Jewish background made him the object of persecution under the Nazi regime from which he fled in 1930. He settled in Nice, France, where he spent the last few years of his life with his long-term companion Karl Giese. Hirschfeld studied Medicine and in 1886 moved to Berlin where he began his campaign for homosexual rights. In *Sappho and Socrates* (1896) he argued for the legalization of homosexuality. Hirschfeld followed Karl Heinrich ULRICHS's medicalized view of homosexuals, or sexual intermediaries as he called them, in regarding homosexuality as innate and the result of some endocrinal malfunction during the development of the embryo. It was on the basis of this diagnosis that he campaigned for the repeal of the laws against homosexuality. In 1897 Hirschfeld co-founded the Wissenschaftlich-humanitäres Komitee that attempted, in vain, to lobby the German parliament to legalize homosexuality. In 1919 Hirschfeld set up the Institute for

Sexual Research in Berlin. The Institute was closed when the Nazis came to power. Hirschfeld published a number of texts on the issue of sexuality and intermediate types including in his journal *Jahrbuch für sexuelle Zwischenstufen (Yearbook on Sexual Intermediaries*), which appeared between 1899 and 1923. His writings include *Berlins drittes Geschlecht* (1904; *Berlin's Third Sex*), *Transvestiten* (1910; *Transvestites*), *Die Homosexualität des Mannes und des Weibes* (1914; *Homosexuality in Men and Women*), and *Women East and West* (1935). In 1919 he appeared in one of the first films that offered a sympathetic portrayal of homosexuals, *Anders als die Anderen* (*Different from the Others*). An enthusiastic supporter of women's emancipation as well as homosexual rights, Hirschfeld nonetheless did not believe in the parity of the sexes, and viewed women as inferior to men.

Hocquenghem, Guy (1946–88). Gay French queer theorist and writer who was born in the suburbs of Paris, educated at the Ecole Normale Supérieure, participated in the 1968 student revolution, and became a member of the Communist Party from which he was expelled for his homosexuality. Hocquenghem was one of the first gay men to join the Front Homosexuel d'Action Révolutionnaire, founded by lesbian separatists who split from the Mouvement Homophile de France in 1971. Hocquenghem produced a considerable body of both theoretical and creative work, most of which remains untranslated into English. His three theoretical texts, *Le Désir homosexuel* (1972), *L'Après-mai des faunes* (1974), and *Le Dérive homosexuelle* (1977), offer a radical critique of Freudian psychology and liberal social theory from a Marxist perspective. In the 1970s he was appointed to a professorship in Philosophy at the University of Vincennes-Saint Denis. Together with another professor, René Schérer, he wrote *Co-ire, album systématique de l'enfance* (1976) and *L'Ame atomique, pour* *une esthétique d'ère nucléaire* (1986). Following a collection of short stories, *Fin de section* (1976), Hocquenghem started to write experimental fiction in the 1980s when he published *L'Amour en relief* (1982) about a blind foreign boy's engagement with French society. *La Colère d'agneau* (1986) is a fictional retelling of the vision of St John the Evangelist. *Eve* (1987) combines the story of Genesis with Hocquenghem's reflections on the decline of his body as a result of AIDS. His final novel, *Les Voyages et aventures extraordinaires du frère Angelo* (1988) describes an Italian monk's travels in America. Hocquenghem died of an AIDS-related illness in 1988.

Holleran, Andrew (b. 1943?). Little is known about this writer who uses only his pseudonym and who has guarded his anonymity to the extent that even his birth date remains unclear – hence the question mark. Interviewed in the *Publisher's Weekly* in 1983, Holleran suggested that the well-to-do white characters in his two novels *Dancer from the Dance* (1978) and *Nights in Aruba* (1983) reflect his own life. Holleran was educated at a private prep school, served in the army in West Germany, and began studying Law but abandoned that in favour of doing Creative Writing at the University of Iowa. He moved to New York in 1971. Especially his second novel reflects that history. His third volume, a collection of writings on AIDS-related topics entitled *Ground Zero*, reveals his preoccupation with the impact of AIDS, which was already beginning to be present in his second novel.

Hollinghurst, Alan (1954–). The British gay author of *The Swimming-Pool Library* (1988), which was one of the most acclaimed first novels of the 1980s, Hollinghurst was selected as one of the Best of Young British Novelists in 1993. *The Swimming-Pool Library* is set in London where a gay man from an upper middle-class background discovers that his grandfather as Director of Public Prosecutions was responsible for sending gay men to prison. Hollinghurst has written for *The Times Literary Supplement* for many years and is the editor of the annual literary competition, 'Nemo's Almanac'. His novel *The Folding Star* (1994) was short-listed for the 1994 Booker Prize and won the James Tait Memorial Prize. It details the life of Edward Manners in a Flemish town where he frequents the gay haunts by night and teaches part-time by day, falling in love with his pupil. Simultaneously Manners gets drawn into research on a nineteenth-century artist whose life and photography raise questions about sexual preferences and practices. Hollinghurst's *The Spell* (1998) was a romantic novel in which two middle-class middle-aged gay men come to terms with and endure their relationships with younger, more fickle men whose interests are less focused on culture and more on sex.

Housman, A.E. (1859–1936). The British poet Alfred Edward Housman was educated at Bromsgrove and St John's College, Oxford, where, in 1877, he met Moses Jackson. Housman formed a passionate attachment to Jackson who became the inspiration for much of his poetry. They and another student shared rooms in their final year. Having inexplicably failed his Greats, Housman worked in the Patent Office of London for ten years, working on classical authors like Ovid and Juvenal, and publishing occasional articles. Jackson was already working in the Patent Office when Housman joined and for three years Housman, Jackson, and Jackson's younger brother Adalbert shared lodgings. In late 1885 a breach occurred between Jackson and Housman, possibly brought about by Jackson's rejection of Housman. Housman subsequently moved out of the lodgings and lived, for the rest of his life, on his own. He continued to be friends with Jackson and to see Adalbert who may have been homosexual himself. Jackson's marriage in the late 1880s and his move to India meant that his and Housman's later contact was entirely by letter. Housman's homosexuality was confirmed by an essay entitled 'A.E. Housman's "De Amicitia"', written by Housman's brother Laurence Housman and deposited in the British Library in 1942, not to be opened until twenty-five years later. In this text Laurence Housman discusses his brother's homosexuality, writes about his life-long love for Moses Jackson, and about his brief relationship with Moses's brother Adalbert, and identifies A.E. Housman's most autobiographical poems. In 1892 A.E. Housman was appointed professor of Latin at London University, and in 1911 he became professor of Latin at Cambridge. He worked on his definitive edition of Manilius, published in five volumes between 1902 and 1930. Prior to that, in 1896 and at his own expense, he had published *A Shropshire Lad*, a collection of poetry that initially had little response but became very popular during the First World War. The collection is supposed to have been inspired by Housman's anger at the Oscar WILDE trial of 1884–5, and Wilde's conviction. He sent Wilde an autographed copy of *A Shropshire Lad* on his release from prison. Housman's brother found a newspaper article about the suicide of a young homosexual Woolwich naval cadet in August 1885 among Housman's papers, which suggested that this case too had contributed to Housman's poetry from the period. Housman's *Last Poems* (1922), too, proved to be a popular success. In 1936 his brother Laurence published *More Poems* posthumously; *Additional Poems* appeared one year later. Housman's poems made coded references to homosexuality. Many of his poems focus on 'lads', 'friends', and other male figures. Some leave the gender of the beloved unspecified. However, especially in his later verse, Housman is increasingly frank in his depiction of homosexuality.

Howard, Richard (1929–). US poet, poetry editor of *The Paris Review*, and Professor of English at Houston, Texas, Howard was brought up in Cleveland and educated at Columbia University and at the Sorbonne. He has translated many French authors including Charles BAUDELAIRE, Jean COCTEAU, and Roland BARTHES, and has produced a number of volumes of poetry in which homosexuality is a significant theme. They include *Quantities* (1962), *The Damages* (1967), *Untitled Subjects* (1969), a collection of dramatic monologues, letters, and journals that won the Pulitzer Prize, *Findings* (1971), *Two-part Inventions* (1974), *Fellow Feelings* (1976), *Misgivings* (1979), *Lining Up* (1984), *No Traveller* (1989), and *Like Most Revelations* (1994).

Hughes, Langston (1902–67). Born in Missouri, Hughes's childhood as a poor black person was characterized by frequent moves as his mother tried to find work. Hughes's experiences as a poor black man in the early part of the twentieth century marked his work throughout his life. In his famous 'A Negro Speaks of Rivers' of the 1920s he expressed the need for spiritual support in the context of economic decline and racism. Hughes attended Columbia University in 1921–2, then travelled extensively in Europe before studying at Lincoln University in Pennsylvania between 1926 and 1929. In 1926 he published *The Weary Blues*; in 1927 *Fine Clothes to the Jew* appeared. Hughes wrote and published in all genres until his death but he never addressed homosexuality openly. His poems invite gay readings but his biographers disagree about his sexuality.

Huysmans, Joris-Karl (1848–1907). Born in Paris, of a French mother and a Dutch father, Huysmans studied Law at the University of Paris and was a civil servant in the Ministry of the Interior where he worked for thirty-two years. He wrote poetic novels, as well as art criticism, essays, short stories, and prose poems. Following early naturalistic novels such as *Marthe* (1976), which explores the world of prostitution, Huysmans became associated with the aestheticist movement and with the decadence of the late nineteenth century through his publication of *A rebours* (1984; *Against Nature*). A forerunner of Oscar WILDE and Aubrey Beardsley, Huysmans's celebration of excessive aestheticism in *A rebours* was taken up in novels such as Oscar Wilde's *Picture of Dorian Gray* in which Huysmans's book is given to Dorian by Lord Henry Wotton. Huysmans's *Là-bas* (1891; *Down There*) focused on the occult, magic rites, and black masses. Huysmans had extensive correspondence with many writers of his day, including the poet Paul VERLAINE whom he met in the summer of 1904 and whose *Religious Poetry* he edited and prefaced in 1906. He himself also wrote a series of four novels centring on the character Durtal and his journey towards Catholicism: *Là-bas* (1891), *En route* (1895), *La Cathédrale* (1898), and *L'Oblat* (1903). Huysmans embraced aestheticism in his own life, collecting antiques and art, and living an elegant life in Paris.

I

Inge, William (1913–73). Born and educated in Kansas, US playwright Inge spent the first few years of his adult life as a small-town teacher in Kansas and Missouri. His homosexuality remained closeted throughout his life, possibly because of fear of reprisals in an era in which homosexuality was considered suspect. He committed suicide in 1973, following increasing problems with alcohol, his repressed sexuality, and extensive psychoanalytic therapy. Inge had four early Broadway successes. *Come Back, Little Sheba* (1950) was followed by *Picnic* (1953), for which he won the Pulitzer Prize for Drama. *Bus Stop* (1955), and *The Dark at the Top of the Stairs* (1957) appeared in quick succession. All were made into Hollywood films. In 1961 he won an Academy Award for Best Original Screenplay for *Splendor in the Grass*. Only one of his plays, *The Boy in the Basement* (a one-act play from the early 1950s that was not published until 1962), focuses on homosexuality as its main theme. Other, especially later, plays include openly homosexual characters such as Pinky in *Where's Daddy?* (1966) and Archie in *The Disposal* (1967).

Irigaray, Luce (1930–). French lesbian feminist, psychoanalyst, and philosopher who was born in Belgium but whose writings have been enormously influential in feminist circles in the USA, the UK, and

Italy. Like several other women theorists residing in France, such as Julia Kristeva and Hélène Cixous, Irigaray has been very much involved in the development of psycholinguistically based critique of heteropatriarchal language, and in the analysis of the relationship between language and gender. Her first book, *Le Language des déments* (1973; *The Language of the Demented*), focused on the collapse of language among those suffering from dementia. Her doctoral thesis *Speculum de l'autre femme* (1974; translated as *Speculum of the Other Woman*, 1985) and the subsequent *Ce sexe qui n'est pas un* (1977; translated as *This Sex Which Is Not One*, 1985) established Irigaray firmly as one of the key thinkers around the notion of an *écriture feminine* or feminine style of writing based on a complex analysis of the relation between the biological body, the unconscious, and women's, and indeed men's, relation to language and systems of symbolic signification. From a lesbian perspective Irigaray's celebration of the multiple sexual and sensual opportunities the female body offers for its own pleasure and that of other women provided a welcome shift from the Freudian notion of woman as lack and inadequate. It is, in fact, to a certain kind of so-called French feminism, which includes the work of Irigaray but also of Julia Kristeva and of Hélène Cixous, that lesbians owe the reintroduction of the notion of pleasure or *jouissance* – as opposed to guilt and self-loathing – into the idea and reality of the female body. The notion of an *écriture féminine*, much celebrated in Anglo-American feminist criticism of the 1980s, has since undergone a rigorous critique, but Irigaray's analysis of the gender/language relation in the context of her analysis of sexual and capitalist regimes has made her one of the foremost feminist critics among Italian feminists, who have embraced her ideas very strongly. Following on from her first two volumes, which made her into an internationally renowned feminist theorist, Irigaray produced a whole range of texts elaborating on her earlier positions. These include *Amante marine: de Friedrich Nietzsche* (1983; translated as *Marine Lover: Of Friedrich Nietzsche*, 1991), *Sexes et parentés* (1987; translated as *Sexes and Genealogies*, 1993), *Je, tu, nous* (1990; translated as *Je, tu, nous: Toward a Culture of Difference*, 1993), *Elemental Passions* (1992), *An Ethics of Sexual Difference* (1993), *I Love to You: Sketch of a Possible Felicity in History* (1995), *The Forgetting of Air* (1999), *Why Different? Collected Interviews* (1999), *To Speak Is Never Neuter* (1999), *To Be Two* (2000), *Democracy Begins between Two* (2001), and *Daily Prayers* (2002). Irigaray is director of research at the Centre National de la Recherche Scientifique.

Isherwood, Christopher (1904–86). The gay novelist Christopher William Bradshaw Isherwood was born in Cheshire, the son of an army captain who was killed in the First World War. He was educated at Repton School, where he met W.H. AUDEN and Edward Upward, and at Corpus Christi College, Cambridge, which he left in 1925 without taking a degree. He then tutored for a time and studied medicine at King's College, London, between 1928 and 1929. After leaving Cambridge he renewed his acquaintance with Auden, and the two had a ten-year unromantic relationship, with sex

enhancing their friendship. Auden, who was two years younger than Isherwood, introduced Isherwood to a fellow Oxford undergraduate, Stephen SPENDER. The three were at the centre of the Auden gang, the angry young writers who dominated the English literary scene of the 1930s. Isherwood's first novels *All the Conspirators* (1928) and *The Memorial* (1932) were influenced by E.M. FORSTER and Virginia WOOLF. From 1930 until 1933 Isherwood lived in Berlin, supporting himself through teaching English, and enjoying the freedom from constraint that living in a foreign country brought with it. He lived in poor districts of Berlin and recorded his experiences of the Berlin demimonde in *Goodbye to Berlin* (1939). His previous novels such as *Mr Norris Changes Trains* (1935) had already represented homosexuality, albeit in terms of its repression. The theme of homosexuality was to emerge more strongly in his later novels, which often centred on certain types of characters such as the weak man unable to combine love and sex in his life, the strong man, etc. Isherwood engaged in a long-term, never realized project to write a long novel entitled *The Lost*, of which *Mr Norris Changes Trains* and *Goodbye to Berlin* were supposed to be the first two parts. An independently published story, 'Sally Bowles' (1937), was turned into an extremely successful stage musical, *Cabaret*, in 1968. It was also made into a film, starring Liza Minnelli. *Cabaret* provides a vivid portrait of Berlin in the 1930s under the threat of Nazidom. After leaving Berlin, Isherwood travelled widely in Europe and to China with Auden about which trip he wrote *Journey to a War* (1939). He published the semi-autobiographical *Lions and Shadows* (1938) in which his friends such as Auden, Spender, and Upward appear under fictitious names. Together with Auden he collaborated on various avant-garde plays such as *The Dog Beneath the Skin* (1935), *The Ascent of F6* (1937), and *On the Frontier* (1938), and supported a variety of left-wing causes. He and Auden emigrated to the USA in 1939. Isherwood settled permanently in Los Angeles and began writing film scripts. In 1940, under the influence of a Hindu monk and surrogate father figure, Isherwood converted to Vedantism, a philosophy that influenced his later work. He edited various works on the subject including *Vedanta for the Western World* (1945) and, together with Swami Prabhavananda translated the *Bhagavad-gītā* (1944) and other Hindu classics. He became a US citizen in 1946. He translated BAUDELAIRE's *Intimate Journals* (1947). In 1953 he fell in love with an 18-year-old college student, Don Bachardy, who achieved independent acclaim as an artist, and with whom Isherwood would have his most enduring relationship. His novel *The World in the Evening* (1954) centres on the plight of the homosexual in a homophobic world. Later works include *A Single Man* (1964), the story of a gay man's grief following the death of his long-term lover, *Kathleen and Frank* (1972), a biography of his parents, and *Christopher and His Kind* (1976), an account of his life as a gay man. His last novel, *A Meeting by the River* (1967), centres on a bisexual movie maker's attempts to stop his younger brother from taking final vows as a swami. Brotherhood, both literal and as the gay community, features here as offering the possibility of an ideal of love.

J

Jacob, Naomi (1889–1964). Born Naomi Ellington Jacob in Ripon, Yorkshire, this lesbian novelist of popular literature, now largely forgotten, wrote prolifically throughout her life, though especially during the 1930s and 1940s when she was also great friends with other lesbian writers including Radclyffe HALL and her partner Una TROUBRIDGE, and the DU MAURIER sisters, Angela and Daphne. Jacob fell for Una Troubridge but was rejected by her. Following her first novel, *Jacob Ussher* (1926), she wrote many more including *The Loaded Stick* (1935), *Honour Come Back* (1935), *Time Piece* (1937), *Straws in Amber* (1938), *The Lenient God* (1938), *Full Meridian* (1940), *Leopards and Spots* (1943), *Barren Metal* (1944), *A Passage Perilous* (1947), *Mary of Delight* (1949), *Morning Will* (1953), *Antonia* (1954), *What's to Come* (1958), and *Strange Beginning* (1961). During the 1930s she also wrote the six-volume Gollantz saga that included *Four Generations* (1934), *The Founder of the House* (1936), *That Wild Lie, Gollantz, London-Paris-Milan*, and *Gollantz and Partners*. Jacob also wrote autobiographies including one of the music hall artiste and male impersonator Marie Lloyd (1936). Of particular interest to lesbian readers are Jacob's autobiographical texts including *Me – Likes and Dislikes* (1954), which includes fascinating chapters on female impersonators revealing Jacob's love for theatre, vaudeville, and cross-dressing, as well as for pets (she wrote several books about dogs), and *Me – and the Swan* (1963), which is much more overtly lesbian in content.

Jahnn, Hans Henny (1894–1959). German writer born in Hamburg as the youngest son of a shipwright who fell in love with a fellow pupil, Gottlieb Harms, while still at school. When the First World War began, the two men fled to Norway to avoid military service. There Jahnn wrote his *Norwegisches Tagebuch* (*Norwegian Diary*). He became interested in organ building and in mysticism. After the war the two men returned to northern Germany. Jahnn founded a religious community. In 1923 he was employed to restore the organ at St Jakobi Church in Hamburg. In 1926 he married a gymnastics teacher, Ellinor Philips, and Harms married her sister. Harms died in 1931. Jahnn had started writing during the first decade of the twentieth century. His novels were lengthy and convoluted, often published in several volumes over extended periods of time. This made them somewhat inaccessible to the general reading public and he remains a minor figure in the history of German literature. Not only did his style militate against his work being taken up by a wider readership; his themes of male union, incest, and a baroque kind of excess also marginalized

Jahnn in the culture of his period. Jahnn's works include *Perrudja*, of which the first volume appeared in 1929 and the second volume in 1968, *Fluß ohne Ufer* (*River without Shore*), published in three volumes in 1949 and 1961, and *Jeden ereilt es* (*Everyone is Overtaken*), published in 1968. During the Nazi period in Germany Jahnn fled to Denmark, fearful for his life because of his homosexuality. In Denmark he lived on the island of Bornholm and studied agriculture. He also continued to write. After the Second World War he returned to Germany and founded the Freie Akademie der Künste (Free Academy of the Arts). Disappointed by the conservative cold-war climate of the 1950s he engaged in animal rights and anti-nuclear war activism. He died of a heart attack and was buried near his friend Harms's grave.

James, Alice (1848–92). US diarist, the younger sister of the writer Henry JAMES and the philosopher William James who, *inter alia*, taught Gertrude STEIN. Alice James led a confined life, plagued, like her brother Henry, by illnesses. However, unlike him and in line with the gendered mores of her time, her physical frailty meant that like Emily DICKINSON, on the one hand, and the first-person narrator of Charlotte Perkins GILMAN's story *The Yellow Wallpaper*, on the other, she spent much of her life laid up on a couch, to some extent a victim of the social conventions governing feminine behaviour in the second half of the nineteenth century. She lived in the USA and in England, following her brother Henry, to whom she was close. She came to more sustained literary and feminist attention when her diary, first published in 1934, was re-edited by Leon Edel in 1964. The diary has become a landmark text for feminist literary criticism, and is of interest from a lesbian perspective because of the light it throws on James's relationships with other women. Jean Strouse's biography of *Alice James* (1981) discusses James's invalid

status as the answer to the conflicting needs James experienced both to live up to certain ideals of femininity and to engage her intellect. She never married and was scathing about marriage and what it did to women. James welcomed her death from breast cancer as a relief from a life she had found difficult to cope with.

James, Henry (1843–1916). Born in New York, brother to Alice JAMES and William James, a famous philosopher and psychologist, Henry James like his siblings was educated in the USA and in Europe, settling in England in 1875, staying in London until 1897 and then moving to Lamb House in Rye, where he lived until his death. James's own sexual identity has been the subject of some speculation. He had close friendships with women but appears also to have had passionate friendships with men as detailed in Fred Kaplan's biography *The Imagination of Genius* (1992). James was fascinated by but not supportive of the plight of his contemporary Oscar WILDE, and refused to sign a petition requesting a pardon for Wilde that was circulated in 1896. His many novels and short fictions problematized both the role of women and relationships between men. Much of his early fiction centred on the impact of European civilization on Americans, both women and men. His first major novel, *Roderick Hudson* (1875), focused on the friendship between a wealthy older man, Rowland Mallett, and his protégé, Roderick Hudson. The friendship is doomed, ending with Hudson's suicide. Within lesbian circles it is his novel *The Bostonians* (1885) that has attracted the most attention since it portrays a so-called Boston marriage, the cohabitation of two spinsters. The novel supposedly draws on the relationship between his sister Alice and her long-term companion Katherine Loring. The relationship between Verena and Olive in this novel is doomed when a young Southern man, Basil Random, comes between the two women. James wrote for magazines such as the *Atlantic Monthly*, many other novels, a few plays that were not very successful, and many short stories as well as some autobiographical texts. Among his best known works are *The American* (1877), *Daisy Miller* (1879), *Washington Square* (1881), *The Portrait of a Lady* (1881), *The Aspern Papers* (1888), *The Tragic Muse* (1890), *What Maisie Knew* (1897), *The Turn of the Shrew* (1898), *The Wings of the Dove* (1902), and *The Ambassadors* (1903).

Jarman, Derek (1942–94). Gay British film-maker, artist, and writer, Jarman was born into a middle-class, Royal Air Force family, spending his early years in public schools and on military bases. He took a degree at King's College, London, before going to the Slade School of Art in London. Jarman was then involved in a variety of projects, designing shops, for theatre and for dance, as well as exhibiting in many art exhibitions. In the 1970s he also wrote a number of film scripts. He conceived of his work as a form of gay activism and focused on the subject of gay relationships. His first feature film, *Sebastiane* (1975), was a great hit. Among the many films which he subsequently made are *Jubilee* (1978), adaptations of Shakespeare's *The Tempest* (1979) and of Christopher Marlowe's *Edward II* (1991), *Caravaggio* (1986), *The Last of England* (1987), *War Requiem* (1989), *The Garden* (1990), and *Wittgenstein* (1992). He continued to produce stage designs for theatre and for ballet, and he also continued to show his art work in a variety of art exhibitions. In 1987 he moved to Prospect Cottage, Dungeness, in Kent, where he created a garden commemorated in *Derek Jarman's Garden* (1995). In 1984 he began to publish autobiographical texts that have become important documents for understanding the experience of gay life from the 1960s onwards. In 1984 *Dancing Ledge* appeared. Two years later he was diagnosed as HIV positive. He

decided to go public about this diagnosis and the effects of this decision are movingly described in his autobiographical texts *Modern Nature* (1991) and *At Your Own Risk* (1992). In 1993 he made his last film, *Blue*, which is autobiographical in tone and constitutes Jarman's response to going blind and undergoing treatment for AIDS-related illnesses. *Chroma* (1994), a book of meditations on colour that also contains the script for *Blue*, was published in 1994.

Jarry, Alfred (1873–1907). French writer, born in Laval, whose mother separated from her husband and took the children to live in Saint-Brieuc (1879) and then in Rennes (1888). Jarry moved to Paris in 1891 and began publishing in 1893. Between 1893 and 1895 he had a brief and passionate friendship with a fellow student from the Lycée Henri IV, the future poet Léon-Paul Fargue. This is Jarry's only known homosexual relationship. It provided material for his semi-autobiographical play *Haldernablou* (1894). He became famous through his play *Ubu roi* (1896), the opening of which with the swear word *merde* caused it to be closed after two performances. The play is considered the inauguration of the theatre of the absurd. Homosexual characters and themes appear in a number of Jarry's writings including *Les Jours et les nuits* (1897; *Days and Nights*), *L'Amour en visites* (1898; *Love Goes Visiting*), *Messaline* (1899; *The Garden of Priapus*), and *Le Surmâle* (1902; *The Supermale*). Jarry was not able to sustain his literary reputation during his lifetime. He died young, a heavy drinker renowned for his eccentric behaviour.

Jewett, Sarah Orne (1849–1909). US fiction writer who enjoyed a 'Boston marriage' with Annie Adams Fields from the early 1880s until Jewett's death. Jewett had been born into a prosperous family in South Berwick, Maine. She adored her father, Theodore H. Jewett, a country physician who encouraged her to make full use of the large library at home. Jewett published her first story in 1868 and was a regular contributor to the *Atlantic Monthly*. Her stories centred on women and their relationships with each other. They included *Deephaven* (1877), *A Country Doctor* (1884), and *The Queen's Twin and Other Stories* (1899), which included a narrative about an elderly woman's fantasy friendship with Queen Victoria. Her story *The Country of Pointed Firs* (1896) features a writer who goes to seek solitude in a small town but finds herself drawn into a deep friendship with her landlady. This text is considered one of the early classics of lesbian writing, portraying what was known as a romantic friendship. In her final year Jewett struck up a friendship with Willa CATHER, whom she encouraged to give up journalism and concentrate on fiction. Cather dedicated her novel *O Pioneers!* (1913) to Jewett. After Jewett's death, her companion Annie Adams Fields, who was fifteen years her junior, published Jewett's letters to her.

Jordan, June (1936–). A black, bisexual activist and writer, Jordan was born in Harlem of Jamaican immigrants and grew up in Brooklyn in an urban black context that taught her early on about racism, and influenced her political work. She was educated at Barnard College where she met and married a white student, Michael Meyer, from whom she was divorced eleven years later. Jordan studied architectural design and in 1964 worked with the visionary architect Buckminster Fuller. Her mother's suicide in 1966 was one of the tragedies in her life. In 1967 she began

her teaching career at the City College of New York. This was followed by several other teaching posts and in 1989 she became professor of African American Studies at the University of California, Berkeley. Jordan has written in a variety of media but is possibly best known for her poetry and her essays. Her 1989 collection of poetry, *Naming our Destiny*, gives full expression to her ideas of self-determination, her rejection of sexual labels, and her views of racial and ethnic violence in a variety of contexts. Her most explicit statement regarding sexual politics is 'A New Politics of Sexuality' (in *Technical Difficulties*, 1993) in which sexual independence and political commitment are presented as going hand in hand.

Juvonen, Helvi (1919–59). Finnish lesbian lyric poet who earned her living variously as a teacher, bank clerk, and translator. Living in Helsinki where she gathered a literary circle of like-minded friends including the lesbian poet Mirkka Elina REKOLA, Juvonen wrote poetry that was inspired both by religious mysticism and by a particular attitude to the nature of the universe. Juvonen's use of symbolic language made her one of the foremost Finnish poets of the 1950s. Although known to be lesbian her sexual identity had to remain hidden since homosexual acts, whether between men or between women, were illegal in Finland until 1971. Among Juvonen's collections of poetry are *Kääpiöpuu* (1949; *The Dwarf Tree*), *Kuningas Kultatakki* (1950; *King Goldcoat*), *Pohjajäätä* (1952; *Deep Ice*), *Päivästä päivään* (1954; *From Day to Day*), and *Kalliopohja* (1955; *Bedrock*).

K

Kallmaker, Karin (1960–). American lesbian writer who was brought up in a middle-class household in Central Valley, California. Aged sixteen she fell in love with another woman with whom she continues to live in Oakland. In 1995 the women had a child. Kallmaker gained a BA at the California State University at Sacramento. Inspired by the film *Desert Hearts*, based on the novel by Jane RULE, Kallmaker began to write popular lesbian romances, publishing with Naiad Press, one of the foremost lesbian presses in the USA. Her first novel was *In Every Port.* This was followed by *Touchwood* (1991), *Car Pool* (1993), *Painted Moon* (1994), *Paperback Romance* (1994), *Wild Things* (1996), *Embrace in Motion* (1997), *The Dawning* (1999), and *Frosting on the Cake* (2001).

Kay, Jackie (1961–). British black lesbian poet, playwright and novelist, Kay was born in Edinburgh and grew up in Glasgow. Following two collections of poetry, *The Adoption Papers* (1991) and *Other Lovers* (1993), both of which won literary prizes, Kay published her first novel *Trumpet* in 1998. *Trumpet* is a fictional construction of the ways in which various characters close to him/her come to terms with the death of Joss Moody, a jazz trumpet player who on his death is discovered to be a woman, having lived his life as a married man with an adopted son. The novel is based on the real-life story of Billy Tipton and deals with the question of what it means to live life as a man when you were born a woman. Its frame, as that of Kay's other work, is the issue of how a mixed-race or black person lives within a white, often racist society. Kay has also written a biographical account of the life of *Bessie Smith* (1997) as well as children's books.

Kellendonk, Frans (1951–90). Gay Dutch writer who died of AIDS and whose novel *Mystiek lichaam* (1986; *The Mystical Body*) caused a major uproar in the Dutch literary community. Featuring a gay protagonist, this family saga was considered homophobic and anti-Semitic by many.

Kenny, Maurice (1929–). Born in upstate New York, to a Mohawk Indian father and a part Seneca mother, the gay poet Kenny lived with his mother in New York after his parents separated when he was nine. Following a brief spell of juvenile delinquency he returned to live with his father, and began to identify with his father's Mohawk heritage. Discovering Walt Whitman as a teenager, Kenny was inspired to write poetry that drew upon the Native oral traditions associated with Native American culture. Kenny was educated at Butler University, in Indiana, at St Lawrence University in New York, and at New York University, where he studied with Louise Bogan. Following his first collection of poems he did not publish again until he settled in Brooklyn in 1967. His poems are strongly incantatory and have been referred to as 'chants'. His collections *North: Poems of Home* (1977) and *Dancing Back Strong the Nation* (1979) reflect his Native heritage. In 1976 Kenny came out as gay with 'Tinselled Buck: An Historical Study in Indian Homosexuality' and with the poem 'Winkte' in *Gay Sunshine*. His 1979 anthology *Only as Far as Brooklyn* combines both a homosexual and a Native Indian consciousness. In 1984 he published *The Mama Poems*, drawing on his childhood and family. For this volume he won the American Book Award. From the 1980s Kenny began to write a series of narrative poems drawing on the histories of particular individuals such as a Jesuit missionary martyred by the Mohawks in 1646 in *Blackrobe* (1982) and Molly Brant, sister of a Mohawk Chief, in *Tekonwatonti/Molly Brant – 1735–1795* (1992). Kenny is one of the most important Native American poets of the twentieth century. His other works include *Between Two Rivers: Selected Poems 1956–1984* (1987), *Wounds beneath the Flesh* (1987), and, most recently, *Tortured Skins and Other Fictions* (2000).

Kerouac, Jack (1922–69). Born in Lowell, Massachusetts, Kerouac had a working-class, French-Canadian background and did not begin to speak English until he went to school at the age of six. His older brother Gerald's death from rheumatic fever in 1926 is said to have influenced his life profoundly, leading to a constant search for the meanings of life and death. Kerouac moved to New York City in 1939, attending Horace Mann Prep School for a year before going to Columbia University on a football scholarship. After leaving Columbia in 1942 he joined the merchant marines, then enlisted in the US Navy but was discharged on psychiatric grounds. Through his first wife, Edie

Parker, he met Allen GINSBERG and William S. BURROUGHS in 1944. Two years later Neal Cassady joined their group and together they formed the nucleus of what is known as the 'Beat Generation'. Kerouac went on the road with Cassady, creating the 'Beat way of life' that involved a rejection of bourgeois values and a search for spiritual values. Following the annulment of his marriage to Parker, Kerouac married Joan Haverty but left her after seven months when he found out that she was pregnant. He never acknowledged their daughter Jan. Kerouac had a number of male lovers including Allen Ginsberg, William Burroughs, and Gore Vidal, but both his relationships with men and with women were doomed. Kerouac's most famous novel, *On the Road* (1957), written in three weeks, became the epitome of the Beat Generation. His writing style relied on improvisation and spontaneity, based on an analogy to jazz music. Kerouac wrote a set of eight novels, designed to be connecting stories featuring the 'Legend of Dulouz', the name he had given himself. His works include *The Town and the City* (1950), *The Dharma Bums* (1958), *Tristessa* (1960), *The Scripture of the Golden Eternity* (1960), *Book of Dreams* (1961), *Visions of Gerard* (1963), and *Visions of Cody* (1969). An alcoholic, Kerouac died in 1969 from complications related to his addiction.

Kleist, Heinrich von (1777–1811). German playwright, born in Frankfurt an der Oder, Kleist was the oldest son of a Prussian army captain. His parents died when he was in his early teens and at the age of fifteen he entered the army at Potsdam, participating in campaigns against the French Revolutionary armies in the Rhineland. Kleist's sexuality has been the subject of recent critical attention; it is assumed that he began having gay relationships while he was in the army, forming in particular life-long close friendships with Ernst von Pfuel and Rühle von Lilienstern. Throughout his life

Kleist had a variety of unconsummated attachments to women and various close relationships with men. In 1799 Kleist resigned his commission and embarked upon the life of a student at Frankfurt University. He got engaged to Wilhelmine von Zenge but left shortly afterwards for the town of Würzburg to seek medical treatment for what seems to have been a sexual disorder. The treatment failed and Kleist was beset by moral and emotional qualms. He broke off his engagement, and a long period of illnesses and breakdowns ensued, coinciding with a period of enormous creative activity. Until his death in 1811 he wrote seven plays, eight novellas, which were published in two volumes, as well as essays on literature and art, poetry, and journalistic pieces. His work was inflected by his preoccupation with the relationship between the individual and society, transgressive sexuality, and destruction. Best known for his play *Der zerbrochene Krug* (1806; *The Broken Jug*), his other works include his first tragic drama *Die Familie Schroffenstein* (1803; *The Schroffenstein Family*); the plays *Amphitryon* and *Penthesilea* (1807); novellas such as *Die Verlobung in St Domingo* (*The Engagement in St Domingo*); *Das Erdbeben in Chili* (*The Earthquake in Chili*); and *The Marquise von O.* In 1811 Kleist entered a suicide pact with Helene Vogel whom he shot before turning his pistol on himself.

Klepfisz, Irena (1941–). Lesbian US poet who was born a Polish Jew in Warsaw during the Second World War and who emigrated to New York in 1949. Klepfisz was educated at City College, New York, and at the University of Chicago, receiving her PhD in English in 1970. She has taught English, Yiddish, and Women's Studies. Her writings have been dominated both by her lesbian and by her Jewish identity. In her collection of poetry *Keeper of Accounts* (1982) Klepfisz articulates her cultural heritage as a Jewish woman of having and wanting to keep

alive memories of both lesbian and Jewish experiences. Klepfisz's poetry has also been collected in *Different Enclosures: Poetry and Prose of Irena Klepfisz* (1985). Klepfisz was one of the founding editors of *Conditions*, a feminist journal. She is also a regular contributor to lesbian feminist journals such as *Sinister Wisdom*. Other writings by Klepfisz include *Periods of Stress* (1977), *Dreams of an Insomniac* (1990), *Jewish Women's Call for Peace* (1990), *A Few Words in the Mother Tongue* (1990), and *The Tribe of Dina* (1992; co-edited).

Krafft-Ebing, Richard, Freiherr von (1840–1902). German-Austrian psychiatrist and sexologist, born in Mannheim to Franz and Klara Antonia Mittermaier, whose father was a famous professor of Law and prosecutor in Heidelberg where Krafft-Ebing himself later studied Medicine. Krafft-Ebing was married and had two sons and a daughter but little is known either about his private life or his therapeutic practice. His abiding importance for lesbians and gays is his volume *Psychopathia sexualis* (1886, expanded and revised repeatedly between 1886 and 1924) in which he attempted to classify various forms of sexual deviation including, prominently, homosexuality, which he represented as innate rather than as a sin. In his writings on homosexuality he drew on his own patients as well as letters and autobiographical accounts of homosexuals with whom he had no direct contact. The case histories that illustrate his classifications are rather melodramatic and frequently suggest degenerative family histories, with astonishing numbers of relatives presented as also having suffered from various forms of deviant behaviour, mental illness, or problem. But Krafft-Ebing was important in attempts to reform the infamous Paragraph 175 in Germany and he supported the homosexual rights movement founded by Magnus HIRSCHFELD in Berlin. He refused to regard homosexuality as immoral and came to accept homosexual desire as natural, i.e. as anchored in nature rather than in some form of moral depravity.

Kramer, Larry (1935–). US writer and gay rights activist who was born into a middle-class family in Bridgeport, Connecticut. Following his BA at Yale University he spent a year in the army before embarking on a career in the entertainment industry where he worked first for the William Morris Agency and then for Columbia Pictures. His first piece of professional writing was a screenplay of D.H. Lawrence's *Women in Love*, which Kramer produced. He received an Academy Award nomination for this film. Kramer's novel *Faggots* (1978), which pre-dated the AIDS crisis, became notorious for its condemnation of a gay community focused on sex rather than on love and long-term relationships. The novel was successfully reissued in 1987 when it became a bestseller. With the advent of the AIDS crisis, Kramer emerged as a powerful spokesman for gay rights. In 1981 he co-founded Gay Men's Health Crisis (GMHC) in New York. This was the first community-based AIDS organization in the USA. Kramer's predilection for campaigning, which came into conflict with those in the lesbian and gay communities who saw themselves as service providers to their own rather than as pre-eminently campaigners, led to a rift between Kramer and others in the management group of GMHC and resulted in Kramer co-founding ACT UP (AIDS Coalition to Unleash Power) in 1988. Since then, both through journalism and through his playwriting, Kramer has vigorously campaigned as an AIDS activist, prompted in part by his own HIV positivity. In 1986 he published *The Normal Heart*, a play that details the fraught history of GMHC, focusing on the character of Ned Weeks, an AIDS activist. The play was an instant international success, resulting in a series of awards including the Dramatists Guild Marton Award and the City Lights Award. The play was followed by *The Destiny of Me* (1992), which again focused on Ned Weeks but this time interwove the narrative of his activism with an engagement with Weeks's family history. Kramer's journalistic writings on HIV/AIDS appeared in 1989 in *Reports from the Holocaust: The Making of an AIDS Activist*. Describing himself as a 'message queen' Kramer has always insisted that since the arrival of AIDS he has not wanted to engage with any other topic than the question of how to fight HIV/AIDS. His vigorous campaigning has not always endeared him to the gay community but he is recognized as the perhaps most important person in activating politicized responses to the AIDS crisis within the gay community.

Kushner, Tony (1956–). Gay US playwright, born in New York City and raised in Lake Charles, Louisiana, Kushner now lives in Brooklyn, New York. He was educated at Columbia University where he graduated in 1978 and attended the New York University graduate theatre programme. Between 1979 and 1985 Kushner worked as a switchboard operator at the United Nations Plaza Hotel. In 1985 Kushner received a National Endowment for the Arts fellowship. He was assistant director of the St Louis Repertory Theatre from 1985 until 1986, and then artistic director of the New York Theatre Workshop from 1987 until 1988. Kushner wrote a series of plays in the 1980s but he gained instant recognition with *Angels in America: A Gay Fantasia on National Themes*, the first part of which, 'Millennium Approaches', was published in 1992 and gained the Pulitzer Prize for Drama and the Tony Award for Best Play. Part II of *Angels in America*, entitled 'Perestroika', was first performed in 1991, and published in 1992. It won the Tony Award for Best Play in 1994. These two plays set Kushner up as one of the most pre-eminent contemporary US playwrights, in particular around the theme of HIV/AIDS. Kushner is a member of ACT UP (AIDS Coalition to Unleash Power). Among his other plays are *La Fin de la Baleine: An Opera for the Apocalypse* (produced 1982), *Yes Yes No No: The Solace-of-Solstice, Apogee/Perigee, Bestial/Celestial Holiday Show* (produced 1985), *The Heavenly Theater* (produced 1986), *In Great Eliza's Golden Time* (produced 1986), *The Illusion* (adapted from the play by Pierre Corneille, produced 1988), and *A Bright Room Called Day* (produced 1990). He has won numerous awards and fellowships, and has taught at various US universities including Yale and Princeton.

Kuzmin, Mikhail Alekseyevich (1872–1936). Gay Russian writer, playwright, and poet, born in Saratov who initially became interested in music and the theatre through attending local operettas. In 1891 he attended Nikolai Rimsky-Korsakov's composition classes at the St Petersburg Conservatory where he stayed for three years. He also learnt German and Italian. In 1895 he travelled to Egypt with his mother where they remained in Alexandria until early 1896. He then went on to Italy. Kuzmin came to accept his homosexuality through the aid of his childhood friend Geogy Vasilevich Chicherin who became foreign minister under Lenin in 1918. Chicherin introduced Kuzmin to Mir iskoustva (the World of Art), an artistic circle centring on Sergei Diaghilev that had a large gay membership and favoured dandyism. In 1905 Kuzmin published his first play *Istoriia rytsaria*

d'Alessio (*The History of the Knight Alessio*). Kuzmin's *Aleksandriiskie pesni* (*Alexandrian Songs*) and his novel *Kril'ya* (1906; *Wings*) were published in the journal *Vesy* (*The Scales*). *Kril'ya* was one of the first Russian novels to deal explicitly with homosexuality. In 1907 Kuzmin published the play *Opasnaia predostorozhnost* (*Dangerous Precaution*), followed by *Seti* (*Nets*), a collection of poetry, in 1908. Much of his work dealt with the love for young men. His own first great love was the poet Vsevolod Knyazev whom Kuzmin met in 1910. Knyazev committed suicide in 1913. Subsequently Kuzmin lived with the poet Yury Yurkin. In 1917 when the Communists came to power, Kuzmin sat on the Praesidium of the association of artists in Petrograd. In 1918 he helped found the daily newspaper *Zhizn iskuostva* (*The Life of Art*) and was one of its editors, together with Viktor Skhlovsky. Kuzmin's writings include *Kuranty lyubvi* (1910; *The Carillon of Love*), a collections of poems set to music; *Osennie ozera* (1912; *Lakes in Autumn*); the play *Venetsianskie bezumtsy* (1915; *The Venetian Madcaps*); and the collections of poetry *Ekho* (1921; *Echo*), *Paraboly* (1922; *Parabolas*), and *Forel' razbivaet led* (1929; *The Trout Breaks Ice*). Kuzmin's own work fell out of favour under Trotsky. In 1934 same-sex relationships were declared illegal in the Soviet Union. Kuzmin died of pneumonia in 1939. Two years later Yury Yurkin and many other writers were arrested and killed under the Stalinist regime.

L

Ladies of Llangollen, the *see* Butler, Lady Eleanor

Larsen, Nella (1891–1964). Born in Chicago, Illinois, to a West Indian father and a Danish mother, Larsen experienced ambivalence throughout her life concerning her dual heritage. Following studies at Fisk University and the University of Copenhagen, she worked as a nurse at Tuskegee, Alabama, before moving to work at hospitals in New York. After a training course she became a librarian at the New York Public Library. In 1919 she married the physicist Elmer S. Imes, and they became active members of the Harlem intellectual elite. She began to write children's literature but her great breakthrough occurred in the late 1920s when she published *Quicksand* (1928) for which she received the Harlem Foundation Bronze Award, and *Passing* (1929). She was the first African American woman to receive a Guggenheim fellowship, which she used to spend a year writing in Europe. On her return to the USA, she faced both a sensationalist press preoccupied with the charge of plagiarism related to her short story 'Sanctuary', a charge she denied, and an increasingly rocky marriage that ended in divorce in 1933. It is unclear whether or not Larsen continued to write after this; for the remaining decades of her life she worked as a nurse at various New York City hospitals,

forgotten by the literary world. She died alone in her apartment. The 1980s saw a revival of interest in her work, prompted by both a feminist and a Black Studies rediscovery of her work. Within this context the issue of her representation of female sexuality came to prominence, partly due to renewed theoretical interests in the idea of passing in lesbian and gay circles. The intense relationship between the two central female characters in *Passing* may be described as lesbian, and her representation of women of mixed race, caught in the dilemma of unstable identities that seek to negotiate hostile worlds, has found a ready reception in lesbian circles.

Lavery, Bryony (1947–). Contemporary lesbian British playwright who, like other lesbian playwrights such as Tash FAIRBANKS and Sarah DANIELS, began to develop her career in the late 1970s when feminist and lesbian theatre were gaining increasing prominence in the British theatre scene. A prolific playwright, many of Lavery's plays have an explicitly lesbian content, often playing with non-naturalistic elements in their exploration of identities, sexual and otherwise. However, she does not want to be seen as a playwright writing for a lesbian audience only. Her plays include *Helen and Her Friends* (1978), *Bag* (1979), *Family Album* (1980), *Missing* (1981), *Hot Time* (1984), *Calamity*

(1983), *Origin of the Species* (1984), *Witchcraze* (1985), *The Headless Body* (1987), *Puppet States* (1988), *Two Marias* (1989), *Kitchen Matters* (1990), *Her Aching Heart* (1990), *Wicked* (1990), and *Flight* (1991). Her plays have been variously published including in the collection *Her Aching Heart, Two Marias, Wicked* (1991), in volume six of the 'Plays by Women' series published by Methuen, and in a collection of plays entitled *Herstory* (1991). Lavery was resident playwright at the Unicorn Theatre for Children in 1986–7. Her work for children includes *The Zulu Hut Club* (1983), *Sore Points* (1986), *Madagascar* (1987), and *The Dragon Wakes* (1988). She has produced some cabaret work including *Female Trouble* (1981), *More Female Trouble* (1982), *The Wandsworth Warmers* (1984), and *The Wandsworth Warmers – Unbridled Passion* (1986). From 1989 until 1991 Lavery was Artistic Director of Gay Sweatshop, the British-based lesbian and gay theatre company. She has also been a tutor in playwriting at Birmingham University. Her play *Frozen* won the 1999 Barclays Theatre Award for Best Play. In 2001 her most recent play *A Wedding Story* was staged in Birmingham and London. Lavery is an extremely prolific writer who has done scripts for radio as well as for the stage. Her work includes adaptations of novels and other texts.

Lawrence, D.H. (1885–1930). English novelist, dramatist, and short-story writer. The son of a Nottinghamshire coal miner and a strong-willed mother, Lawrence grew up in poverty in Nottingham. His mother encouraged him to pursue a higher education, and having successfully sat an examination, he won a full scholarship that enabled him to study at Nottingham University. In his final school years, and while at university, he was involved with Jessie Chambers. Following that relationship he had an affair with Alice Dax, the wife of one of his professors and a mother

of three children. She ended the relationship with him. Lawrence then eloped with Frieda Weekley who came from an aristocratic German background. Although their relationship was stormy it endured through the rest of his life. Lawrence also had relationships with men, and in his writings repeatedly portrayed both lesbians and gay men, in particular in *Women in Love* (1920), which is partly based on Lawrence's relationship with Katherine MANSFIELD and her husband John Middleton Murry. Lawrence's background placed him at odds with the much more middle-class Bloomsbury Group whom he knew. He was the working-class 'other' to their high modernism. His writings played out issues of class and gender within a framework that celebrated a certain brash, supposedly 'earthy', macho masculinity against a frustrating middle-class and/or domineering femininity. Cross-class and cross-gender relationships were constructed as equally fraught. His many novels included *The White Peacock* (1911), *Sons and Lovers* (1913), *The Rainbow* (1915), *Aaron's Rod* (1922), *The Plumed Serpent* (1926), and *Lady Chatterley's Lover* (1928), which gained notoriety through the obscenity trial to which it was subjected. Its unexpurgated edition in English was not published until 1961. Lawrence spent the last part of his life travelling with his wife Frieda to Italy, France, Mexico, and the USA. His health had never been good and he died in 1930 of tuberculosis in Vence, France.

Le Guin, Ursula K. (1929–). Born in Berkeley, California, as the daughter of the anthropologist Alfred Kroeber and the writer Theodora Kroeber, Le Guin attended Radcliffe College and Columbia University, before marrying the historian Charles Le Guin with whom she has three children. They live in Portland, Oregon. Le Guin is best known for her science fiction. She became established as a feminist science fiction writer in the 1970s and 1980s. Apart from the short story

'Quoits' (in *Searoads*, 1991) she has not directly addressed lesbianism. However, her best-known novel, *The Left Hand of Darkness* (1969), features a world in which everyone is human but androgynous and sexually neuter for most of the time. For a few days each month the characters become sexually active and can be either male or female. This kind of experimentation with sexual identity, which was a popular theme in (lesbian) feminist sci-fi of the 1970s and 1980s and had counterparts in the works of Marge PIERCY and Joanna RUSS, for example, has become one of the sources and antecedents of queer, the theory and practice of a particular sexual politics of the 1990s.

Lear, Edward (1812–88). British artist, humorist and traveller who was the twentieth child of Ann and Jeremiah Lear, born in London and educated at home, mainly by his sister Ann. Lear suffered from bouts of depression, epilepsy, asthma, and bronchitis throughout his life. From the age of fifteen he began to make money from drawing and painting. He worked as a draughtsman for the Zoological Society, illustrating a book about parrots. In 1832 the 13th Earl of Derby commissioned him to create a collection of drawings of rare birds in the menagerie at Knowsley Hall on Merseyside. The earl's patronage enabled Lear to travel extensively in Italy and Greece. The drawings and sketches he produced during these travels became part of his travel books, *Views in Rome and its Environs* (1841), *Sketches of Rome* (1842), *Illustrated Excursions in Italy* (1846), and *Journals of a Landscape Painter in Greece and Albania* (1851). His work is collected both in the Tate Gallery and the Victoria and Albert Museum. Lear entertained the Earl of Derby's children with nonsense limericks that were eventually published as *A Book of Nonsense* in 1846 under the pseudonym Derry Down Derry. Lear's ill health led the Earl of Derby to organize a subscription for him so that he could travel to Rome where Lear stayed for ten years. He supported himself by drawing and selling paintings. In 1845 he met the 22-year-old Chichester Fortesque with whom he had a close friendship. Although Fortesque married they remained friends until Lear's death. In 1846 he gave drawing lessons to Queen Victoria at Osborne House and at Buckingham Palace. In 1848, when he was in Malta, he met Franklin Lushington, a barrister and brother of the Government Secretary in Malta. They toured Greece together and Lear developed a passionate attachment to Lushington that the latter did not reciprocate. However, they remained friends throughout Lear's life. Lear returned to London and studied painting at the Royal Academy where he met and grew friendly with Holman Hunt. When Lushington was appointed to the Supreme Court of Justice in the Ionian Islands in 1855, Lear accompanied him and set up home there. He employed a servant, Giogio Kokali, who stayed with him for twenty-seven years. Lear spent the next two decades travelling around the Mediterranean and the Middle East. He met John Addington SYMONDS for whose daughter Janet he composed 'The Owl and the Pussycat'. In 1870 he published *Nonsense Songs, Stories, Botany, and Alphabets*. This was followed, in 1871, by *More Nonsense Rhymes*. In 1872 he published *More Nonsense Pictures, Rhymes, Botany etc.*, and in 1876 *Laughable Lyrics*. Lear eventually settled in San Remo, building Casa Emily, named after Emily Tennyson, the wife of the Poet Laureate. Lear had become very friendly with Emily after his sister Ann's death in 1861. In 1873–4 he made a year-long trip to India and Ceylon. His final trip to England occurred in 1880 when he stayed at Lushington's home in Norfolk Square, and mounted an exhibition of his work. After his death Lady Strachey published

Letters to Edward Lear (1907) and *Later Letters to Edward Lear* (1911).

Leaton, Anne (1932–). Lesbian US writer who was born in Texas, attended university, and then spent twenty years travelling and working in Europe, the Middle East, South Africa, and Canada before settling in Fort Worth, Texas. She has written many radio plays, short stories, and poems, mostly with a lesbian content and featuring lesbian characters within a heterosexually defined world. Her works include the novel *Good Friends, Just* (1983), *Pearl* (1985), *Blackbird, Bye, Bye* (1989), and a collection of short stories, *Mayakowsky, My Love* (1984).

Leavitt, David (1961–). Born in Pittsburgh, the son of a professor and a liberal political activist, Leavitt grew up in Palo Alto, California. He was educated at Yale University and graduated with a BA in English in 1983. While at university he published his first story, 'Territory', in the *New Yorker*, followed by another one, 'Out Here'. His first collection of stories, *Family Dancing*, appeared in 1984 and was nominated for the National Book Critics' Circle Award as well as the PEN-Faulkner Award. This collection interweaves gay issues with middle-class US life, and established Leavitt as a gay writer. His novel *The Lost Language of Cranes* (1986), a father-and-son coming-out story, was made into a film for the BBC. His next novel *Equal Affections* (1989) also featured a gay central character. The text has often been read as autobiographical though Leavitt dismisses such readings. In 1989 Leavitt received a Guggenheim fellowship and spent time in Barcelona as foreign-writer-in-residence at the Institute of Catalan Letters. Leavitt's second collection of short stories, *A Place I've Never Been* (1990), about Americans in Europe, was followed by the novel *While England Sleeps* (1993). This novel, centring on a politically inflected homosexual romance between an upper-class

writer and a communist worker in 1930s England, became the object of some debate when Stephen SPENDER alleged that it had been based on his memoir *World within World* (1951) and sued Leavitt. Leavitt's publisher agreed to withdraw the novel and publish it with some revisions. Since then Leavitt has continued to produce various texts including *The Page Turner* (1999) and *Marble Quilt* (2001). He has also co-edited *The Penguin Book of Gay Short Stories* and *Pages Passed from Hand to Hand: The Hidden Tradition of Homosexual Literature in English from 1748 to 1914* (1998).

Leduc, Violette (1907–72). Born in Arras as the illegitimate daughter of Berthe and the son of the couple Berthe worked for, the lesbian French autobiographer and writer Leduc was close to her grandmother Fideline and her maternal aunt Laure during her childhood. Leduc's formal education was interrupted by the First World War after which she entered the Collège de Douai where she had lesbian relationships with a fellow pupil and a music instructor who, as a consequence of the affair, was expelled. In 1926 Leduc went to Paris and enrolled in the Lycée Racine. She failed her baccalaureate and began working as a telephone operator and secretary at the Plon publishing house. The gay writer Maurice Sachs encouraged her to write, and from 1932 she began a freelance career as a journalist and writer. In 1939 she married Gabriel Mercier who was then drafted into the army. After the Second World War Leduc divorced Mercier. In 1946 Leduc published her first novel, *L'Asphyxie* (*In the Prison of Her Skin*), aided by Simone de BEAUVOIR, whom she had met and with whom she had fallen in love. De Beauvoir did not reciprocate emotionally but mentored Leduc as a writer. Leduc's infatuation with de Beauvoir found expression in her novel *L'Affamée* (1948; *Starved*). Leduc published several other novels including *Ravages* (1955; *Devastation*) and *La*

Vieille Fille et le Mort (1958; *The Old Maid and the Dead Man*) before she achieved acclaim and commercial success with the autobiographical *La Bâtarde* in 1964. One section of this novel, entitled 'Thérèse et Isabelle', was removed prior to publication due to its explicit lesbian sex scenes. In 1966 Leduc sent this section as a pink pamphlet to Janet FLANNER. It was published separately in the same year and made into a film in 1968. The commercial success of *La Bâtarde* enabled Leduc to buy a house in Faucon in the Vaucluse region. There she wrote the second and third volumes of her autobiography, *La Folie en tête* (1970; *Mad in Pursuit*) and *La Chasse à l'amour* (1972; *The Hunt for Love*). She developed breast cancer of which she died after two operations in 1972. Leduc was a passionate woman whose infatuations with both women and, occasionally, gay men like Jean GENET were often not met or not met with the ardour she invested in them. In lesbian circles her work has not received the critical attention it deserves.

Lee, Vernon (1856–1935). Born Violet Paget near Boulogne in France, the lesbian essayist, novelist, and short-story writer Lee came from a privileged, cosmopolitan background and spent her youth travelling around Europe being educated by various governesses. Interested in writing from an early age she completed the *Biographie d'une monnaie* (1879; *Biography of Money*) in French when she was fourteen. Publishing in *Frazer's Magazine* in 1878 and 1879 she adopted the male pseudonym Vernon Lee, a common occurrence among Victorian women writers who thought that a male pseudonym would aid the publication and acceptance of their ideas. In her writings Lee on the whole did not engage with the issue of sexuality and passionate female friendships although her drama *Ariadne in Mantua* (1903) featured a cross-dressing heroine. Instead she focused on aesthetics, travel, art and artists. Her *Studies of the Eighteenth Century in Italy* (1880) brought her some acclaim and her essay collections *Belcaro* (1881) and *Euphorion* (1884) were also well received. She became well known for her impressionistic travel sketches that attempted to portray the *genius loci* or 'spirit of places'. Between 1897 and 1925 she produced seven volumes of such sketches, of which the perhaps best known one is *Genius Loci: Notes on Places* (1899). Lee's collection of aesthetic essays, *Beauty and Ugliness and Other Studies in Psychological Aesthetics* (1912), introduced the notion of 'empathy' into aesthetics. *The Beautiful* (1913) continued this theme. Not all her writings were equally successful. Her first novel, *Miss Brown* (1884), was not well received. Neither was her thinly disguised portrayed of Henry James, 'Lady Tal' (in *Vanitas*, 1892). Her pacifist trilogy *Satan the Waster* (1920) was condemned on publication though it received a better press when it was re-issued in 1930. Throughout her life Lee had emotional attachments to women. Her relationship with her companion Annie Meyers, which ended in 1881, was followed by a close friendship with Mary Robinson between 1881 and 1887. When Robinson married James Darmsteter, Lee was devastated. Lee then began a new friendship, with Clementina (Kit) Anstruther-Thomson, which lasted from 1887 until 1897, a period in which Lee was both very productive as a writer and seemingly happy in her personal life. Lee spent most of her life in Europe, partly to avoid scandals about her lesbianism. In Paris she was a frequent visitor to Natalie Clifford BARNEY's famous rue Jacob salon.

Lehmann, Rosamond (1901–90). UK novelist and short-story writer, born in Buckinghamshire, the daughter of the Liberal MP R.C. Lehmann and of Alice Lehmann. Educated privately and at Girton College, Cambridge, where she studied modern languages, Lehmann came to public attention with her first novel,

Dusty Answer (1927), which deals with the sexual awakening of 18-year-old Judith Earle, and was the first of several of Lehmann's novels to explore female sexuality and lesbianism. In *Dusty Answer* Judith, who in her childhood focuses on the family who live next door, becomes passionately attached to Jennifer, a beautiful fellow student at Cambridge. Jennifer rejects Judith in favour of an older, more 'mannish' lesbian, leaving Judith, who in turn rejects a proposal of marriage, to face an uncertain future. Lehmann herself had two marriages that ended in divorce and a long-term friendship with the poet C. Day Lewis. Lehmann's second novel *A Note in Music* (1930) dealt with the topic of homosexuality. She then produced two novels featuring the character Olivia Curtis, *Invitation to the Waltz* (1932) and *The Weather in the Streets* (1936). *The Ballad and the Source* (1944) presented adult passion through the eyes of a child. Rebecca Landon, the child, and Sybil Jardine from this novel re-appear in Lehmann's much later novel *A Sea-Grape Tree* (1976). After *The Echoing Grove* (1953) she did not produce a novel for some years. Her daughter Sally's unexpected death from poliomyelitis in Java in 1958 had a profound influence on Lehmann who became preoccupied with spirituality and mysticism. *The Swan in the Evening: Fragments of an Inner Life* (1967) was a response to that event. A collection of Lehmann's short stories, *The Gypsy's Baby*, appeared in 1946. She also translated Jean COCTEAU's *Les Enfants terribles*. Lehmann's interest for lesbian readers lies in her depiction of lesbian relationships and of homosexuality in her earlier work. In the 1980s she was rediscovered by feminist critics, and many of her novels were re-issued by Virago.

Lewis, Matthew G. (1775–1818). English writer of the Gothic whose novel *The Monk* (1795) brought him literary acclaim. Lewis was born to well-to-do, loving parents, and acted as emissary

between his mother and father from the age of six, when his parents divorced. He was educated at Westminster School and at Christ Church College, Oxford. At eighteen he left university and went to the Hague to pursue a diplomatic career but while there he completed *The Monk*, which caused something of a scandal on publication. The novel focuses on male attraction. Ambrosio, the hero of the novel and a monk, becomes involved with a young male novice to whom he is greatly attracted. The 'dilemma' of this attraction is resolved by the novice turning out to be a woman. *The Monk* belongs to the genre of the Gothic that enabled the exploration of divergent and transgressive sexualities and was therefore particularly suited to the representation of same-sex love. In his own life, Lewis may never have had sexual relationships with other men but he was deeply attached to William Kelly, an author, with whom he corresponded and whom he included in his will. Lewis was appointed to Parliament and served as an MP from 1796 to 1802. He was censured in Parliament for *The Monk*. He spent his time writing other texts. Of these *The Castle Spectre* (1797) became a successful stage play.

Lezama Lima, José (1910–76). Cuban writer who was born in Havana and, apart from two short trips to Mexico and to Jamaica, never left that city. In 1938 he gained a Law degree from the University of Havana. His first poetic composition, *Muerte de Narciso* (1937; *Death of Narcissus*) signalled the beginning of a long career as one of Cuba's leading writers. Its baroque style and allegorical symbolism was replicated in the many other collections of poems and essays Lezama published. He also founded and edited a number of important literary journals such as *Orígenes* (1944–56). However, it was his novel *Paradiso* (1966) that brought Lezama international fame. The novel centres on the childhood and adolescence of Jose Cemí, and his friendship with two boys, Fronesis and Foción, with whom he has long discussions, including about homosexuality. In this novel homosexuality is constructed as depraved and set against a more desirable heterosexuality. The novel's complete lack of commitment to the Cuban Revolution and its frank discussions of homosexuality in chapters nine and ten in particular made it a daring text at a time when the Cuban regime was conducting purges of homosexuals. Despite significant obstacles and censorship the book was published. Before his death Lezama was working on a new novel entitled *Oppiano Licario*, which remained incomplete and which was published posthumously in 1977. This novel took up as its central protagonist one of the characters from *Paradiso*, Fronesis, now living in Paris and attracting both women and men. In this novel homosexuality was no longer opposed to heterosexuality but constructed as a split subject, divided into the 'good' and the 'bad' homosexual. While these representations of homosexuality remain problematic, one of the significances of the novels is that they discussed homosexuality in some considerable detail, thus allowing the subject to surface.

Lister, Anne (1791–1840). Lesbian English upper-class woman who lived at Shibden Hall, Halifax, West Yorkshire, and whose faithfully recorded lesbian relationships were described in her diary of several million words, which was only published in excerpts in the 1980s. Lister was one of six children, born to Jeremy Lister, who served as a captain in the American War of Independence, and Rebecca Battle, a woman from the East Riding in Yorkshire. All the family's sons had died by 1813, which meant that Anne inherited Shibden Hall. She took up residence there in 1815 with her unmarried Uncle James and Aunt Anne. Lister was allowed great freedom and known in the area as 'Gentleman Jack' because of her masculine attire and behaviour. By 1817

when she was twenty-six she had clearly come to terms with her sexuality and had no difficulty in attracting a number of women lovers with whom she had passionate sexual affairs. An early relationship with M (Marianne, or Mary Lawton, née Belcombe), which had begun in 1812, was reciprocated and continued for several years despite M's marriage to Charles Lawton of Lawton Hall, Cheshire. Another relationship from the same period was with Isabella Norcliffe who, like Anne, remained unmarried. After her uncle's death in 1826 Anne Lister became a woman of independent means, which enabled her to travel widely. The life companion upon whom she eventually settled was a Miss Anne Walker, a local heiress who lived at Lightcliffe on the outskirts of Halifax. Once her domestic life was organized Lister started travelling again. In 1840, while in Russia, she contracted a virulent fever and died at Koutalis near the Caucasian mountains. A distraught Anne Walker ensured the return of her body to England. Lister's diaries were written in code whenever she wanted to remain private. It was not until the publication of Helena Whitbread's *I Know My Own Heart* (1988) that parts of Lister's diaries became available to a wider public. This was followed by Muriel Green's *Miss Lister of Shibden Hall* (1992) and Whitbread's *No Priest but Love* (1992). Apart from providing a fascinating account of provincial life of the early nineteenth century, Lister's diaries are important in revealing a clearly defined lesbian identity, including a fully lived lesbian sexuality, at a time when the term 'lesbian' was not common currency.

Livia, Anna (1955–). Born in Dublin, Anna Livia spent her childhood in Africa before returning to London in her teens. Her schooling included a boys' boarding school in the Swazi mountains. She studied French and Italian at university, taught French and English for a while at the University of Avignon, and lived in

London as a radical lesbian and writer. She then moved to the San Francisco Bay Area. Anna Livia came to public attention in the 1980s when she published several successful volumes of novels and short stories. Her publications include *Relatively Norma* (1982), a novel which was very successful. It features Minnie, a lesbian feminist from Brixton in London who goes to Australia (where Livia's own mother lives) in order to come out to her mother Beryl, but finds herself embroiled in her mother's quest for a new identity. This was followed by *Accommodation Offered* (1985), her second novel, and by a collection of short stories entitled *Incidents Involving Warmth* (1986). Her other writings include *Saccharine Cyanide* (1990), *Angel and the Perverts* (1995), which she translated from French, and *Bruised Fruit* (1999). She also edited *A Perilous Advantage: The Best of Natalie Clifford Barney* (1992) for which she translated Barney's texts. Her novel *Minimax* (1992) features Natalie Barney and Renée VIVIEN in a comic take on vampire life and the notion of the lesbian as vampire.

Lorca, Federico García (1898–1936). Renowned Spanish poet and dramatist whose homosexuality was suppressed until well after his untimely death at the hands of General Franco's fascistic supporters. Born in Fuente Vaqueros into a wealthy land-owning family, Lorca grew up in comfortable surroundings. In his early years he showed an interest in puppetry, music, and painting. In 1909 the family moved to Granada where Lorca studied music with Don Antonio Segura Mesa, a disciple of Verdi's. Granada's population of gypsies, who have lived in the caves of Sacromonte for centuries, inspired his *Gypsy Ballads* (1924–7; published in 1928) and his *Poem of the Deep Song* (1921; published in 1931). In 1919 Lorca went to study at the University of Madrid, living at the Residencia de Estudiantes, a student residence for gifted students

founded in 1910. There he met Salvador Dali, with whom he fell deeply and unhappily in love, and Luis Buñuel. Following a somewhat mysterious emotional crisis, brought on apparently by Dali's rejection and by a stormy relationship with a young sculptor, Emilio Aladrén Perojo, Lorca travelled to New York in 1927. This trip inspired a series of poems, later collected under the title *Poet in New York* (1940). From New York, Lorca went to Cuba for three months and, liberated by his geographical distance from his family and Spain, he began writing his most openly homosexual work, 'Ode to Walt Whitman', in which he contrasts a pure, de-sexualized homosexuality epitomized by Whitman with the depraved sexuality of effeminate gay men. He also wrote two incomplete pieces of 'impossible' theatre, *The Public* and *The Destruction of Sodom*. Of the latter only the first page survives. Two scenes apart, which appeared in a Spanish magazine, *The Public* was not published until 1978, and then in incomplete form. In 1930 Lorca returned to Spain. Between 1930 and 1936 he completed some of his best-known dramatic works including *The Blood Wedding, Lament for Ignacio Sáchez Mejías, Yerma,* and *The House of Bernarda Alba*. He also wrote his *Sonnets of Dark Love* (1935), which remained unpublished until the appearance of a clandestine edition of 250 copies in 1983. In 1936 generals Franco and Yoldi Orgaz seized control of Las Palmas, which marked the beginning of the bloody Civil War that lasted until 1939. Lorca was arrested by fascist extremists, and two or three days later shot. The precise circumstances of his death remain unclear but his homosexuality may have played a role in his arrest. It was not until the 1980s that it was possible to discuss Lorca's homosexuality or its impact on his work.

Lorde, Audre (1934–92). Lesbian poet, novelist, essayist, and feminist political activist who was born in New York City of Grenadian parents. She was educated at Hunter College and Columbia University where she completed a Masters degree in library studies in 1961. Following initial work as a librarian, from 1968 she held a variety of academic positions including at John Jay College of Criminal Justice where she fought for the establishment of a Black Studies department. She became Professor of English at Hunter College in 1980. Her marriage in 1962 to Edwin Ashley Rollins, by whom she had two children, Elizabeth and Jonathan, ended in divorce in 1970. Subsequently she had several long-term relationships with women. She died of breast cancer in 1992. Among her writings, three texts from the 1980s in particular generated much public response, identifying her as a key figure in lesbian feminist writing. *The Cancer Journals* (1980) recorded her experiences of breast cancer. Like the British lesbian photographer and autobiographer Jo Spence, Lorde dealt with breast cancer in a creatively transformative manner at a time when women's engagement with their bodies was increasingly prominent. Lorde's novel *Zami: A New Spelling of My Name* (1982), which as a 'biomythography' simultaneously explored issues of racial and sexual identity, established Lorde as an important black lesbian writer. Her collection of essays, *Sister Outsider* (1984), included several of her most frequently anthologized essays including one on 'The Uses of the Erotic' and 'The Master's Tools will Never Dismantle the Master's House'. The former constituted her intervention in the pornography debates from the 1970s and early 1980s; the latter is a key intervention in feminist politics. Other works by Lorde include *The First Cities* (1968); *Cables to Rage* (1970); *From a Land Where Other People Live* (1973); *New York Head Shop and Museum* (1975); *The Black Unicorn* (1978); *Chosen Poems: Old and New* (1982); *Our Dead behind Us* (1986); and *A Burst of Light* (1988).

Louÿs, Pierre (1870–1925). Pseudonym of Pierre Louis, French novelist and poet who was born in Ghent, Belgium, of French parentage. Educated in Paris, he was a disciple of the poet Heredia whose youngest daughter he married. Together with André GIDE and others he co-founded the literary journals *La Conque* (1891) and *Le Centaure* (1896). He became (in)famous with the publication of *Chansons de bilitis* (1894), which he passed off successfully as prose poems *d'amour antique* that he had translated from the Greek original of a contemporary of SAPPHO. These poems, which have a lesbian content, reflect the interest of some male poets of the late nineteenth century such as BAUDELAIRE with lesbian relationships. Louÿs followed this with *Aphrodite: moeurs antique* (1896), *La Femme et le pantin* (1898), *Les Aventures du roi pansole* (1900), and *Poésies* (1927), which included 'Astarté', twenty-five poems '*sur la femme et sur l'eau*'. His diaries were published as *Journal intime 1882–1891* (1929).

Lowell, Amy (1874–1925). Lesbian US poet and critic, born into a distinguished Boston family in Massachusetts. Lowell was the child of Augustus and Katherine Lawrence Lowell. Much younger than her siblings she grew up in the intellectually and socially sophisticated environment of grown-ups on the family's large estate, Sevenels. Born to a genteel lifestyle, Lowell attended a private girls' school until the age of seventeen when she left school to care for her by then elderly parents. She read widely at home and, after her parents' death, bought Sevenels from the estate and there devoted herself to her two great loves: poetry and dogs. She became famous for her divergent self-presentation, smoking cigarillos and wearing men's clothes. In the latter respect she was not unlike a whole number of lesbians from the turn of the nineteenth to the twentieth century who expressed their sense of their sexual identity through wearing men's clothes. Lowell's first poem was published in the influential *Atlantic Monthly* when she was thirty-six years old. Her first volume of poetry, *A Dome of Many-colored Glass* (1912) was influenced by Keats whose autobiography she wrote in 1925. From the publication of her first volume of poetry onwards she published on average a volume per year, including during her final decade of ill health. *Sword Blades and Poppy Seeds* (1914) and *Can Grande's Castle* (1918) established Lowell as a modernist poet who identified in particular with the work of another of the great US modernist lesbian poets, H.D. Her work experimented with unrhymed cadences, and she developed a 'polyphonic prose'. Lowell's poetry was inspired by two 'muses': her partner of thirteen years, Ada (Dwyer) Russell, who survived Lowell, and the stage actress, Eleonora Duse, whom she adored and to whom she wrote dozens of poems. With her volume *Pictures of the Floating World* (1919) Lowell's lesbian images and conceits became more explicit. She is one of the most important lesbian poets of the early twentieth century. Lowell promoted poetry as much as she wrote it. She introduced imagism from the UK into the USA, and published three volumes of *Some Imagist Poets* between 1915 and 1917, making imagism one of the major developments in US poetry. After a decade of ill health Lowell died of a stroke on her estate. With her own final volume of poetry, *What's O'clock* (1925), published posthumously, she received the Pulitzer Prize in 1926.

Lynch, Lee. Pen name of Beverly Lynch, contemporary US author of lesbian popular fiction including romance and lesbian thrillers. Her publications include *Old Dyke Tales* (1984), a collection of short stories, *The Swashbuckler* (1985), *Home in Your Hands* (1986), *The Amazon Trail* (1988), *Sue Slate, Private Eye* (1989), *The Old Studebaker* (1991), *Morton River Valley* (1992), and *Rafferty Street* (1998).

M

McAlmon, Robert (1896–1956). US writer and publisher who was born in Clifton, Kansas, and moved to London and later to Paris in 1921. In London, McAlmon entered a marriage of convenience with the lesbian writer BRYHER (pseudonym of Annie Winifred Ellerman), who became the lifelong partner of the poet H.D. Bryher was the daughter of an English shipping magnate and when her and McAlmon's marriage broke up he received a large settlement that enabled him to publish modernist work. He founded the Contact Editions, and published, *inter alia*, Gertrude STEIN's *The Making of Americans* (1925) and Djuna BARNES's *The Ladies' Almanack* (1928). McAlmon did not acknowledge his own homosexuality although he explored homoerotic relationships in various short stories and novels. These include the collections *A Hasty Bunch* (1922) and *The Distinguished Air* (1925), as well as the novel *The Village* (1924). He also published his poetry in the volumes *Explorations* (1921), *The Portrait of a Generation* (1926), *North America, Continent of Conjecture* (1929), and *Not Alone Lost* (1929). His autobiographical *Being Geniuses Together* (1938) was re-edited by his friend, the writer Kay Boyle, in 1984. McAlmon did not write about his own homosexual relationships but one of his partners, John Glassco, with whom he had a relationship between 1927 and 1929, wrote about this relationship in his *Memoirs of Montparnasse* (1970). McAlmon returned to America in 1940 and died almost unknown. His partial rehabilitation is in part due to the intense interest in modernism and the lesbian and gay scenes of the modernist period, which began to surface in the 1980s.

McCrary Boyd, Blanche (1945–). Lesbian US writer, born in Charleston, South Carolina, whose work is informed by being a lesbian in a Southern context. McCrary Boyd teaches writing at Connecticut College, New Jersey. Her novels, several of which centre on the kinds of family dramas often associated with Southern writers, tend to focus on female characters who, at some point in their lives, become lesbian, and who react against the oppressiveness of their environment. McCrary Boyd's first novel, *Nerves* (1973), was published by Daughters Inc., the lesbian publishing house, now defunct, co-founded by June ARNOLD. Subsequent novels include *Mourning the Death of Magic* (1977), *The Revolution of Little Girls* (1991), and *Terminal Velocity* (1999). McCrary Boyd has also published a collection of short stories, *The Redneck Way of Knowledge: Down-Home Tales* (1981).

McCullers, Carson (1917–67). The publication of her first novel, *The Heart is a*

Lonely Hunter, in 1923 made US lesbian writer Carson McCullers (Lula Carson Smith), then twenty-three years old, an instant literary celebrity in New York. Married to Reeves McCullers, who preferred his own sex just as Carson did, she spent her life, dressed in men's clothes, trying to establish long-term relationships with the women she adored. In 1940 she met Annemarie SCHWARZENBACH in the company of Erika MANN and Klaus MANN, and fell into long-term unrequited love with her, as both Janet FLANNER and Solita SOLANO, two of her close friends, testified. She dedicated her second book, *Reflections in a Golden Eye*, to Schwarzenbach. In 1940 Carson McCullers moved into a house in Brooklyn inhabited, among others, by W.H. AUDEN, Paul BOWLES, and Jane BOWLES. She repeatedly fell in love with figures such as Katharine Ann Porter, Hilda Marks, and Djuna BARNES, and spent the final years of her life supported by Mary Mercer, a doctor.

McDermid, Val. Contemporary British writer and journalist who grew up in a Scottish mining village and read English at Oxford before taking up a career as a journalist. In this capacity she has worked for papers such as the *South Devon Times*, the *Sunday Independent* (Exeter), the *Scottish Daily Record*, and the *People* in Manchester, outside which she now resides. McDermid is one of those crime and detective writers like Sarah DREHER, Katherine V. FORREST, Kate CALLOWAY, Barbara WILSON, and other, often lesbian, female writers who, from the late 1970s, have created the figure of the lesbian sleuth in a strategic appropriation of a traditionally very masculine popular genre. McDermid, a prolific writer, has produced three series of crime fiction, each with its own key investigator who in two cases is a lesbian detective. Her earliest series is the one featuring Lindsay Gordon, around whom she has produced five novels to date: *Report for Murder* (1987), *Common Murder* (1989), *Final*

Edition (1991), *Union Jack* (1993), and *Booked for Murder* (1996). In 1993 the first of McDermid's mystery novels featuring Kate Brannigan appeared, to be followed by five more to date. They were *Kick Back* (1993), *Dead Beat* (1994), *Crack Down* (1994), *Clean Break* (1996), *Blue Genes* (1997), and *Star Struck* (1998). McDermid has also written two crime thrillers featuring Dr Tony Hill: *The Mermaids Singing* (1995) and *The Fire in the Blood* (1997). In 1995 McDermid was awarded the Golden Dagger Award of the British Crime Writers Association for Best Crime Novel for *The Mermaids Singing*. McDermid writes weekly crime fiction reviews for the *Manchester Evening News*.

McEwen, Christian (1956–). Lesbian writer and editor, born in London, who grew up in the Scottish Borders. She studied Social Anthropology and English Literature at King's College, Cambridge, and English and American literature at Berkeley, California. In 1979 McEwen moved to the USA where she settled in New York. She has worked as a teacher and editor, and her writings have appeared in publications such as the lesbian journals *Sinister Wisdom* and *Feminary*. In 1988 she edited an important anthology of lesbian poetry, *Naming the Waves: Contemporary Lesbian Poetry*, which was published by Virago Press. Together with Sue O'Sullivan she edited *Out the Other Side: Contemporary Lesbian Fiction* (1988), and she has also written *Jo's Girl: Tomboy Tales of High Adventure* (1997).

MacInnes, Colin (1914–76). Gay Anglo-Australian writer, the son of the novelist Angela Thirkell who was brought up in Australia for a time. MacInnes attended art school, and was in the army during the Second World War, before he embarked upon a career as a writer and journalist. He became well known with his novels of youth and black immigrant culture, indicating his fascination with 'the other' and with boys. *City of Spades* (1957) and *Absolute Beginners* (1957) describe life in London's Notting Hill, specifically a new Bohemian culture of drugs, drink, homosexuality, and jazz clubs.

McKay, Claude (1889–1948). Jamaican-American writer, born into a poor family in Sunny Ville, whose early interest in Jamaican folk tales translated into his first volume of poetry, *Songs of Jamaica* (1912). His second book, *Constab Ballads* (1912), led to his receiving a medal from the Jamaican Institute of Arts and Sciences. The prize money he received enabled him to move to the USA where he became a revered figure of the Harlem Renaissance. His volume *Harlem Shadows* (1922) is a key text of that period. His subsequent novel *Home to Harlem* (1928) became a bestseller. The scenes depicted in that novel reveal a Harlem in which gay men and lesbians move easily. McKay's later novels *Banjo* (1929) and *Banana Bottom* (1933) do not reference homosexual life. McKay published a range of writings including the poetry collection *Spring in Hampshire* (1920), a collection of short stories entitled *Gingertown* (1932), as well as the non-fiction volumes *A Long Way from Home* (1937) and *Harlem: Negro Metropolis* (1940). McKay's private life is only sketchily known though it would appear that he had relationships with both women and men.

Mackay, John Henry (1864–1933). Born in Scotland as the son of a marine insurance broker and a mother from a well-to-do German background, Mackay was taken to Germany by his mother upon his father's premature death and brought up there, with German as his first language. He initially made his name as a lyric poet and as a writer of naturalist novellas but became famous with his novel *Die Anarchisten* (1891; *The Anarchists*). In 1901 he wrote *Der Schwimmer*

(*The Swimmer*), an early sports novel. His mother's death the following year brought on an intense depression that he sought to alleviate by dedicating himself to the project of gaining recognition for man--boy love. Mackay himself apparently had a preference for boys between the ages of fourteen and seventeen. He began a campaign under the pseudonym Sagitta, intent upon publishing a series of volumes in different literary forms, all extolling the virtues of same-sex love. Charges were brought against his publisher when the first books appeared and, in 1909 after a nineteen-month trial, they were declared obscene. This did not deter Mackay from publishing *Die Bücher der namenlosen Liebe von Sagitta* in 1913 (*Sagitta's Books of Nameless Love*), which he sold underground. Within this collection is the story 'Fenny Skaller', a coming-out story of a boy-lover. In 1920 Mackay published a sequel to *Die Anarchisten, Der Freiheitsucher* (*The Freedom Seeker*). In 1923 his fortune was wiped out by the galloping inflation of the period. Mackay continued to write and in 1926 published *Der Puppenjunge* (*The Hustler*), a story set in the milieu of boy prostitutes in Berlin during that period. Mackay published most explicitly on homosexuality under his pseudonym, and 'Sagitta's' writings were banned by the Nazis. Occasionally, though, homosexuality also appeared in his other work. His 1931 novella *Der Unschuldige* (*The Innocent*), for instance, featured obviously homosexual characters. By the time of his death Mackay's identity as Sagitta was well known. He gave instructions that after his death his writings should all appear under his actual name rather than his pseudonym.

MacKenzie, Compton (1883–1972). Prolific British writer who portrayed gays and lesbians in his work. Educated at St Paul's and at Magdalen College, Oxford, Sir Edward Morgan Compton MacKenzie became a writer of travel books, biography, essays, poetry, fiction, and journalism. He variously lived on Capri, in the Channel Islands, and in Scotland. His popular two-volume novel *Sinister Street* (1913; 1914) presented the life of a semi-autobiographical figure, Michael Frane, as he passed from a public school and university background to low life in London. Both his novels *Vestal Virgins* (1927) and *Extraordinary Women* (1928) contained lesbian characters. Both novels are set on the Mediterranean island of Sirene, and depict a hedonistic culture. MacKenzie also wrote two volumes of war memoirs, *Gallipoli Memories* (1929) and *Greek Memories* (1932). During the Second World War MacKenzie brought out a six-volume account of the life of John Ogilvie from the time of the Boer War to the advent of Scottish nationalism, entitled *The Four Winds of Love* (1937–45). MacKenzie's novel *Thin Ice* (1956), about the homosexual relationship between an older man and his 'secretary', was serialized on BBC Radio 4 in 2001. Between 1963 and 1971 MacKenzie produced an extended autobiography, *My Life and Times*. Though out of favour at present, MacKenzie was a highly popular writer during his lifetime and was knighted for his services to literature.

MacLane, Mary (1881–1929). Born in Winnipeg, Minnesota, to James MacLane, a boatsman who carried cargo to the Canadian Arctic, MacLane was one of four children. In 1884, after the Riel rebellion, the family moved to Fergus Falls, western Minnesota, and then, when MacLane was eight years old and her father died, to Butte in Montana Territory where MacLane attended school and was inspired by her teacher to read widely. She graduated in 1899 from Butte High School and began writing her first book in 1901. When *The Story of Mary Mac Lane* appeared in 1902 it gained notoriety for its frank depiction of female sensuality and lesbian relationships. With the money she earned from this book she left Butte and set herself up in New York where she

lived between 1903 and 1908. In 1903 she published *My Friend, Annabel Lee*, which is written as a series of conversations with a small porcelain statue of a Japanese woman. MacLane's *The Devil's Letters to Mary MacLane, by Himself* also appeared in the same year. In early 1909 MacLane returned to Butte where she fell ill with scarlet fever and nearly died. The success of her first book encouraged her to re-issue that text, complete with a further chapter, in 1911, and in 1917 she published *I, Mary MacLane: A Diary of Human Days*. She then left Butte for Hollywood where she wrote and starred in a film entitled *Men Who Have Made Love to Me* (1918), based, apparently, on six of her affairs. She died in Chicago but was buried, in accordance with her mother's wishes, at Fergus Falls next to her father. MacLane's writings reveal her deep desire to be loved and a, possibly tongue-in-cheek, sense of herself as 'genius'. She described her adoration of women as 'the man-love, set in the mysterious sensibilities of my woman-nature'.

McNab, Claire. Contemporary US writer, specializing in lesbian popular fiction. McNab, like Katherine V. FORREST, Sarah DREHER, and a number of other writers, has contributed significantly to the establishment of the lesbian detective novel, a genre that gained prominence in the 1970s and 1980s when a number of writers invented lesbian sleuths, appropriating a predominantly male genre and resituating its narratives in lesbian and gay, or all-female, settings. McNab's Detective Inspector Carol Ashton is one such lesbian sleuth. Beginning with *Lessons in Murder* (1988), McNab progressed to write a series of lesbian thrillers including *Fatal Reunion* (1989), the second Carol Ashton thriller, *Death Down Under* (1990), *Cop Out* (1991), *Dead Certain* (1992), *Body Guard* (1995), *Inner Circle* (1996), *Chain Letter* (1997), *Under Suspicion* (2000), *Set Up* (2000), and *Death Club* (2001). McNab also wrote the lesbian romances *Under the Southern Cross* (1992) and *Silent Heart* (1993).

McWilliam, Candia (1955–). Born in Edinburgh, Candia McWilliam is a British novelist whose work features gay couples. *A Case of Knives* (1988), joint winner of the Betty Trask Award and short-listed for the Whitbread Best First Novel Prize, centres on a gay surgeon and the effects of his attempts to keep his young lover by procuring a wife for him. In *Change of Use* (1996) two men look after the grandmother of one of them. McWilliam has also published *A Little Stranger* (1989) and *Debatable Land* (1994), for which she won the Guardian Fiction Prize.

Mahyère, Eveline (1925–57). Born in Geneva to a Protestant school teacher mother and a father who was a bank manager, Mahyère was sent to a convent following her expulsion from the Voltaire Lycée in Geneva. She returned to Geneva to take her *Maturité*. Subsequently she went to Paris and won a scholarship to study in Madrid for a year. She then took a degree in Spanish at the Sorbonne and lived most of the rest of her life in Paris where she worked as a translator for the publishers Stock, translating crime fiction from English into French. Her only novel, *Je jure de m'éblouiré* (*I will not serve*) was published posthumously in 1958. It is a boarding-school fiction of sorts that centres on the passionate love of Sylvie, a rebellious convent schoolgirl, for her teacher, the nun Julienne. The schoolgirl finally commits suicide. Shortly after its completion Mahyère, who had suffered from bouts of depression throughout her life, herself committed suicide. In 1959 her novel was translated into English by Antonia WHITE, herself the author of a boarding-school fiction, and the translator of the work of COLETTE.

Mann, Erika (1905–69). The eldest daughter of the German writer Thomas MANN, Erika Mann was an actress, writer, and political activist whose close relationship with her gay brother Klaus MANN was the subject of much speculation. She and Pamela Wedekind, daughter of the playwright Frank Wedekind, took the lead roles in the 1925 world première of Klaus Mann's play about a lesbian couple, *Esther and Anja*. Erika Mann had a number of associations with lesbian writers and playwrights such as the Swiss writer Annemarie SCHWARZENBACH and the actress Therese Giehse. She had two marriages of convenience, one with the actor Gustaf Gründgens (1926–9) and one with the poet W.H. AUDEN, the latter in 1935 to enable her to obtain a British passport. Throughout the 1930s she had a personal and professional relationship with Therese Giehse with whom she founded a cabaret entitled 'The Pepper Mill'. In 1938 Erika Mann published her bestseller, *School for Barbarians: Education and Youth in the Third Reich*. From 1933 she lived first in Switzerland, then in the USA, and then again in Switzerland.

Mann, Klaus (1906–49). The gay German writer Klaus Mann, eldest son of the writer Thomas MANN and his wife Katia, was born in Munich into a well-connected patrician family. Early on he decided that he wanted to be famous and he started to write poems and novellas. In 1925 he went as a theatre critic to Berlin and was noted for the experimental theatre that he was involved with. Together with his sister Erika MANN, Pamela Wedekind, daughter of the playwright Frank Wedekind, and the gay actor Gustaf Gründgens, who rose to fame during the Nazi regime, Mann founded a theatre ensemble and engaged in literary cabaret. Erika and Pamela Wedekind took the lead roles in the 1925 world première of Klaus Mann's play about a lesbian couple, *Esther and Anja*. In 1929 he and Erika, his sister, went on a world tour together that Mann wrote about in *Rundherum* (*Roundabout*). In 1932 he published his autobiography *Kind dieser Zeit* (*Child of this*

Time). In the spring of 1933 he emigrated, initially to Paris. There he published his most famous work, the novel *Mephisto* (1936), which focuses on an actor's deep involvement with the Nazi regime through his refusal to understand that art, too, is political. The novel caused something of a sensation as it was considered to indict Gustaf Gründgens, who had played Mephisto in a famous *Faust* film, to whom Erika Mann had been unhappily married, and who was regarded as having sold out to the Nazis for the sake of his artistic career. In fact, like Mann, Gründgens was homosexual and, like him, he eventually committed suicide (in 1963). However, Gründgens had managed to become one of the darlings of the Nazi film industry and to rise again as a star in post-Second World War Germany. The novel became the source of a persistent controversy and was banned in Germany in 1968 but finally allowed to appear in 1981. In 1934 Mann wrote 'Homosexualität und Faschismus' ('Homosexuality and Fascism'). In 1936 Klaus Mann moved to New York. He joined the US Army and took part in campaigns in North Africa and Italy during the Second World War. He published the novel *Flucht in den Norden* (1934; *Flight to the North*) and later a further novel, *Der Vulkan* (1939; *The Volcano*). While in exile he wrote about great homosexual figures of the past for his novels on *Alexander, Symphonie Pathétique* (1935; *Pathetic Symphony*; on Tchaikovsky), and *Vergittertes Fenster* (1937, *Barred Window*; on King Ludwig II of Bavaria). In 1942 he published his autobiography *The Turning Point: Thirty-five Years in this Century*, which was published in English in the first instance. In 1945 he visited Austria and Germany as a reporter for the army newspaper *Stars and Stripes*. In 1948 he undertook a lecture tour in Europe during which he appealed to those who had railed against the Nazis to conjoin in order to secure the future peace of Europe. Mann had been desperate to become famous but like his siblings suffered from the seemingly unattainable status his father held as one of the patricians of German literature and probity. Drug abuse, unhappiness about political developments in the post-Second World War period, and lack of literary success all combined and led to his suicide in Cannes, France, in 1949.

Mann, Thomas (1875–1955). Born in the Hanseatic town on Lübeck, a background which was to influence much of his later work, Mann and his mother settled in Munich when he was nineteen years old. There he met his wife Katia whom he married in 1905 and with whom he had six children including Golo Mann, now an eminent German historian, Klaus MANN, and Erika MANN, both of whom were gay. After a brief spell at university he joined his brother Heinrich in Italy to be a writer. Heinrich Mann was also a writer and much famed for his novel *Professor Unrat* (1905), which was made into a world-famous film under the title *Der blaue Engel* (*The Blue Angel*, featuring Marlene Dietrich as the cabaret artist who leads the teacher Professor Unrat astray). Mann's first novel, *Die Buddenbrooks*, established him as one of the most important German writers of his generation. Always preoccupied with the relationship between a cool, rational north, and a passionate but supposedly enervating south, Mann then continued to write a series of novellas, essays, and novels. His stories *Tonio Kröger* (1902) and *Tristan* (1903) were followed by *Königliche Hoheit* (1909; *Royal Highness*) and then the text which established him as an icon of gay literature, *Der Tod in Venedig* (1913; *Death in Venice*), which centres on a man's attraction for a boy and which was made into a very successful film featuring Dirk BOGARDE as Gustav von Aschenbach, the fatally infatuated man. Mann's many novels all have overtly homoerotic and homosocial themes. His *Zauberberg* (1924; *The*

Magic Mountain) earned him the Nobel Prize for Literature in 1929. In 1930 *Mario und der Zauberer* (*Mario and the Magician*) appeared, prefiguring a certain experience in Nazi Germany through its portrayal of the appalling influence of a hypnotic mountebank on a susceptible youth during a circus performance. In 1933 Mann was forced to flee Nazi Germany; both he and his brother Heinrich settled in the USA but, while Mann was fêted in the White House and elsewhere and acted as a member of the high establishment, his brother had a difficult time. Mann settled in the USA in 1936 and became a US citizen in 1944. In 1947 he moved to Switzerland while his brother eventually moved to what was to become and remain until 1989 East Germany. Mann's other work includes *Lotte in Weimar* (1939), *Appel an die Vernunft* (1930; *Appeal to Reason*), a collection of anti-Nazi broadcasts (1945), *Leiden und Größe der Meister* (1933; *The Sufferings and Greatness of the Masters*), *Die vertauschten Köpfe* (1940; *The Transposed Heads*), *Joseph und seine Brüder*, a tetralogy (*Joseph and his Brothers*), *Doktor Faustus* (1947), *Der Erwählte* (1951; *The Chosen*), *Die Betrogene* (1953; *The Deceived*), *Bekenntnisse des Hochstaplers Felix Krull* (1954; *Confessions of Felix Krull: Confidence Man*), and *Letzte Aufsätze* (1959; *Last Essays*). Mann was always a darling of the establishment and a *grand seigneur* of German literature. This does not detract from the homoeroticism of his work.

Mannin, Ethel (1900–84). English writer assumed to be lesbian who frequented lesbian circles. Mannin was of Irish descent, committed to the women's cause, and a member of the Independent Labour Party during the 1930s. Like Clemence DANE she was an extremely prolific writer who produced work, often centring on women's oppression, in a variety of genres. She had an interest in child psychology and wrote among other texts

Common Sense and the Child (1931). Her travel writings include *Women also Dream* (1937) and *South to Samarkand* (1936). In *Women and the Revolution* (1938) she argued for the emancipation of women through the overthrow of capitalism, and her novel *Red Rose* (1941) was based on the life of Emma Goldman. Her many other novels include *Lover under Another Name* (1963). Among her autobiographical texts are *Confessions and Impressions* (1930), *Privileged Spectator* (1939), the sequel to *Confessions and Impressions*, as well as *Stories from My Life* (1973).

Manning, Olivia (1908–80). Born in Portsmouth to a naval officer and an Ulster-Irish mother, Manning had a middle-class upbringing, marred slightly when she was five years old by the arrival of her younger brother Oliver by whose birth she felt sidelined. He was killed, much to her dismay, in 1941 while on active service. Manning went to London in her early twenties and had a variety of jobs before getting married to a British Council lecturer, R.D. Smith, who later became a radio producer and then Professor at the New University of Ulster. The poet Stevie Smith, with whom Manning had a lifelong friendship, was her bridesmaid. Until 1946 the couple lived abroad in Bucharest, Greece, and Egypt. Manning was press officer to the United States Embassy in Cairo. Between 1941 and 1945 she worked in Jerusalem as press assistant at the Public Information office there. Her first published novel was *The Wind Changes* (1937). After the Second World War Manning became a distinguished writer who used her wartime experience to produce works such as the so-called Balkan trilogy *The Great Fortune* (1960), *The Spoilt City* (1962), and *Friends and Heroes* (1965), the novel *The Rainforest* (1974), and the so-called Levant trilogy *The Danger Tree* (1977), *The Battle Lost and Won* (1978), and *The Sum of Things* (1980). She also wrote *Artist among the*

Missing (1949), *School for Love* (1951), *A Different Face* (1953), and *The Doves of Venus* (1955). In 1969 she published a rather curious novel entitled *The Playroom*. This novel, apparently in part an exploration of Manning's relationship with her brother, is a novel about rather threatening forms of sexual transgression that bear some resemblance to the notion of 'queer' as a play upon sexual identity and practice, as that term has come to be used in the 1990s. In the first part of the novel the protagonist Laura and her brother spend a holiday with their former char lady, now living off men, on the Isle of Wight, where one afternoon they stray into a garden where a Mrs Toplady, who might be a transvestite, introduces them into her 'playroom' full of large, life-like naked dolls. Later in the novel, Laura develops a devotion for her rich, spoilt, and sexually curious classmate Vicky Logan, somewhat in the manner of girls' (boarding-)school fictions that constitute a sub-genre of lesbian writing. Laura herself has a fascination with the much older working-class lad and lout Clarrie. There is a suggestion in the novel that Vicky has masochistic tendencies, which the brutally macho Clarrie responds to. In a terrible twist to the story, he finally rapes and kills Vicky who, when found, reminds Laura of the dolls in the 'playroom' she saw during her visit to the Isle of Wight.

Manning, Rosemary (1911–). British lesbian writer who came out in 1980 on television following her retirement from teaching in 1972. Most of her writing is autobiographical. Her novel *The Chinese Garden* (1962) is a classic of the girls' boarding-school fiction genre to which texts such as Henry Handel RICHARDSON's *The Coming of Wisdom* and Olivia's (see STRACHEY BUSSY, DOROTHY) *Olivia* also belong. *The Chinese Garden* is a story of the awakening to lesbian identity by the protagonist and its betrayal in the school, which culminates in

the dismissal of the two girls who are discovered having a lesbian affair. Manning's other novels are *Look, Stranger* (1960), *Man on a Tower* (1965), *A Time and a Time* (1971), first published under the pseudonym Sarah Davys, which deals with a broken lesbian love affair and is highly autobiographical, various books for children, and an autobiography, *A Corridor of Mirrors* (1987).

Manrique, Jaime (1949–). Born in Barranquilla, Colombia, Manrique has written in a variety of genres in both Spanish and English. He was awarded the Colombian National Poetry Award in 1975 for his collection *Los adoradores de la luna* (*The Moon Worshippers*). His novella *El Cadaver de Papa/Dad's Corpse* (1978) became a best seller in Colombia and was followed by *Colombian Gold: A Novel of Power and Corruption*, published in English in 1983. The principal character in both novels is one Santiago Martinez, whose adventures reflect the violence associated with the repression of same-sex relationships in a patriarchal, machismo society. Manrique has subsequently published *Latin Moon in Manhattan* (1992) and *Twilight at the Equator: A Novel* (1997), again focusing on Santiago, now living in Manhattan in the time of AIDS. In 1999 appeared *My Night with Federico García Lorca*, a book of poems. *Eminent Maricones: Arenas, Lorca, Puig, and Me* (1999) is an innovative autobiographical work of non-fiction. In a series of independent chapters, Manrique intersperses his own experiences, first during his childhood and teenage years in Colombia and later as an adult in New York, with critical discussions of the three Latino writers from the perspective of their influence on him.

[David Garnes]

Mansfield, Katherine (1888–1923). New Zealand short-story writer who was born in Wellington into a middle-class colonial family, one of six children. Initially Mansfield grew up in a semi-pastoral landscape in New Zealand but in 1903 she and her older sisters were taken to London to be educated there. At Queen's College Mansfield became close friends with Ida Constance Baker, a friendship that continued throughout her life and on which the notion that Katherine was lesbian, or at least had emotional and erotic interests in women, has been founded. Baker was not the only woman in Mansfield's life. On her return from London to New Zealand in 1907 she met the artist Edith Kathleen Bendall for whom she developed passionate feelings. Her story 'Leves Amores', written a year after she had met Bendall, has an unmistakable lesbian content. Other stories like 'Bliss' also dealt with homoeroticism. Mansfield returned to England from New Zealand in 1908. She never returned to New Zealand. Instead she spent her time both in England and in France where she hoped to find relief from her frail physical constitution. In London Mansfield led a Bohemian lifestyle, marrying George Bowden, only to leave him the next day, touring with musical cabarets and writing. Vera BRITTAIN and Rebecca West remember seeing her in 1913 in a performance at the lesbian nightclub 'the Cave of the Golden Calf'. Around 1910 Mansfield began to submit stories to *Rhythm*, a new journal edited by John Middleton Murry. Through this work she met writers like Virginia WOOLF and D.H. LAWRENCE with whom, apparently, she talked about her lesbian relationships. In 1918, after having worked and lived together for some years, Mansfield married Middleton Murry but was forced to spend much time in the better climate of France due to her ill health. Several collections of her work were published including *In a German Pension* (1911); *Prelude* (1918); *Bliss and Other Stories* (1921); *The Garden Party and Other Stories* (1922); *The Doves' Nest and Other Stories* (1923); *Poems* (1924); and *Something Childish and Other Stories* (1924). Middleton

Murry documented her life by publishing her edited journal (1924) and letters (1928, 1929). In 1971 Ida Constance Baker published *Katherine Mansfield: The Memories of LM*.

March, Caeia (1946–). British lesbian writer, born to working-class parents on the Isle of Man, who grew up in the industrial south of Yorkshire and attended university in London from 1964. She graduated in the social sciences in 1968 and married in the same year. She had two sons. In 1980 she left her marriage and began living as a lesbian. Her sons stayed with her father, living in close proximity to her in London. March has supported herself by teaching in adult education and conducting writing classes for women. Her first novel, *Three Ply Yarn*, appeared in 1986 and *The Hide and Seek Files* came out in 1988. Her poetry has been variously anthologized including in *Naming the Waves: Contemporary Lesbian Poetry* (1988, edited by Christian MCEWEN). Other works by March include *Fire! Fire!* (1991), *Between the Worlds* (1996), *Knowing ME* (1998) a book about the disease ME which March edited, and *Spinsters' Rock* (1999).

Marchessault, Jovette (1938–). Canadian lesbian writer, born in Montreal, who spent her early childhood in the countryside near Montreal where her father had a job as a munitions worker. The end of the Second World War and the father's consequent job loss forced the family to move into one of the poorest areas of Montreal, a move that initiated in Marchessault the strong sense of a paradise lost that haunts so many of her writings. The most important early influence on Marchessault was her half-Indian herbalist grandmother whose creativity included painting and playing the piano. Marchessault left school at thirteen and spent her life until the age of thirty-one in a number of jobs, intermittently escaping on long Greyhound trips to Mexico and to the West

Coast. Before becoming a freelance artist and writer upon her grandmother's death, she spent four years working for the Grolier encyclopaedia firm. She then worked as a painter, achieving one-woman shows in Montreal, New York, Paris, and Brussels. In 1975 the first volume of her three-volume autobiography, *Le Crachat solaire* (translated in 1988 as *Like a Child of the Earth*) appeared. This was followed by *La Mère des herbes* (1980; translated as *Mother of the Grass*, 1989) and by *Des cailloux blancs pour les forêts obscures* (1987; translated as *White Pebbles of the Dark Forests*, 1990). These three volumes of autobiography, published collectively as *Comme une enfant de la terre*, won the Prix France-Québec in 1976. They constitute both a working-class autobiography and an attempt to reclaim myth for women in general and lesbians in particular. In 1980 Marchessault published *Tryptique lesbienne*, a three-part representation of coming out as a lesbian in Roman Catholic Québec, and a celebration of a female-centred universe. The three sections, 'A Lesbian Chronicle from Medieval Québec', 'Night Cows', and 'The Angel Makers', constituted an unambiguous statement of Marchessault's lesbianism. Since then she has written extensively for theatre, producing imaginative portraits of women artists and writers, often lesbians.

Marlowe, Christopher (1564–93). English poet and playwright whose work is permeated by homoerotic images and encounters. Born in Canterbury, in the same year as SHAKESPEARE, Marlowe was the son of a cobbler who earned a scholarship to Cambridge where he took a BA in 1584 and an MA in 1587. One result of his education was his love of classical literature, especially Ovid whose work he translated. Marlowe's own writings veer between the Christian condemnation of homoeroticism and its acceptance in classical culture. Marlowe was frequently in conflict with the pre-

vailing political authorities. There are suggestions that Marlowe may have acted as a spy for Sir Francis Walsingham. Then, in 1593, he was accused by Elizabeth I's Privy Council of heresy and blasphemy. He was murdered in a tavern in Deptford, now part of London, before he could answer the charges. The circumstances of Marlowe's death remain the object of much speculation. After his death the playwright Thomas Kyd and Richard Baines in the 'Baines libel' testified against Marlowe for holding outrageous beliefs and for blasphemy, possibly to exonerate themselves. In the Baines libel the statements that 'St John the Evangelist was bedfellow to Christ and leaned alwaies in his bosome, that he used him as the sinners of Sodoma' and 'That all they that love not Tobacco & Boies were fooles' were attributed to Marlowe. *The Tragedie of Dido, Queene of Carthage* (1594) was probably written while Marlowe was still at Cambridge. It opens with a comic scene in which Jupiter is discovered 'dandling Ganimed upon his knee'. Part I of his play *Tamburlaine* was probably written by 1587 and the second part of this play in the following year. The most significantly homoerotic of Marlowe's plays, *Edward II*, was published in 1594. It features the love between Edward II and Gaveston, famously transcending rank and class. The play also contains the infamous putting to death of the homosexual Edward II through sodomizing him sadistically with a red-hot poker. Marlowe's play *Massacre at Paris* survives only as a fragment. His erotic narrative poem *Hero and Leander*, which contains the lyrical idealization of youthful male beauty, was completed by G. Chapman and published in 1598. This was followed by *The Passionate Pilgrim* (1599), which contains the potentially homoerotic song 'Come live with me and be my love', and *England's Helicon* (1600). His *Dr Faustus* came out in 1604. Marlowe's *Jew of Malta* was not published until 1633. Marlowe's portrayal of homoeroticism stood in powerful contrast to the condemnation of homosexuality in Renaissance England.

Mars-Jones, Adam (1954–). Gay British writer, born into an upper middle-class family, Mars-Jones was educated at Westminster School and Cambridge University. He has acted as film critic for the *Independent* newspaper. His first book, *Lantern Lectures* (1981), contained three novellas, written in a postmodern style, and containing a mixture of fiction and documentary. In 1983 he edited *Mae West is Dead*, a collection of lesbian and gay fiction. Since 1986 Mars-Jones has been producing AIDS narratives, often in a realist style. The first one appeared in a collection with Edmund WHITE entitled *The Darker Proof: Stories from a Crisis* (1987), which was followed by *Monopolies of Loss* (1992), edited by Mars-Jones. His novel *The Waters of Thirst* (1993) centres on a man waiting for a kidney replacement operation who develops a fantasy relationship with a porn star.

Martinac, Paula (1954–). Born in Pittsburgh, Pennsylvania, lesbian writer Martinac was educated at Chatham College, Pittsburgh, where she gained a BA in 1976, and at the College of William and Mary, Williamsburg, Virginia, where she completed an MA in 1979. Between 1988 and 1990 she was editor of the magazine *Conditions*. She has also been co-chair of the Board of Directors of the New York City Lesbian and Gay Community Services Center, and is a member of the International Women's Writing Guild. In 1990 she won the Lambda Literary Award for lesbian fiction. In the same year the Puffin Foundation awarded her a grant for teaching lesbian writing. Martinac has an interest in the ways in which lesbians and gays have been treated at various historical moments in time. Her first novel, *Out of Time* (1990), centres on a woman who steals a photo album from an antiques shop, becomes curious

about the four women represented in it, and as she gets to know these women she gets drawn into their 1920s world of lesbian life. Martinac's second novel, *Home Movies*, appeared in 1993. She has also written a number of short stories that have appeared both in journals such as *Sinister Wisdom* and in collections of lesbian writings. She herself has edited and contributed to the anthologies *The One You Call Sister: New Women's Fiction* (1989) and *Voyages Out I: Lesbian Short Fiction* (1989), which she edited with Carla Tomaso. In 1998 she wrote *The Lesbian and Gay Book of Love and Marriage*.

Mason-John, Valerie. Contemporary Black British lesbian writer and performer whose work has done much to produce a Black lesbian history in/of Britain. Born in Cambridge she lived with a single-parent white foster mother until the latter retired when Mason-John was four years old. She was then placed in a Barnardo's home in Essex, disastrously re-united for a time with her mother whom she describes as treating her sadistically, resulting in Mason-John being taken back into care at the age of twelve, and then being fostered again from the age of thirteen. Educated at Ilford County High School for Girls and Leeds University, where she read Politics and Philosophy, she also completed a postgraduate course in Journalism with Business Press International. Since then she has written for the black national newspaper, the *Voice*, and has been a staff reporter on the lesbian and gay national newspaper, the *Pink Paper*. She has also contributed articles to various other newspapers like the *Guardian* and *Social Work Today*. Her book *Making Black Waves* (1993) was the first to record the experiences of black lesbians in Britain. It was followed by *Talking Black* (1995), a collection of texts by lesbians of African and Asian descent. Her volume *Brown Girl in the Ring* (1998) introduces her creative writing, including autobiography, poetry, and performance pieces. In it she records the importance Barbara BUR-FORD's collection *The Threshing Floor* had on her work. The texts engage with the sexual and racial politics in lesbian circles of the 1980s and 1990s, raising complex questions about black women's sexual relationships with white women, the politics of queer and sado-masochism, and the history of black lesbian experiences in Britain. Mason-John is also known as Queenie, a name apparently given to her by San Francisco gays who thought she was a bigger queen than any of them.

Matthiessen, F.O. (1902–50). Gay US literary critic, born in Pasadena, California, to William Frederick and Lucy Orne Matthiessen. After his parents' divorce in 1915, Matthiessen lived on his grandfather's farm in Illinois, attended boarding school in Tarrytown, New York, and joined the Canadian Air Force towards the end of the First World War. He went to Yale University in 1919, graduating in 1923. Subsequently he became a Rhodes scholar at Oxford University, receiving a BLitt in 1925. He met the painter Russell Cheney with whom he had a relationship until Cheney's death in 1945. Under Cheney's influence Matthiessen developed his interest in lesbian and gay literary figures such as Walt WHITMAN and Sarah Orne JEWETT on whose relationship with Annie Fields he and Cheney modelled their own relationship. In 1925 Matthiessen went to Harvard Graduate School, gaining an AM in 1926 and a PhD in 1927. He then had a brief spell teaching at Yale University before returning to Harvard University where he taught until his premature death by suicide in 1950. In his critical works Matthiessen focused predominantly on lesbian and gay figures or on those whose sexuality was in question. His works include *Sarah Orne Jewett* (1929), *Translation: An Elizabethan Art* (1931), *The Achievement of T.S. Eliot: An Essay on the Nature of Poetry* (1935,

1947), and, most notably, *American Renaissance: Art and Expression in the Age of Emerson and Whitman* (1941). He also published a catalogue of Cheney's work, *Russell Cheney, 1881–1945: A Record of His Work* in 1947. His depression about his partner's death and the increasingly homophobic atmosphere of late 1940s USA led him to commit suicide in 1950.

Maugham, Robin (1916–81). Robert Cecil Romer Maugham, second Viscount Maugham of Hartfield, was an English author who produced short stories, fiction, non-fiction, autobiographies, plays, and screenplays. Born in London, the son of Herbert Maugham, a Lord Chancellor of England, and nephew of the popular novelist W. Somerset Maugham, Robin Maugham went to Eton and Trinity College, Cambridge, a classic educational route for the upper middle classes. He then read Law at Lincoln's Inn and followed the family tradition of practising law. During the Second World War he served as an intelligence officer in North Africa and the Middle East but was retired as a consequence of being hit in the head by a shell fragment. This caused blackouts and prevented him from continuing to practise law. Instead he became a prolific writer though he was never as successful as his uncle. Maugham wrote many texts that deal with homosexuality both directly and indirectly. Among these are *The Wrong People* (1967), *Search for Nirvana* (1975), *The Man with Two Shadows*, *The Rough and the Smooth*, *Behind the Mirror*, *Come to Dust*, and *The Intruder*. His first autobiography, *Escape from the Shadows* (1972), began to detail his often difficult relationship with his family and his uncle. His perhaps best-known work is the novella *The Servant* (1948), which centres on the triangular relationship between two men who served in the army together and one of these men's servants, and on the compulsive, destructive, and sexualized relationship between that man and his servant. The novella was made into a highly successful film in 1963, directed by Joseph Losey, for which Harold Pinter wrote the screen version and in which Dirk BOGARDE starred as the servant. The novella was adapted for the stage again by Neil BARTLETT in 2001.

Maugham, W. Somerset (1874–1965). English writer, born in Paris, the son of a solicitor and legal adviser to the British embassy. He was orphaned by the age of ten and sent to Whitstable, Kent, to live with his aunt and uncle. He attended King's School, Canterbury, and later Heidelberg University and St Thomas's Hospital, London. In 1897 he received his medical MRCS and LRCP but his success as a novelist with his first novel, *Liza of Lambeth* (1897), diverted him from medicine to literature. The novel drew on his experiences of London slums and the inadequacy of medical attention to those dwelling there. He achieved fame with *Lady Frederick* (1907), a comedy of marriage. His playwriting proved so successful that in 1908 he had four plays running simultaneously in London. He continued to write plays until 1933 but stopped when he thought that his themes were no longer of interest to theatre managers. Among his best-known plays are *Our Betters* (1917), *The Circle* (1921), *East of Suez* (1922), *The Constant Wife* (1926), and *For Services Rendered* (1932), an anti-war play. In his work Maugham avoided all discussion of homosexuality but his private life was dominated by his relationship with Gerald Haxton, eighteen years his junior, whom Maugham had met in 1914 in Flanders, and who became his secretary and companion until his death in 1944. Before that, in 1911, Maugham met Syrie Wellcome, the daughter of Dr Barnardo (of Barnardo Homes for orphans) who was then the wife of a US businessman. Their child Liza was born in 1915, and in 1917 they married. The marriage was rather unorthodox, with much time spent apart.

It ended in divorce in 1927. By that time Maugham had established a permanent relationship with Haxton, with whom he spent much time travelling to the South Seas, to China, Mexico, South-east Asia, and a number of other countries. In 1926 Maugham bought a house, the Mauresque, in Cap Ferrat, France, where he lived for most of the rest of his life. Apart from plays he wrote a thinly disguised autobiographical novel entitled *Of Human Bondage* (1915), *The Moon and the Sixpence* (1919), based on the life of the painter Gauguin, *Cakes and Ale* (1930), based on the life of Thomas Hardy, and *The Razor's Edge* (1944). He produced a number of other volumes, novels, short stories, and plays. In his autobiography *The Swimming Up* (1938) he described himself as 'in the first row of second-raters'.

Maupin, Armistead (1944–). Gay US writer who was born into a conservative North Carolina family as Armistead Jones Maupin Jr. He attended the University of North Carolina, gaining a BA in 1966. While at university, he wrote for the *Daily Tar Heel*. After dropping out of law school, he worked at Raleigh television station whose then manager, Jesse Helms, gained notoriety for his conservative television commentaries. Maupin went on several tours of duty with the Navy. Working for a Charleston newspaper eventually facilitated his move to California where the *San Francisco Chronicle* began publishing his *Tales of the City*, the basis for a series of books about life in 28 Barbary Lane on San Francisco's Russian Hill. Serialized for publication in the paper, the stories were put together into several novels, all revolving around the lives of the characters inhabiting this house, presided over by Anna Madrigal. An important aspect of these novels is that Maupin places his lesbian and gay characters within a wider community rather than into a specifically gay and lesbian one. The novels are *Tales of the*

City (1978), *More Tales of the City* (1980), *Further Tales of the City* (1982), *Baby-cakes* (1984), *Significant Others* (1987), *Sure of You* (1989), *28 Barbary Lane* (1990; contains the first three volumes of *Tales* as a collection), *The Complete Tales of the City* (1991), and *Back to Barbary Lane: The Final Tales of the City* (1991). Maupin has written a variety of other texts, including *Maybe the Moon*, a novel, in 1992. He lives in San Francisco with his partner Terry Anderson.

Mead, Margaret (1901–78). Born in Philadelphia, Margaret Mead is one of the most renowned anthropologists of the twentieth century. Throughout her life, and despite being married three times, Mead maintained close relationships with women. In *With a Daughter's Eye* (1984), a memoir of her parents Margaret Mead and Gregory Bateson, Mead's daughter Mary Catherine Bateson indicated that Mead's relationship with the anthropologist Ruth BENEDICT had been far more intimate than Mead had led people to believe during her lifetime. During her studies Mead lived with a group of women including the anthropologist Ruth Bunzel and the poet Leonie Adams. The women were known as the 'Ash Can Cats'. They remained close after their studies and continued to meet regularly. Among Mead's fellow students was Marie Erle Eichelberger who was to become one of her closest friends, an intermittent co-habitant, and an educator for Mead's daughter. Eichelberger looked after Mead's household and finances while the latter pursued her career as an anthropologist. Until her death in 1948 Ruth Benedict was probably the most important woman in Mead's life. In 1940 she met Rhoda Bubendey Metraux, then a student at Vassar College, with whom Mead undertook a series of anthropological projects. When both women were on their own in 1955 they decided to share a house, bought by Rhoda and in which Mead rented one floor. Mead, one of the

most famous anthropologists of the twentieth century, is a prolific writer. Her many anthropological works began as inquiries into so-called primitive societies but towards the end of the twentieth century turned increasingly towards Western societies as an object of anthropological investigation. Her many works include *Inquiry into the Question of Cultural Stability in Polynesia* (1928), *Growing Up in New Guinea* (1943), *Coming of Age in Samoa: A Psychological Study of Primitive Youth* (1961), later complemented by *Coming of Age in Samoa: A Psychological Study of Primitive Youth for Western Civilization* (2001 reprint), *Sex and Temperament in Three Primitive Societies* (1963), *Science and the Concept of 'Race'* (1968), *Ruth Benedict* (1975), *Blackberry Winter: My Earlier Years* (1972), *Male and Female: The Classic Study of the Sexes* (1949), *Continuities in Cultural Evolution* (1964), and *And Keep Your Powder Dry: An Anthropologist Looks at America* (1942).

Melville, Herman (1819–91). Well known and successful during the early years of his writing career, Melville was largely forgotten until a revival of critical interest in the 1920s. Now considered one of the giants of US letters, he is increasingly embraced as an icon of gay literature as well. Along with Walt WHITMAN, his contemporary, Melville reveals in his work a preoccupation with male bonding that, while less pervasive than Whitman's, is nonetheless compelling. Born in New York, Melville spent several years as a sailor on merchant ships, whalers, and US Navy vessels after a reversal of fortune in the family's business. His experiences during this period are vividly reflected in the novels that established his initial popularity and reputation: *Typee* (1846), *Omoo* (1847), *Redburn* (1849), and *White-Jacket* (1850). Ironically, it was after the publication of *Moby Dick*, a novel now regarded as a masterpiece, in 1851 that he began a slow decline into the relative obscurity that lasted for the remainder of his long life. Other major writings include the novel *Pierre* (1852); the lengthy poem *Clarel* (1876); numerous short stories such as 'Benito Cereno', 'Bartleby the Scrivener', and 'The Encantadas'; and, notably, the short novel *Billy Budd*, published posthumously in 1924. The exact nature of Melville's own sexuality remains ambiguous, as difficult to pin down as the allegorical complexities of his tale of the white whale. His long marriage to Elizabeth Shaw Melville has been increasingly revealed to have been troubled. Much has also been made of Melville's intense friendship with writer Nathaniel Hawthorne. In a published review of Hawthorne, Melville wrote provocatively that '(Hawthorne) dropped germinous seeds in my soul... and shoots his strong New England roots into the hot soil of my Southern soul.' Their relationship ended under unexplained circumstances in the summer of 1851. Whatever the circumstances of his personal life, there is throughout Melville's writing a pervasiveness of same-sex bonding and a preoccupation with male physicality and other gender issues. These elements argue persuasively for his inclusion in the gay canon. Descriptions of native islanders in both *Typee* and *Omoo* are striking in their emphasis on the beauty of the men, lovingly described as 'Polynesian Apollos'. Homoerotic descriptions of sailors are notable in *White Jacket*, and particularly in the depiction of the sailor Harry Bolton in *Redburn*. *Moby Dick* abounds with episodes of male bonding that, read today, are startling in their intimacy and sexual implications. Passages ranging from the extended 'marriage bed' scene between Ishmael and Queequeg ('You had almost thought I had been his wife...') to the extraordinary 'Squeeze of the Hand' whale harvesting account ('I squeezed that sperm till a strange sort of insanity came over me; and I found myself unwittingly squeezing my co-laborers' hands in it, mistaking their hands for the gentle globules') are

unmistakable in their homoerotic content. The novella *Billy Budd* is Melville's most sustained presentation of the ambiguities of male sexuality, although here the mood is dark and the outcome tragic. Descriptions of the handsome Billy suggest a mix of gender characteristics: he is variously seen as Apollo, Hercules, and 'as feminine in purity of natural complexion'. The attraction of master-at-arms Claggart to Billy is clear in terms of its sexual nature, and his demise may be interpreted as the result of failed desire. Written at the end of his life, *Billy Budd* is Melville's strongest statement about the consequences of repressed sexuality, a depiction very different from the romantic ruminations of his earlier works. It was the inspiration for the gay British composer Benjamin Britten's opera *Billy Budd*. The libretto was co-written with E.M. FORSTER.

[David Garnes]

Merrill, James (1926–95). Gay US novel writer and poet who was born into a wealthy stock-broking family. His parents divorced when he was twelve. While he was still at high school his father collected some of his writings and published them under the title *Jim's Book*. Merrill graduated from Lawrenceville School and enrolled at Amherst College. His studies were interrupted by a spell in the army during the Second World War. He graduated in 1947. However, after the publication of his first collection of poetry, *First Poems* (1951), he experienced writer's block and went to Rome to seek treatment. He then settled in Stonington, Connecticut, dividing his time between his home there and Greece. Merrill was never secretive about his homosexuality, which is both a persistent theme in his writings, and was said by him to have fuelled his work. In 1959 he published another collection of poetry, *The Country of a Thousand Years of Peace*, to be followed by *The Fire Screen* in 1969. In 1955 he began experimenting with Ouija boards. Out of those experiences, which involved his lover David Jackson and Jackson's wife Doris, and involved the calling upon various figures from Merrill's past as well as poets like W.H. AUDEN and W.B. Yeats, came a trilogy published collectively under the title *The Changing Light at Sandover* in 1982. It contained the volumes *Divine Comedies*; *Mirabell: Books of Number*; and *Scripts for the Pageant*. Merrill also published two novels, *The Seraglio* (1957) and *The (Diblos) Notebook* (1965), an experimental text. From 1979 Merrill divided his time between Stonington and Key West, where his lover David Jackson had a house.

Mew, Charlotte (1869–1928). British writer Charlotte Mary Mew was born in London to an architect and his wife Anna Maria Kendall Mew, who was the daughter of the head of the firm in which Charlotte Mew's father worked. Mew was brought up rather strictly in a family beset by tragedies: three of her siblings died during childhood, and two went insane in their twenties. Mew began writing stories and verses during her teens. Her story 'Passed' was accepted by Henry Harland for *The Yellow Book* in 1894. He refused a second story, 'The China-Bowl', but Mew continued publishing occasional stories and poems to supplement her family's dwindling income. Most of her poems were written between 1909 and 1916. In 1912 Henry Massingham's radical paper the *Nation* published her poem 'The Farmer's Bride' about a young woman who is so scared of him that she runs away. She is recaptured and from then on resides with him happily 'so long as men-folk keep away'. It is through lines such as these that Mew's lesbianism is indicated in her work. Mew was taken up by the hostess Catherine Scott at whose teas she read. She published a chapbook entitled *The Farmer's Bride* under the imprint of the Poetry Bookshop in 1916. This volume was noticed by Sidney Cockerell, director of the Fitzwilliam Museum, Cambridge, who sent it to literary friends

such as Thomas Hardy and Siegfried SASSOON. Cockerell's patronage eventually enabled Mew to receive a Civil Pension in 1923. In her personal life Mew was rather thwarted. Her passionate love of the writers Ella D'Arcy and May Sinclair came to nothing. Sinclair in fact broadcast Mew's affection for her, making Mew the butt of sustained ridicule. In her later years Mew stopped writing verse. Her mother died in 1923. Worse, her sister Anne with whom she had lived all her life died in 1927 after a long battle against cancer. Mew was deeply affected by these deaths and in February 1928, suffering from the strain of these bereavements, Mew was put into a nursing home. In March of the same year she committed suicide by drinking a bottle of disinfectant. Alida Klementaski Monro, of the Poetry Bookshop, published a volume entitled *The Rambling Sailor* posthumously in 1929.

Millay, Edna St Vincent (1892–1950). Born in Rockland, Maine, Millay was the oldest of three girls, brought up by their divorced mother who worked as a district nurse. Those close to Millay always called her Vincent. A poet and playwright, Millay attended Vassar College from where she graduated in 1917. She then moved to Greenwich Village in New York, where she wrote poetry and plays as well as journalistic pieces. In late 1921 she spent some months in Vienna, Austria, travelled through Italy and Albania, and went to Paris where she met Djuna BARNES, with whom she had previously collaborated at the Provincetown Theatre. Their relations were strained, partly for reasons of literary rivalry but also partly because Millay embarked on an affair with Barnes's partner, the sculptress Thelma Woods. In the winter of 1922 Millay met the poet Elinor Wylie who became one of her close friends. Through Wylie, Millay met Ruth BENEDICT and the poet Leonie Adams. In 1923 she married the widower of the feminist Inez Mulholland. However, at the centre of Millay's work are female figures and female relationships. During the 1920s her poetry was very popular but its lack of formal experimentalism at a time – high modernism – when experiments in form were central to much writing led to a decline in her popularity as a poet. Millay published many volumes of poetry and some plays including *Renascence and Other Poems* (1917), *A Few Figs from Thistles* (1920), *Aria da Capo* (1920; a pacifist play), *Second April* (1921), *Two Slatterns and a King* (1921), *The Harp Weaver* (1922), for which she won the Pulitzer Prize, *A Distressing Dialogue* (1924), *The King's Henchmen: A Play in Two Acts* (1927), *Fear* (1927), *The Fatal Interview: Sonnets* (1931), *The Princess Marries the Page: A Play in One Act* (1932), *Wine from These Grapes* (1934), *'There Are No Islands Anymore'* (1940); *Make Bright the Arrows* (1940), *1940 Notebook* (1940), *Invocation to the Muses* (1941), *The Murder of Lidice* (1942), *Poem and Prayer for an Invading Army* (1944), and *Mine the Harvest* (1954).

Miller, Isabel (1924–). US writer Isabel Miller was born Alma Routsong in Traverse City, Michigan. Miller went to college in 1942, interrupted her studies to serve for two years in the US Navy, but then received a BA in art from Michigan University in 1949. By that time she had also married Bruce Brodie with whom she lived for fifteen years. In the 1950s Miller published two novels under her own name, Routsong, *A Gradual Joy* and *Round Shape*. For a lesbian readership, however, her key work is *A Place for Us* (1967), originally printed in a 1,000-copy edition financed by Miller herself and later republished by McGraw-Hill as *Patience and Sarah*. The book received the American Library Association's first annual Gay Book Award. The novel was inspired by the relationship of Mary Ann Wilson and Miss Brundidge who lived together in Greene County, New York, in

the 1820s. Their story bears a mild resemblance to the Ladies of Llangollen (see BUTLER, LADY ELEANOR). *Patience and Sarah* is a historical cross-class romance in which the educated painter Patience White sets up home together with the cross-dressing farmer Sarah Dowling. Miller produced an uncompleted sequel to the novel with 'A Dooryard Full of Flowers', which appeared in 1993 in a collection of her stories bearing the same name. In *Side by Side* (1990) Miller to some extent replicated the story of *Patience and Sarah* with the depiction of the relationship between artist Patricia and herbalist Sharon. Miller's work celebrates lesbian partnerships.

Millett, Kate (1934–). US feminist and lesbian whose first work, *Sexual Politics* (1970), her PhD thesis for Columbia University, became a landmark text of second-wave feminism and feminist literary criticism. Born in St Paul, Minnesota, Millett graduated from the University of Minnesota in 1956 and then read English at St Hilda's College, Oxford, prior to embarking on her PhD at Columbia University. Millett's critique of D.H. Lawrence and Norman Mailer's work for their sexism and misogyny in *Sexual Politics* started a long career of publishing feminist critiques of patriarchal structures and institutions. Millett's interest in women's (auto)biographies was demonstrated in her documentary *Three Lives* (1970). Her own autobiographical novels, *Flying* (1974) and *Sita* (1977), describe her lesbian relationships and her political involvement in feminist politics. When *The Loony Bin Trip* (1991) was published, it received much critical attention for its engagement with women's mental breakdowns. A prolific and always very politically engaged writer with an activist focus in many of her writings, other work by Millett includes *The Prostitution Papers* (1973), *The Basement: Meditations on Human Sacrifice* (1979), *Give Sorrow Words: Maryse Holder's*

Letters from Mexico (1979), which Millett edited, *Going to Iran* (1982), *The Politics of Cruelty* (1994), *A.D. A Memoir* (1995), and *Mother Millett* (2001).

Mishima, Yukio (1925–70). Born into a family dominated by his grandmother Natsu, Mishima was taken from his mother at two months of age to spend all his time with his grandmother. The latter disliked boys' behaviour and brought him up in a feminizing way. This may have been the source of Mishima's misogyny. His father's lack of interest in his son's situation, on the other hand, led to an absence of a male role model in Mishima's life, and may account for the obsession he felt with masculinity in his later life. Until the age of thirty he was rather feminized and weak but he then embarked on a quest of masculinizing himself. In 1949, with his novel *Confessions of a Mask*, he had already come out as gay. In the 1950s he started weight-lifting, martial arts, and wearing particularly male attire such as sports gear, uniforms, and leather; he also organized the Shield Society, a private military group dedicated to traditional Japanese masculine ideals. *Confessions* is considered to be the first Japanese novel dealing with homosexuality. This was followed in 1951–3 by *Forbidden Colors*, a more sociological exploration of Tokyo's homosexual society. In this as in his other works such as 'Patriotism' (1960), *The Sailor Who Fell from Grace with the Sea* (1963), *Sun and Steel* (1968), and *Runaway Horses* (1969) Mishima represented ideals of a muscular masculine beauty, often achieved through pain and suffering. He was keenly interested in the restitution of certain traditional Japanese male values. In November 1970, together with four young men whom he had chosen for the purpose, he attempted a *coup d'état* at the Ichigaya, Tokyo, the headquarters of the Japanese Self-Defence Forces. This *coup* proved unsuccessful and Mishima killed himself immediately, committing *harakiri* (disembowelling himself).

Mohin, Lilian. Contemporary editor and publisher of lesbian and feminist poetry and other writings in the UK. Mohin, who has been the driving force behind the Onlywomen Press in London, published the first anthology of lesbian feminist poetry in the UK, *Beautiful Barbarians: Lesbian Feminist Poetry*, in 1986. This volume was important in promoting the work of lesbian feminist poets such as Jackie KAY, Bernardine EVARISTO, Suniti NAMJOSHI, Gillian HANSCOMBE, Judith BARRINGTON, and Mary DORCEY. She also previously edited *One Foot on the Mountain: An Anthology of British Feminist Poetry 1969–1979* (1979), a volume which appeared at a time when the women's movement was in full swing and cultural activism was considered an important part of mapping and reclaiming women's cultural heritage. Together with Sheila Shulman she has also edited *The Reach and Other Stories – Lesbian Feminist Fiction* (1984), and with Anna Livia she edited *The Pied Piper: Lesbian Feminist Fiction* (1989). In 1987 her *Not for the Academy: Lesbian Poets* appeared, and in 1992 she edited *An Intimacy of Equals*.

Monette, Paul (1945–). Gay US writer born in Lawrence, Massachusetts, educated at the Phillips Academy, Andover, Massachusetts, and at Yale University where he gained a BA in 1967. He subsequently taught at the Milton Academy and at Pine Manor College before settling into the life of a writer. Initially closeted he became an advocate of gay and lesbian rights, and an active supporter of ACT UP (AIDS Coalition to Unleash Power). He received international acclaim for *Borrowed Time: An AIDS Memoir* (1988), which deals with his lover Roger Horwitz's diagnosis of AIDS and subsequent death. The memoir stands as one of the great testimonies of the first decade of the AIDS epidemic. It was followed by the novel *Afterlife* (1990), which records the work of AIDS activists and reactions of the gay and lesbian community to AIDS. His subsequent memoir, *Becoming a Man: Half a Life Story* (1992), won him the National Book Award. Monette has published a series of volumes of poems including *The Carpenter at the Asylum: Poems* (1975); *No Witnesses: Poems* (1981); *Love Alone: Eighteen Elegies for Rog* (1988); and *West of Yesterday, East of Summer: New and Selected Poems 1973–1993* (1994). His other novels include *Taking Care of Mrs Carroll* (1978); *The Gold Diggers* (1979); *The Long Shot* (1981); *Lightfall* (1982); and *Halfway Home* (1991). He has also written various film scripts. His essays have appeared in a collection entitled *Last Watch of the Night: Essays too Personal and Otherwise* (1994) and *The Politics of Silence: The National Book Week Lectures* (1994). He has also published *Havana* (1991) and *Sanctuary: A Tale of the Woods* (1997).

Monnier, Adrienne (1892–1955). Born in Paris, this French lesbian book dealer and writer was a significant member of the modernist avant-garde in Paris in the early twentieth century. Monnier was born and died in Paris. In 1915 she opened her renowned bookshop La Maison des Amis des Livres. Four years later she moved her shop to the rue de l'Odéon where her partner, the book dealer Sylvia BEACH, had opened a bookshop for British and US books, Shakespeare and Company. Monnier and Beach shared a flat from 1921 until 1937 when Beach moved out, possibly because Monnier had become involved with a German *émigrée*, the photographer Gisèle Freund, whom she and Sylvia had taken in and who was living with them in their flat. Freund exhibited her work in Monnier's bookshop in 1939. In 1940 Freund fled to the south of France where she lived until 1942, and later moved to Argentina. Beach's and Monnier's friendship contin-

ued until Monnier fell seriously ill and, suffering from excruciating pain, decided to kill herself in 1955. Monnier was an experimental writer, with definite views about what being a bibliophile meant. Her writings have largely been forgotten, and she is now known mostly for her influential bookshop and her relationship with Sylvia Beach. Monnier's works, most of which were published after her death, include *Les Gazettes d'Adrienne Monnier 1925–1945* (1953); *Rue de l'Odéon* (1960), *Trois agendas d'Adrienne Monnier* (1960), *Dernières gazettes et écrits divers* (1961), *Les Poésies d'Adrienne Monnier* (1962), and her autobiography *The Very Rich Hours of Adrienne Monnier* (1976).

Moore, Honor. Contemporary lesbian US poet who lives and writes in Connecticut and New York City. Her poetry has been widely anthologized. Many of her poems focus on lesbian experiences and relationships. Her autobiographical verse play *Mourning Pictures* resulted in her receiving a CAPS Grant from the New York State Council for the Arts in 1976. That play is included in the volume she edited the following year entitled *The New Women's Theatre: Ten Plays by Contemporary American Women* (1977). In 1976 Moore also edited *Write Poems Women*. Other collections of poetry by Moore include *Leaving and Coming Back* (1981), *Memoir* (1988), and *Darling: Poems* (2001). In 1996 Moore published a biography of her grandmother, the painter Margarett Sargent, entitled *White Blackbird: A Life of the Painter Margarett Sargent by her Granddaughter*.

Moraga, Cherríe (1952–). Lesbian US essayist, poet, dramatist, and editor who was born in Whitter, California, to an Anglo father and a Chicana mother. Moraga describes her childhood as having been spent listening to women telling stories in the kitchen. In her work Moraga combines a lesbian sensibility with a

Chicana consciousness. In the 1980s she emerged as one of the most important voices in lesbian-Chicana literature in the USA. During her time as a graduate student at San Francisco State University, where she took an MA in Feminist Writing in 1980, she met Gloria ANZALDÚA with whom she edited *This Bridge Called My Back: Writings by Radical Women of Color* (1981), a volume which became a key text in the discussion about the position of women of colour in feminism, and was – and continues to be – much used on Women's Studies courses. It was published by the Kitchen Table/Women of Color Press, which Moraga helped co-found. This landmark text was followed by *Loving in the War Years* (1983), the first volume of poetry by an openly lesbian Chicana poet. In 1984 a women's theatre in Minneapolis staged a reading of Moraga's explicitly lesbian play *Giving up the Ghost*, published in 1986. Moraga then wrote two further plays, *The Shadow of Man* and *La extranjero*. Her work constantly engages with questions of sexuality and Chicana identity. It includes *Shattering the Myth* (1993), which she edited with Linda Feyder, *Heroes and Saints, and Other Plays* (1994), and *Hungry Woman* (2001).

Morgan, Claire *see* Highsmith, Patricia

Mori, Mari (1903–87). Japanese novelist and essayist who was born in Tokyo, the daughter of the novelist Ogai Mori. In 1957 she was awarded the Japanese Essayist Club Prize for her collection of essays *My Father's Hat*. She then began to work as a writer full-time and her novel *The Forest for Lovers*, which centres on homosexual love, won her the Tamura Toshiko Prize in 1961. *The Room Filled with Sweet Honey* won the Izumi Kyouka Prize in 1975. Her work combines romanticism with a strong sense of the erotic.

Moritz, Karl Philipp (1757–93). Gay German writer whose autobiographical novel

Anton Reiser (1785–90) portrays a young man suffering from psychological deprivation, who cross-dresses for the stage (at which he excels), and who longs to meet the famous German writer Goethe in order to serve him. Moritz also edited a journal of psychology, *Magazin zur Erfahrungsseelenkunde* (1783–93), which published first- and third-person accounts of psychological anomalies, among them homosexuality.

Murdoch, Iris (1919–99). Anglo-Irish philosopher and writer, Iris Jean Murdoch was born in Dublin but grew up in London, where she was educated at Badminton School and at the Froebel Institute. She then went to Somerville College, Oxford, where she read Classics, Ancient History, and Philosophy. During the Second World War Murdoch worked for a time as an Assistant Principal at the Treasury, and with UNRRA in London, Belgium, and Austria. She then undertook postgraduate work at Newnham College, Cambridge, returning to Oxford at the end of the Second World War and becoming a fellow of St Anne's College, Oxford, in 1948. In 1956 she married John Bailey, a literary critic and writer. He wrote a memoir of her, *Iris: A Memoir of Iris Murdoch* (1998), in which he describes their marriage and Murdoch's decline into Alzheimer's disease. He commented on Murdoch's attraction for members of both sexes and stated that while at St Anne's, an all-female college, 'she never went to bed with any of her colleagues, or indeed with any other woman, although the novelist Brigid BROPHY tried very hard to persuade her. That was both before and after we were married.' Murdoch clearly knew and had friendships with a number of lesbian women. When Esmé Ross Langley died in 1992, she wrote her obituary, commenting that she knew her from 'Arena Three' days, *Arena Three* being a journal for lesbians founded in 1963. However, in Murdoch's fiction it is gay men rather than lesbians who make an appearance and, indeed, in her fiction, men are more central to the action than women. Nevertheless, it is for her portrayal of gay and lesbian characters that Murdoch is included here. Her husband maintained in his memoir that Murdoch had 'an odd streak of romanticism about gay men' and they had close gay friends. One of the strengths, from a lesbian or gay perspective, of Murdoch's treatment of lesbians and gays is that she portrayed their relationships as of equal importance to relationships between heterosexuals, apt to be equally successful or unsuccessful. In her novel *An Unofficial Rose* (1962) a lesbian couple is depicted. In *The Bell* (1958) the relationship between a homosexual who has retreated into the performance of religion and a boy who comes to his community, Tobias, is explored. In *A Fairly Honourable Defeat* (1970) there is an extended representation of a gay couple, Simon and Axel, in which the fun-loving, slightly effeminate, younger Simon's relationship with the older, sterner Axel is tested but does not fail, and the novel, in the end, finds them happily on holiday in Paris. The couple, as do the other gay and lesbian characters in Murdoch's fiction, become an emblem of Murdoch's idea of human love as needing to be self-less rather than selfish.

Murdoch has written many other novels as well as philosophical writings. The novels include *Under the Net* (1954), *The Flight from the Enchanter* (1956), *The Sandcastle* (1960), *A Severed Head* (1961, dramatized by J.B. Priestley in 1963), *The Unicorn* (1963), *The Italian Girl* (1964), *The Red and the Green* (1965), *The Time of the Angels* (1968), *Bruno's Dream* (1969), *The Black Prince* (1973), for which she won the James Tait Black Memorial Prize, *A Word Child* (1975), *Henry and Cato* (1976), *The Sea, the Sea* (1978), for which she won the Booker Prize, *Nuns and Soldiers* (1980), *The Philosopher's Pupil* (1983), *The Good Apprentice* (1985), *The Philosopher's Stone* (1983), *The Book and the Brotherhood* (1987), *The Message to the Planet* (1989), *The Green Knight* (1993), and *Jackson's Dilemma* (1995). Among her philosophical works are *Sartre: Romantic Realist* (1953), an essay on 'The Moral Decision about Homosexuality' that appeared in *Man and Society* (vol. 7, 1964), *The Sovereignty of Good* (1970), *The Fire and the Sun: Why Plato Banished the Artists* (1978), *Acastos: Two Platonic Dialogues* (1986), *The Existentialist Political Myth* (1989), *Metaphysics as a Guide to Morals* (1993), and *The One Alone* (1995).

N

Namjoshi, Suniti (1941–). Born in India into an Indian noble family, Namjoshi, the only daughter of five children in the family, worked as an officer in the Indian Administrative Service before moving to Canada. There she completed her PhD on Ezra Pound's *Cantos* before becoming an Associate Professor in the Department of English at the University of Toronto. The long-term companion of the writer Gillian HANSCOMBE, Namjoshi now lives and writes in Rousdon, Devon. Namjoshi is a lesbian writer whose work has been influenced by her movement between East and West, her feminist stance, and by her lesbian identity. Her poetry is lyrical, and she has an interest in myth and legend that finds expression in her writings. Her work has been widely anthologized. In 1981 Namjoshi published *Feminist Fables*, a text that rewrote fairytales from a feminist perspective. This kind of reclamation of a literary history that had undervalued women and put them in marginal roles was a major preoccupation of feminist writers in the late 1970s and early 1980s, resulting famously in work by Anne Sexton, Michelene Wandor, and Angela Carter, among others, all engaging in this reclamation of fairytales and myths. Namjoshi also published *The Authentic Lie* (1982), *From the Bedside Book of Nightmares* (1984), *The Conversations of Cow* (1985), *Aditi and the One-eyed Monkey* (1986), *The Blue Donkey Fables* (1988), *Because of India: Selected Poems* (1989), *The Mothers of Maya Diip* (1989), *Saint Suniti and the Dragon* (1993), *Building Babel* (1996), and, in 2000, *Goja: An Autobiographical Myth*. Automythography has become an important form of writing for lesbians, promoted in particular through the publication of Audre LORDE's *Zami*. In her autobiographical myth Namjoshi engages in imaginary conversation with both Goja, a servant who helped bring her up, and Goldie, her grandmother. Her emotional attachments to both are presented as Namjoshi tries to explore the vast class differences between the two women, and her own experiences of moving from India to the West. The text attempts a reconciliation of the seemingly irreconcilable. It also details Namjoshi's sexual abuse, as a child, by a servant, and it analyses her later relationships with women. Together with Gillian Hanscombe, Namjoshi has also produced two volumes, *Flesh and Paper* (1986) and *Kaliyug, or Circles of Paradise* (1993).

Nestle, Joan (1940–). Lesbian US writer, archivist, and activist who was born in the Bronx in New York City, Nestle was brought up by her Jewish mother Regina. Her father died before she was born. After graduating from Martin van Buren High School in Queens, New York, she took a BA in English at Queens College,

Flushing, New York, in 1963 and an MA in English at New York University in 1968. She then began a PhD but never completed it. She took up teaching writing at Queens College, New York City, in 1966, retiring from teaching due to cancer in 1995. Nestle has been an important force in the lesbian and gay movement of New York and beyond. In 1972 she helped set up the Gay Academic Union (GAU). Importantly, she was the co-founder of the Lesbian Herstory Archives. In 1979 Nestle started to write erotic stories. In a context where lesbian feminism and socialist feminism had produced sustained critiques of the sexual objectification of women in unequal power relationships, Nestle's stories, which evoked the butch–femme relationships that were a key feature of lesbian culture and representation in the 1950s, made her an object of attack from members of the anti-pornography movement. Nestle continued to celebrate lesbian sex in her work, and continued to do so within the framework of butch–femme relations. Such relations, decried in the 1970s and early 1980s for their seeming replication of both heterosexual relationships and unequal power relations, have had something of a revival as part of the rise of queer in the late 1980s and 1990s. Her two key works on this are *The Persistent Desire: A Butch– Femme Reader*, which she edited in 1992, and her collection of stories, *A Restricted Country*, which came out in 1996. Like Pat CALIFIA and Dorothy ALLISON, Nestle belongs to a generation of women who have resisted the ideological dominants within lesbian culture, celebrating instead both lesbian relations and a lesbian sexuality that acknowledge working-class roots, unequal relations between women, and the importance of sex. Together with Naomi Holoch, Nestle has also edited three volumes of *Women on Women: An Anthology of American Lesbian Short Fiction* (1990; 1993; 1996), and *The Vintage Book of International Lesbian Fiction* (1999).

With John Preston she has edited *Sister and Brother: Lesbians and Gay Men Write about Their Lives* (1995).

Newman, Lesléa (1955–). Born in Brooklyn, New York, this Jewish lesbian writer has created something of a controversy with her books for children such as *Heather has Two Mommies* (1989), which centres on a girl brought up by a lesbian couple. Newman went to the University of Vermont where she gained a BS in 1977, and in 1980 earned a certificate in Poetics from the Naropa Institute. Since then she has developed her writing career as well as working in a variety of jobs. In 1982 she acted as a manuscript reader for *Mademoiselle* and for *Redbook* in New York City. Between 1983 and 1987 she was a book reviewer and writer at the *Valley Advocate* in Hatfield, Massachusetts. She also taught in continuing education at the University of Massachusetts, and, between 1986 and 1988, directed and taught Creative Writing on the summer programme for high-school women at Mount Holyoke College, South Hadley, Massachusetts. In 1987 she founded the 'Write from the Heart: Writing Workshops for Women' in Northampton, Massachusetts. Newman is a regular contributor to lesbian journals such as *Sinister Wisdom* and *Heresies*. In her own work the issues of being a woman, a lesbian, and Jewish are paramount. She has written in a variety of genres. Her works include the novels *Good Enough To Eat* (1986), about a young woman's experience of bulimia, and *In Every Laugh a Tear* (1992), which centres on a middle-aged Jewish lesbian dealing with her grandmother's admission to a nursing-home, and coming to terms with the priorities in her own life, including her ultimate commitment to her lesbian lover. Newman's short stories have been collected under the titles *A Letter to Harvey Milk* (1988), itself the title of one of her short stories that was produced as a play at York University, Canada, in 1990, and

Secrets (1990). Newman has written *Fat Chance!* (1993) for young adults, and *Gloria Goes to Gay Pride* (1991), *Belinda's Bouquet* (1991), and *Saturday is Pattyday* (1993) for children. Her collections of poetry include *Just Looking for My Shoes* (1980), *Love Me Like You Mean It* (1987), and *Sweet Dark Places* (1991). Her play *After All We've Been Through* was produced in Durham, North Carolina, in 1989, and her play *Rage* was produced in New York in 1991. Her nonfiction includes *Somebody to Love: A Guide to Loving the Body You Have* (1991) and *Writing from the Heart: Inspiration and Exercises for Women Who Want to Write* (1993). She is editor of *Bubbe Meisehs by Shayneh Maidelehs: Poetry by Jewish Granddaughters about Our Grandmothers* (1989), *Eating Our Hearts Out: Personal Accounts of Women's Relationship to Food* (1993), and *Bearing the Unbearable: Stories of Losing Loved Ones to AIDS* (1994). She has also published *Every Woman's Dream: Short Fiction* (1994), *The Femme Mystique* (1995), and *Out of the Closet and Nothing to Wear* (1997). In 1989 Newman was awarded a Massachusetts Artists' Foundation fellowship in poetry. She also won the Lambda Literary Award for *Gloria Goes to Gay Pride* and the Highlights for Children fiction writing award for her story 'Remember That' (1992). Newman is a member of several writers' organizations including the Society of Children's Book Writers, the Authors' League of America, the Feminist Writers' Guild, and the Academy of American Poets.

Nichols, John Beverley (1898–1983). Gay British writer, born in Bower Ashton, Bristol. Nichols went to Marlborough College and Balliol College, Oxford, where, for a time, he was president of the Oxford Union. He was editor of *Isis*, and founder and editor of *Outlook*, an Oxford journal. Nichols wrote a variety of texts during his life. He was both a broadcaster and a columnist. In the latter capacity he was a rival of Godfrey Winn, a fellow columnist. Nichols involved himself in anti-racist campaigns in the 1950s, and spoke out against anti-homosexual legislation and homophobia. He was relatively open about his own homosexuality. He earned his living through writing. In 1920 he published *Prelude*, a story of schoolboy love. In 1926 he published his autobiography *Twenty-Five*. He then wrote his most successful volume, *Down the Garden Path*, a gardening book. *Merry Hall* (1950) was the story of the transformation of a derelict house and garden. In 1958 he published *The Sweet and Twenties*. When *A Case of Human Bondage* (1966) appeared, a volume which defended Syrie Maugham, the wife of W. Somerset MAUGHAM, Nichols fell out seriously with Winn, who had been a lover of Maugham's and regarded the book as an attack on his character. Nichols had a companion for forty years.

Nin, Anaïs (1903–77). Bisexual French-born writer and diarist who was the only daughter and oldest child of the Spanish composer and pianist Joaquín Nin and the Cuban-born opera singer Rosa Culmell. Her father abandoned the family when Nin was ten years old but she had already been abused by him. Her mother took Nin and her two siblings to New York when she was eleven years old. On the journey Nin began her diaries that would grow to 150 volumes during her lifetime. Although the diaries themselves did not appear until 1966 Nin published poetic fiction based on those diaries from 1936 onwards. In 1923 Nin married Hugh Guiler and they lived in Paris from then until 1939. During this period Nin became increasingly prolific. Her personal life grew more complicated when, in 1931, she met and fell in love with, first, Henry Miller's wife June and, then, Miller himself. Her first book, *D.H. Lawrence: An Unprofessional Study* (1932) had been completed just prior to meeting the Millers. Based on her diaries from the period she then wrote *The House of Incest* (1936) and *The Winter of Artifice* (1939), a volume of short fiction that features a central character named after Djuna BARNES. Djuna Barnes also reappears in Nin's *Cities of the Interior* (1959). *Diary I* (1966) covers Nin's early years. Initially, it was heavily censored and two sections from it, *Henry and June* (1986) and *Incest* (1992), appeared some time after her death. The title of *Incest* harked back to her relation with her father, with whom she was reconciled in 1932, only to re-enter into an incestuous relationship with him. She finally managed to free herself from his hold over her through psychoanalysis. He died in Cuba in 1949. Most of Nin's work explores the relationship between sexuality and identity. Her inability to make it in the literary establishment in New York during the 1940s led her to set up her own press in Greenwich Village where she published the books she had written in Paris and a collection of short fiction, *Under a Glass Bell* (1944). She also wrote erotica to make ends meet. She produced six novels based on her diaries, *Ladders to Fire* (1946), *Children of the Albatross* (1947), *The Four Chambered Heart* (1950), *A Spy in the House of Love* (1954), *Seduction of the Minotaur* (1961), and *Collages* (1964), before finally beginning to publish the diaries themselves. She divided the last thirty years of her life between New York and Hugh Guiler and Los Angeles and Rupert Pole. Her intermittent relationships with women, and her openness towards sexual self-determination, make her interesting for a lesbian readership. Some of her works have been considered feminist in content.

O

O'Hara, Frank (1926–66). Gay US poet and art critic who was born in Baltimore. When he was one year old his family moved to Grafton, Massachusetts, where O'Hara was privately educated until 1944. He served two years in the Navy before entering Harvard to study music. He switched to English, gaining a BA in 1950, and then completing an MA at the University of Michigan in 1951. While at Michigan University he wrote two plays, *Try! Try!* and *Change Your Bedding*, and won the Hopwood Award in Creative Writing. He then took a job at the Museum of Modern Art in New York, spent two years as an associate editor at *Art News* (1953–5), and eventually, in 1960, became curator of paintings and sculptures at the Museum of Modern Art. O'Hara published both art criticism, such as a definitive study on Jackson Pollock in 1959, and poetry. In his poetry he sometimes collaborated with artists, and was interested in translating the techniques of Dadaist art into poetry. In 1952 he published his first major collection of poetry, *A City Winter and Other Poems*. This was followed by *Stones* (1958) and *Odes* (1960). O'Hara's poetry drew on urban gay culture. O'Hara also collaborated on two experimental films, *The Last Clean Shirt* (1963) and *Philosophy in the Bedroom* (1965). He died prematurely in 1966, having been hit by a dune buggy on Fire Island.

Olivia *see* Strachey Bussy, Dorothy

Orton, Joe (1933–67). Gay British novelist and playwright, born John Kingsley Orton in a working-class area of Leicester as the oldest of five children to William and Elsie Orton. Orton moved to London when he was eighteen to go to the Royal Academy of Dramatic Arts, where he auditioned and was accepted in 1951. There he met Kenneth Halliwell, then twenty-five, who was to be Orton's mentor and lover for sixteen years. Halliwell encouraged Orton to read literature. Halliwell and Orton moved in together in 1951, first in West Hampstead and then in 1959 in Islington. Orton worked as an actor and stage manager for a while. During the 1950s he and Halliwell collaborated on several novels, which were not published during their lifetimes. They included *The Boy Hairdresser* (1954), *Between Us Girls* (1957, published posthumously in 1998), and *Lord Cucumber* (1960, published posthumously, together with *The Boy Hairdresser*, in 1999). Orton and Halliwell used public libraries to borrow books that they either stole and used to decorate their flat, or defaced in obscene ways. In 1962 they were arrested and sent to prison for six months for this offence. Following their release from prison, Orton began writing seriously, producing the novel *Head to Toe* (published posthumously in 1971) but, more importantly, embarking on writing plays which were dark satiric comedies and which made his name. His first play, *The Ruffian on the Stair* (1963), was based on Harold Pinter's early work. Orton then wrote *Entertaining Mr Sloane* (1963), *The Good and the Faithful Servant* (1964), *Loot* (1966), which was the *Evening Standard*'s Best Play of that year, and *What the Butler Saw* (1967, published posthumously in 1969). During the 1960s Orton thus became established in London's literary and theatrical circles while Halliwell failed to become a success. Orton was commissioned to write a movie script for the Beatles entitled *Up against It* (posthumously published in 1979). As Orton became more and more successful and Halliwell did not make a name for himself, the latter became more and more disenchanted and alienated. On 9 August 1967 Halliwell bludgeoned the sleeping Orton to death before committing suicide by taking an overdose of Nembutals. Subsequent to his death, Orton has been the object of several biographical texts and a film, *Prick Up Your Ears* (1987), based on John Lahr's biography of Orton.

Owen, Wilfred (1893–1918). Gay British poet, born Wilfred Edward Salter Owen in Shropshire. His father was a railway worker. He was educated at the Birkenhead Institute in Liverpool and at Shrewsbury Technical College. For a while he worked as a pupil-teacher. Interested in poetry from an early age, he began experimenting with verse form. He failed to get into university and went to work in a poor country parish for a while before leaving England in 1913 to teach English at the Berlitz School of Languages in Bordeaux. He returned to England in 1915 and was soon commissioned, going to France as an officer towards the end of 1916. Suffering from shell shock and trench fever, he was sent back to England in June 1917. He was treated at Craiglockhart War Hospital in Edinburgh. This period of Owen's life has been fictionalized by Pat BARKER in a trilogy that eventually won her the Booker Prize. At Craiglockhart, Owen met the poet Siegfried SASSOON who encouraged him to work on his poetry. When Owen was discharged from Craiglockhart, Sassoon gave him a letter of introduction to London's literary circles where he met Oscar WILDE's friend Robert Ross, the poet Osbert Sitwell, and others. When Sassoon returned wounded from the front in 1918, Owen felt he should take his place. He was posted back to France in August 1918 where he was killed in action, leading his men across the Sambre Canal, a week before the Armistice was signed. He was awarded the Military Cross posthumously for leadership. During his lifetime only five of his poems were published. His poetry, most of which was written between the summer of 1917 and the autumn of the following year, makes him one of the outstanding war poets of his generation, though his reputation was slow to grow. His work was first collected in 1920 by Sassoon. Much of it celebrates and mourns the beauty of dead young men. Owen wrote about the waste of young men's lives during the war, combining homoeroticism with acute observations of the horror of trench warfare. Benjamin Britten used some of his poems for his *War Requiem*, which was made into a film by Derek JARMAN in 1988. C. Day Lewis edited Owen's collected poems in 1967. In 1974 Jon Stallworthy published his biography and in 1985 Stallworthy edited a further edition of Owen's poems. His work is now routinely taught in schools and universities.

P

Parnók, Sofia Iakovlevna (1885–1933). Russian lesbian poet, born in Taganrog. Her mother, a physician, died when Parnók was six years old, and her father, a pharmacist, remarried shortly afterwards. Parnók did not get on with her new stepmother or with her father, who was to disapprove of her lesbianism. She began to write poetry early, favouring traditional forms such as the sonnet. During her last two years at the gymnasium, a grammar school, (1901–3) she wrote extensively about her lesbian sexuality and her love affairs. In 1905 Parnók left home to spend a year travelling in Europe with an actress lover. Lack of funds forced her to return home and in order to escape from her father's house she married a fellow poet and settled in St Petersburg. She found the marriage constraining both from a creative point of view and in terms of her personal life, and therefore decided, in 1909, to leave her husband and brave the financial problems and social censure that would ensue, in order to free herself. She then settled in Moscow, making money through journalism, translations, and as an opera librettist. She published under the male pseudonym Andrei Polianin. In 1914 she met and fell in love with the poet Marina TSVETÁEVA. Both women's poetry was abidingly influenced by their relationship. They broke up in 1916, the year that Parnók's first volume of *Poems* appeared,

which focused on lesbian desire. Parnók acquired a new lover, the actress Lyudmila Erarskaya, with whom she left Moscow in 1917 to live in the Crimean town of Sudak during the Civil War years. There Parnók wrote the libretto for Alexander Spendiarov's opera *Almast*. Several collections of Parnók's poetry were published in the 1920s. They include *Roses of Pieria* (1922), *The Vine* (1923), *Music* (1926), and *Half-voiced* (1928). In 1923 Parnók met Olga Tsuberbiller, a mathematician who taught at Moscow University. The two women embarked on a relationship and lived together from 1925 until Parnók's death. Parnók's last few years were weighed down by ill health and by the fact that the Russian censor made the publication of her poetry impossible. In late 1931 she met and fell in love with another scientist, this time the physicist Nina Vedeneyeva. Their affair inspired Parnók's final verse cycles 'Ursa Major' and 'Useless Goods'. Parnók died of a heart attack in a village outside Moscow. Her collected works finally appeared in Russia in 1979.

Pasolini, Pier Paolo (1922–75). Gay Italian artist whose openly homosexual lifestyle and art roused much controversy during his lifetime. Like Derek JARMAN, Pasolini was both a writer and a filmmaker. Pasolini was born in Bologna and brought up in the rural area of Friuli. His first poems, published in 1942, were written in Friulian dialect. During the Second World War he began working as a school teacher. In 1945 he joined the Communist Party. When Pasolini was arrested for corrupting minors and obscene acts in public places in 1949, he was expelled from the party and suspended from his job. He left Friuli for Rome. Pasolini's diaries from this period describe his life in Friuli, and his relations with boys from the area. In some respects similar to Jean GENET, Pasolini had a fascination with sub-proletarian youths. They reappear throughout his work, including in some of his films where he gave them bit parts. Before going to Rome Pasolini drafted his first novel, *Il sogno di una casa* (1988; *A Dream of Something*), first published in 1962. Pasolini's adventures with boys in Rome were captured in *Ali dagli occhi azzuri* (1965). A selection of the stories can be found in the translated collection, *Roman Nights* (1986). Pasolini's two major novels, *Ragazzi di vita* (1955; *The Ragazzi*, 1968) and *Una vita violenta* (1959; *A Violent Life*, 1968), both caused a stir because of their celebration of a certain kind of working-class and street-based masculinity. In Rome Pasolini began his life as a film-maker. His first film, *Accattone*, appeared in 1961. It was followed by *The Gospel According to St Matthew* (1964), *Teorama* (1968; *Theorem*), *The Decameron* (1971), *The Canterbury Tales* (1972), *The Arabian Nights* (1973), and *Salò* (1975), based on the Marquis de Sade's *The 120 Days of Sodom*. Pasolini continued to write during these years. His film *Theorem*, for example, was also published as a novel. Pasolini was murdered in 1975 by a hustler he had picked up at Rome central station.

Pass, Gail. Contemporary lesbian US writer, born in Toledo, Ohio, who attended Smith College and graduated from the University of California, Berkeley, in 1962. She worked and lived in the San Francisco Bay area for about fifteen years before moving to Portsmouth, New Hampshire. Her first lesbian novel, *Zoe's Book* (1976), centres on a young woman's involvement with now ageing members of the Bloomsbury group, including Virginia WOOLF. Pass lived in New England for four years where she taught fiction writing in the Department of Continuing Education at the University of New Hampshire. She also helped to establish a battered women's shelter. Pass's second novel, *Surviving Sisters* (1981), deals with the impact of the Vietnam War on a family of Greek extraction who lose a son in that war. One of the surviving sisters becomes involved with a woman archaeologist, uncovering an ancient female-centred past. Both Pass's novels reveal the author's interest in the impact of the past on the present, and the ways in which the past can ultimately help to free individuals from the constraint of the present.

Pater, Walter (1839–94). Walter Horatio Pater was born in Stepney as the son of a surgeon who died when Pater was three years old. He was educated at King's School, Canterbury, and Queen's College, Oxford. He became a fellow of Brasenose College, Oxford, in 1864. A homophile aesthete and celebrant of beauty and of art for art's sake, he was a forerunner of Oscar WILDE. From 1869 he lived with his unmarried sisters Hester and Clara, first in Oxford and then in London, embracing a style that was much influenced by the Pre-Raphaelites, some of whom such as SWINBURNE and Dante Gabriel Rossetti were among his friends. Pater produced both critical writings on art and on literature and fiction. His *Studies in the History of the Renaissance* (1873) contained a series of celebrated essays, including one on Johann Joachim WINCKELMANN, whose interest in Greek art and sculpture, driven by his homoerotic interests in boys, Pater acknowledged. Pater suppressed the conclusion of this work that encouraged the celebration of experience and living for/in the moment in the second edition of 1877 because it was thought to incite inappropriate behaviour in young men. The 'Conclusion' was restored in the third edition of 1888. In 1878 Pater published 'The Child in the House' in *Macmillan's Magazine*, a text considered to be an autobiographical representation of his own childhood. His historical novel *Marius the Epicurean* (1885; revised 1892), set in Rome during the reign of the emperor Marcus Aurelius, reflected Pater's engagements with paganism, Greek philosophy, Christianity, and Rome, where he had travelled in 1882. In 1887 Pater's *Imaginary Portraits* was published. It, like his previous novel, utilized a hybrid of historical and mythological sources, to dwell on notions of early promise and premature death, a favourite theme among the decadent aesthetes of the second half of the nineteenth century. In 1889 *Appreciations* appeared, a collection of essays on various literary figures and on style. *Plato and Platonism* (1893) was a volume of prose poetry. After Pater's death his writings on Greek culture appeared as *Greek Studies* (1895). His unfinished novel, *Gaston de Latour*, was published (1896), with the subtitle 'An Unfinished Romance'. This novel, as well as other shorter pieces such as the historical romances 'Emerald Uthwart' (*The New Review*, 1892) and 'Apollo in Picardy' (*Harper's New Monthly*, 1893), showed Pater's interest in a rather morbid cruelty, beauty, and sensibility that he associated romantically with the past.

Patrick, Robert (1937–). Gay US playwright, born in Texas and raised in the South before he began life in the experimental and gay theatre circles of New York in the mid-1960s, working initially at the Caffe Cino. Using his adopted name Una O'Connor, Patrick worked as a typist in the city morgue during the day and in the theatre at night. His first play,

The Haunted Host, was produced at the Caffe Cino in 1964. When Joe Cino died in 1967, Patrick moved to the Old Reliable Tavern Theatre. His most famous play, *Kennedy's Children* (1973), in which a group of five characters in a bar remember where they were the night that Kennedy was assassinated, played briefly on Broadway. In this play he appears as Sparger, a drag queen, recounting what seems to be the history of the Caffe Cino. A figure who resembles Patrick appears in many of his plays. London's Gay Sweatshop Theatre included two of his plays, *The Haunted Host* and *One Person*, in their first season in 1975. His plays present satires of gay life in New York, drawing on parody, camp, and monologues, all stalwarts of certain kinds of experimental theatre of the 1960s and early 1970s. *T-shirts* (1978) depicts the sexual economy of gay city life. His one-act plays were published as *Untold Decades* (1988). He has also published a novel, *Temple Slave*, about life at the Caffe Cino.

Penelope, Julia (1941–). Lesbian US writer and linguist whose work has been important in promoting lesbian perspectives on language and culture. Penelope completed her BA at the City University of New York in 1966 after having been kicked out of Florida State University and the University of Miami. She then went on to do her PhD at the University of Texas at Austin, completing it in 1971. She taught in universities for twenty years before settling down to a life of writing in Massachusetts. She lists as her hobbies cooking, gardening, weight-lifting, and rock hunting. Her publications, many of which she co-edited, include *The Original Coming out Stories* (1980, 1989) which she co-edited with Susan J. Wolfe under the name of Julia Penelope Stanley. With Wolfe she also edited *Sexual Practice/Textual Theory: Lesbian Cultural Criticism* (1993) and *Lesbian Culture: An Anthology* (1993). Her anthology *For*

Lesbians Only: A Separatist Anthology (1988), which she co-edited with Sarah Lucia Hoagland, has been very influential in preserving key documents from the lesbian movement. With Sarah Valentine she edited *Finding the Lesbians* (1990) and *International Feminist Fiction* (1992). With Morgan Grey she co-authored *Found Goddesses: From Asphalta to Viscera* (1988). She has also authored *Speaking Freely: Unlearning the Lies of the Fathers' Tongues* (1990) and *Call Me Lesbian: Lesbian Lives, Lesbian Theory* (1992). In 1994 she published *Out of the Class Closet: Lesbians Speak*, and in 1995 her *Crossword Puzzles for Women* appeared.

Penna, Sandro (1906–77). Italian poet whose work centres on boys as his source of inspiration and love. Born in Perugia into a middle-class family, his parents' unhappy marriage led to his mother abandoning the family to go to Rome in 1920. This affected Penna deeply. Always prone to illness and depression Penna saw himself very much as an outsider who never really became part of the Italian literary establishment despite winning major literary prizes. After leaving school he initially worked for his father but was sacked from his job in 1929 when he moved to Rome to live there for most of his adult life. His poetry was championed by Pier Paolo PASOLINI, Elsa Morante, and Alberto Moravia. Literary friends such as the poets Umberto Saba and Eugenio Montale helped Penna to get published. In 1939 Penna's volume of poetry *Poesie* came out. He eked out a precarious living in a variety of jobs during the Second World War and in 1950 published *Appunti*, a volume containing some thirty-seven poems of his. This was followed in 1956 by *Una strana gioia di vivere* for which he received the Le Grazie Prize. In 1957 a second volume entitled *Poesie* appeared, presenting a collection of his poems from the period 1927 to 1957. This won him the Viareg-

gio Prize, which, since he shared it with his friend Pasolini, caused an outcry as it seemed to point to the ascendancy of left-wing homosexual artists. The re-issue of Penna's work in 1970 led to the Fiuggi Prize. However, possibly due to the specificity of his thematic focus and his sexual interest in boys, expressed clearly in his poems, his writings achieved little by way of wider recognition. To date his work has not been disseminated in English. Penna died shortly after winning the Bagutta Prize for his last collection of poetry, *Stranezze*, which contained work from the period 1957 to 1976.

Peri Rossi, Cristina (1941–). Uruguayan writer, born in Montevideo to Italian immigrants, who was educated at the University of Montevideo. She was persecuted by the Uruguayan government for her opposition to oppression and moved to Barcelona in Spain in 1972. In her work Peri Rossi addresses both the situation of women under patriarchy and transgressive sexual relationships. Her first two books were volumes of short stories, exploring women's situation in patriarchal society. *Viviendo* (1963; *Living*) was followed by *Los museos abandonados* (1969; *The Abandoned Museums*) for which Peri Rossi won the Arca Prize for young Uruguayan authors in 1968. Her novel *El libro de mis primos* (1969; *The Book of My Cousins*) was also successful and won a prize from *Marcha* magazine. Peri Rossi's subsequent book, *Indicios pánicos* (1970; *Signs of Panic*), however was banned by the Uruguayan military government when it seized power in 1973. Peri Rossi's first volume of poems, *Evohé* (1971), has been read as a text that presents lesbian sexual desire in coded form. Many of Peri Rossi's poems celebrate the female body. Her subsequent volumes of poetry, written in Barcelona, took up the theme of lesbian love and marine images, a theme not uncommon during the period in lesbian writing. Thus, shortly after Adrienne RICH, for instance, had published her collection *Diving into the Wreck* (1973), Peri Rossi published *Descripción de un naufragio* (1975; *Description of a Shipwreck*). The marine images used in this volume (again, it is worth noting that some time later the French lesbian theorist Luce IRIGARAY published her volume *Marine Lover*) are transfigured in *Diáspora* (1976; *Diaspora*), where the objectified woman at the centre declares her lesbian identity openly. This collection won the 1973 Inventarios Provisionales. Peri Rossi's later works include *La tarde del dinosaurio* (1976; *The Afternoon of the Dinosaur*); *La rebelión de los niños* (1980; *The Children's Rebellion*); *El museo de los esfuerzos inútiles* (1983; *The Museum of Useless Endeavours*); *La nave de los locos* (1984; *The Ship of Fools*); *Una passión prohibida* (1986; *A Forbidden Passion*); and *Desastres íntimos* (1997; *Intimate Disasters*).

Pessoa, Fernando (1888–1935). The sexual identity of Portugal's greatest modernist poet has been the object of some speculation since little is recorded regarding his personal relationships. However, writings such as the long poem 'Antinous', published with *35 Sonnets* (1918), suggest homoerotic interests in his work. Pessoa was born in Lisbon where he lived for most of his life though he grew up in Natal, South Africa, receiving an English education. He was a student at the University of the Cape of Good Hope, Cape Town, before returning to Portugal in 1905 where he earned his living writing letters in foreign languages for companies exporting abroad. Like the Greek writer CAFAVY, Pessoa developed a number of voices, styles, and pseudonyms under which he wrote including Alberto Caeiro, Alvaro de Campos, and Ricardo Reis. He coined the term heteronym to describe these distinct personalities. Viewed by some as the expression of a schizophrenic imagination, queer theory has rehabilitated this style as an expression of perfor-

mativity. Pessoa lived a fairly reclusive, slightly dandyish life.

Philips, Katherine (1632–64). Born as the daughter of the London merchant John Fowler, Philips married James Philips of Cardigan, Wales, when she was sixteen years old. Her husband was thirty-eight years her senior, a wealthy Welsh Puritan and supporter of Oliver Cromwell. With him Philips had two children. Her son died in infancy but her daughter survived Philips's early death from smallpox. Philips is known predominantly as a poet. Her earliest poems were prefixed to the poems of Henry Vaughan (1651). A well-educated woman who knew several languages Philips translated Corneille's *Pompée*, which was performed in Dublin in 1663 to great acclaim. She also translated *Horace*, which, however, remained uncompleted at the time of her death. Her own collected poems appeared first in an unauthorized version in the year of her death, 1664, and then in an authorized one in 1667. These poems established her as a poet who used the conventional language of courtship to describe relationships between women. Philips had a 'Society of Friendship', a correspondence circle that was active for about ten years between 1651 and 1661. In this society members adopted classical names. The society appears to have included Mary Aubrey (or 'Rosania') and Anne Owen (also known as 'Lucasia'). Philips's poems suggest that she was what one might now term a woman-identified woman. Known as the 'matchless Orinda' in her female friendship circles many of her poems were addressed to 'Lucasia', with whom she seems to have had a ten-year relationship between 1652 and 1662.

Picano, Felice (1944–). Gay US writer and publisher, born as the third of four children to Anne and Felice Picano, both of Italian descent, in New York City and educated at Queens College of the City University of New York, where he gained a BA in 1964. Between 1964 and 1966 he worked as a social worker in East Harlem, New York. He then left for Europe, a break with the States that enabled him to 'become a homosexual'. On his return he worked in various capacities for several bookshops including the Doubleday Bookstore in New York City (1969–70) and Rizzoli's Bookstore, New York (1972–4). He also undertook freelance writing. Between 1980 and 1983 he was book editor for the *New York Native*. From 1977 he founded a variety of gay publishing houses including SeaHorse Press Ltd, and became one of the leading figures of the contemporary US gay literary scene. His first novel, *Smart as the Devil* (1975), was a finalist for the Ernest Hemingway Award. He then published two novels that had no gay content, *Eyes* (1976) and *The Mesmerist* (1977), which proved to be commercial successes. In 1979 he wrote an openly gay thriller, *Lure*. After the founding of SeaHorse Press, the first wholly gay publishing house in New York, Picano joined forces with two other gay presses to form Gay Presses of New York (GPNY), which has been very influential on the gay literary scene and published, among others, bestsellers such as Harvey FIERSTEIN's *Torch Song Trilogy*. Picano's publishing activities led to the configuration of a group of gay writers including Edmund WHITE and Andrew HOLLERAN, which became known as the Violet Quill Club. In the 1970s Picano decided to become a writer. Following the commercial success of his first three 'straight' novels, he began to write openly about gay life, both his own and fictional ones. In 1980 he published *An Asian Minor: The True Story of Ganymede*. This was followed by *Late in the Season* (1981), *House of Cards* (1984), and *To the Seventh Power* (1989). His two autobiographical accounts, *Ambidextrous: The Secret Lives of Children* (1985) and *Men Who Loved Me: A Memoir in the Form of a Novel* (1989), detail Picano's sexual awakening, the first covering

the period when he was between ten and fourteen years old, the second describing his experiences in his twenties. Picano has published two volumes of poetry, *The Deformity Lover, and Other Poems* (1978) and *Window Elegies* (1986). He has also written *Like People in History* (1995), *Dryland's End* (1995), a science fiction narrative, *A House on the Ocean, a House on the Bay* (1998), and *Onyx* (2001). He has contributed to many anthologies of gay writing including *Aphrodisiac: Fiction from Christopher Street* (1980, ed. Michael Denneny), *The Christopher Street Reader* (1983, eds. Charles Ortleb and Michael Denneny), *The Penguin Book of Homosexual Verse* (1983, ed. Stephen Coote), *The Male Muse, Number Two* (1983, ed. Ian Young), *Men on Men* (1986, ed. George Stambolian), and *The Gay Nineties* (1991, eds Phil Wilkie and Greg Baysans). He himself has also edited various collections including *A True Likeness: An Anthology of Lesbian and Gay Writing Today* (1980), *Slashed to Ribbons in Defense of Love, and Other Stories* (1983), and *New Joy of Gay Sex* (1992, with Charles Silverstein).

Piercy, Marge (1936–). US writer, born in Detroit, Michigan, into a working-class Jewish family. In 1958 Piercy gained an MA from Northwestern University. Married three times, Piercy's writing has been infused by her left-wing politics and her desire for a better world. In the 1960s she became active in the women's movement. Her early novels reflected her engagement with the interrogation of conventional gender roles as evidenced in *Small Changes* (1973). This position led to one of the key novels of the feminist science fiction wave of the 1970s and early 1980s: *Woman on the Edge of Time* (1976) is probably Piercy's best-known and most widely read novel. In its representation of a futuristic world that transcends conventional gender roles, it has both a place in the history of lesbian literature that deals with precisely this topic and prefigures in some respects the emergence of 'queer' through its playing with gender roles. Embracing a particular kind of femininity Piercy subsequently wrote *The Moon is Always Female* (1980). She has written many other works including *Breaking Camp* (1968), *Hard Loving* (1969), *Going down Fast* (1969), *Dance the Eagle to Sleep* (1970), *The Grand Coolie Damn* (1970), *The Earth Smiles Secretly: A Book of Days* (1970), *A Work of Artifice* (1970), *When the Drought Broke* (1971), *To Be of Use* (1973), *Small Changes* (1973), *Living in the Open* (1976), *The Twelve-spoked Wheel Flashing* (1978), *The High Cost of Living* (1978), *Vida* (1979), *The Last White Class: A Play About Neighbourhood Terror* (1980, with Ira Wood), *Parti Colored Blocks for a Quilt* (1982), *Circles on the Water* (1982), *Braided Lives* (1982), *Stone, Paper, Knife* (1983), *Fly away Home* (1984), *My Mother's Body* (1985), *Gone to Soldiers* (1987), *Available Light* (1988), *Summer People* (1989), *He, She, and It . . .* (1991), *Mars and Her Children* (1992), *The Longings of Women* (1994), *City of Darkness, City of Light* (1996), *Storm Tide* (1998, with Ira Wood), *The Art of Blessing the Day* (1999), and *Three Women* (2000).

Pizarnik, Alejandra (1936–72). Argentinian writer, born into a Jewish immigrant family from Eastern Europe in Buenos Aires. She painted and wrote poetry from an early age, producing translations of surrealist poets such as André Breton and Paul Eluard. In 1960 she went to Paris where she lived for four years, writing and moving in literary circles. Little is as yet known about her private life though she had relationships with men and women while in Paris. She has been described as a poet *maudite* because her work references poets such as RIMBAUD and BAUDELAIRE. Her volumes of poetry gesture towards what one would now term queer sexuality. Her works include

La tierra más ajena (1955; *The Most Alien Land*), *Arbol de Diana* (1962; *Diana's Tree*), *La condesa sangrienta* (1965; *The Bloody Countess*), which is about the Hungarian countess Erszebet Báthory who sexually tortured and murdered numerous young women in her quest for eternal youth, *Extracción de la piedra de locura* (1968; *Extraction of the Stone of Folly*), *El infierno musical* (1971; *Musical Hell*), and *Textos de sombra* (*Shadow Texts*), published posthumously in 1982. In 1966 Pizarnik won the Buenos Aires First Prize for Poetry. She also held a Guggenheim Fellowship in 1968 and a Fulbright scholarship in 1971. Despite her increasing recognition as a poet, Pizarnik suffered from depression and repeatedly tried to commit suicide. She eventually died of an overdose. In 1987 Frank Graziano edited a collection of her writings, including poems and essays in a volume entitled *Alejandra Pizarnik 1936–1972*.

Ponsonby, Sarah *see* Butler, Lady Eleanor

Pool, Maria Louise (1841–98). Born in Rockland, Massachusetts, into a well-to-do manufacturing family, the third child of Lydia Lane Poole and Elias Poole, Pool's literary talent was recognized and encouraged by her father at an early stage. She taught in the local school for a year before settling down to a life of writing. Her first stories were published by Moses Dow in the *Waverly Magazine* when she was sixteen years old. Dow also supplied her with copies of the *Atlantic* and *Harper's Magazine*. A contemporary described her as a puritan maiden whose work was melodramatic. During her twenties Pool met Caroline M. Branson who, in the tradition of lesbian romantic friendships as described by Lillian FADERMAN, was to become her life-long companion. The two women lived together for thirty-two years. They moved to Brooklyn in 1870 but in 1877 returned to Massachusetts where they settled in a house that had been a station of the underground railroad in the town of Wrentham, the place where Caroline Branson had grown up. Pool was a great lover of Yorkshire terriers, and the two women had a succession of dogs. These also appeared in many of Pool's stories. During this period Pool began to write 'Random Sketches' for the *New York Tribune*, stories about life in New England. Pool's novels were very popular in her day. They included *Tenting at Stony Beach* (1888), *Dally* (1891), *Roweny in Boston* (1892), *Mrs Keats Bradford* (1892), the sequel to the previous novel, *Katherine North* (1892), *The Two Salomes* (1893), *Out of Step* (1894), *Mrs Gerald* (1896), *In a Dike Shanty* (1896), *In Buncombe County* (1896), *Boss and Other Dogs* (1896), a collection of short stories, *The Red-Bridge Neighbourhood* (1898), *A Widower and Some Spinsters* (published posthumously in 1899), *Chums* (published posthumously in 1899), *Sand n' Bushes* (published posthumously in 1899), and several undated novels including *Friendship and Folly*, *Little Bermuda*, and *In the First Person*. Pool's and Branson's happy years in Wrentham came to an end in 1894 when Pool felt impelled to move back to Rockland due to her mother's old age and her sister Amelia's ill health. Branson and Pool built a new house near Pool's childhood home. Pool was at her most productive, writing novels and short stories in quick succession. She was unexpectedly struck down with pneumonia in the spring of 1898, dying in May that year. Branson (1837–1918) survived Pool by many years but was buried, at her request, next to Pool in Mount Pleasant Cemetery in Rockland.

Pratt, Minnie Bruce (1946–). Lesbian US writer, born in Selma, Alabama. Pratt attended the University of Alabama in Tuscaloosa and the University of North Carolina at Chapel Hill. Her work in grassroots organizations and her teaching experiences in traditionally black universities strongly influenced her political activism. Pratt married and had two sons before coming out as lesbian. For five years she was a member of the editorial collective of *Feminary: A Feminist Journal for the South, Emphasizing Lesbian Vision*. This journal started as a newsletter in 1969, focusing on literature. Together with Elly BULKIN and Barbara Smith she co-authored *Yours in Struggle: Three Feminist Perspectives on Anti-Semitism and Racism* (1984). Prior to that she had already published her first collection of poetry, *The Sound of One Fork* (1981). This was followed by a second collection, *We Say We Love Each Other* (1985). *Crime Against Nature* (1989) focused on Pratt's experiences as a lesbian mother with two sons who had to deal with a custody battle with her husband when she came out as lesbian. It was awarded the Lamont Poetry Selection by the Academy of American Poets. In 1991 the book also won the American Library Association Gay and Lesbian Book Award for Literature. When *Rebellion: Essays 1980–1991* came out in 1992 Pratt was granted a Creative Writing Fellowship in Poetry by the National Endowment for the Arts. The same year saw a significant change in her personal life. Pratt attended a talk in Washington, DC, by Leslie FEINBERG, a novelist, historian and transgender activist. They fell in love and Pratt describes Feinberg as her 'beloved lesbian husband'. The relationship led to Pratt's collection of stories *S/he* (1995), which explores fluid gender roles. *Walking Back up Depot Street*, another collection of poetry, was nominated Best Lesbian/Gay Book of the Year in 1999. Pratt teaches Women's Studies, Creative Writing, and Lesbian/ Gay/Bisexual/Transgender Studies in the Graduate Faculty of the Union Institute, an alternative PhD-awarding university. In 2000 she was the New York City Writers'

Community Writer-in-Residence as part of the YMCA National Writer's Voice Program.

Prime-Stevenson, Edward Irenaeus (1868–1942). Gay US writer who was born into a middle-class, literary family in New Jersey and who studied Law before devoting his life to writing and editing magazines such as *Harper's* and *The New York Independent*. Initially Stevenson wrote books for boys, centring on romantic teenage friendships. These included *White Cockades: An Incident of the 'Forty-five'* (1887) and *Left to Themselves: Being the Ordeal of Gerald and Philip* (1891). In the first decade of the twentieth century he also published a series of texts that were overtly homosexual under the pseudonym Xavier Mayne. His volume *The Intersexes* (1908) offered a defence of homosexuality. *Imre: A Memorandum* (1906) was a story of the relationship between two men that, amazingly for its time, had a happy ending. In 1913 Stevenson published a collection of short stories, including homoerotic ones, under the title *Her Enemy, Some Friends – and Other Personages*. By this time he had already moved to Europe. He wrote less and less and died in Lausanne in Switzerland.

Proust, Marcel (1871–1922). Born into an intellectual, middle-class family, the French writer Proust enjoyed a cosseted childhood, particularly after the onset of the asthma attacks that left him a physically weak man and turned him into a virtual recluse in his later life. Proust's background enabled him to lead a comfortable, financially secure existence that did not require him to work for his living. After completing degrees in Law (1893) and Philosophy (1895) at the Sorbonne, he devoted himself to his literary activities, beginning with an autobiographical novel, *Jean Santeuil*, which was an early version of his most famous work, *A la recherche du temps perdu*, and which he

never finished. An episodic text, it was published posthumously in 1952 and translated into English in 1955. For most of his life Proust worked on *A la recherche du temps perdu*, a modernist classic that presents French society through the medium of gossip, hearsay, and third-hand evidence. Homosexuality is a key theme in this novel in which the sexual identity and proclivities of some of its main protagonists are the object of constant scrutiny. The inverts in Proust's novel, to use the terminology of the period, are like those in Radclyffe HALL's *The Well of Loneliness*, divided into 'true' and involuntary inverts, those born to be homosexual and those turned invert through opportunity. Both male and female homosexuals figure in the novel, in particular Robert de Saint-Loup, the Baron Palamède de Charlus, Albertine de Simonet, and the narrator. Like Proust himself, these characters have romantic liaisons and affairs with both women and men, their sexuality permanently in question and the object of continued speculation. André GIDE turned the volume down for publication by the Nouvelle Revue Française because he considered it to be superficial and because he disliked the ways in which Proust represented inverts in the text.

Puig, Manuel (1932–90). The Argentinian writer Manuel Puig was born in General Villegas, an isolated town in Buenos Aires Province where, from an early age, he visited the local cinema regularly to escape the boredom of his surroundings. It was here that his love affair with the glamorous world of Hollywood movies, reflected in his novels, began. Puig was sent to boarding school in Buenos Aires and, from 1950, attended the University of Buenos Aires without, however, completing his degree. In 1956 he was awarded a scholarship to study Film at the Centro Sperimentale di Cinematografía but he was unsuccessful in his attempt at pursuing a film career. In 1963 he

moved to New York where he started to
write his first novel, *La traición de Rita
Hayworth* (*Betrayed by Rita Hayworth*).
The portrayal of its main character, Toto,
as effeminate and sexually ambivalent,
resulted in the novel encountering censorship problems before its publication in
Argentina in 1968. A year later it was
published in French by the renowned
publishing house Gallimard, and voted
one of the best novels of 1968–9, thus
making Puig's reputation. Puig's novels
became identified with stylistic innovation
through his use of mass popular cultural
phenomena as a site of interrogation of
his characters' identities. Puig wrote a
further seven novels after *La traición de
Rita Hayworth*, as well as plays and film
scripts. They were *Boquitas pintadas:
folletín* (1969; *Heartbreak Tango: A Serial*);
The Buenos Aires Affair: novela political
(1973; *The Buenos Aires Affair: A Detective Novel*); *El beso de la mujer araña*
(1979; *Kiss of the Spider Woman*); *Pubis
angelical* (1979; *Pubis Angelical*); *Maldi-
cíon eterna a quien lea estas páginas*
(1980; *Eternal Curse on the Reader of
These Pages*); *Sangre de amor correspon-
dido* (1982; *Blood of Requited Love*); and
Cae la noche tropical (1988; *Tropical
Night Falling*). Of these *Kiss of the
Spiderwoman* is without doubt the most
famous. In 1985 it was made into a very
successful Hollywood film. The novel
features two prisoners incarcerated in a
Buenos Aires prison during Argentina's
military dictatorship in the 1970s. Molina, an ageing queen imprisoned for
'corrupting minors', seduces the younger,
macho political activist Valentín Arregui
Paz by telling him stories derived from
film plots. Gradually their relationship
changes, and Paz falls in love with Molina. Their relationship is cast in conventional terms, with Molina taking on the
role of the flamboyant female and Paz
that of the 'real' man. Despite the somewhat muted reception of the novel in
Argentina where homosexuality is something of a taboo, the roaring success of

the film has guaranteed this novel a place
in the canon of gay literature.

Purdy, James (1923–). Born in Ohio,
James Purdy went to the University of
Chicago and the University of Puebla,
Mexico, before teaching at Lawrence
College in Wisconsin between 1949 and
1953. Having spent some years abroad he
returned to the USA where he settled in
Brooklyn, New York. Purdy initially began publishing stories in magazines.
When he began writing novels he had
difficulties finding a publisher, possibly
because of the rather savage nature of his
writing. *63: Dream Palace* (1956), his
first novel, dealt with obsession, homosexuality, and urban alienation. That urban alienation can be found in many of
his other novels in which violence becomes the answer to the isolation and
inability to form relationships his characters experience. His male characters have
difficulty expressing their love for other
men because they are intensely homophobic and cannot imagine having a homosexual relationship. The result of this
explosive mixture of desire and denial is
violence as described in *Eustace Chisholm
and the Works* (1967) and *Narrow
Rooms* (1978). Other works by Purdy
include *The Nephew* (1960), *Children is
All* (1962), *Cabot Wright Begins* (1964),
Jeremy's Version (1970), *In a Shallow
Grave* (1975), *In the Hollow of His Hand*
(1986), and *Out with the Stars* (1992).
Some of these novels portray small-town
life in the Midwest. The bleak outlook
that characterizes much of Purdy's relatively prolific work has not enhanced his
popularity as a writer. Novels apart, he
has written plays, poetry, and short stories
but he remains a marginalized figure on
the literary scene. His other works include
Malcolm (1960), *Color of Darkness, and
Malcolm: Eleven Stories, One Novella,
and a Novel* (1974), *A Day after the Fair*
(1977), *Mourners Below* (1984), *Garments
the Living Wear* (1989), *The House of the
Solitary Maggot* (1986), *The Candles of*

Your Eyes: And Thirteen Other Stories (1991), *I am Elijah Thrush* (1996), *Gertrude of Stony Island Avenue* (1998), and *Moe's Villa and Other Stories* (2000).

Puttkamer, Marie Madeleine von (1881–1944). Born Marie Günther in Eydtkuhnen, East Prussia, Puttkamer married the much older Major-General and aristocrat Baron Georg Heinrich von Puttkamer when she was nineteen. They then moved to Berlin where she published a first and highly successful volume of verses, *Auf Kypros* (1900; *On Cyprus*). This collection contained erotic poems of both a heterosexual and a lesbian kind, and went into more than thirty editions in a period of ten years, aided, not unlike Mary MACLANE, by the notoriety that both her poetry and the writer gained. Puttkamer published six further successful collections of poetry as well as writing short stories and novels. They include *Die drei Nächte* (1901; *The Three Nights*), *An der Liebe Narrenseil* (1902; *A Fool in Love*), *In Seligkeit und Sünde* (1905; *In Bliss and Sin*), *Die Kleider der Herzogin. Roman* (1906; *The Duchess' Clothes – A Novel*), *Katzen: drei Liebesspiele* (1910; *Cats: Three Plays about Love*), *Die rote Rose Leidenschaft* (1912; *The Red Rose of Passion*), and *Taumel* (1920; *Dizziness*), which features a female Don Juan.

R

Rachilde (1860–1953). Born Marguerite Aymery this French novelist adopted male clothing and became interested in the issue of sexual inversion, possibly because her father wanted a son instead of a daughter and taught her to associate femininity with worthlessness. She began a career in journalism and married Alfred Vallette, the then editor of the *Mercure de France*. In 1884 she published her first novel, *Monsieur Vénus*, which deals with gender role inversion and cross-dressing, and might be described as belonging to a tradition of queer rather than lesbian literary history. Throughout Rachilde's *œuvre* there is an interest in androgyny, incest, homoeroticism, and complex emotional relationships of dependency and passion. *Monsieur Vénus* was considered pornographic and banned in Belgium where it first appeared. It is for this work that Rachilde is most remembered today. In its decadence it is not unlike some of the other novels she produced. They include *Mme Adonis* (1888), *Les Hors nature* (1897; *Nature's Outcasts*), *L'Heure sexuelle* (1898; *The Sexual Time*), *La Tour d'amour* (1899; *The Tower of Love*), *La Jongleuse* (1900; *The Juggler*), and *La Souris japonaise* (1912; *The Japanese Mouse*). In 1928 she published a frank autobiographical text entitled *Pourquoi je ne suis pas féministe* (*Why I'm not a Feminist*).

Raffalovich, Marc-André (1864–1934). Russian-British writer, born into a wealthy family in Paris who came to England in 1882. He began to live in London and became a patron of the arts, encountering Oscar WILDE, who made fun of him. Raffalovich wrote several volumes of poetry, novels, and articles but he did not receive any recognition for his literary efforts. In 1892 he met the poet John Henry GRAY with whom he fell in love and whom he supported. In 1895 Raffalovich published an essay in Paris in which he attacked Wilde. He then published a series of articles defending homosexuality as equal to heterosexuality. In 1896 he entered the Roman Catholic Church, and became a devout Catholic. He paid for Gray to study at the Scots College in Rome, following him to Edinburgh in 1905. There he partly financed St Peter's Church in Morningside where Gray became rector. He maintained his friendship with Gray and the two men died within a few months of each other.

Rapi, Nina. Contemporary Greek-British lesbian playwright who was born in Argos Orestiko in Greece and moved to the UK when she was twenty. Rapi studied Sociology at the London School of Economics and then completed an MA in Drama at the University of Essex. In 1989, her first full-length play, *Ithaka*, received a rehearsed reading at the River-side Studios, Hammersmith. In 1991 her one-woman play *Johnny is Dead* was produced as part of a festival at the ETC Theatre. In 1991 her play for the Oval House in London, *Dream House*, was commissioned and produced by the As-pect Theatre Company. Since then Rapi has written a number of other plays including *Dance of the Guns* (1992), *Dangerous Oasis* (1993), and *Confession* (1999), which is an extract from *Angelstate*, written in 1998 while on a theatre writing bursary from the Arts Council of Great Britain. *Confession* won a prize at the London Writers' Competition in 1999. Her most recent plays are *Lovers and Other Enemies* (2000), *Josie's Restroom* (2000), a monologue performed at the ICA, *Edgewise: I.T.L.* (2000), performed at the Eros Theatrou in Athens, Greece, and *No Trouble* (2001), for the Soho Theatre. Between 1993 and 1995 Rapi was editor of the lesbian and gay theatre journal *GLINT*. Together with Maya Chowdhry she edited *Acts of Passion: Sexuality, Gender and Performance* (1998), a special issue of the *Journal of Lesbian Studies*. She teaches Creative Writing part-time at Birkbeck College, London.

Rattigan, Sir Terence Mervyn (1911–77). Gay British playwright, the son of a diplomat, educated at Harrow and Trinity College, Oxford. He began his playwriting career early, driven by an ultimatum from his father who enabled him to write over a period of two years to see if he could make a career of playwriting. Ratti-gan's first West End success was a co-medy, *French Without Tears* (1936). This was followed by many others, including *The Winslow Boy* (1946) about a father who fights to clear his naval-cadet son of the accusation of petty theft; *The Browning Version* (1948), set in a boys' board-ing school and featuring Crocker Harris, a repressed and unpopular schoolmaster; *The Deep Blue Sea* (1952), in which the heroine, a judge's wife, suffers from a passionate attachment to a test-pilot; *Separate Tables* (1954), two one-act plays set in a hotel, about emotional failure; *Ross* (1960), based on the life of T.E. Lawrence; and *Cause Célèbre* (1977), about a murder trial. Rattigan kept his private life and sexual identity private, partly because of fear of public scandal. Though he lived with men like Kenneth Morgan for periods of time, his love was not always met with the same ardour by those whom he fell in love with, and that experience is recorded, albeit in hetero-sexual, coded form, in his plays.

Rechy, John (1934–). Born in El Paso, Texas, into a Mexican aristocratic family, Rechy and his parents fled persecution during the purges of Pancho Villa. Rechy attended Texas Western College where he studied Journalism, and the New School for Social Research in New York. He then served in Germany in the US Army. On leaving the Army he moved to New York where a period of drifting and hustling inspired his first novel, *City of Night* (1963). This novel documents the life of an unnamed male hustler, drifting be-tween El Paso, New York, Los Angeles, and New Orleans. The narrative contains character sketches of the people the hus-tler meets and recollections of his child-hood. Whereas in *City of Night* sex is treated as a job, in later novels Rechy grapples with questions of gay sexual identity as much as gay sexual activity. These novels include *Numbers* (1967), centring on the characters of Johnny Rio whose aim it is to have sex with a certain number of men in Griffith Park, Los Angeles; *This Day's Death* (1969); *Rushes* (1979); and the 'documentary' *The Sexual Outlaw: A Documentary* (1977). More recently Rechy has taken female hetero-sexual characters as the protagonists of his novels *Marilyn's Daughter* (1988) and *The Miraculous Day of Amalia Gomez* (1991). Other writings include *The Fourth Angel* (1972), *Bodies and Souls*

(1984), *Our Lady of Babylon* (1996), and *The Coming of the Night* (1999).

Reid, Forrest (1875–1947). Irish writer who spent his life in and near Belfast. He wrote a number of not very successful novels, two collections of short stories, and two autobiographies (*Apostate*, 1926, and *Private Road*, 1940). Reid's writings, which centre on the worlds of boys, are permeated by the quest for the ideal playmate and friend. The celebration of a Greek ideal of male friendship in his works placed Reid's characters in a pagan, lyrical world. The inability of some of his heroes such as Denis Bracknel (first published as *The Bracknels* in 1911, re-published as *Denis Bracknel* in 1947) to cope with modern society emphasized the creation of the sensitive, homosocial figures who peopled Reid's novels. Reid's fictions include *The Kingdom of Twilight* (1904), *The Garden God: A Tale of Two Boys* (1905), *Following Darkness* (1912), *Demophon: A Traveller's Tale* (1927), *Brian Westby* (1934), which was inspired by Thomas MANN's novella *Death in Venice*, and the trilogy *Uncle Stephen* (1931), *The Retreat* (1934), and *Young Tom* (1944). These last three were published as *Tom Barber* in one volume in 1955.

Reinig, Christa (1926–). Lesbian German writer, born in Berlin, where her mother worked as a cleaner to bring up her illegitimate daughter. Reinig grew up in Nazi Germany, and after the end of the Second World War worked in a factory in the East German part of Berlin. She studied art and archaeology at the Humboldt University and then began work on a satirical magazine, the *Ulenspiegel*. Reinig was forced to live outside the East German literary mainstream, publishing with the West German publishing house Fischer. In 1964, following the publication of a collection of poems entitled *Gedichte* (*Poems*), Reinig won the Bremen Prize for Literature and was allowed to emigrate to West Germany. She moved to Munich. In 1971 Reinig had an accidental fall that permanently disabled her. This event became the centre of her first novel, *Die himmlische und die irdische Geometrie* (1975; *The Geometry of Heaven and Earth*). From this period her writing also became more and more explicitly concerned with lesbian issues. A trial in 1974 in Germany of two lesbians who had conspired to murder the husband of one of them, a trial that led to the expression of much anti-lesbian sentiment in the German press, became the source of her second novel, *Entmannung: die Geschichte Ottos und seiner vier Frauen* (1976; *Emasculation, or the Story of Otto and his Four Women*). In 1980 she published a collection of essays, *Der Wolf und die Witwen* (*The Wolf and the Widows*). Subsequent fiction includes *Mädchen ohne Uniform* (1979; *Girls without Uniform*), a novel inspired by Christa WINSLOE's novel *Girls in Uniform*, *Die ewige Schule* (1982; *The Eternal School*), *Nobody* (1989), *Glück und Glas* (1991; *Fortune and Glass*).

Rekola, Mirkka Elina (1931–). Finnish lesbian writer who, due to the illegality of homosexual acts in Finland for both women and men until 1971, only began to come out fully in the 1990s. Brought up in Tampere, Rekola was early on made aware of social injustice and inequalities through the industrial environment in which she found herself. Since she was often ill, Rekola turned to literature for entertainment and support. In 1954 she published her first collection of poetry, *Vedessä palaa* (*Burning/Returning in the Water*). At the same time she moved to Helsinki where she was introduced to Helvi JUVONEN, another lesbian poet, and her literary circle among whom she found her first lover. In 1969 Rekola published *Muistikirja* (*A Notebook*), a collection of aphorisms, and in 1987 *Maskuja*, a collection of stories centring on Masku, a creature of indeterminate gender. This text is not unlike others of the 1970s and

1980s such as June ARNOLD's *The Cook and the Carpenter*, which also played with gender by obliterating gender definitions through pronouns and names. Rekola first began publishing lesbian poetry in the lesbian poetry anthology *Ääriviivasi ihollani* (1991; *Your Contours on My Skin*), which was published by the lesbian publishing house Meikänainen. In 1995 Rekola won the Suomi Prize. Interviews with her about her lesbian identity were published in the women's magazine *Anna* (1996) and the lesbian and gay journal *Z* (1997). In 1996 her poetry collection *Taivas päivystää* (*The Sky on Duty*) appeared.

Renault, Mary (1905–83). Born Eileen Mary Challans in London to Frank Challans, a physician, and Clementine Baxter Challans, Mary Renault initially wrote under her own name. She adopted the pen name under which she would become famous from Thomas Otway's tragedy in blank verse, *Venice Preserved* (1682). Renault was educated in London and Bristol before reading English at St Hugh's College, Oxford, from where she graduated in 1928. In 1933 she embarked on a training course for nurses at the Radcliffe Infirmary, Oxford, where she met Julie Mullard, also a nurse, who was to become Renault's life-long companion. Renault's first novel, *Purposes of Love* (1939) and her subsequent novels *Kind are Her Answers* (1940), *The Friendly Young Ladies* (1944), and *The Middle Mist* (1945), all drew on her experiences as a nurse. Her fourth novel, *Return to Night* (1947), gained her the Metro-Goldwyn-Meyer Prize of $150,000. All these novels were written under her own name. In 1948 Renault published *North Face*. In the same year she emigrated to South Africa. It was there that she wrote the novels for which she would become famous – historical novels, written mostly in the first person, and focusing more or less explicitly on male rather than female homosexuals. Many of these novels were set in ancient Greece where male homosexuality was celebrated rather than suppressed. *The Charioteer* (1953), set in 1940s England, centres on a young soldier wounded at Dunkirk who is coming to terms with his homosexuality. *The Last of the Wine* (1956), Renault's first classical novel, indicates meticulous Hellenist scholarship. It, together with *The King Must Die* (1958), established her reputation as a historical novelist and scholar of ancient Greece. In her historical novels Renault portrayed men as capable of both homosexual and heterosexual relationships, and suggested that homosexual relationships bring out the best in a man. In *The Mask of Apollo* (1966) Renault began to chronicle the life of Alexander the Great, which was explored in her subsequent novels *Fire from Heaven* (1970), *The Persian Boy* (1972), and *Funeral Games* (1981). Renault's other novels include *The Bull from the Sea* (1962), *The Lion in the Gateway* (1964), and *The Praise Singer* (1975), and in an unpublished play, *The Day of Good Hope* (1955). Unusually for a lesbian woman, she is much better known for her portraits of male homosexuality in ancient Greece than for her much more restrained depictions of lesbians in her early novels.

Reve, Gerard (1923–). Dutch writer whose representations of masturbation and homosexuality caused scandals in the Netherlands in the 1940s and the 1960s, thus ensuring his long-term reputation as an innovator of Dutch literature. Reve was born in Amsterdam where he attended grammar school. During the Second World War he studied Graphic Design and worked as a reporter for the daily newspaper *Het Parool* from 1947 until 1949. In 1947 he published his first novel, *De avonden* (*The Evenings*), which was a critical success and earned him the Reina Prinsen Geerligs Prize as best young writer in the Netherlands. When the Minister of State denied Reve a travel grant for having written on masturbation in what was considered a pornographic way, Reve emigrated to England in protest. There he worked as a hospital attendant and wrote a series of plays. However, his first publication in English, *The Acrobat and Other Stories* (1956), was a failure and he returned to the Netherlands to work as an editor and writer for *Tirade*, a literary journal. In *Op Weg naar het Ende* (1963; *Approaching the End*) and *Nader tot U* (1966; *Nearer to You*) Reve broached the subject of homosexuality openly. After his much publicized conversion to Roman Catholicism Reve was the object of a great scandal centring on an official charge of blasphemy brought about by his description, in an article published in the journal *Dialoog*, of Christ as a donkey with whom Reve wished to have sexual intercourse. The case was eventually dismissed but gained Reve a certain notoriety. In 1968 Reve was awarded the P.C. Hooft Prize for Literature. A year later he emigrated to France.

Rich, Adrienne (1929–). Rich is the USA's perhaps most famous twentieth-century lesbian feminist poet, as well as being a renowned essayist. She was born into an intellectual middle-class household in Baltimore, Maryland, and was encouraged to write by her father from an early age. In 1951 she graduated with an AB from Radcliffe College. She published *A Change of World*, which was selected for the Yale Younger Poets Award by W.H. AUDEN. In 1953, Rich married Alfred Conrad, an economist at Harvard University. She had three sons between 1955 and 1959. She and her family lived in Cambridge, Massachusetts, until 1966 when they moved to New York City. She and her husband became very active in anti-Vietnam War campaigns. In 1970 Rich left her husband who committed suicide later that year. Rich's partner is the writer Michelle CLIFF, with whom she has lived since 1976, first in Montague, Massachusetts, and, from 1984, in Santa Cruz,

California. Together Rich and Cliff have edited the lesbian journal *Sinister Wisdom*. Rich has published numerous volumes of poetry and several collections of essays. Following her collection of poems, *The Diamond Cutters and Other Poems* (1955), Rich published *Snapshots of a Daughter-in-law* (1954–62). With this latter volume she inaugurated her interrogation of women's position in society, which gained increasing and politicized prominence from the late 1960s onwards, fuelled by the Women's Liberation Movement of that time. She published the collections *The Will to Change* (1971) and *Diving into the Wreck* (1973), for which she won the National Book Award in 1974. *The Dream of a Common Language: Poems 1974–1977* (1978) contained her lesbian love poem sonnet sequence 'Twenty-one Love Poems'. That volume, together with *A Wild Patience Has Taken Me this Far: Poems 1978–1981* (1981) established Rich's preoccupation with the issue of women's relation to language. This subject was much debated in the late 1970s and early 1980s when the notion of a specifically female or feminine or, indeed, feminist language was widely interrogated, most famously perhaps in the concept of *écriture féminine* in France. During the 1970s and 1980s Rich also published some of her famous collections of essays including *Of Woman Born: Motherhood as Experience and Institution* (1976), *On Lies, Secrets and Silence: Selected Prose 1966–1978* (1979), and *Blood, Bread and Poetry: Selected Prose 1966–1978*. Her most famous essay from the period is without doubt 'Compulsory Heterosexuality and Lesbian Existence' (1980) in which she discusses the pervasiveness of heterosexuality and its normatizing effects, hence the still much-used phrase 'compulsory heterosexuality', and describes what she calls the 'lesbian continuum' of women's relations with each other which range from platonic emotional affinities to clearly articulated and lived sexual preferences for women. The notion of the lesbian continuum has been the object of much debate in lesbian feminist circles, with some claiming that a lesbian identity is tied unequivocally to lesbian sexual activity and others suggesting that 'romantic friendships' between women, even if sexually not consummated, are sufficient to classify women engaged in such relationships as lesbian. From the mid-1980s Rich moved towards an examination of her Jewish heritage. *Your Native Land, Your Life* (1986) and *An Atlas of the Difficult World: Poems 1988–1991* (1991) pay homage to this. In 1991 Rich was awarded the Commonwealth Poetry Prize. She became a member of the founding editorial group of *Bridges: A Journal of Jewish Feminists and Our Friends* (1990). In 1989 *Time's Power: Poems 1985–1988* was published and in 1995 *Dark Fields of the Republic: Poems 1991–1995* appeared. These reveal Rich's engagement with world politics, as does her *What Is Found there: Notebooks on Poetry and Politics* (1990). Recent collections by Adrienne Rich include *Midnight Salvage* (1999) and *Arts of the Possible* (2001). Rich's poetry has consistently been characterized by a specific use of spacing, often leaving gaps within lines signalling pauses and silences, and by the very sparing use of punctuation. She is considered one of the great innovators of twentieth-century US poetry. Her work has won her numerous awards, fellowships, honorary doctorates, and literary prizes. These have never detracted from her political and feminist commitments.

Richardson, Henry Handel (1870–1946). Australian writer whose real name was Ethel Richardson. Her experience of being educated at the Presbyterian Ladies' College at Melbourne is reflected in her best known lesbian work, *The Getting of Wisdom* (1910), a boarding-school fiction which centres on the expulsion of a schoolgirl for writing a romantic novel, deemed to indicate her depraved imagina-

tion. Richardson moved to Leipzig in Germany in 1888 to study music, and wrote *Maurice Guest* (1910), which offers a comment on this experience. Following her marriage to J.G. Robertson, she lived a life of social isolation with her husband and her companion Olga Roncoroni. Her trilogy *The Fortunes of Richard Mahony* (1930) is considered an Australian classic. She was nominated for the Nobel Prize in 1932.

Rimbaud, Arthur (1854–91). The French poet Jean Nicolas Arthur Rimbaud was born in Charleville in northern France where he attended the Institution Rossat and the Collège de Charleville. He was academically very gifted and started writing from an early age, first in Latin and then in French. Encouraged by a young professor who taught him, Georges Izambard, Rimbaud had written and published many poems by the time he was seventeen years old. His image has been that of a Romantic poet, an individual genius whose flights of imagination led him to create magical worlds in his poetry, celebrating freedom and the life of the senses. His most famous poem, 'Le Bateau Ivre' ('The Drunken Boat'), was written in 1871. In 1870 Rimbaud travelled to Paris where it is suggested he had his first sexual experiences with soldiers in a barracks. While in Paris Rimbaud met Paul VERLAINE, who invited him to return to Paris in 1871. The two men began an affair which lasted for one and a half years, and which has been much celebrated since, for instance in Bertolt BRECHT's various versions of his play *Baal*. Rimbaud's poetry from that time was strongly influenced by his relationship with Verlaine. While they were together, they were active in Paris's literary salons and travelled to Brussels and to London together. During this time Rimbaud produced *The Illuminations* (1872), an autobiographical text in verse, and *A Season in Hell* (1873). His affair with Verlaine ended in 1873 when the latter shot him in the wrist during a violent fight. Following this incident Rimbaud lost interest in his poetry and began to travel extensively. He briefly enlisted in the Dutch army in 1876 but then resumed his travels, trading variously in coffee and in guns. Rimbaud, as befits the image of the Romantic genius immortalized in Verlaine's *Rimbaud* (1872), died prematurely at the age of thirty-seven.

Rive, Richard (1931–89). Gay South African writer, born and brought up in Cape Town in the coloured area of District Six. Rive attended Hewat Training College where he also later taught, the University of Cape Town, and Columbia University, before writing a doctorate on Olive SCHREINER at Magdalen College, Oxford. In his writings Rive never discussed homosexuality. His first novel, *Emergency* (1963), focused on the Sharpeville massacre. The topic of apartheid was central to his work. His autobiography, *Writing Black*, appeared in 1981. His novel *'Buckingham Palace', District Six* (1986) was adapted for the stage, and his last novel, *Emergency Continued*, had just been completed when Rive was stabbed to death by some rent boys in his home.

Rochefort, Christine (1917–). French novelist and essayist whose work is very popular in France and whose subject matter is frequently the repression of female sexuality, both lesbian and heterosexual. Her first novel, *Le Repos du guerrier* (1958; *Warrior's Rest*, 1959) centred on the love affair of a middle-class woman and an alcoholic, a topic considered *risqué* at the time. Her second novel, *Les Petits Enfants du siècle* (1961; *Children of Heaven*, 1962) about a deprived childhood in the working-class suburbs of Paris, the author's own background, won the Prix du Roman Populiste. This text is now widely taught in French schools. In 1963 Rochefort published *Les Stances à Sophie* (*Cats Don't Care for Money*, 1965), which features a

brief lesbian relationship between two married women. Rochefort also published a dystopian novel, *Une Rose pour Morrison* (1966; *A Rose for Morrison*), and a utopic novel, *Archaos ou le jardin étincelant* (1972; *Archaos, or The Glittering Garden*). However, most of her novels are realist. They include *Printemps au parking* (1967; *Spring in the Car Park*), *Encors heureux qu'on va vers l'été* (1975; *Still Happy that Summer is Coming*), and *Quand tu vas chez les femmes* (1982; *How to Deal with Women*). In 1988 Rochefort received the Prix Médicis for *La Porte du Fond* (*The Far Door*).

Rochester, John Wilmot, Earl of (1647–80). Born at Ditchley in Oxfordshire to a Cavalier hero and a deeply religious Puritan mother, John Wilmot, Earl of Rochester, was a poet, satirist, and member of the court wits surrounding Charles II. Rochester wrote very frankly and deeply misogynistically about sex, specifically heterosexual sex. It is this that suggests he had homosexual inclinations. He was educated at Wadham College, Oxford, and went on a European tour before returning to court in late 1664. There he gained a reputation for debauchery and for satirizing courtly life and mores. When he was eighteen he abducted the heiress Elizabeth Malet to whom, despite her parents' resistance, he was married some eighteen months later, and with whom he had four children. Rochester divided his life between his mother's estate where Elizabeth and their children resided and the London court scene where he was renowned for his sexual adventures. He was exiled from the court by the king on a number of occasions for his libellous poetry and scandalous behaviour. He is, nonetheless, regarded as one of the last of the so-called metaphysical poets of the seventeenth century. With the Augustans such as Alexander Pope, also something of a misogynist, he shared an appetite and aptitude for satire. His poems include 'A Satyr on Charles II',

'Satyr against Reason and Mankind', and 'The Maimed Debauchee', which recalls a *ménage à trois* with his mistress and a page boy. In his early thirties he became very ill and began to correspond with a number of theologians, among them the Anglican chaplain G. Burnet, who later wrote of Rochester's deathbed conversion. Since he died young, Rochester's *œuvre* remained small but he influenced many later poets such as Swift, Dryden, and Pope.

Roellig, Ruth Margarete (1878–1969). Lesbian German writer, born in Schwiebus, who moved to Berlin with her parents when she was nine years old. After finishing school, Roellig initially worked in her parents' hotel but then, in 1911, took up an apprenticeship with a Berlin publisher and worked as an editor. She began publishing poems and short stories in various magazines. Her first novel, *Geflüster im Dunkeln* (*Whispers in the Dark*) appeared in 1913. She published *Liane. Eine sonderbare Geschichte* (1919; *Liane: A Strange Story*) and *Traumfahrt. Eine Geschichte aus Finnland* (1919; *Dream Journey; A Story from Finland*), as well as *Lutetia Parisiorum* (1920), and a collection of short stories, *Die fremde Frau* (1920; *The Strange Woman*). From 1927 Roellig worked for two popular lesbian-feminist magazines in Berlin, *Die Freundin* (*The Girlfriend*) and *Garçonne*. In 1928 she published a guide to lesbian Berlin, *Berlins lesbische Frauen* (*Lesbian Women in Berlin*), reprinted as *Lila Nächte: die Damenklubs der zwanziger Jahre* (*Lavender Nights: Ladies' Clubs of the 1920s*) in 1981 and 1994. This volume provided details of fourteen clubs and dance halls of the lesbian scene in 1920s Berlin. Roellig also contributed a chapter on lesbians and transvestites to Agnes Countess Esterhazy's collection *Das lasterhafte Weib* (1930; *Women's Vices*). A story from 1930, *Ich klage an* (*I accuse*) and *Die Kette im Schoß* (1931; *The Chain in her Lap*) both centre on lesbian prota-

gonists. Roellig survived the Nazi regime without being persecuted, or discouraged from publishing. She produced a murder mystery, *Der Andere* (1935; *The Other One*) and a novel about the First World War, *Soldaten, Tod, Tänzerin* (1937; *Soldiers, Death and Dancer*). In 1937 her flat in Berlin was bombed and she moved to Silesia where she stayed until 1945, when she returned to Berlin where she lived until her death.

Roffiel, Rosamaria (1945–). Mexican author and journalist, born in Veracruz, whose novels explore lesbian relationships. Roffiel's volume of poetry, *Corramos libres ahora* (1986), centres on the female body and sexuality. Her autobiographical, *¡Ay, Nicaragua, Nicaraguita!* (1987), details Roffiel's experiences in Nicaragua during the Sandinista revolution. *Amora* is a lesbian novel which features Claudia and Lupe, and the development of their lesbian relationship, attacking the prejudices against lesbian relationships prevalent in Latin American society.

Rolfe, Frederick William (1860–1913). Eccentric British gay writer born in London who worked in a number of schools in England before taking up something of an itinerant lifestyle, moving between Italy and England. In his mid-teens Rolfe converted to Catholicism and attempted to pursue his dream of becoming a Roman Catholic priest. However, he was thrown out both of St Mary's College, Oscott (Birmingham), and, later, the Scots College in Rome for being unsuitable for the priesthood. Rolfe was a great admirer of male beauty and adolescent male youths. His first works, *Stories Toto Told Me* (1898) and *In His Own Image* (1901), are told from the perspective of a servant narrating saints' lives. Subsequently he wrote *Hadrian the Seventh* (1904) in which the narrator, George Rose, who is expelled from a seminary, later becomes the Pope. Both the style of this novel and the style of *Chronicles of the House of Borgia* (1901) established Rolfe as a decadent writer. Rolfe's novels *Nicholas Crabbe* (1904; not published until 1958) and *The Desire and Pursuit of the Whole* (1909–10; published in 1934) reveal his admiration for male beauty. Rolfe's own life seems to have been continuously beset by disappointments, poverty, and lack of success in sexual relations. In 1890 he returned from Rome to England, adopting the title Frederick, Baron Corvo, which, he maintained, had been bestowed on him by the Duchess of Sforza-Cesarini. In the last few years of his life, Rolfe lived in Venice, a city he loved and which, through Thomas MANN's later novella *Death in Venice*, is linked with the ideas and ideals of adolescent male beauty and a fatal attraction to male youth. Rolfe died of exposure after having been thrown out of his hotel for failing to pay his bills. His life has been the object of some interest, beginning with A.J.A. Symons's biography *Quest for Corvo* (1934).

Roosevelt, Eleanor (1884–1962). US autobiographer and humanitarian reformer, born into a wealthy New York family. In 1905 she married her distant cousin Franklin Delano Roosevelt, with whom she had six children, and to whom she ministered for many years. Roosevelt led an active political and social life, independent from her husband. She was active in the League of Women Voters, the Women's Trade Union League, and the women's division of the Democratic Party. Once her husband was elected president in 1933, Roosevelt continued to be politically active supporting the poor, African Americans, and women. After her husband's death she was appointed as a member of the US delegation to the United Nations. She became chair of the committee that produced the Universal Declaration of Human Rights. She had a wide circle of friends, including lesbians, and her letters to Lorena Hickok suggest a lesbian relationship. She published two autobiographies, *This is My Story* (1937) and *This I Remember* (1949).

Rorem, Ned (1923–). Gay US composer and diarist, born in Richmond, Indiana, whose musical and literary talents were fostered from an early age. When he won the Gershwin Memorial Award in 1948, he used it to spend time in Paris where he began his diaries, which, among other things, detail homosexual love affairs with a frankness unusual for its time. *The Paris Diary of Ned Rorem* appeared in 1966, and was followed by several more such volumes including *New York Diary* (1967), *The Final Diary: 1961–1972* (1974), *An Absolute Gift: A New Diary* (1974), and *Knowing When to Stop* (1994). These diaries chronicle Rorem's rise to being one of the best-known contemporary US composers, especially of the art song, a form he has used to set to music the work of many gay and lesbian writers, in particular Walt WHITMAN, but also Gertrude STEIN, Adrienne RICH, Paul MONETTE, Thom GUNN, and John ASHBERY. Rorem has also published on music, e.g. his *Pure Contraption: A Composer's Essays* (1974). During the late 1970s and early 1980s Rorem wrote a regular column for the New York journal *Christopher Street*. He has never made a secret of his homosexuality.

Ross, Sinclair (1908–96). Gay Canadian writer who earned his living working in banks until his retirement in 1968, and who was 'outed' only after his death. His relatively small output of short stories and novels often features characters who have attachments to young boys, or whose gender identity is in some way ambiguous. Ross himself was born and brought up on Saskatchewan farms by his divorced mother. His career with the Royal Bank of Canada entailed various stays in small prairie towns, but also, later, enabled periods abroad in Spain and Greece before Ross's final settling down in Vancouver where he died from Parkinson's disease. Small-town life and its prejudices are extensively explored in Ross's novels such as *As for Me and My House* (1941), *The Well* (1958), *Whir of Gold* (1970), and *Sawbones Memorial* (1974). Ross also published two collections of short stories.

Rossetti, Christina (1830–94). English poet whose inclusion in this volume rests on one of her best-known poems, 'Goblin Market', which had been variously read as an allegory of temptation and redemption in a Christian mould, and as a fairy-tale, before being rediscovered as a representation of the eroticism and endurance of female-to-female relations in the 1980s. Rossetti was born to Anglo-Italian parents and brought up in a deeply religious as well as arts-oriented family. The family turned Anglo-Catholic in the 1840s. Rossetti's sister Maria, who eventually became an Anglican nun, wrote a study of Dante. Her brother Dante Gabriele became a painter and poet at the centre of the so-called Pre-Raphaelite movement, and her brother William wrote the family history. Rossetti herself seems to have lived a life of renunciation and illness. Twice she refused suitors for religious reasons, in one case breaking off an engagement because her fiancé, James Collinson, had converted back from Catholicism. In her late teens Rossetti suffered from various illnesses, at one point described as religious mania. Some of her verse was published under the pseudonym Ellen Alleyne in the Pre-Raphaelite's *The Germ* in 1850. However, it was only with the publication of 'Up-Hill' by *Macmillan's* in 1861 that Rossetti gained some public recognition as a poet. Macmillan then published her first volume of poetry, *Goblin Market and Other Poems*, and *The Prince's Progress* in 1866. In 1872 *Sing Song: A Nursery Rhyme Book* appeared. A year later, in 1873, Rossetti contracted Graves' disease and became virtually a recluse. Her later work is mainly religious in tone and subject matter. She published *Seek and Find* (1879), *Called to Be Saints* (1881), and *The Face of the Deep* (1892). Her 'Sonnet' with the opening line 'Remember me when I am gone away' is still frequently read at funerals in England. On one level Rossetti is part of a tradition of reclusive and laid-up women writers such as Emily DICKINSON and Alice JAMES, for example. However, it is not so much the circumstances of her private life as the intense emotional and sensual attachment between the sisters Laura and Lizzie in 'Goblin Market' that have made her of interest for lesbian readers.

Rukeyser, Muriel (1913–80). US poet, essayist, and playwright, born and brought up in an upper middle-class Jewish family in New York, where she lived for most of her life. Rukeyser was educated at the Ethical Culture School in New York City, at Vassar College, and at Columbia University. A writer as well as a political activist of the left Rukeyser attended the 1933 trial of the Scottsboro Nine in Alabama, covered the Antifascist Olympics in Barcelona in 1936 for the London magazine *Life and Letters Today*, was imprisoned during the Vietnam protests, and travelled to Hanoi in 1975 to protest against the poet Kim Chi-Ha's death sentence. She published some twenty volumes of poetry, which appeared as *The Collected Poems of Muriel Rukeyser* in 1978. The first of these volumes, *Theory of Flight* (1935), won the Yale Younger Poets Prize of the same year. In 1945 she was briefly married, and in 1947 had a son by another man. Rukeyser was always silent about her own sexual orientation though in later years she seemed to accept a more publicly lesbian identity. In 1967 she was elected to the National Institute of Arts and Letters. Her poetry has been much heralded by lesbian and feminist readers due to its preoccupations with what in the 1970s and 1980s were regarded as 'women's issues', in particular single motherhood, and female bodily experiences such as menstruation, breast-feeding, and female to female relationships. Her line in a tribute to the sculptor Käthe Kollwitz 'the world (...) split open' became the title of a famous women's poetry anthology.

Rule, Jane (1931–). Lesbian Canadian novelist, essayist, and short-story writer, Jane Rule moved to Vancouver in 1956 to live with her partner Helen Sonthoff, who died in 1999. She taught at the University of British Columbia and then moved to Galiano Island, British Columbia, in 1976. All her writing has centred on lesbian relationships. Her novel *Desert of the Heart* (1964), a lesbian love story, was made into a highly successful feature film in 1985. This novel was followed by *This Is not for You* (1970), *Against the Season* (1970), *The Young in One Another's Arms* (1977), *Contract with the World* (1980), *Memory Board* (1987), a novel dealing with the rarely discussed topic of lesbian love and relationships in old age, and *After the Fire* (1989). Her short stories have been collected in *Theme for Diverse Instruments* (1975), *Outlander* (1981), and *Inland Passage* (1985). The essay collection *Lesbian Images* (1975) offers biographical accounts of the lives of several famous lesbian writers. A further essay collection, *A Hot-Eyed Moderate*, was published in 1985.

Russ, Joanna (1937–). Lesbian US novelist and prose writer who was born and grew up in the Bronx. In 1953 Russ became one of the top ten Westinghouse Science Talent Search Winners, an indication perhaps of the feminist and lesbian science fiction writing she would engage in later

on in her life. Russ gained a BA in English from Cornell University (1957), and an MFA from the Yale University School of Drama in 1960. Russ subsequently taught at Cornell University, the State University of New York at Binghampton, and at the University of Colorado at Boulder before becoming Professor of English at the University of Washington, Seattle. Russ's science fiction was first published in 1959. Her work has been central to the questioning of established gender roles that dominated feminist thinking of the 1970s and early 1980s (e.g. in *The Female Man*, 1975), as well as to the genre of science fiction (e.g. the 1969 story 'When it Changed', which appeared in 1972 and won the Nebula Award). One series of Russ's sci-fi novels features the character Alyx. These novels include *Picnic on Paradise* (1968), *Alyx* (1976), and *The Adventures of Alyx* (1986). She has also written other novels such as *And Chaos Died* (1970) and *The Two of Them* (1978). Among her collections of short stories, which include *Extraordinary People* (1984), *The Zanzibar Cat* (1984), and *The Hidden Side of the Moon* (1987), it is particularly the first one which caused a stir among lesbian feminists as some of its stories belong to what one might describe as a first generation of queer people. Russ's feminist criticism has been outspoken and forceful, attacking the oppressiveness of gendered regimes and patriarchal structures. These volumes include *On Strike against God* (1980) and *How to Suppress Women's Writing* (1983). Both volumes were important texts in the period when the canon of English literature was under attack for being virtually exclusively male.

S

Saba, Umberto (1883–1957). Born Umberto Poli, Saba was brought up by his Jewish mother in the Jewish quarter of Trieste after his mother had been deserted by his Christian father. From 1902 Saba earned his living by writing for newspapers. He did military service in Salerno in 1908 and then returned to Trieste where he got married and, in 1919, bought a bookshop. In 1921 he began publishing his own poetry under the title *Il canzoniere* (*The Songbook*). Over the years he added to this collection, which might be read as a lyrical autobiography, publishing revised and expanded editions in 1945, 1951, and 1961. During the Nazi occupation of Italy Saba was forced to flee Trieste and stayed in Florence, moving frequently to avoid arrest and deportation. While Saba's poetry is celebrated for the poems written to his wife and his daughter, it also contains representations of friendships between men, and between young boys and older men, which is why they are of interest to gay readers. Late in life Saba began a novel, *Ernesto*, published posthumously in 1975 and made into a successful film. That novel deals with a boy's sexual awakening, his first sexual experience with a man, and his later emotional and sexual relationships both with women and men.

Sackville-West, Vita (1892–1962). English writer, born the daughter of the third Baron Sackville, who was brought up at the family home Knole, in Kent, and was educated privately. Her parents were cousins, her mother being the illegitimate daughter of Lionel Sackville-West and a Spanish gypsy dancer, Pepita, immortalized in Sackville-West's eponymous biographical novel *Pepita* (1937). Sackville-West met her later husband, Harold Nicolson, a career diplomat, in 1910. They were married in 1914, and had two sons, Ben, born in 1914, and Nigel, born in 1917. Their marriage lasted for fifty years, punctuated but not put into question by the lesbian and homosexual affairs both Sackville-West and her husband engaged in. Of Sackville-West's affairs the two most famous ones are possibly her relationship with Violet Keppel (later TREFUSIS) which lasted from 1918 until 1921, and which is documented in a text published as part of *Portrait of a Marriage* (1973) by Sackville-West's and Nicolson's son Nigel Nicolson. *Portrait of a Marriage* was made into a highly successful BBC television series. The other famous affair was her relationship with Virginia WOOLF, an affair that inspired Woolf's novel *Orlando* (1928) in which Sackville-West features as the heroine. Sackville-West was a passionate writer, biographer, and gardener. In 1915 she and Nicolson bought a cottage, Long Barn, near Knole, and eventually, in 1930, Sissinghurst Castle, which they made their home and where Sackville-West cultivated the gardens. Sackville-West's passion for the house manifested itself in *Sissinghurst* (1931), and in *English Country Homes* (1941). Sackville-West was unable to inherit Knole due to the system of patrilineage. She wrote about this in *Knole and the Sackvilles* (1922) as well as, indirectly, in her first novel *Heritage* (1922). Her novel *Challenge* (1923) is considered to be a *roman à clef* about her relationship with Violet Trefusis. Similarly, *Dark Island* (1934) is supposed to be about her relationship with Gwen St Aubyn. However, only in her very last novel, *No Signposts in the Sea* (1961), are there any direct references to lesbianism. Sackville-West's long pastoral poem *The Land* (1927) established her as a poet. Her interest in mysticism and the lives of saints led to *Saint Joan of Arc* (1936), *Solitude* (1938), and *The Eagle and the Dove* (1943), about St Theresa of Avila and St Thérèse of Lisieux. Her *The Edwardians* (1930) was a bestseller. She also wrote *All Passion Spent* (1931), *Grey Wethers* (1923), *Passenger to Teheran* (1926), *Aphra Behn* (1927), *The Easter Party* (1953), and *Daughter of France: The Life of Anne Marie Louise d'Orléans* (1959). Her letters to Violet Trefusis, Virginia Woolf, and Andrew Reiber were published in collected volumes. To her chagrin, Sackville-West did not receive the literary recognition she had hoped for. In some respects her writings were too rooted in a literary past that did not match the experimentation of the high modernists with whom she had contact. She died of cancer.

Sade, Donatien Alphonse François, Marquis de (1740–1814). Born into an impoverished French aristocratic family, the Marquis de Sade, as he is now commonly referred to, was brought up by the de Condé family and married, by his parents, to Pélagie de Montreuil, a woman from a rich family able to counteract the de Sade's diminishing family fortune. With

his wife de Sade had two sons and a daughter. However, for most of his adult life de Sade was embroiled in scandals, either for immoral behaviour, or for the obscenity of his work, or for treason against the state. These scandals resulted in his repeated arrests and long-term imprisonments, ending finally in his death in 1814 in a lunatic asylum in Charenton. De Sade, whose name is the basis of the term sadism coined by the nineteenth-century sexologist Richard von KRAFFT-EBING, was a defender of sexual libertinism of a kind that included such extremes of sexual behaviour as to defy any easy acceptance, in particular in relation to the cruel treatments inflicted on women for the sexual gratification of men. His father had been arrested for cruising men in the Tuileries Gardens, and de Sade, too, became the object of legal censure for his sexual behaviour. In 1768 he abducted a seamstress, Rosa Keller, from the street, held her captive, and asked her to blaspheme and to whip him. When she refused he whipped her. She escaped and brought charges against him. He was imprisoned and then banished to his castle in La Coste. In 1772 he visited a brothel in Marseilles where he gave the prostitutes aphrodisiacs that they mistook for poison. He also had his manservant sodomize him. For this he and his servant were sentenced to death and their effigies burnt. In 1777, de Sade was arrested in Paris. His capital punishment was revoked but he was held in prison until 1790 under a *lettre de cachet*, or order of confinement, requested by his family. During the French Revolution his aristocratic background made him an object of attack. Imprisoned for treason and sentenced to death, he escaped that fate through the fall of the Jacobin regime. Following Napoleon's ascent to the throne de Sade was arrested for the obscenity of his work, and confined to the Charenton asylum where he eventually died. Most of de Sade's writings were produced during his various terms of incarceration. They

include a number of infamous pornographic works such as *Justine, ou les
infortunes de la vertu* (1791; *Justine, or
the Misfortunes of Virtue*), *Philosophie
dans le boudoir* (1795; *Philosophy in the
Boudoir*), and *Les Cint Vingt Journées de
Sodome* (published 1904; *The 120 Days
of Sodom*).

Saikaku, Ihara (1642–93). Japanese writer
about whose personal history little is
known. It is assumed that he may have
been called Hirayama Togo, that he was
born into the urban merchant class, and
that his family may have been sword
makers, hence his privileged knowledge
of the samurai class that he would otherwise have had little access to, and which
features prominently in his writing. Following the death of his wife in 1675
Saikaku gave up business to concentrate
on writing haikai poetry, and in the 1680s
he focused on writing the prose for which
he is now famous in Japan. In his works
he covered three subjects: love, samurai
life, and merchant life. Among his works
is *Nanshoju okagami* (1687; *The Great
Mirror of Male Love*), a collection of
stories that centre on male love, dividing
its protagonists in two groups, 'women
haters' or 'true' homosexuals, and 'con-
noisseurs of boys' or men who enjoy boys
as well as women sexually. He also wrote
Koshoku ichidai otoko (1682; *The Life of
an Amorous Man*), which featured con-
noisseurs of boys, *Koshoku ichidai onna*
(1684; *The Life of an Amorous Woman*),
which contained a lesbian scene; and
Shoen okagami (1684; *The Great Mirror
of Loves*). His representations of sexuality
and love were constructed to fit the aims
of his texts rather than as an expression of
personal preference.

Saisio, Pirkko Helena (1949–). Lesbian
Finnish writer whose plays and novels,
sometimes written under pseudonyms,
have dealt with lesbian identity, though
not invariably so. Her novel *Betoniyö*
(1981; *The Concrete Night*) deals with
homophobia and violence. *Kainin tytär*
(1984; *Daughter of Cain*) is considered to
be the first lesbian novel in Finnish.
Saisio's play *Hissi* (1987; *The Lift*) is set
in a prison and addresses the theme of
lesbian love. In the late 1980s and early
1990s Saisio used two pseudonyms, a
male one, 'Jukka Larson', and a female
one, 'Eva Wein'. Under the former name
she published a trilogy which was much
praised: *Kiusaaja* (1986; *The Tormentor*),
Viettelijä (1987; *The Tempter*), and *Kan-
taja* (1991; *The Bearer*). As Eva Wein she
wrote *Puolimaailman nainen* (1990; *Woman of the Half-world*), and *Kulkue*
(1992; *The Procession*), which was nominated for the Finlandia Award. Saisio lives
with her partner Pirjo Honkasalo, a film-
maker, with whom she is raising her
biological daughter. She has been a supporter of lesbian and gay rights for which
she campaigned during the mid-1990s.

Saki (1870–1916). Saki was the *nom de
plume* of Hector Hugh Munro, English
short-story writer, one of three children of
the Inspector General of Police in Burma
where Saki was born and where his
mother died shortly after his birth. He
was sent to England to be brought up by
two aunts and, following a period at a
private school in Exeter, he was sent to
Bedford Grammar School when he was
fifteen. Between the ages of seventeen and
twenty-three he travelled with his retired
father to France, Switzerland, and Germany. In 1893 he took up a post in the
police force in Burma but had to give that
up after fifteen months due to ill health.
He moved to London, after having recup-
erated in Devon, and began his life as a
writer. He had some success as a political
satirist for the *Westminster Gazette*
(1900–2). There followed a spell as foreign correspondent for the *Morning Post*
(1902–8), during which time he undertook trips to the Balkans, to Warsaw, St
Petersburg, and Paris. In the first decade
of the twentieth century Saki published
The Rise of the Russian Empire (1900),

The Westminster Alice (1902), the short-story collection *Reginald* (1904), and *Reginald in Russia and Other Sketches* (1910). He then wrote *The Chronicles of Clovis* (1911), a collection of short stories, the novel *The Unbearable Bassington* (1912), *When William Came: A Story of London under the Hohenzollerns* (1913), and *Beasts and Superbeasts* (1914). He was considered something of a chronicler of the Edwardian period. At the beginning of the First World War he enlisted in the 22nd Royal Fusiliers, going to the front in France in 1915. He died at the front. His *The Toys of Peace, and Other Stories* (1919) and *The Square Egg, and Other Sketches* (1924) were published posthumously. Noël COWARD considered himself to have been influenced by Saki's work.

Sánchez, Luis Rafael (1936–). Puerto Rican writer, born into a middle-class family and educated at the University of Puerto Rico, New York University, and at the University of Madrid. An academic, Sánchez is best known for a story entitled 'Jum!' in *En cuerpo de camisa* (1966; *Body Show*), and the novels *La guaracha del Macho Camacho* (1976; *Macho Camacho's Boat*), *La importancia de llamarse Daniel Santos* (1988; *The Importance of Being Named Daniel Santos*), and *La guagua áerea* (1994; *The Bus Station*). Sánchez's texts explore homosexuality through the simultaneous celebration of a certain Puerto Rican masculinity and the expression of homophobia. This entails both the creation of space to represent a more effeminate homosexuality and the disavowal of that homosexuality. In a country that, in 1974, passed a penal code that gave homosexual practices a particular criminal status this mode of representing homosexuality may be the only way of giving it a literary presence.

Sandel, Cora (1880–1974). Pseudonym of Sara Fabricius, a Norwegian writer, whose understanding that women artists need to live alone and whose woman-centred life make her of interest to lesbian readers. Initially Sandel wanted to become a painter. She studied painting and travelled to Paris in 1905 in pursuit of a life as an artist. In 1913 she married the Swedish sculptor Anders Jönsson, with whom she had a son in 1917. The complete disruption all this brought to her artistic life led her eventually to separate from her husband and, in 1926, the year that she left him, she published her first novel, *Alberte og Jakob* (*Alberte and Jacob*). Two further novels featuring Alberte, a character who shares many of the life experiences Sandel herself had, were published: *Alberte og Friheten* (1931; *Alberte and Freedom*) and *Bare Alberte* (1939; *Alberte Alone*). Her other writings include *Kranes Konditori* (1945; *Krane's Café*) and *Kjøp ikke Dondi* (1958; *The Leech*). Many of her characters are women struggling to survive situations that do not allow their creativity any space.

Sappho (seventh–sixth century BC). Greek poet from the island of Lesbos, born there in the town of Eresus, the daughter of Scamandronymus and Cleis, who had three brothers. She seems to have lived most of her life in Mytilene, the main town on Lesbos but was exiled to Sicily for several years because of her family's political activities. It appears that Sappho may have been married and had a daughter named Cleis although this is not certain. Sappho was a famous poet in her own day. Her work survives only in fragments but many of these are concerned with love for young girls. Sappho appears to have had a circle of young unmarried aristocratic girls whom she may have taught the arts of beauty, music, poetry, and dance. She repeatedly invoked the goddess of love and sexuality, Aphrodite. Sappho's surviving fragments centre on the delights of the sensual world. Her name is the source of the phrase 'sapphic love' and her birthplace Lesbos lent the term 'lesbian' to homosexual women.

Sarduy, Severo (1937–93). Cuban writer, born in Camagüey in rural poverty. Sarduy studied medicine and, like the gay writer Reinaldo ARENAS who castigated Sarduy for his support of the Castro regime in his autobiography *Before Night Falls*, initially supported the Revolution. However, soon afterwards he fled to Paris where he lived for the remainder of his life, supporting Castro from the safe distance of France. Sarduy's texts advocate free-floating identities in a quasi-postmodern, queer fashion. They include *De donde son los cantantes* (1967; *Where the Singers Come From*), *Cobra* (1972), and *Colibrí* (1983; *Hummingbird*). As well as novels Sarduy produced anthologies of poetry and of literary criticism, and published articles in journals such as *Tel Quel*. He remained relatively closeted about his own homosexuality until the end of his life when, in his final volume, *Pájaros en la arena* (1993; *Birds on the Sand*) he addressed the topic of AIDS. He died from an AIDS-related illness in Paris.

Sargeson, Frank (1903–82). Born Norris Frank Davey in the small town of Hamilton, the New Zealand writer Sargeson moved as a young adult to Auckland, where he studied Law. He later travelled in Britain and Continental Europe. Sargeson is significant for his depiction of aspects of regional life and for his influence on later generations of New Zealand writers, including Janet Frame. A repressed but unmistakable gay sub-text in a number of his novels and short stories offers an interesting parallel to the travails of the inarticulate and often alienated characters who populate these works. After an arrest for indecent assault, he changed his name and moved to a small house in the suburbs of Auckland, where he lived the rest of his life. He remained largely silent about his homosexuality, speaking out only in his later years, when he had become a major figure in New Zealand literature. Many of Sargeson's characters are involved in a variety of

same-sex relationships, sometimes acknowledged as homosexual but often depicted as an aspect of what they refer to as 'mateship'. The novella *That Summer* (1946) delineates such a situation, in which the gay sexuality of the two main characters, Billy and Terry, is unacknowledged but strongly felt. Other stories containing a variety of gay sexual situations and tensions include 'I've Lost My Pal', 'A Great Day', and 'A Pair of Socks'.

[David Garnes]

Sarton, May (1912–95). Lesbian writer, born in Belgium, the daughter of Mabel Sarton, an artist and designer, and George Sarton, a historian of science. When May was two years old, her father became a professor at Harvard University, and the Sartons moved to the USA. Sarton began publishing poetry when she was still a teenager but was initially interested in a career in theatre. She joined Eva Le Gallienne's Civic Repertory Theatre Company and later founded her own theatre company, which, however, folded during the Great Depression. It was this that prompted her to turn to writing. In 1937 *Encounter in April*, her first collection of poems, appeared. Throughout her life Sarton published poetry, novels, and eight journals, and it is perhaps for the last, especially the ones dealing with old age such as her final one, *At Eighty-Two* (1994), that she will mostly be remembered. In these texts she explores issues such as the difficulties of living alone (*Journal of Solitude*, 1977) and coping with illness (*After the Stroke*, 1988). In her novel *As We Are Now* (1983) she describes the life of a seemingly lesbian older woman as she faces life in an old people's home. In this novel, as in *The Magnificent Spinster* (1986), Sarton describes single older women, 'old maids', who are strong characters and fighters. *A Reckoning* (1984) focuses on an older woman facing death and reconciling herself with her life. Two of her novels, *Mrs Stevens Hears the Mermaids Singing*

(1965) and *The Education of Harriet Hatfield* (1989), are narratives of lesbian awakening. On the whole, Sarton's writing has become more overtly lesbian as she has grown older. Sarton's long-term relationship with Judith Matlack is celebrated in *Honey in the Beehive* (1988). Sarton has also published essays and interviews (*Writings on Writing*, 1980), and in 1982 a first film about her, *May Sarton: A Self-Portrait*, appeared. This was followed in 1991 with another film about her, *May Sarton: Writing in the Upwards Years*. Sarton saw herself as inspired by a female muse, often one of her lovers.

Sassoon, Siegfried (1886–1967). Born into a wealthy Jewish family, the writer Siegfried Louvain Sassoon was at educated at Marlborough and at Clare College, Cambridge. Initially he lived a life of country pursuits, fictionalized in his semi-autobiographical trilogy *Memoirs of a Fox-hunting Man* (1928), *Memoirs of an Infantry Officer* (1930), and *Sherston's Progress* (1936). In 1937 the three volumes appeared together as *The Complete Memoirs of George Sherston*, the latter being the central character of the novels. Sassoon is now best known as one of the so-called War Poets, among them Wilfred OWEN whom he met when both were hospitalized at Craiglockhart in Scotland, suffering from shell shock. Sassoon's attitude towards war changed during the course of the First World War. Wounded twice, he wrote publicly in protest against the war, and escaped court martial only through the intervention of Robert Graves. Sassoon's experiences at Craiglockhart were fictionalized in Pat BARKER's novel *Regeneration*, as well as in a play by Stephen MacDonald entitled *Not about Heroes* (1983). In his early years Sassoon appears to have been attracted to men. During the First World War at least two of these men lost their lives. In 1933 Sassoon married and had a son. His early

poems appeared in *The Old Huntsman* (1917) and in *Counter-attack* (1918). During the 1920s he published a number of other collections of poems, and his reputation as a poet rose. He increasingly thought of himself as a religious poet, and collections such as *Vigils* (1935) and *Sequences* (1956) testify to that. Sassoon became a Catholic in 1957. Poetry apart, Sassoon published a number of memoirs and his diaries appeared in 1982 and 1983. He also published a biography of George Meredith.

Schreiner, Olive (1855–1920). South African writer, born Olive Emilie Albertina in Cape Colony to a German Lutheran missionary. She tried to escape the Christian confines of her early life, which included working as a governess, by moving to England in 1881 where she hoped to publish the three novels she had written by then. Throughout her life Schreiner was a feminist, rejected Christianity, and took an anti-imperialist and anti-racist stance. Once she was in England Schreiner developed close friendships with free thinkers such as Havelock ELLIS and Edward CARPENTER. Her most famous work, the novel *The Story of an African Farm* (1883), which brought her great success on publication under the pseudonym 'Ralph Iron', was influenced by ideas on identity and sexuality also found in Ellis's and Carpenter's work. It is this novel that makes her of particular interest to lesbian and gay readers for in it Schreiner explores and explodes conventional gender roles, showing the typically feminine woman as long-suffering and oppressed, presenting in the characters Waldo and Gregory men who do not wish to inhabit traditional masculine roles, and portraying in Lyndall, one of the central female characters, a woman striving to move beyond the conventional constraints for women. Both Waldo and Lyndall represent versions of a third or intermediate type, constructed as 'higher' beings due to their yearning for a kind of soul companionship. In 1889 Schreiner returned to South Africa where she married the politician Samuel Cron Cronwright. She returned to England in 1914, leading a miserable life on account of her German surname, which at the time of the First World War made her the object of much hostility. She returned to South Africa in the last stages of her life. Apart from *The Story of an African Farm* Schreiner published two novels with a feminist theme, *From Man to Man* (1927), on which she worked for most of her life, and *Undine* (written between 1875 and 1877, but published only posthumously in 1929). Schreiner also wrote some allegories, *Dreams* (1890), *Dream Life and Real Life* (1983), and *Stories, Dreams and Allegories* (1923). Among her best-known non-fiction writing is *Woman and Labour* (1911). Other works include *Trooper Peter Halket of Mashonaland* (1897), *An English South African's View of the Situation* (1899), *Closer Union* (1909), and *Thoughts on South Africa* (1923).

Schulman, Sarah (1958–). Lesbian US novelist and political activist, born in New York City where she lives in Manhattan. Schulman was educated at Hunter College of the City University of New York and has worked variously as a waitress, stagehand, secretary, and teacher. As a political activist working for lesbian and gay rights she was a co-founder of ACT UP and of the Lesbian Avengers. Schulman's writings eschew the realist tradition that many lesbian novelists have embraced in favour of a mainly postmodern, experimental style of writing. Satirical and witty, her work refuses linear narratives, relying instead on an episodic structure. They often feature adventurous, feisty lesbian heroines who are street-savvy and the very opposite of the notion of lesbian as victim. Schulman's first novel, *The Sophie Horowitz Story* (1984), features Sophie as a feminist investigative reporter parodying the

Search for Woman. Her second novel, *Girls, Visions and Everything* (1986), takes its title from a passage in Jack Kerouac's *On the Road* and centres on Lila Futuransky, a female *flâneuse* who travels the streets of New York. *After Dolores* (1988) is about losing a woman lover to another woman. This book won the Library Association's Gay and Lesbian Book Award. *People in Trouble* (1990) was a novel about people being confronted by an AIDS organization. It won the Gregory Kolovakos Memorial Prize. In 1991 Schulman and Della Grace, a queer photographer who has since become a drag king, published *Love Bites*. *Empathy* (1992), Schulman's next novel, was another experimental novel featuring Anna O., named after one of Freud's most famous case histories, and it explores and refuses the notion that lesbians hate men or want to be men. Since then she has published *Rat Bohemia* (1995), *Shimmer* (1998), and *Stagestruck* (1998). Schulman has been a prolific contributor to many magazines, newspapers, and journals both mainstream and specifically lesbian and gay ones such as *Advocate*, *Mother Jones*, the *Village Voice*, and many others. A collections of her essays appeared in 1994 under the title *My American History: Lesbian and Gay Life during the Reagan and Bush Years*. Schulman has also written a number of plays including *Art Failures* (with Robin Epstein, produced 1983); *Whining and Dining* (with Robin Epstein, produced 1984); *Epstein on the Beach* (with Robin Epstein, produced 1985); *Hootenanny Night* (produced 1986); *Salome/Psychology* (produced 1992); *Empathy* (produced 1993); *The Group, Guilty with an Explanation* (produced 1993). Schulman is probably one of the best-known contemporary lesbian experimental writers. She has held a Fulbright fellowship (1984).

Schwarzenbach, Annemarie (1908–42). Treated as 'her little pageboy' by her mother, the Swiss lesbian writer Annemarie

Schwarzenbach grew up as one of three children in a materially secure, middle-class environment. In 1930 she met Erika and Klaus MANN, and fell in love with the former. She completed her doctorate and in 1931 published her first novel, *Friends of Bernhard*. In 1931 she went to Berlin where she was introduced to morphine and became a drug addict. In the spring of 1933 her *Lyrical Novella* was published; shortly afterwards she went on her first voyage to Turkey, the Lebanon, Iraq, and Syria, described in *Winter in Asia Minor: Diary of a Journey*. Having met Maud von Rosen in 1934, Annemarie Schwarzenbach travelled to Teheran and married the French diplomat Claude Clarac in 1935, a common move in this period to avoid questions about sexual preferences. In 1936 she completed her unpublished novel *Death in Persia* and in 1936 she went to the USA where she collaborated with Barbara Hamilton-Wright on various journalistic projects. During the 1930s her drug addiction led to repeated bouts of illness as well as attempts to cure her addictions, which proved fruitless. Involved with various women, she met Carson MCCULLERS in 1940 who fell madly in love with her. Annemarie Schwarzenbach, however, had an association with Margot Opel and when they fell out she attempted suicide by cutting her wrists. Carson McCullers took care of her. In 1941 she worked on her new novel *The Miracle of the Tree* but died a year later aged thirty-four following a bicycle accident. Her work was rediscovered and republished by the Swiss publishing house Lenos in the 1980s.

Scott, Sarah (1732–95). English novelist and writer who was born as Sarah Robinson into an established Yorkshire family and who was the sister of Elizabeth Montagu, a famous Bluestocking. In 1748 Scott met Lady Barbara Montagu, the daughter of the first Earl of Halifax and Lady Mary Lumley. The two women began a relationship that lasted until Lady

Montagu's death in 1765. In 1751 Sarah Robinson married George Lewis Scott, separating from him the following year. Writing became a way of sustaining herself financially. In 1750 Scott's first novel, *The History of Cornelia*, appeared. After separating from her husband, Scott and Lady Barbara Montagu moved to Bath to set up a female community at Batheaston and to teach poor children. This formed the basis of Sarah Scott's most famous novel, *Millennium Hall* (1762), which is a utopian novel depicting an all-female community where a series of previously distressed ladies cohabit, regulating their own affairs after having been the victims of men's financial mismanagement. *Millennium Hall* advocates rational virtues and the ability of women to manage their lives successfully, given the opportunity. For contemporary readers the attitudes towards the poor expressed in the text may seem sanctimonious and patronizingly philanthropic but this novel is the first to celebrate a separatist female community and as such prefigures some of the lesbian feminist science fiction of the twentieth century, including texts such as Charlotte Perkins GILMAN's *Herland* and Sally Miller GEARHART's *The Wanderground*.

Sedgwick, Eve Kosofsky (1950–). US academic and theorist whose work, together with that of Judith BUTLER, has been highly influential both in establishing queer theory during the 1990s, and in rethinking the role of the homosexual in Western culture and literature. Sedgwick gained a PhD at Yale University. That PhD formed the basis of her first publication, *The Coherence of Gothic Conventions* (1980). It was with *Between Men* (1985) that Sedgwick achieved a major intervention in the reading of the sexual politics of nineteenth-century fiction. In that volume she investigated the notion of the 'homosocial', male bonding in literature that always gestures towards the homosexual, even if homoeroticism remains unacknowledged or fiercely repressed. In Sedgwick's reading the paradigm of social relations of nineteenth-century fiction was the 'homosocial triangle' in which the plot developed as an exchange between men, with women frequently figuring as the object of exchange. Sedgwick's breakthrough with a wider gay and lesbian audience came with *Epistemology of the Closet* (1990), which analysed the ways in which sexual knowledge functions as a key to understanding knowledge *per se*. The closet, so powerfully associated with the repression of lesbian and homosexual desire, came to stand both for the notion of having a secret and having a *telling* secret. In 1993 Sedgwick published *Tendencies*, which continues the investigations begun in her two previous works of the relation between sexual identity, sexual knowledge, and literary representation. In 1994 a collection of poetry by Sedgwick, *Fat Art, Thin Art* appeared. Sedgwick remains one of the key theorists of queer. She has also published *Novel Gazing: Queer Reading in Fiction* (1997; edited), and *A Dialogue on Love* (1999).

Seward, Anna (1747–1809). English writer, mainly of poetry, born as the eldest daughter in the village of Eyam, Derbyshire, to Thomas Seward who was a rector there, and was to become the Canon of Lichfield. His daughter, known as the 'Swan of Lichfield', never married and looked after him until his old age. Seward had a series of intense involvements with women, beginning with her foster sister Honora Sneyd who entered the Seward household when Anna was thirteen, and became Anna's closest companion after the death of her sister Sarah in 1763. Seward was deeply affected by Honora's marriage to Richard Lovell Edgeworth in 1773, and went into mourning for the loss of her friend. Seward attended Lady Anne Miller's literary circle in Batheaston, beginning to write in her mid-thirties. Her poetry expressed an excess of sentiment, was dedicated to her female friends, and sometimes presented her deep affections for other women. She had close friendships with Penelope Weston and Elizabeth Cornwallis, and was a correspondent of the Ladies of Llangollen (see BUTLER, LADY ELEANOR) for whom she wrote the long poem 'Llangollen Vale'. Some of her poetry was published in the *Gentleman's Magazine*. She came to public attention with her elegies on David Garrick and on Captain Cook. In 1784 her novel *Louisa* appeared. Her collected *Poems* were published in 1810. Much attention has focused on Seward's relation with John Saville, vicar choral at Lichfield, who was separated from his wife. Seward did not marry him even after his wife had died and she was deeply upset by Saville's death in 1803. However, her most intense emotional attachments appear to have been with women. Seward was well known and widely connected in literary circles in the 1780s and 1790s. Seward bequeathed her writings to Sir Walter Scott who published her poems in three volumes in 1810.

Shakespeare, William (1564–1616). English playwright and poet, the son of John Shakespeare and Mary Arden who had eight children of whom five survived early childhood. Shakespeare was baptized in Stratford-upon-Avon and probably educated there. In 1582 he married Anne Hathaway of Shottery, close to Stratford. They had three children, Susanna, Hamnet, and Judith. Shakespeare may have been a schoolmaster in his early adulthood. He is first referred to as a playwright and theatre person in 1592. He became a leading member of the Lord Chamberlain's Men in 1594. The company became very prosperous, occupying the Globe Theatre in London from 1599. On the accession of James I the company became the King's Men. They used Blackfriars as their winter quarters in 1608.

Shakespeare's family remained in Stratford while he resided in London. Shakespeare's inclusion in this dictionary rests upon the reclamation of both some of his plays and his sonnets by literary critics who regard the representation of cross-dressing and of close male companionship in his plays, as well as the possibility that his sonnets may have been addressed to men rather than to women, as opening this work to readings that suggest homoeroticism and gay sensibilities, all the more so because in Shakespeare's day his plays were performed by boy companies. The all-male environment of such companies itself lends added interest to such readings. However, unlike his contemporary Christopher MARLOWE, who was fairly directly accused of sodomy soon after his death, there is no evidence that Shakespeare was thought of as homosexual or a sodomite in his lifetime or thereafter. Among the plays in which boy actors dressed as women cross-dress as men are *The Two Gentlemen of Verona* (1594), *As You Like It* (1598), and *Twelfth Night* (1601). In *Troilus and Cressida* (1603), *Coriolanus* (1608), and *Henry V* (1599), close male friendship is represented. Many of Shakespeare's other plays also feature close friendships, either between women, or between men, including *A Midsummer Night's Dream* (1594–5), *The Merchant of Venice* (1596–7), *Othello* (1603–4), *Antony and Cleopatra* (1606), *The Winter's Tale* (1609–10), and *The Two Noble Kinsmen* (1613). In 1593 and 1594, respectively, Shakespeare published his only works written directly for the press, two long narrative poems entitled *Venus and Adonis*, and *The Rape of Lucrece*. These poems were dedicated to H.W., thought to be Henry Wriothesley, the Earl of Southampton. In *Venus and Adonis*, the man's body is the object of erotic attention rather than the woman's. In 1609 Shakespeare's 154 sonnets were printed as a group but it appears that Shakespeare himself was not involved in that publica-

tion. Subsequent scholarship has suggested that the first 126 sonnets seem to be addressed to a fair-complexioned man, possibly a nobleman, and the last twenty-eight sonnets to a dark-complexioned woman, the speaker's mistress. Shakespeare's plays are notoriously difficult to date since they were not published at the time they were played. His other works include the trilogy on the reign of Henry VI: *Henry VI Parts 1, 2,* and *3. Richard III* is also one of his early plays. His first Roman tragedy, *Titus Andronicus*, appeared in print in 1594 as did *The Taming of the Shrew* and *The Comedy of Errors*. *Love's Labour's Lost* was printed in 1598. These were followed by *Richard II* (printed 1597), *The Merry Wives of Windsor* (1602), *Much Ado about Nothing* (printed 1600), *Romeo and Juliet* (written in the 1590s), and *Henry V* (1599). Shakespeare's tragedies *Julius Caesar* (1599), *Hamlet* (1600–1), *King Lear* (1605), and *Timon of Athens* (date uncertain) belong to his later period. It also includes *All's Well that Ends Well* (first decade of 1600) and *Measure for Measure* (1604). *Pericles* (1609), *Cymbeline* (1611), *The Winter's Tale* (1611), and *The Tempest* (1611) were among his last plays. It is possible that he wrote his final three plays, *Henry VIII, The Two Noble Kinsmen*, and a lost play, *Cardenio*, in collaboration with J. Fletcher. A collection of his work, known as the First Folio, appeared in 1623.

Shchépkina-Kupérnik, Tat'iana L'vovna (1874–1952). Russian prose writer, dramatist, translator, and memorist whose work advocated emotional attachments between women, and art, as the sources of happiness. Shchépkina-Kupérnik was the great-granddaughter of the famous Russian actor Mikhail Shchépkin. On the centennial of his birthday, in 1886, she published her first poem. She joined the Korsh Theatre troupe in Moscow in 1891, following in the family tradition. Her mother had been a professional musician.

In 1892 she wrote *Summer Picture*, a vaudeville one-act play that was staged at the Malyi Theatre. Subsequent plays by her attracted the leading actors of her day. *A Happy Woman* (1911), a play about the mother of a revolutionary student, won her the Griboedov Prize. As well as plays, Shchépkina-Kupérnik published a number of volumes of poetry including *From Women's Letters* (1898), *My Poems* (1903), *Clouds* (1912), and *Echoes of War* (1915). She also published several volumes of short stories of which *Legends of Love* won an honourable mention for the Pushkin Prize. *Sappho* (1894) was a light-hearted story unlike many of Shchépkina-Kupérnik's other works, which focused on social injustice. Shchépkina-Kupérnik translated many classics, among them the works of Shakespeare, Goldoni Calderón, Lope de Vega and Victor Hugo, into Russian. In 1944 she received the Order of Labour of the Red Banner.

Shilts, Randy (1951–94). Born in Davenport, Iowa, Shilts was educated at the University of Oregon where he gained a BS in 1975. During his college years he was already an openly out gay reporter. In 1975 he went to San Francisco to work on the *Advocate*. From 1981 until 1987 he was a staff reporter for the *San Francisco Chronicle*. His writings culminated in three volumes all in different ways chronicling contemporary gay and lesbian life in the USA. In 1982 he produced the gay political biography *The Mayor of Castro: The Life and Times of Harvey Milk*. This was followed by his perhaps best-known but also highly controversial representation of HIV/AIDS in *And the Band Played on: Politics, People, and the AIDS Epidemic* (1987). In this text he charted a history of the spread of HIV/AIDS, which he infamously linked to the so-called Patient Zero, a Canadian air steward, who was supposed to have introduced the virus into the US. Shilts then published *Conduct Unbecoming: Lesbians and Gays in the U.S. Military,* *Vietnam to the Gulf War* (1993) in which he addressed another controversial topic, that of the experiences of lesbians and gays in the military. Shilts won numerous awards and prizes for his investigative journalism, among them the American Society of Journalists and Authors' Outstanding Author Award in 1988, the Bay Area Book Reviewers' Association Award for Nonfiction (1988), the named University of Oregon Outstanding Young Alumnus (1993), and the California Public Health Association's Outstanding Print Media Award (1993). He died in 1994 of an AIDS-related illness.

Shockley, Ann Allen (1927–). Born in Louisville, Kentucky, the daughter of social workers Bessie Lucas and Henry Allen, Shockley was educated at Fisk University, Nashville, Tennessee, where she also later worked as an archivist, librarian, and professor, and where she gained a BA in 1948. She then attended Western Reserve (now Case Western Reserve) in Cleveland, Ohio, receiving an MSLS in 1959. In 1949 she married William Shockley, a teacher, whom she has since divorced. She has a son and a daughter. Shockley is considered to be the first writer to put a black lesbian at the centre of her narratives. *Loving Her* (1974) focuses on the inter-racial relationship between Renay, a black woman, and Terry, a white one. This novel, like Shockley's subsequent writings, explores the oppressions black lesbian women experience in a homophobic society. Shockley's collection of short stories, *The Black and the White of It* (1980), has been widely critiqued for representing black lesbians in defeatist ways, constructing them as victims of both homophobia and racism, and portraying them as succumbing to alcohol and denial of their lesbian identity. In 1982 *Say Jesus and Come to Me*, Shockley's second novel, appeared, attacking the black middle classes in the USA for their prejudices and pretensions. Shockley has published many short stories in magazines and journals. She is the recipient of a variety of awards including the American Association of University Women Short Story Award (1972), the American Library Association Black Caucus Award (1975), the Martin Luther King Jr. Black Author Award (1982), the Susan Koppelman Award (1988), the Outlook Award for outstanding pioneering contributions to lesbian and gay writing (1990), and the American Library Association Black Caucus Award for professional achievement (1992).

Sitwell, Edith (1887–1964). Edith Louisa Sitwell, the daughter of Lady Ida and Sir George Sitwell, was brought up at Renishaw Hall where her rather unhappy childhood was mediated by her close relationship with her brothers Osbert SITWELL and Sacheverell Sitwell. All three became writers, publishing in the main poetry. In 1903 Helen Rootham, who had translated Arthur RIMBAUD's writings into English was engaged as a governess for Edith Sitwell. Rootham, who became Sitwell's companion until her death in 1938 in Paris, introduced Sitwell to the French symbolist poets whose influence permeated Sitwell's work. In 1913 Rootham and Sitwell left Renishaw Hall to set up home together in London. Sitwell's first published poem, 'Drowned Suns', appeared in the same year in the *Daily Mirror* newspaper. In 1915 her first collection of poetry, *The Mother and Other Poems*, was published. A great supporter of modernist writing, Sitwell and her brothers, who were anti-Georgian, set up *Wheels*, an avant-garde annual literary anthology that first published Wilfred OWEN's poetry. *Wheels* came out yearly from 1916 until 1921. In 1923 Sitwell gave a celebrated performance of *Façade*, a piece that involved verses set to syncopated music by William Walton, which Sitwell performed from behind a screen. The performance focused on the sounds of individual words, employing eccentric diction and utilizing popular dance music

as part of its score. It made her part of the modernist movement. *Gold Coast Customs* (1929) compared modern Europe with an ancient and barbaric Africa. Sitwell intermittently wrote prose works in an attempt to make some money. These included a study of Alexander Pope (1930), *English Eccentrics* (1933), an abiding bestseller, and *Victoria of England* (1936). In 1932 she and Rootham, then already terminally ill, moved to Paris where Rootham died in 1938. The year before, Sitwell's fantastic, only novel *I Live under a Black Sun* appeared but did not receive much critical acclaim. While in Paris Sitwell was a member of a variety of literary circles there, championing the work of Gertrude STEIN, and being friends with many of the lesbian writers and exiles of the Left Bank, including BRYHER Ellerman, who became a lifelong supporter of Edith Sitwell, Natalie BARNEY, Adrienne MONNIER, and Sylvia BEACH. Sitwell's poems about the blitz and the atom bomb published as *Street Songs* (1942), *Green Song* (1944), *The Song of the Cold* (1945), and *The Shadow of Cain* (1947) were highly successful as they captured the mood of the hour. They led to a very successful lecture tour in the USA. Her poem 'Still Falls the Rain' (1942) was set to music by the gay composer Benjamin Britten and performed by his partner Peter Piers. During the 1950s Sitwell's reputation began to fade. In 1955, sponsored by the writer Evelyn WAUGH, Sitwell converted to Catholicism. Throughout her life, Sitwell had close friendships with gay men including W.H. AUDEN, James PURDY, and Ronald FIRBANK. Her last poem, 'The Outcasts' (1962), was written in support of the reform of British anti-homosexual legislation. Sitwell was made Dame Commander of the British Empire in 1954. Her autobiography, *Taken Care Of*, was published a year after her death. Though her work is not currently in vogue she is remembered as one of the most stylish eccentrics of the first part of the twentieth century, eminently photographable.

Sitwell, Osbert (1892–1969). Sir Francis Osbert Sacheverell Sitwell, gay British writer, brother of Edith SITWELL and the poet Sacheverell Sitwell, son of Lady Ida and Sir George Sitwell, who was born and brought up at Renishaw Hall, Derbyshire, which he later inherited. He was educated at Eton and then, reluctantly, served in the First World War. His early poems are both satirical and pacifist in tone. Sitwell had a close relationship with his siblings. In the mid-1920s Sitwell met David Horner who was to become his long-term companion. Unlike his sister, Osbert did not mix in homosexual circles and kept his private life separate from his writing. He wrote in a variety of genres but gained lasting fame with his autobiographical sequence *Left Hand, Right Hand!* (1945), *The Scarlet Tree* (1946), *Great Morning* (1948), *Laughter in the Next Room* (1949), and *Noble Essences* (1950). To these was later added *Tales My Father Taught Me* (1962). Sitwell's other works include *Triple Fugue* (1924), the words for William Walton's *Belshazzar's Feast* (1926), *Before the Bombardment* (1926), a novel about the impact of the shelling of Scarborough in Yorkshire in 1914, *Winters of Content* (1932), and *Escape with Me!* (1939), both of which are travel books about travels in Italy and in China and the Far East respectively.

Smyth, Dame Ethel Mary (1853–1944). English composer, suffragist, and autobiographer, born in Sidcup in the UK, one of several children of a French mother and a father who was a general. She was brought up in Frimley near Aldershot and became interested in composing after she had heard a new governess, who had studied music at Leipzig, play. In 1877, her father finally allowed her to go to Leipzig where she met various composers, including Clara Schumann. She met and fell in love with the wife of her music

teacher, Lisl von Herzogenberg, and had seven happy years in Germany, returning home during the summer months. In 1882, she met Henry 'Harry' Brewster, a writer, in Florence and they became close friends and collaborators. In 1883 Smyth visited Lisl's sister Julia and her husband Henry Brewster in Florence. She was attracted to both and remained in regular contact with Henry Brewster until his death. Her 'Mass in D' (1891), a choral work, established her reputation as a composer when it was performed at the Albert Hall. Another composition of hers, *Der Wald* (1902; *The Forest*), was performed at New York Metropolitan Opera, making it the first opera by a woman to be performed there. Smyth became interested in the suffrage movement in 1910 after hearing Emmeline Pankhurst at a meeting of the Women's Social and Political Union. In 1911 she composed 'March of the Women', which became the suffragettes' anthem. A year later, in 1912, she spent three months in Holloway Prison for participating in suffrage activities, in particular for smashing the windows of the building housing the Colonial Secretary. While in prison she famously led the prisoners' singing of the 'March of the Women' by directing with her toothbrush. In 1922 she was made a Dame Commander of the British Empire. Smyth fell in love with a number of women including Winnaretta Singer, Edith Somerville (see SOMERVILLE AND ROSS), and Virginia WOOLF. In her memoirs and autobiographical texts she comments on these attachments. These writings include *Impressions that Remained* (1919), *Streaks of Life* (1921), *Female Pipings in Eden* (1933), *As Time Went On* (1936), and *What Happened Next* (1940). Her later years were marred by an increasing deafness that prevented her from composing. A famous biography of her was written by another lesbian, a contemporary of Ethel Smyth, Christopher St. John (1959).

Solano, Solita (1888–1975). US writer and life-long companion and friend of Janet FLANNER who was born in Troy, New York State, as Sarah Wilkinson. In 1903, following her father's death, her two younger brothers were made executors of his will. In 1904 Solano ran away from home and married Oliver Filley, an engineer. They spent the next four years in the Philippines, China, and Japan, but Solano left the marriage, returning to New York in 1908. After an attempt to earn money in the theatre, Solano moved to Boston where she became a successful journalist. In 1918 she moved back to New York to be theatre critic for the New Yorker *Tribune*. In the winter of 1919 Solano met and fell in love with Janet Flanner and together the two women moved to Europe where they travelled widely. Solano had a commission from the *National Geographic* to write about Constantinople. Between 1924 and 1927 Solano wrote and published three novels but since these were not successful she refocused on her journalism. Her partner Flanner's work as the Paris correspondent for the *New Yorker* meant that Solano increasingly worked for Flanner, doing background research and writing up her notes. They continued to work together throughout their lives. While Solano's and Flanner's relationship continued, the latter especially became repeatedly deeply involved with other women. In the 1940s Solano eventually met and fell in love with Elizabeth (Lib) Jenks Clark. They moved together, first to the US, and then after the Second World War to Orgeval in France, to look after the singer Noel Haskins Murphy, one of Flanner's great loves. Solano and Flanner had a large circle of lesbian friends throughout their lives and never abandoned each other. Solano preserved many of Flanner's writings.

Somerville and Ross. Somerville and Ross were a lesbian Irish writing couple, in some respects rather like the Michael FIELDs who were also blood-related. Somerville (1858–1949) was born Edith Anna Oenone Somerville in Corfu. She was brought up in her family's eighteenth-century house in West Cork. This background served as material for her later writing. Somerville trained as an illustrator, studying art in London and Paris. For a while she adopted the pseudonym Guilles Herring. She was an accomplished huntswoman who in 1903 served as the first female master of foxhounds, and was master of the west Carberry pack between 1912 and 1919. She was also actively involved in the suffrage movement and was president of the Munster Women's Franchise League. After the First World War she exhibited her work as an artist and in 1926 she made a radio appearance reading her own poetry. In her later life she was a close companion of the lesbian composer Ethel SMYTH. Ross (1862–1915) was born Violet Florence Martin and educated in Dublin. She assumed the pseudonym Martin Ross. Somerville met Ross in 1886 and they became life-long companions. Although they did not describe their relationship as lesbian they made it clear that they thought of themselves as married. Ross and Somerville were second cousins. They set up house together in Drishane, County Cork, and collaborated on a series of humorous novels about the rural Irish gentry. Their work includes *An Irish Cousin* (1889), *Naboth's Vineyard* (1891), *In the Vine Country* (1893), *Through Connemara in a Governess Cart* (1893), *Beggars on Horseback* (1895), *The Silver Fox* (1897), *Some Experiences of an Irish R.M.* (1899), which was turned into a successful TV series in 1983–4, and their most famous novel, *The Real Charlotte* (1894), which features two cousins. They also wrote *A Patrick's Day Hunt* (1902), *All on the Irish Shore* (1903), *Further Experiences of an Irish R.M.* (1908), and *Dan Russell the Fox* (1911). Following Ross's death Somerville continued to write under their joint name. Their joint legacy includes thousands of letters and 116 volumes of diaries. After Ross's death Somerville published *In Mr Knox's Country* (1915), *Mount Music* (1919), *The Big House at Inver* (1925), *The Sweet Cry of Hounds* (1936), and *Sarah's Youth* (1938). In 1981 Somerville and Ross's life was dramatized for BBC radio by Maureen DUFFY in *Only Goodnight*. A further version of their lives, also by Maureen Duffy, was broadcast by BBC radio in 1986 under the title *On the Hunt for Somerville and Ross*.

Sontag, Susan (1933–). Lesbian US writer, cultural critic, and political activist whose work has not articulated a concern with female homosexuality but has consistently investigated gay culture. In 1963 she published her first novel, *Benefactor*, and in 1967 the novel *Death Kit*. In between one of her most important essays, 'Notes on "Camp"' (1964) appeared, a key text both for its engagement with gay subculture and for its discussion of a gay aesthetic. During the 1960s and 1970s Sontag published many essays in which she wrote about leading modernist and structuralist European thinkers of the day including Walter Benjamin and Claude Lévi-Strauss. Some of her essays were collected in *Against Interpretation* (1966), *Styles of Radical Free Will* (1969), and *Under the Sign of Saturn* (1980). Sontag wrote and directed two films, *Duet for Cannibals* (1969) and *Brother Carl* (1971), during a period she spent in Sweden. These were followed by a documentary, *Promised Lands* (1974), about the aftermath of the 1973 Arab–Israeli war. Her short fiction, *I, Etcetera* (1979) was published two years after her volume *On Photography* (1977) came out. In 1978 she also published the highly influential *Illness as Metaphor* in which she offered a critique of the ways in which illness is culturally encoded. This text proved, in a sense, to be prophetic since the emergence of HIV/AIDS into the public limelight three years later brought precisely this issue to the cultural fore-

front as gay and lesbian activist organizations began to attempt to counter the cultural stereotyping that accompanied HIV/AIDS. In 1989 Sontag then duly published *AIDS and Its Metaphors*, in which she focused the debates from her earlier work specifically on HIV/AIDS as a cultural as well as a medical syndrome. In 1992 Sontag's novel *The Volcano Lover: A Historical Romance* was published. She has since published other novels including *In America* (2001). Sontag continues to be one of the major cultural commentators of her time.

Spender, Sir Stephen (1909–95). The British poet and critic Sir Stephen Harold Spender was born in London, the second son of E.H. Spender, a distinguished journalist. On his mother's side he was partly of German-Jewish descent. Spender was orphaned in his teens. He was brought up in Hampstead and educated at University College School, London, and at University College, Oxford, where he met W.H. AUDEN, and which he left without taking a degree in 1931. In his autobiography *World within World* (1951) Spender described the destructive influence his father, who was very puritanical, had on his own perception of his body, and the guilt and shame he felt about his bodily desires. These feelings were not alleviated until he met W.H. Auden at Oxford in 1928. In 1928 Spender printed his and Auden's first books of poems on his own hand press. The liberation from his father's attitudes figures prominently in Spender's autobiographical novel *The Temple*, which was written in 1929 but not published until 1988. In 1930 Spender published *Twenty Poems*; some of his work also appeared in *New Signatures* in 1932. At Oxford Spender also made friends with Christopher ISHERWOOD. Both Auden and Isherwood became Spender's mentors. The relationship among the men is characterized by Spender as *Freundschaft* (friendship) in his journal of 1939 in which he recounts the period of the late 1920s. Following university Spender travelled extensively. For a time he lived in Barcelona with Helmut, the apparent subject of his poem 'Helmut'. Originally published in the 1933 edition of Spender's *Poems*, which T.S. ELIOT accepted for Faber & Faber, it was not included in the later *Collected Poems 1928–1953* but appeared again in *Collected Poems 1928–1985*. In September 1933 Spender met Tony Hyndman, an unemployed working-class lad from Cardiff, who features as Jimmy Younger in *World within World*. They lived together for three years but in 1936 they broke up and Spender announced his marriage to Inez Pearn to whom he was engaged for only three weeks. David LEAVITT adapted many of the details from Spender's autobiography in his novel *While England Sleeps* (1993). This resulted in a charge of unlawful use against Leavitt and his publisher, Viking Press, by Spender but the case was settled out of court in February 1994. During the Spanish Civil War Spender went to Spain and worked as a propagandist for the Republicans. In 1937 Spender joined the Communist Party and got much involved in left-wing politics, writing essays such as *Forward from Liberalism* (1937) and *The New Realism* (1939). His volume of poems *The Still Centre* was published in 1939. Spender divorced in 1939 and two years later married the pianist Natasha Litvin with whom he had two children, Matthew, born 1945, and Lizzie, born 1951. With Cyril Connolly, Spender acted as co-editor of *Horizon* (1939–41) and of *Encounter* (1953–67), which he co-founded with Irving Kristol. Spender held various university posts both in the USA and in the UK, including being Professor of English at University College, London, between 1968 and 1973. Among his other works are a play, *Trial of a Judge* (1938), many translations of writers such as Federico García LORCA, Rainer Maria Rilke, and Ernst Toller, a novel, *The Backward Son* (1940), his *Collected*

Poems (1955), a volume of poetry entitled *The Generous Days* (1971), and several books of criticism such as *The Destructive Element* (1935) and *The Struggle of the Modern* (1963). He also wrote *Love-Hate Relations* (1974) and *The Thirties and After: Poetry, People, Politics* (1978) and a *Chinese Journal* (1982), illustrated by the gay painter David Hockney, with whom he undertook the journey to China. He was knighted for his services to literature in 1983.

Spicer, Jack (1925–65). Gay US poet, born in Hollywood, California, and educated at the University of California at Berkeley. After university Spicer embarked on a series of low-paid jobs in various cities, apparently because he refused to sign the 'Loyalty Oath' required of all state employees of California. He returned to San Francisco in 1957, publishing *After Lorca*, his first collection of poetry, in 1957, and eleven further volumes afterwards, including *The Heads of the Town up to the Aether* (1960–1) in which some of his gay love poetry appears. During his lifetime Spicer gathered a circle of openly homosexual friends around him. Unlike his contemporary Allen GINSBERG, however, he never achieved mainstream status and his poetry was circulated in small editions by local presses. In 1965 he decided to leave San Francisco to move to Vancouver in British Columbia; however, he died on the poverty ward of San Francisco General Hospital beforehand.

Split Britches (1981–). Lesbian US theatre company consisting of Peggy Shaw, Lois Weaver, and Deb Margolin. Shaw and Weaver met and fell in love in Berlin in 1979 when both were there touring with different theatre companies, Shaw with the male drag show Hot Peaches, and Weaver with Spiderwoman, a multi-ethnic, feminist theatre company. Shaw left Hot Peaches to work with Weaver in Spiderwoman but in 1981 they began touring together with a show entitled *Split Britches*. This title came from the pants women working in the fields wore so that they could urinate without stopping to work, and Weaver and Shaw adopted this name to signify the labour that is associated with working in the arts. They use the name Split Britches both as a collective and individually. Apart from touring as Split Britches, they have been associated with the WOW Café in the Allcraft Center, St Mark's Place, which they helped establish in 1980 and which opened in 1982 on 330 East 11th Street. Its function is to promote women's theatre projects, and Split Britches have both performed there and helped to put programmes together. Always lesbian-focused in their own work, and interested in gender roles as well as queer performance, Split Britches have explored butch–femme relationships, reworked Tennessee WILLIAMS's *A Streetcar Named Desire*, and produced a number of plays that they have devised and toured both in the USA and in the UK, as well as elsewhere. Their work includes *Beauty and the Beast* (1982), *Upwardly Mobile Home* (1984), *Dress Suits to Hire* (1987), *Little Women* (1988), *Belle Reprieve* (1991, with the troupe Bloolips), *Lesbians Who Kill* (1992), about the Aileen Wuornos case, *Lust and Comfort* (1995). In addition Shaw, Weaver, and Margolin have also pursued separate projects. Weaver has acted as Artistic Co-Director of the London-based Gay Sweatshop company, and has been visiting lecturer in performance at various universities. Shaw has toured with one-woman shows including *You're Just Like My Father*. Margolin has also toured with one-woman shows including *Gestation* (1991), *Of Mice, Bugs, and Women* (1994), and *Carthieves! Joyrides!* (1995). In 1996 a volume of their plays was published including *Split Britches, Beauty and the Beast, Upwardly Mobile Home, Little Women, Belle Reprieve, Lesbians Who Kill*, and *Lust and Comfort*.

Stefan, Verena (1947–). German-speaking Swiss writer who was closely involved in the student movement in Berlin in the 1960s. Her main claim to fame is her experimental novel of 1975 *Häutungen* (translated as *Shedding* in 1978), which is a radical feminist statement combining poetry, autobiography, and experimental, dream-like passages. The text is an outstanding example of *écriture féminine* (a feminine way of writing, or 'writing the body') as celebrated in the 1970s and early 1980s. The novel involves a move from a heterosexual to a lesbian identity. Since then Stefan has published a number of other writings including *Mit Füssen und Flügeln: Gedichte und Zeichnungen* (1980; *With Feet and Wings: Poems and Drawings*), *Wortgetreu ich träume: Geschichten und Geschichte* (1987; co-published with the re-issued *Shedding* as *Literally Dreaming* in 1994), *Es ist reich gewesen: Bericht vom Sterben meiner Mutter* (1993; *It Was Bountiful: An Account of My Mother's Death*) and *Rauh, wild und frei: Mädchengestalten in der Literatur* (1997; *Rough, Wild and Free: Girls in Literature*).

Stein, Gertrude (1874–1946). Lesbian US author and one of the most widely respected modernist authors, born in Allegheny, Pennsylvania, into a progressive and intellectual middle-class German-Jewish family. After the early deaths of her parents, while Stein was still a teenager, she was left in the care of her older brother Michael. She was educated privately and in public school. In 1893 she accompanied her brother Leo, to whom she was then very close, to Harvard University where she studied psychology under William James, the brother of Alice JAMES and Henry JAMES. She became very interested in character typology and published two articles on the topic in the *Harvard Psychological Review*. In 1897 Stein gained a BA from Harvard University. Between 1897–1901 she attended Johns Hopkins Medical School at Baltimore. Her experiences of delivering babies in the African American community there became the basis for her story 'Melanctha', published in *Three Lives* (1909). At Baltimore, Stein was involved with a circle of women including Mabel Haynes and Grace Lounsbury whose lesbianism was expressed in terms of a romantic friendship. Haynes dropped Lounsbury in favour of another student, Mary Bookstaver, with whom Stein also fell in love. Both Haynes and Bookstaver later married. Stein's experiences in this trio found their literary counterpart in her novel *Q.E.D.* (1903), initially published posthumously under the title *Things as They Are* (1950). Both *Q.E.D.* and *Fernhurst* (1904), another early unpublished work, centre on lesbian triangles and employ conventional narrative styles, much unlike her later high modernist writing in which she experimented with style, structure, language, and punctuation in radical and innovative ways. After Baltimore Stein followed her brother Leo to Paris. Paris in the early twentieth century became a haven for many lesbian and gay writers who set up salons there and were able to live their lives in relative openness. Leo and Gertrude set up together at 27 rue de Fleurus, and began collecting modernist art including the work of painters such as Picasso, Cézanne, and Matisse. During the same period that Stein sat for her portrait by Picasso, she wrote *Three Lives*. She then began *The Making of the Americans* (published 1925), a volume that details the lives of the families Hersland and Dehning and offered Stein a way of engaging with her background. Stein first met Alice B. TOKLAS, the woman who was to become her life-long companion, in 1907 when Toklas was on a visit to Paris. Toklas, like Stein, came from a prosperous Jewish background and had been disappointed in her love for another woman with whom she had, in fact, come to Paris. Gertrude's blossoming relationship with Toklas caused friction between Gertrude and Leo, recorded in *Two* (1908–12), a novel about a conflict be-

tween a brother and a sister. In 1913, Leo moved out of the apartment and Gertrude and Toklas became ensconced there as a lesbian couple in which Toklas featured as the wife, secretary, and barrier between Stein and the outside world and Stein acted as the creator/writer. In her writings Stein addressed lesbianism both directly and indirectly. The play *Ada*, included in *Geography and Plays* (1922) is a tribute to Toklas. Repetition and variation became the hallmarks of Stein's work as demonstrated in the lesbian story 'Miss Furr and Miss Skeene' (1922), which was based on Maud Hunt Squire and Ethel Mars, a lesbian couple who came to see Stein and Toklas in Paris. In the celebrated *Tender Buttons: Objects, Food, Rooms* (written in 1912, published in 1914) Stein tried to find a vocabulary for expressing lesbian sexuality. Stein also wrote *Portrait of Mabel Dodge at the Villa Curonia* (1912), *A Book Concluding with As a Wife Has a Cow, a Love Story* (1926), and *Ida, a Novel* (1941) while, between 1912 and 1925, turning to the shorter form of the poem as her favourite mode of writing. These poems are frequently about domestic or erotic adventures. They record Stein's happiness in her relationship with Toklas, especially 'Lifting Belly' (published in 1953), an amazing poetic account of lesbian love-making, celebrating the female body. Stein's radically divergent writing made it difficult for her to find publishers for it during her lifetime. In the 1920s she began to write commentaries on her work, beginning with 'Composition as Explanation' (1926). In 1933 she published *The Autobiography of Alice B. Toklas* in which she assumed Toklas's voice and described herself and her relationship with Toklas through Toklas's eyes. In it she unabashedly describes herself as a genius, sharing with a contemporary writer like Jeanette WINTERSON a sense of importance that may be a function of simultaneously understanding oneself to be part of a socially marginalized group, lesbians. *The*

Autobiography of Alice B. Toklas was a great success and launched Stein on a much publicized lecture tour through England and the USA. Her lectures from this tour were included in *Writings and Lectures 1911–1945* (1976), republished as *Look At Me Now and Here I Am: Writings and Lectures* in 1971. Made aware of the issue of audiences by her lecture tour, in *The Geographical History of America* (1936) and *Everybody's Auto-biography* (1937), Stein explored the notion of writing for a public and writing from the self. During the Second World War Stein and Toklas lived in their country house in Bilignin and in Culoz, a town nearby. They returned to Paris in 1944 where Stein died from cancer, leaving a grief-stricken Toklas behind who, as happens so often with lesbian and gay couples, then found herself embroiled in a struggle with Stein's family over the inheritance. During her lifetime Stein was a prodigious writer, producing, among other things, a whole series of plays including *A Village Are You Ready Yet Not Yet A Play in Four Acts* (1928), *Operas and Plays* (1932), *In Savoy; or, This Is For A Very Young Man (A Play of the Resistance in France)* (1946), *Last Operas and Plays* (1949, edited by her longstanding friend and advocate Carl van Vechten), and *Lucretia Borgia: A Play* (1968). Stein also wrote librettos including *Four Saints in Three Acts: An Opera to be Sung* (1934), *A Wedding Bouquet: Ballet Music by Lord Berners* (1938), *Capitals, Capitals: Four Men and a Piano* (1947), *The Mother of Us All* (1947), a libretto about Susan B. Anthony, *Preciosilla: For Voice and Piano* (1948), and *In a Garden: An Opera in One Act* (1951). Other texts include *Useful Knowledge* (1927), *Lucy Church Amiably* (1930), *Before the Flowers of Friendship Faded Friendship Faded, Written on a Poem by Georges Hugnet* (1931), *Portraits and Prayers* (1934), *Is Dead* (1937), *Picasso* (1939), *The World Is Round* (1939), *Paris France* (1940), *What Are Masterpieces*

(1940), *Wars I Have Seen* (1945), *Brewsie and Willie* (1945), *Four in America* (1947), *Blood on the Dressing Room Floor* (1948), *I am Rose* (1970), and *Money* (1973). Stein's avant-garde experimental writings made her a difficult author to read. Her work had a great revival in the 1970s and 1980s when a number of her plays and operas were performed, and her work reissued by main publishing houses. She is both one of the great writers of the modernist period and one of the most important lesbian writers of the twentieth century.

Stoddard, Charles Warren (1843–1909). Gay US writer, born in Rochester, New York, as one of five children, to Sarah Freeman and Samuel Burr Stoddard. His father was a paper merchant, and although initially prosperous, the family's fortunes gradually declined and in 1854 they moved to San Francisco. Stoddard regarded California as his home, entering literary circles after he finished his education. In 1867 his *Poems* appeared. Shortly afterwards he converted to Catholicism. His later autobiography, *A Troubled Heart* (1885), became very popular. Stoddard taught at various Catholic education institutions including Notre Dame, from which he resigned after arguments about his attentions to his students, and the Catholic University of America. Stoddard was much influenced by Walt WHITMAN's 'Calamus' poems. He had his first sexual experiences in Hawaii and Tahiti. His best stories, *South Sea Idylls* (1874, 1892) and *The Island of Tranquil Delights* (1904), were written about these. The most homoerotic ones of these were republished in 1987 under the title *Cruising the South Seas*. Edward PRIME-STEVENSON remarked upon the significance of these stories in his *The Intersexes* (1908). Stoddard's personal sexual preferences were for youths. In 1895 he adopted Kenneth O'Connor, then fifteen years old, who lived with him in Washington until 1903 when Stoddard's health began to fail and their relationship deteriorated. Stoddard returned to California, settling in Monterey where he eventually died of a heart attack. Among his other works are *Mashallah!* (1880), *A Cruise under the Crescent* (1898), *Lepers of Molokai* (1885), and *For the Pleasure of His Company: An Affair of the Misty City* (1903). His collected *Poems* were posthumously published in 1917.

Strachey, Lytton (1880–1932). Born in London as one of thirteen children to Jane Maria Grant and Richard Strachey, among them Dorothy STRACHEY BUSSY, the gay English biographer and essayist Strachey was named after his grandfather, the first earl of Lytton and viceroy of India. Strachey had a relatively miserable childhood, and after a year at Liverpool University went to Trinity College, Cambridge, where he met the friends that would later be at the centre of the Bloomsbury Group, including Virginia WOOLF's husband Leonard Woolf. Not very happy or successful in his homosexual relationships he eventually lived in a *ménage à trois* with the painter Dora Carrington who adored him, and her husband Ralph Partridge. Strachey wrote extensively for periodicals such as the *Spectator*, the *Edinburgh Review*, and *Life and Letters*. His collection of essays *Landmarks in French Literature* (1912) was well received but he became famous with his collection of four portraits, *Eminent Victorians* (1918), in which he set out to debunk certain prevalent notions about the Victorian era. This was followed by *Queen Victoria* (1921) and *Elizabeth and Essex: A Tragic History* (1928), considered by some to be slightly salacious since it focused on Elizabeth's relationship with her father and its impact on her subsequent relationship with Essex. Strachey's essays were variously collected during his lifetime and afterwards. He rarely wrote about homosexuality.

Dora Carrington committed suicide after Strachey died from cancer in 1932.

Strachey Bussy, Dorothy (1865–1960). Born in London as one of the older of thirteen children to Jane Maria Grant and Richard Strachey, the sister of Lytton STRACHEY and wife of the painter Simon Bussy, Dorothy Strachey Bussy published *Olivia* (1949), a version of girls' boarding-school fiction, anonymously. The novella was reissued in 1981 as being authored by 'Olivia'. It purports to be an autobiographical account of a year the author spent at a school in France during which she falls in love with one of her school mistresses, Mlle Julie, who in turn has a relationship with another school mistress, Mlle Cara. The hothouse emotions that the confines of the school arouse in teachers and pupils alike culminate, predictably for that type of fiction during that period, in the expulsion of all the women from this same-sex paradise. The story is apparently based on Strachey Bussy's own experiences at Les Ruches, a girls' school in Fontainebleau that she attended. This school was run by Marie Souvestre for whom Strachey Bussy developed a strong attachment. Her one novel apart, Strachey Bussy also translated most of the work of the gay French writer André GIDE whom she met in 1918 and with whom she maintained a life-long friendship.

Strindberg, August (1849–1912). Swedish playwright and author, Johan August Strindberg was born in Stockholm as the son of a steamship agent who married his housekeeper after she had already three sons, a fact that informed the title of Strindberg's autobiography, *The Son of a Servant* (1886). Although his reputation rests on his plays including *Master Olaf* (written 1872–7, first performed in 1881), *The Father* (1887), *Miss Julie* (1888), and *Creditors* (1889), he is of interest to lesbian and gay readers because in a series of non-dramatic writings he engaged, albeit in many respects homophobically, with the issues both of male homosexuality and lesbianism. The latter was prompted by his divorce from his first wife (he was married three times), Siri von Essen, whose lesbian relationships made her in his eyes unfit to be a mother. Suffering from severe hallucinations and feelings of guilt and insecurity, Strindberg described Siri von Essen and her friends as lesbian in *A Madman's Defence* (1895). Before that, both in *Getting Married I* (1884) and in *Getting Married II* (1887) Strindberg attempted to account for homosexuality as something that occurred in the context of sexual segregation when men find themselves in a same-sex environment and as a consequence, expressed in 'The Last Word on the Question of Women' (1887), of the increasing equality between the sexes. Strindberg manifested neurotic responses to issues of religion, class, and sexuality. He accused many of his friends of harbouring homoerotic feelings for him, and it has been suggested that he himself was a repressed homosexual. In the mid-1890s Strindberg, then in Paris, underwent a terrible crisis, described in *Inferno* (published in French in 1897). In the aftermath of his crisis he produced symbolic dramas, fraught with tension and suffering, and the longing for redemption. These included *To Damascus* (1898–1901; a play in three parts), *The Dance of Death* (1901), *A Dream Play* (1902), and *The Ghost Sonata* (1907).

Sturgis, Howard Overing (1855–1920). Of US descent and with an independent income, this gay writer spent his life in England where he was friendly with other writers such as Henry JAMES and Edith Wharton. Sturgis himself embodied the notion of the sensitive, effeminate male that informs his writings. Of Sturgis's three novels, *Tim: A Story of Eton* (1891), *All that Was Possible* (1894), and *Belchamber* (1904), the first and the last in particular centre on a gay sensibility

and the difficulties of being regarded as an outsider and a sensitive male. *Tim: A Story of Eton* is concerned with the romantic attachment between two schoolboys. *Belchamber* explores the problems of a gay upper middle-class man in fulfilling the expectations of his class and status, including getting married. Apart from a few short stories Sturgis produced no further writing. He had a long-term relationship with William Haynes-Smith, to whom *Belchamber* is dedicated.

Swenson, May (1913–89). Born in Logan Utah, Swenson, who was of Swedish descent, became renowned for her innovative poetry that included many lesbian love poems. A number of these were posthumously collected under the title *The Love Poems of May Swenson* (1991). During her lifetime she published ten volumes of poetry including *Another Animal* (1954), *To Mix with Time* (1963), *Iconographs* (1970), *New and Selected Things Taking Place* (1978), and *In Other Words* (1987). In her poetry Swenson conjoined notions of nature and sexuality, 'naturalizing' lesbian sexuality through the imagery she used to convey what was being described. Swenson also translated the poems of the Swedish psychologist and poet Tomas Transtromer, which appeared as *Windows and Stones: Selected Poems of Tomas Transtromer* (1972). She died in Ocean View, Delaware.

Swinburne, Algernon Charles (1837–1909). The son of Jane and Charles Swinburne, descended from an old Northumbrian family, Swinburne was brought up on the Isle of Wight. He was a sickly child, with a nervous temperament. Educated for four years at Eton where he is said to have acquired a taste for flagellation, he then had a series of private tutors before going to Balliol College, Oxford, in 1856 where he became acquainted with Dante Gabriel Rossetti and the Pre-Raphaelite circle. Swinburne wrote in a variety of genres and showed great skill in his use of metrical verse. He was also influential in reviving interest in Elizabethan and Jacobean drama. His first publication, *The Queen-Mother; Rosamund* (1860) was followed by *Atalanta in Calydon* (1865), which brought him to critical attention for his use of the classic Greek dramatic form. It was followed by *Chastelard* (also 1865), one of three dramas about Mary Queen of Scots. In 1866 his first set of *Poems and Ballads* (1866) provoked a great scandal and was withdrawn from circulation by its publisher. Among the more notorious poems in this collection were 'Dolores', a poem about masochism, 'Hermaphroditus', which effectively centred on bisexuality, 'Anactoria', an address by SAPPHO to her lover, and 'Faustine'. The collection and Swinburne's later writings suggested that divergent sexuality might be viewed as a form of rebellion against prevailing morals. That, together with his open renunciation of Christianity – he did not want the Christian burial service read at his funeral, for example – made him a controversial figure. Through *A Song for Italy* (1867) and *Songs before Sunrise* (1871) Swinburne sought to express his support for the Italian struggle for independence. He also produced two further collections of *Poems and Ballads: Second Series* (1878) and *Poems and Ballads: Third Series* (1889). In the 1870s Swinburne became an alcoholic, with serious health problems. He was saved by his friend Theodore Watts (later Watts-Dunton), a solicitor who gave up his career for literature, producing several minor novels and being one of the main writers for the *Athenaeum*. With Watts-Dunton he moved to the Pines in Putney, South London in 1879 where Watts-Dunton weaned him off his alcohol addiction and generally watched over him until his death. Their intimate household remained uninterrupted by Watts-Dunton's marriage, in 1905, to a woman who was much younger than himself. Swinburne's other writings included two long novels,

A Year's Letters (serialized pseudonymously in 1877) and *Lesbia Brandon* (published posthumously in 1952). He also wrote long verse dramas such as *Marino Faleriero* (1885), other volumes of poetry such as *Tristram of Lyonesse and Other Poems* (1882), and translated the ballads of François Villon. His letters were edited posthumously in six volumes (1959–62), and many of his writings remain unpublished, possibly because they were considered unpublishable.

Symonds, John Addington (1840–93). Born in Bristol as the son of an eminent physician who strongly disapproved of 'male friendships', Symonds was educated at Harrow and at Balliol College, Oxford, eventually becoming a fellow at Magdalen College. At Harrow Symonds had contributed to the downfall of one of its headmasters, Dr Vaughan, when he told a family friend about the sexual relationships the headmaster had with several boys. It took Symonds many years to come to terms with his own homosexuality. He married in 1864 and had children. Together with his wife and children he resided for much of his adult life in Italy and Switzerland in order to combat his tuberculosis. However, from 1881 until Symonds's death, the gondolier Angelo Fusato was his lover. Symonds advocated homosexuality, which he viewed as a congenital condition, and campaigned for legal reform discreetly through his privately circulated pamphlets entitled 'A Problem in Greek Ethics' (1883) and 'A Problem in Modern Ethics' (1891). These were partly reproduced in Havelock ELLIS's *Sexual Inversion* (1897). Symonds also produced many volumes of literary and cultural criticism, chief among them his seven-volume *Renaissance in Italy* (1875–86). He translated the *Autobiography* of Benvenuto Cellini (1888) and the *Life of Michelangelo Buonarroti* (1892). His many works on literary figures such as Ben Jonson, Shelley, and Walt WHITMAN, as well as his collections of poetry such as *Many Moods* (1878) and *New and Old* (1880), and his translations of Greek and Italian poetry, did not, in the end, result in the same success as his contemporaries Walter PATER and Algernon SWINBURNE enjoyed.

T

Takahashi, Mutsuo (1937–). Gay Japanese poet and dramatist, educated at Fukuoka University of Education who has received much acclaim for his work and won a variety of prestigious literary prizes including the Reketei Prize, the Yomiuri Prize, and the Tamaki Jun Prize. His poetry collections that explicitly celebrate homosexuality include *You Dirty Ones, Do Dirtier Things* (1966), *Poems of a Penisist* (1975), *The Structure of the Kingdom* (1982), *A Bunch of Keys* (1984), *Practice/Drinking Eating* (1988), *The Garden of Rabbits* (1988), and *Sleeping Smiling Falling* (1992). His representation of homosexuals presents them as outsiders, particularly from the family structures and daily rituals that govern Japanese life. Takahashi won the Yamamoto Kenkichi Prize for his play *Princess Medea* in 1987.

Tennyson, Alfred Lord (1809–92). English poet and playwright, born in Somersby, Lincolnshire, the third surviving son of Elizabeth Fytche Tennyson and a rector, George Clayton Tennyson. Tennyson's father was a violent alcoholic, and all three brothers suffered under his regime, experiencing periods of melancholia and breakdown in later life. Tennyson was educated first by his father and then at Trinity College, Cambridge, where he met Arthur Henry Hallam who became a close friend and to whom Tennyson's elegy *In Memoriam* (1850) is dedicated. In 1832 he and Hallam travelled on the Continent; a year later Hallam died prematurely abroad. This death initiated a period of intense grief for Tennyson who began writing *In Memoriam* in the year of Hallam's death but did not complete and publish it until 1850. It is in part due to this long poem that Tennyson is of interest to gay readers. In several of his other works, as well as in this poem, Tennyson celebrates close male friendship that is passionate and intense though not necessarily sexual. Significantly, Hallam's father burnt all letters between Hallam and Tennyson after his son's death and Tennyson's eldest son and executor, named after Tennyson's great friend Hallam, destroyed many more documents that could have shed light on their relationship. Tennyson wrote many other collections of poems. In some of these poems a homoerotic or homosocial content are evident. They include 'Morte d'Arthur' (1842), 'Sir Galahad' (1842), *The Princess* (1847), and 'The Holy Grail' (1869). His collections were published as *Poems by Two Brothers* (1827), which contains his early writings, *Poems* (1832), and *Poems* (1842). From 1845 Tennyson received £200 annually as a civil list pension. When *In Memoriam* appeared in 1850, Tennyson became a favourite with Queen Victoria whose grief for her husband Albert found a mirror in Tennyson's mourning for his loss of Hallam. She made him Poet Laureate. In the same year Tennyson married Emily Sellwood to whom he had been engaged for many years. Established as a poet and entering a period of stability, Tennyson published *Maud and other Poems* (1855), *Idylls of the Kings* (1859), *Enoch Arden etc* (1864), *The Holy Grail and Other Poems* (1869), *Gareth and Lynette etc* (1872), *Ballads and Other Poems* (1880), *Tiresias, and Other Poems* (1885), and *The Foresters* (1892). His plays include *Queen Mary* (1875), *Harold* (1876), *The Falcon*, *The Cup*, and *Becket*, all published in 1884. He died of influenza and was buried in Westminster Abbey.

Thoreau, Henry David (1817–62). US writer, born in Concord, Massachusetts, where he attended Concord Academy and then Harvard where he graduated in 1837. During his lifetime only two books he wrote were published, and he earned no money from his literary work, supporting himself instead through a variety of jobs such as surveying, school-teaching, and as a maker of lead pencils, which had also been his father's occupation. The books that were published during his lifetime were *A Week on the Concord and Merrimack River* (1849), which centres on a canoe trip Thoreau undertook with his brother John in 1839, and *Walden, or Life in the Woods* (1854), an account of a period of two years which Thoreau spent living self-sufficiently at Walden Pond where he built himself a hut. These works did not achieve much acclaim during his lifetime but were recognized as literary masterpieces subsequently. Thoreau's essays also became very influential. The most famous of these is perhaps ' Civil Disobedience', originally published as 'Resistance to Civil Government'. This essay was concerned with the right of the individual to refuse to pay poll tax if his or her conscience so dictated. Thoreau and Bronson Alcott had refused to pay the poll tax in 1843

in protest against the Mexican War and slavery. Thoreau was imprisoned for a day on account of this. Thoreau's sexuality has remained a matter of speculation but the absence of reference to women in his work and the discussion of love between men in some of his essays such as 'Chastity and Sexuality' and 'Friendship' have gained him a place in the history of gay writing. His *Journal* (fourteen volumes) and his collected *Writings* (twenty volumes) were published in 1906.

Toklas, Alice B. (1877–1967). US writer and, famously, the life-long companion of the lesbian writer Gertrude STEIN whose nickname between them was 'Baby'. Toklas grew up in a well-to-do middle-class Jewish family in San Francisco. When her mother died in 1897 she looked after the family home for a while. In 1907 Toklas visited Paris, meeting Gertrude Stein the day after she arrived. They considered themselves married, with Toklas taking on the role of wife, typing Stein's manuscripts and running their household while Stein held her literary salons and worked on her writings. Toklas was always enormously supportive of Stein's work, convinced as Stein was that she was a genius and deserved more critical acclaim than she received. Although as Jews they were under threat from the Nazis Toklas and Stein decided to stay in France throughout the Second World War. Following Stein's death from cancer in 1946 Toklas went through a battle with Stein's relatives over her inheritance, and at one point faced sustained poverty. She published *The Alice B. Toklas Cookbook* in 1954 in order to make some money. To write it she asked various friends to send her recipes. The volume is a mixture of anecdotes and recipes. She also published a further cookbook, *Aromas and Flavours of Past and Present* (1958). Toklas also published a volume of autobiography, *What Is Remembered: An Autobiography* (1963) and her letters were edited posthumously by Edward Burns in 1973 under the title, *Staying on Alone: Letters of Alice B. Toklas*. Toklas promoted Stein's work tirelessly after Stein's death, and began writing articles on art and fashion for various US magazines. She converted to Catholicism late in her life. After her death she was buried alongside Gertrude Stein at the Père Lachaise cemetery in Paris.

Tondelli, Pier Vittorio (1955–1991). Gay Italian writer from a middle-class background who studied at the University of Bologna under Umberto Eco, and between 1980 and 1990 published four novels, the last three of which engage directly and centrally with homosexuality. *Altri Libertini* appeared in 1980. It was followed by *Pao Pao* (1982), *Rimini* (1985), and *Camere separate* (1989). In this last novel Tondelli explores among other things the impact of AIDS on a gay couple. At the time he himself already suffered from the AIDS-related illnesses that would kill him two years later. Although he had been engaged in many public debates and was well established on the literary scene he chose to remain silent about his illness. His essays were published under the title *Un weekend post-moderno* (1990).

Townsend Warner, Sylvia (1893–1978). Lesbian English poet and novelist, born in Harrow, the daughter of the Head of the Modern Side, a housemaster, at Harrow School. Townsend Warner was interested in early music and worked as one of the editors of *Tudor Church Music* (ten volumes; 1922–9). Her first volume of poetry, *The Espalier*, was published in 1925. It was followed by *Opus 7* (1931) and later by *Whether a Dove or a Seagull* (1933), written in collaboration with her lover Valentine ACKLAND, and her *Collected Poems*, which were published posthumously in 1982. Townsend Warner is best known, however, for her novels and short stories. *Lolly Willowes* (1926) features a spinster who realizes her vocation

as a witch. That novel, and the following two, *Mr Fortune's Maggot* (1927) and *The True Heart* (1929), established Townsend Warner's reputation as a novelist. In 1929 Townsend Warner visited New York as a guest critic for the *Herald Tribune*. She also contributed short stories to the *New Yorker* for several decades thus ensuring her reputation both in the USA and in the UK. Townsend Warner met Valentine Ackland in Dorset through Theodore Powys. Both women were committed to the anti-fascist struggle. They were to spend their lives together. In the 1930s Townsend Warner was a member of the Executive Committee of the Association of Writers for Intellectual Liberty, and she also acted as a representative for the Congress of Madrid in 1937. Altogether Townsend Warner published seven novels, four volumes of poetry, a volume of essays, a biography of T.H. White (1967), and eight volumes of short stories. In her work she combined a concern with feminist issues with a sense of alternative realities and worlds. Her novels were often set in other countries and other times. Thus *Summer Will Show* (1936) was set in the revolutionary Paris of 1848, *After the Death of Don Juan* (1938) in eighteenth-century Spain, and *The Corner that Held Them* (1948) in a fourteenth-century abbey. Townsend Warner's other texts include *A Moral Ending* (1931), *The Salutation* (1932), *More Joy in Heaven* (1939), *The Museum of Cheats* (1947), *Jane Austen* (1951), *The Flint Anchor* (1954), *Winter in the Air* (1955), *The Innocent and the Guilty* (1971), *Kingdoms of Elfin* (1977), and *Scenes of Childhood* (1981). Her *Letters* were published in 1982. Townsend Warner and Ackland lived most of their lives either in Dorset or in Norfolk. They died within a year of each other.

Trefusis, Violet (1894–1972). English novelist, born in London as the first child to Allice Frederica and George Keppel, the third son of the 7th Earl of Albemarle.

Trefusis's mother became the mistress of the Prince of Wales, later to become King Edward VII. Trefusis is known mainly for her stormy relationship with the writer Vita SACKVILLE-WEST, which the latter described in a brief autobiographical account published by her son Nigel Nicolson in *Portrait of a Marriage* (1973). Trefusis and Sackville-West had met at school when they were both children. Their later affair when both were already married caused much unhappiness. They eloped together in 1919, shortly after Trefusis's marriage to Denys Trefusis. The relationship was finished by 1921. Trefusis returned to her husband, who died of tuberculosis in 1929, and lived in Paris where she wrote novels including *Sortie de Secours* (1929), *Echo* (1931), *Hunt the Slipper* (1937), *Pirates at Play* (1950), and *Broderie Anglaise* (published posthumously in 1985). Her autobiography, *Don't Look Around*, appeared in 1952. She wrote two other novels, *Tandem* and *Les Causes perdues*, and a further volume of autobiography, *Prelude to Misadventure*. Trefusis returned to England during the Second World War but later lived in France and Italy, moving in the upper-class expatriate communities there, and dying in Florence in 1972. She did not remarry. She was awarded the Légion d'honneur and the Italian Order of Merit. *Violet to Vita: The Letters of Violet Trefusis to Vita Sackville-West* were published in 1989. Sackville-West's letters to Trefusis do not survive since Trefusis's husband destroyed them at the height of their affair.

Tremblay, Michel (1942–). Canadian writer, born in Montreal, who originally trained as a typesetter, thus following in his father's footsteps, but gave this work up when he achieved literary acclaim. He has written plays, novels, and autobiographical texts that centre on a range of issues including feminist concerns and, especially in his autobiographical texts, histories of becoming and being gay.

Among his plays are *Les Belles Soeurs* (1972; *The Beautiful Sisters*), *A toi pour toujours ta Maria* (1972; *Yours Always, Maria*), and *Albertine en cinq temps* (1984; *Albertine in Five Stages*). Chronicling the life of the characters in his plays prior to their staged lives, Tremblay produced five novels, the *Chroniques du Plateau Mont-Royal* (*Chronicles of the Plateau Mont-Royal*). Tremblay's most recent writings are autobiographical and address his gay history. They include *Les Douze Coups de théâtre* (1992), *Un Ange cornu avec des ailes de tôle* (1994), and *La Nuit de princes charmants* (1995). His recent work, *Un Objet de beauté* (1997), deals with schizophrenia.

Troubridge, Lady Una (1887–1963). English writer, best known for her long-term relationship with the famous English lesbian novelist Radclyffe HALL. Troubridge was married to the widowed Admiral Troubridge in 1907 with whom she had a daughter, Andrea, in 1910. Her life remained that of a typical woman of her class until 1915 when she met and fell passionately in love with Radclyffe Hall, then in a relationship with Mabel Veronica Batten, known as Ladye. Her death in 1916 paved the way for Radclyffe's and Una's relationship. Troubridge and Hall moved between France and England where they had circles of lesbian friends including the lesbian painter Romaine Brooks who produced a famous portrait of Una. In the early 1930s Una began to experience a series of health problems and a nurse, the Russian expatriate Evguenia Souline, was engaged to look after her. Hall fell in love with Evguenia, and Una was to share Hall with her until Hall's death in 1943. Una herself was the object of several other women's affections, including the writer Naomi JACOB, but she refused any other liaison. Following Hall's death Una moved first to Florence and then to Rome. In 1961, two years before her own death, Una's biography of Radclyffe Hall, *The Life and Death of*

Radclyffe Hall, appeared, a biography which makes interesting reading for its omissions as much as its inclusions. It is best read alongside other biographies of Radclyffe Hall since that process gives a greater insight into the difference between how Una wanted to see her life with Hall, and how others view it. Troubridge was buried in the Verano Cemetery in Rome, contrary to her wishes to be buried next to Hall at Highgate Cemetery in London.

Tsvetáeva, Marina Ivanovna (1892–1941). Russian poet, prose writer, and dramatist, born in Moscow to a mother who was a pianist and a father who was an art professor. Tsvetáeva started to write poetry early on in her life. Her first volume of poems, *Evening Album*, appeared in 1910. It was followed by *The Magic Lantern* in 1912. Her poetry, which at that time celebrated childhood, was regarded as autobiographical. By 1914 Tsvetáeva had married Sergei Efron with whom she had a daughter. In that year she also met the poet Sofia PARNÓK with whom she began a passionate affair. This inspired a verse cycle entitled 'Girlfriend' (1914–15), published only in the 1970s and a classic of lesbian love poetry. Tsvetáeva was deeply traumatized by the break-up of her relationship with Parnók in 1916. She returned to her husband and became immediately pregnant with her second daughter who was born in 1917. Tsvetáeva spent the Civil War years in Moscow alone with her two daughters. Her husband was an officer in the White Army. Desperate for money and food, she was forced to put her second daughter in an orphanage where the little girl died of starvation. Tsvetáeva herself worked with the Third Stage, an avant-garde theatre group in Moscow, between 1918 and 1920. This led to a passionate attachment to the actress Sonya Holliday, recorded in the prose work 'The Tale of Sonechka', and a cycle of poems, 'Poems to Sonechka'. She also published *The Tsar's Maiden* (1920), and a response to the Civil War, *The Demesne of the Swans* (1921). Immediately after her most famous collections of poems, *Mileposts I*, was published in Russia in 1922, Tsvetáeva left Russia to be reunited with her husband in Prague. In 1923 her collection *Craft* appeared in Berlin. She had a son in 1925 and the family moved to Paris where they lived for the next fourteen years. Initially part of the Russian *émigré* circles in Paris, Tsvetáeva became increasingly isolated there, partly because of her husband's pro-Soviet activities. Her last work to be published during her lifetime, *After Russia*, came out in 1928. However, her work was not well received in Paris, and when she felt rejected by Natalie Clifford BARNEY's circle in the rue Jacob she wrote her 'Lettre à l'Amazone' (1932, revised 1934), addressed both to Barney and to Parnók, the two lesbians who had rejected her. 'Lettre' deals with a lesbian love affair between a young girl and an older woman. At the end of the 1930s Tsvetáeva finally returned to Russia. Her remaining daughter was arrested in August 1939 and sent to a concentration camp. Then her husband was arrested and executed as an enemy of the people. She herself was sent to live near Golitsyno. She became involved in a relationship with Tatyana Kvanina, the wife of a poet. When the German offensive against Russia began, Tsvetáeva and her teenage son were evacuated to Yelabuga in the Tartar Autonomous Republic. Tsvetáeva could not find work or support there. Completely desperate, she committed suicide by hanging herself in her house. She was buried in an unmarked grave in Yelabuga Cemetery.

U

Ulrichs, Karl Heinrich (1825–95). German sexologist, born in Aurich, Hanover, whose father died when he was ten years old, and whose mother brought him up in the Lutheran household of her own parents. Ulrichs studied law in Göttingen and Berlin, but had to resign his subsequent position in the civil service when his homosexual activity was noted. He then worked as a reporter for the *Allgemeine Zeitung* and lived off the small inheritance he received upon his mother's death in 1856. Under the pseudonym Numa Numantius Ulrichs published five booklets, collectively entitled *Forschungen über das Rätsel der mannmännlichen Liebe* (*Researches on the Love between Men*) between 1864 and 1865. He published a further seven booklets on the topic under his own name. In all of these he argued for the biological origin of homosexuality and the notion that the male homosexual had a woman's soul imprisoned in a man's body. Ulrichs used the term 'Urning' to describe homosexual men. He campaigned unsuccessfully for the repeal of anti-homosexual legislation. In 1880 he left Germany for Italy where he remained until the end of his life, promoting Latin, in which he wrote, as an international language.

V

Van Vechten, Carl (1880–1964). Gay US cultural critic and writer, born in Cedar Rapids, Iowa, where his father cofounded a school for African American children. Van Vechten moved to Chicago where he attended the University of Chicago between 1899–1903. Here he developed his interest in black music and ragtime about which he wrote for *Vanity Fair* and the *New York Times*. He supported many black artists and musicians, writing eight books of music and art criticism once he had moved to New York in 1906. From the early 1920s Van Vechten began to write novels, celebrating the gay, Bohemian culture of New York City. His seven novels are *Peter Whiffle: His Life and Works* (1922), *The Blind Bow-boy* (1923), *The Tattooed Countess* (1924), *Firecrackers* (1925), *Nigger Heaven* (1926), *Spider Boy* (1928), and *Parties* (1930). Van Vechten is in part remembered for being an ardent admirer of Gertrude STEIN whose work he championed.

Verlaine, Paul (1844–96). Born into a well-to-do family in Metz, France, as the only son of a military father and a mother, Stéphanie, who supported her son throughout his life despite his intermittent violence towards her, Verlaine gained notoriety through his relationship with the younger poet Arthur RIMBAUD whose work he championed. Verlaine had a calm childhood. In 1862 he took his baccalaureate, then embarked on studying Law, a career he abandoned to become, for a time, a civil servant in Paris, while writing poetry. His first collection of poetry, *Poèmes saturniens* (1866), showed the influence of Charles BAUDELAIRE on his work. In 1868 he published *Les Amies*, an erotic work focusing on lesbian sexuality. He published this collection under a pseudonym in Brussels to avoid French censorship. In 1869 *Fêtes galantes* appeared, a collection of pastoral poems. In 1870, while still enamoured of a friend, Lucien Viotti, Verlaine married Mathilde Mauté, with whom he had a son, Georges. However, a year later Verlaine began his stormy relationship with Rimbaud who had written to him admiringly from the French provinces and turned up in Paris. Their attraction on meeting was instant and Verlaine was torn between his relationship with his wife, whom he treated rather badly, and his affair with Rimbaud, which was also not without its difficulties. *La Bonne Chanson* (1870) celebrates Verlaine's wife. His *Romances sans paroles* (1874), in contrast, focused on the sensual experiences he had had with Rimbaud, with whom he had something of a sadomasochistic relationship. Verlaine and Rimbaud travelled in England and Belgium where their relationship came to a violent end when, in 1873, Verlaine shot Rimbaud in his wrist during an argument and was sentenced to two years' imprisonment for this assault. During his imprisonment he had a religious conversion. He composed *Cellulairement* (1875, published in its complete form only in 1992). After his release Verlaine tried to effect a reconciliation, first with Rimbaud, and then with his wife Mathilde. Both attempts failed, and Verlaine had an itinerant existence for a time, teaching in France and in England. In 1878 he met Lucien Létinois with whom he fell in love. They settled on Létinois's parents' farm in the Ardennes, and in 1881 Verlaine published his first collection of religious poems, *Sagesse*. In 1882 Verlaine returned to Paris; a year later Létinois died. Verlaine returned with his mother, now providing financial and emotional support for him, to the country, and Verlaine published a collection of both old and new poetry, *Jadis et naguère* (1884), which was not nearly as successful as his portraits of poets, *Poètes maudits*, of the same year. He wrote a second series of *Poètes maudits* in 1888 in which he included a self-portrait. Arrested and imprisoned for one month for violence against his mother, Verlaine returned to Paris after his release, where he lived in reduced circumstances. He was eventually reconciled with his mother and she joined him in Paris. He published more volumes of religious verse, including *Amour* (1888) and *Bonheur* (1891), but also a more sensually inspired collection, *Parallèlement* (1889). In 1888 he fell in love with the younger painter Frédéric-Auguste Cazals with whom he had a relationship. The last ten years of Verlaine's life were plagued by rheumatism affecting one of his legs, and periods in and out of hospital. He produced the autobiographical works *Mes hôspitaux* (1891) and *Mes prisons* (1893), detailing his experiences of institutional confinement. In *Confessions* (1895) he revisited his early life and career. In 1895 he also published Rimbaud's *Poésies complètes*. His own *Hombrès* (published posthumously in 1904)

contained fifteen poems celebrating the male body and homosexuality. Verlaine's work as a poet has to some extent been overshadowed by the mythologizing of his relationship with Rimbaud. This relationship has been the object of several representations, including Bertolt BRECHT's play *Baal* and Christopher HAMPTON's play *Total Eclipse*.

Viau, Théophile de (1590–1626). Born in Clairac into a Huguenot family that had only recently been promoted to the status of lesser nobility, de Viau, a French poet and thinker variously derided in his day as a libertine, studied medicine in Bordeaux and in the Netherlands. For a time he also joined a troupe of actors, writing plays for them. He was banished from Paris in 1619 for his libertine morals and scandalous poetry. He went to his family estate at Boussères where he wrote free verse and translated Plato. He was brought back to Paris at the request of the King's favourite, the Duke de Luynes and for a time was a major court poet. The first volume of his *Works*, which established him as a significant poet of his time, appeared in 1621. In 1622 de Viau converted to Catholicism for political reasons but, accused by one Father Garasse of libertinism and atheism, de Viau was convicted of the crime of *lèsemajesté divine* in 1623, and burnt as an effigy at the stake. He was arrested in September 1623 and imprisoned in the Conciergerie where he remained for nearly two years. Cleared of all charges, he and one of his adversaries, Father Voisin, were banished from France. De Viau went into hiding and died not long thereafter at the home of his protector the Duke of Montmorency, in Paris. De Viau is generally acknowledged as having been a man who loved men but little is known about his personal relationships other than through inferences drawn from comments by contemporaries and through his poetry. De Viau advocated following 'Nature's law' and enjoying oneself as

Vidal, Gore (1925–). Gay US writer whose work has sought to challenge prevailing stereotypes of homosexuals, and who has lived, since the 1960s, mostly in Italy with his companion Howard Austen. Vidal's parents divorced when he was young but he was much influenced by his grandfather, a blind US senator. Vidal served in the armed forces during the Second World War and afterwards worked briefly as an editor for E.P. Dutton. Later he was a Democratic Party candidate for Congress in 1960, and engaged in various forms of political activism in the 1960s and 1970s. Vidal has written in a variety of genres including mystery novels such as *Death in the Fifth Position* (1952), *Death before Bedtime* (1953), and *Death Likes It Hot* (1954) under the pseudonym Edgar Box. His first novel *Williwaw* appeared in 1946. It was followed by *In a Yellow Wood* (1947) and *The City and the Pillar* (1949, revised and reissued in 1965, and in 1995). The latter text generated much critical attention due to its supposedly scandalous portrayal of homosexuality. It was panned in the *New York Times* but sold well. The novel ends tragically with a death but constitutes an important coming-out narrative within mainstream literature. Vidal published many subsequent novels. Of these *Myra Breckinridge* (1968) proved to be another challenging text as it dealt with a central character who was having a clinical sex change. Vidal produced a follow-up text in *Myron* (1974). Other novels include *The Season of Comfort* (1949), *A Search for the King: A Twelfth-Century Legend* (1950), *Dark Green, Bright Red* (1950), *The Judgment of Paris* (1953), *Messiah* (1954), *Julian* (1964), *Washington D.C.* (1967), *Two Sisters: A Novel in the Form of a Memoir* (1970), *Burr* (1973), *1876* (1976), *Kalki* (1978), *Creation* (1981), *Duluth* (1983), *Lincoln* (1984), *Empire* (1987), *Holly-*

wood: A Novel of America in the 1920s (1990), and *Live from Golgotha* (1992). His collection of short stories, *A Thirsty Evil: Seven Short Stories* (1956), contains some stories with a homosexual theme. Vidal has also published many plays including *The Best Man: A Play of Politics* (1960), *Weekend* (1968), and *An Evening with Richard Nixon* (1972). His screenplays, essays, and television scripts have made him one of the most prolific writers of his generation. He has won a number of prizes for his writing including the Mystery Writers of America Edgar Allan Poe Award for Television Drama (1955), the Cannes Critics Prize for his play *The Best Man* (1964), and the National Book Critics' Circle Award for *The Second American Revolution, and Other Essays* (1982).

Virgil (70–19 BC). Publicus Vergilius Maro, born on a farm near Mantua and suffering from poor health during his life, was nicknamed 'the Virgin' as a consequence of being considered shy and awkward. He is one of the most important Roman poets whose work includes some exultation of male friendship and love. His early patron Asinius Pollio encouraged him to write about the rural life. According to the biography of Virgil that is part of the *Commentary* of Donatus, Virgil fell in love with a slave boy called Alexander owned by Pollio. In *Eclogues*, Virgil's first significant set of poems, rural life is presented in idealized form. In the second eclogue Virgil portrays the love of Corydon for Alexis, for whom the slave Alexander was apparently the model. Virgil's *Georgics* are a panegyric on Italy and the Italian countryside. Patronized by Augustus, Virgil was then commissioned to write an epic intended to rival the Greek *Iliad*. Virgil produced the *Aeneid*, which incorporates the story of Nisus and Euryalus, two warriors, between whom there is a bond of pious male love and who die a heroic death. Virgil's poetry was highly influential in the Middle Ages when Dante, for example, chose him as the guide figure through Hell and Purgatory.

Vivien, Renée (1877–1909). Lesbian Anglo-French poet and novelist, born Pauline Tarn in Paddington, London, into a well-to-do merchant family. She and her sister Antoinette went to school in Paris until the death of their father John when Vivien was nine years old. Their mother decided to return to England, and even attempted to have Vivien declared insane so that the latter's inheritance should come directly to her. However, Vivien was made a ward of court when the courts sided with her. When she reached her majority in 1898 she returned to Paris. There she changed her name, began writing in French, and lived for the most part of her life in France. Vivien wrote openly about lesbian relationships in her work. Her poetry, published in two volumes as *Poèmes* in 1923, was influenced by poets such as Charles BAUDELAIRE and Paul VERLAINE. Vivien was ambivalent about her lesbianism, exalting both the female form and simultaneously regarding lesbian relationships as perverse and impure. In 1904 she published her only novel, *Une Femme m'apparut* (*A Woman Appeared to Me*), which fictionalizes her relationship with Natalie BARNEY and provides a fascinating account of life in the lesbian circles of turn-of-the-century Paris. She also produced plays based on the life of SAPPHO, and wrote a life of Anne Boleyn. She appears to have been a rather unhappy and lonely woman, prone to depression. She died of alcoholism and starvation. During her ten years or so as an adult in Paris she wrote many volumes of poetry, two novels, three volumes of short stories, and prose poems. They included *Etudes et préludes* (1901; *Etudes*

and Preludes) and *Cendres et poussières* (1902; *Dust and Ashes*), *Evocations* (1903), *A l'heure des mains jointes* (1906; *At the Hour of the Joined Hands*), *Sillages* (1908; *Wakes*), and *Flambeaux éteints* (1908; *Extinguished Torches*). Vivien also collaborated with the Baroness Hélène de Zuylen de Nyevelt, whom she met in 1901 and with whom she had a relationship, under the pseudonym Pauline Riversdale, on two novels and two volumes of poetry. Despite her prolific output, Vivien's œuvre has not stood up well to the ravages of time. At present it is her novelistic account of her relationship with Natalie Barney, *A Woman Appeared to Me*, for which she is best known.

Vogel, Bruno (1898–1983). Gay German writer who, shortly after the First World War, co-founded a local branch of the Scientific-Humanitarian Committee, which worked for homosexual emancipation in his hometown of Leipzig. Through Magnus HIRSCHFELD, the national founder of this Committee, Vogel was given a job at the Berlin headquarters of the Committee and elected to its board of directors in 1929. In the same year he published the novel *Alf*, a narrative about the love between two schoolboys, Alf and Felix. Vogel had already established himself as a writer with his anti-war *Es lebe der Krieg!* (1924; *Long Live the War!*), which caused him to be tried for blasphemy. His collection of stories, *Ein Gulasch und andere Skizzen* (1928; *Gulash and Other Sketches*), portrays gay men as sympathetic to the cause of others who suffer. As a pacifist, socialist, and homosexual Vogel understood the dangers of the Nazi regime from early on and went into exile in 1931, first living in various European cities and then emigrating to South Africa, which he left in 1952 to move to London where he lived for the rest of his life.

W

Walker, Alice (1944–). Born Alice Mal-senior Walker in Eaton, Georgia, to an African American sharecropper family, Walker attended Spelman College be-tween 1961 and 1963. While at Sarah Lawrence College, from where she grad-uated in 1965, she travelled to Africa and began to write poetry. In 1967 she mar-ried Melvyn R. Leventhal, a civil rights lawyer – with whom she had a daughter, Rebecca, in 1969 – and whom she di-vorced in 1976. She has had relationships with women as well as men. Today Walker is renowned for her feminist work as a poet, short-story writer, novelist, and essayist. She herself has used the term 'womanist' (see *In Search of Our Mothers' Gardens*, 1983), as opposed to feminist, to describe her work and posi-tion. Her writings focus on the racist and sexist experiences that dominate African and African American women's lives. Among her many volumes of writing her best-known work is perhaps the novel *The Color Purple* (1982), which was made into a commercially very successful Hollywood movie by the film director Stephen Spielberg in 1985. In *The Color Purple* the central character, Celie, a black girl variously sexually and physically abu-sed by her father and other males, is led towards liberation and self-transformation through her affair with Shug, a black, bisexual singer whose compelling sensual-ity and indomitable personality enable her

to resist the oppressive treatment from men that figures like Celie are made to suffer. This novel, as well as other work by Walker, was controversial not only for its representation of lesbianism as sexu-ally and otherwise liberating but also for its representation of black men as oppres-sive and abusive. Walker's earlier novels, *The Third Life of Grange Copeland* (1970) and *Meridian* (1976), had dealt with issues of African American politics and the Civil Rights Movement more generally while her later work, including *The Temple of My Familiar* (1989) and *Possessing the Secret of Joy* (1992), have explored her African heritage, and issues of spirituality, as well as sexual and racial identity in that context. Walker has had many fellowships and won a variety of prizes for her work, including the Amer-ican Book Award and the Pulitzer Prize for *The Color Purple*. Her other works include *Once: Poems* (1968), *In Love and Trouble: Stories of Black Women* (1973), *Revolutionary Petunias* (1979), *Good Night Willie Lee, I'll See You in the Morning* (1979), *You Can't Keep a Good Woman Down: Stories* (1981), *In Search of Our Mothers' Gardens: Womanist Prose* (1983), *Horses Make the Land-scape More Beautiful* (1985), *Living By the Word: Selected Writings 1973–1987* (1988), *Her Blue Body Everything We Know* (1992), *Warrior Marks: Female Genital Mutilation* (1993, with P. Parmar), the autobiography *The Same River Twice: Honoring the Difficult* (1996), *Anything We Love Can Be Saved: A Writer's Activism* (1997), *By the Light of My Father's Smile: A Story of Requited Love* (1998), *The Complete Stories* (2000), and *The Way Forward is with a Broken Heart* (2001).

Warren, Patricia Nell (1936–). US writer whose work has centred extensively on gay US culture, celebrating homosexual relationships between men, and placing these in the context of popular US writing. Warren was an editor of *Reader's Digest* for twenty years before becoming a freelance writer. She published five novels under the pseudonym Patricia Kilina including *The Last Centennial* in 1971. She became established as a writer of gay novels with *The Front Runner* (1974), which focuses on Billy Sive, an athlete who is assassinated. In this novel the gay culture depicted is one of the male-dominated sports. This novel was followed by *The Fancy Dancer* (1976), featuring the growing relationship between two unlikely men, a biker and a priest, and *The Beauty Queen* (1978), a fictionalization of the figure of Anita Bryant, a singer who indulged in anti-gay campaigns during the 1970s and who is here recast as Jeannie Laird Colter. *Harlan's Race* (1994) is a sequel to *The Front Runner*, now set in the age of HIV/AIDS. Warren's *Billy Boy* was published in 1998. She received the Walt Whitman Award for Excellence in Gay Literature in 1978.

Waugh, Evelyn (1903–66). English novelist and satirist of upper-class society, born in Hampstead, London, the son of Arthur Waugh who became managing director of the publishing firm Chapman & Hall. Waugh was brought up in London and educated at Lancing and at Hertford College, Oxford. During his time at Oxford he appears to have had homosexual affairs but he subsequently married and

had six children. Several of his novels feature homosexual characters, sometimes in a sympathetic and sometimes in a homophobic manner. The best known of these is probably *Brideshead Revisited* (1945), which details the affair of Sebastian Flyte and Charles Ryder. In *Put out More Flags* (1942) the character Ambrose Silk is constructed as an intellectual and aesthetic queen. Waugh's other writings include *Decline and Fall* (1928), *Vile Bodies* (1930), *A Handful of Dust* (1934), *Scoop* (1938), *The Loved One* (1948), *The Ordeal of Gilbert Pinfold* (1957), which is an autobiographical account of an author's crisis, and *Sword of Honour* (1965), a trilogy about male military life during the Second World War consisting of *Men at Arms* (1952), *Officers and Gentlemen* (1955), and *Unconditional Surrender* (1961). In 1964 his autobiography *A Little Learning* was published. He also wrote journalistic accounts of his travels including *Remote People* (1931) about a journey through Africa, *Ninety-two Days* (1934), and *Waugh in Abyssinia* (1936). His *Diaries* appeared posthumously in 1976, his *Letters* in 1980.

Weirauch, Anna Elisabet (1887–1970). Born in Galatz, Romania, Weirauch, her sister, and her mother moved to Germany when her father died in 1891, moving to Berlin where Weirauch studied acting and, between 1906 and 1914, was a member of Max Reinhardt's ensemble of the Deutsches Theater. Weirauch wrote prolifically, including plays, novellas and novels. Of these a three-volume series, entitled *The Scorpion* (1919, 1921, 1931), is of abiding interest to lesbian and gay readers because it presents a novel of the development of the central lesbian character, Mette, who moves from a sense of difference in childhood, to an exploration of the lesbian and gay world of Berlin, to an acceptance of herself as a lesbian. The author avoids the usually negative explanations for the character's lesbian identity common in the period in favour of Mette seeing her identity as something natural. It is partly for this reason that this three-volume series proved highly successful, going into multiple editions and translations into other languages.

Welch, Denton (1915–48). Born in Shanghai into a business family, Maurice Denton Welch was educated in England. He went to art school but was paralysed and crippled at age twenty when he was run over by a car while he was riding a bicycle. His injuries led to his premature death. He spent the rest of his life writing, producing poems, stories, some paintings, and, most importantly, three autobiographical novels that established him as a gay writer. In *Maiden Voyage* (1943), *In Youth is Pleasure* (1945), and the posthumously published, incomplete *A Voice through a Cloud* (1950), Welch focused on his experiences and his physical suffering. Locked into his own world through his injuries, he created a style of writing which was that of a queen.

White, Antonia (1889–1930). English novelist, and translator of French writers such as COLETTE and Eveline MAHYÈRE. Her first novel, *Frost in May* (1933), is considered, together with texts such as Henry Handel RICHARDSON's *The Getting of Wisdom*, Rosemary MANNING's *The Chinese Garden*, and OLIVIA's *Olivia*, to belong to the category of girls' boarding-school fiction, a genre preoccupied with the awakening of sexual and emotional passions in adolescent girls in single-sex educational settings. Often both oppressive and brooding, these fictions almost invariably feature a heroine who is ultimately expelled from the paradise that the school in some respects represents because of her articulation of passionate feelings and attachments, often to another pupil or a teacher. White's *Frost in May* is no exception in that the heroine Nanda Grey, attending a Catholic convent, produces a passionate novel which results in her

being expelled from school, even though she tries to defend her writings as fantasy. Boarding-school fictions, including this one, frequently have homoerotic currents though these are occasionally hinted at rather than made explicit. In *Frost in May*, begun when White was sixteen years old, White retold her own experiences of her parents' and her own conversion to Catholicism, and her experience of being expelled from school for writing novels. After her education at the Convent of the Sacred Heart in Roehampton, South London, and at St Paul's School for girls where her father was a classics master, White had a number of clerical and secretarial jobs before attending drama school in 1919, and becoming an actress in provincial theatres. Her first marriage ended in annulment. During that marriage she suffered from mental breakdowns and was in an asylum for nine months. Her second marriage was more secure, and it was during that marriage that she finished *Frost in May*. Her subsequent novels take up the fate of Nanda Grey, reborn as Clara Batchelor, after her expulsion from school. They are *The Lost Traveller* (1950), *The Sugar House* (1952), and *Beyond the Glass* (1954). In *The Hound and the Falcon* (1966) White described her relation to the Catholic faith. Other works by White published posthumously include *Three in a Room* (1947), *Strangers and Other Stories* (1981), and *Living with Minka and Curdy* (1970).

White, Edmund (1940–). One of the best-known contemporary gay US writers, White was born Edmund Valentine White III to middle-class Texan parents in Cincinnati, Ohio. His father, Edmund White Snr, a businessman, and his mother, Delilah Teddlie, a child psychologist, divorced when White was seven years old, and he and his sister spent their childhood alternately with their mother and father. White went to the exclusive Cranbrook Academy, then studied Chinese at the University of Michigan, and subsequently worked as a journalist and arts editor for a variety of magazines in New York between the 1960s and 1983. He also taught Creative Writing at various prestigious universities in the USA including Johns Hopkins University, Columbia University, Yale University, and, more recently, Princeton University. White was a member of the Violet Quill writers' group in New York. From 1983 White lived mostly in Paris. In 1985 he was diagnosed as HIV-positive. Whilst in Paris he met Hubert Sorin, an architect, then married, but soon to move in with White on a permanent basis. Their relationship was widely covered in the media, especially once Sorin had been diagnosed as suffering from full-blown AIDS. In 1994 White and Sorin went on a final trip to Morocco where Sorin died at a hospital in Marrakesh. White devoted his novel of 2000, *The Married Man*, to a depiction of their relationship. In 1995 White embarked on his relationship with the writer Michael Carroll (born 1965) with whom he moved to New York in 1999. White took some time to come to terms with his homosexuality but in the course of the 1970s he gradually emerged as one of the key writers on gay life and culture. Thus he collaborated with Charles Silverstein on *The Joy of Gay Sex: An Intimate Guide* (1977). He then produced *States of Desire: Travels in Gay America* (1980). His early fiction was less expressly focused on gay life. It included *Forgetting Elena* (1973) and *Nocturnes for the King of Naples* (1978). During the 1980s, fuelled by the emergence of HIV/AIDS, White became increasingly involved in gay men's activism, and was, like the playwright Larry KRAMER, one of the co-founders of the Gay Men's Health Center. He announced that he had tested HIV-positive in 1985. He began publishing autobiographical narratives exploring his history as a gay man in the USA in novels such as *A Boy's Own Story* (1982), *The Beautiful Room is Empty* (1988), and *A Farewell Symphony* (1997), which, like Paul MON-

ETTE's *Borrowed Time*, pays tribute to the death of White's partner Sorin from HIV/AIDS. Simultaneously with these novels White published non-fiction dealing both with HIV/AIDS and other issues in the gay community. With Adam Mars-Jones he published *The Darker Proof: Stories from a Crisis* (1987). He edited the *Faber Book of Gay Short Fiction* (1991), *The Burning Library: Writings on Art, Politics and Sexuality 1969–1993* (1994), and *Skinned Alive: Stories* (1995). In the 1990s he also published two biographies, *Genet: A Biography* (1993), for which he won the National Book Critics Circle Award, and *Proust* (1999).

White, Patrick (1912–90). Gay Australian writer, born in London as the only son of Ruth Withycombe and Victor Martindale who were second cousins. His parents' well-to-do background as members of the Hunter Valley grazier society of New South Wales embedded White in the conservative upper middle-class society of Sydney from whom he was able to dissociate himself only late in life. As a boy he was sent to Cheltenham College to be educated, a period that was one of intense misery. He began to understand his homosexuality but also felt that he had to keep it hidden, and this closeted attitude impacted both on his life and on his writing. In 1932 White went to King's College, Cambridge, to study modern languages. Subsequently he lived in London, mixing in artistic and homosexual circles. In 1940 he joined the Royal Air Force and, as part of the British Army Intelligence Unit in Alexandria in 1941, he met a Greek soldier, Manoly Lascaris, who was in the Royal Greek Army, and who was to become his life-long companion. In 1948 White returned to Australia for good. Lascaris followed him a month later, and the two set up house together in Sydney where they lived until White's death. Although they were open about their relationship White did not write directly about homosexuality until quite late in his

life, and he did not support gay rights activism. His closetedness may have guaranteed his place in society and his position as a writer at a time when homosexuality was much reviled, particularly in a relatively macho society such as Australia can be. Between 1939 and 1986 he wrote twelve novels that earned him a reputation as one of the great Australian writers of the twentieth century. His works include *The Aunt's Story* (1948), *Voss* (1957), *The Vivisector* (1970), and *The Twyborn Affair* (1979). In 1973 he was awarded the Nobel Prize for Literature. White finally came out as gay in 1981 with his autobiography *Flaws in the Glass*. His final novel *Memoirs of Many in One* (1986) proved controversial to homophobic critics.

Whitman, Walt (1819–92). Born in West Hills, Long Island, New York, the US poet and writer Whitman had little formal education and was the product of an unstable, poor background. Mainly self-taught, he had a variety of jobs, working as an office boy, printer, school teacher, and editor before gaining recognition for his work. His early writings include the short story 'The Child's Champion' (1941), reprinted as 'The Child and the Profligate'. This story was the first of his writings to contain a homoerotic content, interweaving issues of moral reform with a tale of male love and friendship. Whitman's novel *Franklin Evans* (1942) also dealt with the issue of temperance. Whitman became active in politics as a Democrat and in 1848 he travelled to New Orleans where he wrote for the *Crescent*. Whitman's fame rests on a collection of poetry entitled *Leaves of Grass*, which he first published as a collection of twelve poems and an eighteen-page preface in 1855, and in which he celebrated the USA as an open country characterized by a certain outdoor, rugged masculinity in contrast to the more 'feminine' culture of Europe. During his lifetime Whitman continued to work on this volume, revis-

ing and enlarging it. In 1856 he published a second edition which added twenty-one poems, and in 1860 he produced the third edition which had 122 further poems, including the sequence 'Calamus', celebrated as Whitman's key expression of his love for men, the male body, and male friendship. During Whitman's lifetime six further editions appeared. Whitman worked as a clerk in Washington during the Civil War. He also acted as a volunteer hospital visitor for the war wounded. This experience was retold in his prose work *Memoranda during the War* (1875), and in the poems *Drum-taps* (1865). The *Sequel* (1865–6) of these poems contained his famous elegy for President Lincoln, 'When Lilacs Last in Dooryard Bloom'd'. Whitman's work did not find the recognition it deserved during his lifetime, partly because of his outspoken celebration of the male body and of homosexuality, and partly because of his representation of a certain kind of working-class masculinity that he embraced. However, he was taken up by a number of other gay writers including Edward CARPENTER, and proved highly influential among later generations of writers such as E.M. FORSTER whose *Passage to India* is a response to Whitman's poem of 1871 of the same title. In 1873 Whitman had a stroke and went to live in Camden, New Jersey. He continued to write until the end of his life.

Wickham, Anna (1884–1947). Born in Wimbledon and educated in Queensland and New South Wales, Australia, Wickham was a poet whose real name was Edith Alice Mary Harper. Wickham came to London in 1905 and studied singing at Tree's Academy of Acting. She then went to Paris to continue her coaching for opera. In 1906 she married Patrick Hepburn, a solicitor and astronomer. Her marriage and the birth of her first child led Wickham to develop an interest in supporting working-class mothers. She had four sons altogether but, after the unexpected death of her 4-year-old son, she moved to Paris where she became involved with the lesbian writer and critic Natalie BARNEY with whom she conducted a passionate correspondence between 1926 and 1937. Wickham's first collection of poems, *Songs of John Oland* (1911), were privately published but she was then taken up by Harold Monro of the Poetry Bookshop, which, from 1914, published her work. Wickham's poetry dealt openly with women's sexuality as well as satirizing the English middle classes, and critiquing marriage. Her work was widely anthologized during her lifetime though she has since been largely forgotten. Her publications include *Poetry and Drama* (1914), *The Contemplative Quarry* (1915), *The Man with a Hammer* (1916), *The Little Old House* (1921), and *Richards' Shilling Selections* (1936). Wickham committed suicide in 1947. Subsequently her work was republished as *Selected Poems* (1971), and as *The Writings of Anna Wickham: Free Woman and Poet* (1984).

Wilde, Oscar (1854–1900). Born in Dublin, Ireland, the son of Jane Francesca Elgee who published under the pseudonym Speranza and of Sir William Wilde, an Irish surgeon, Oscar Fingal O'Flahertie Wills Wilde has become the key figure in the literary canon of gay literature for the late nineteenth century. He owes his fame as much to his brilliantly witty writing as to his dandyish and aestheticist lifestyle that resulted in the famous trials of 1895. Wilde was a brilliant classical scholar who went to Trinity College, Dublin, and then to Magdalen College, Oxford. In 1878 his poem 'Ravenna' won the Newdigate Prize. Wilde considered himself a disciple of Walter PATER and while at Oxford had already begun the flamboyant camp existence that was to prove his downfall. A satirist of late Victorian society he nonetheless cultivated as well as derided that society. In 1882, following the publication of his first collection of *Poems*, he undertook a lecture tour of the

USA. His play *Vera* (1883) did not prove a success. Perhaps because in some respects he wanted to be part of the upper-class society he also despised he married Constance Lloyd with whom he had two sons. He wrote a collection of fairy-tales, *The Happy Prince and Other Tales* (1888), for his sons. From 1886 he became seriously involved in homosexual life when he met the Canadian Robbie Ross who became a close friend and executor of his literary will. Wilde's story of 1889, 'The Story of Mr H.W.', which he revised repeatedly and which was finally published in 1921, was a speculation about the young man addressed in SHAKESPEARE's sonnets and constitutes an interrogation of homosexuality. During the same period Wilde also wrote and published *Lord Arthur Savile's Crime, and Other Stories* (1891) and *The Picture of Dorian Gray*, which appeared in *Lippincott's Magazine* (1890) causing something of a scandal. In 1891 Wilde published a further collection of fairytales, *A House of Pomegranates*. His play *The Duchess of Padua* appeared in the same year. His *The Soul of Man under Socialism*, a plea for individualism and artistic freedom, was published in the same year. The year 1891 was also marked by Wilde meeting Lord Alfred DOUGLAS, then twenty-one, with whom he became involved in a passionate affair and through whom he was introduced into the homosexual world of London. The early 1890s, Wilde's period of intense homosexual activity, were also his most productive ones from a literary point of view. He wrote a series of plays that were great successes due to their epigrammatic style and witticisms. They were *Lady Windermere's Fan* (1892), *A Woman of no Importance* (1893), *An Ideal Husband* (1895), and *The Importance of Being Earnest* (1895). *Salomé* (1894) was refused a licence in England but performed by Sarah Bernhardt in Paris in 1896. In his plays Wilde did not address homosexuality directly but produced arch satires on contemporary upper and upper middle-class society. His interest in his writings in leading double lives, secrets, and mysterious situations can all be viewed as expressions of a gay sensibility. Lord Alfred Douglas's father, the Marquis of Queensbury, disapproved of his son's relationship with Wilde, insulting the latter publicly so as to draw him out into action. Encouraged by Douglas, Wilde initiated proceedings that ultimately resulted in his imprisonment for homosexual offences in 1895, having been sentenced to two years of hard labour that left Wilde bankrupt, debilitated, and distressed, and led to his exile in Paris in 1897. During his period of imprisonment Wilde wrote *De Profundis* (1905), which is in part a letter of reproach to Lord Alfred Douglas for having deserted him and in part an account of Wilde's suffering during his imprisonment. In 1898 he published *The Ballad of Reading Gaol*, a text inspired by his prison experiences. While in Paris he adopted the name Sebastian Melmoth, from the Irish writer Charles Robert Maturin's Gothic novel, *Melmoth, The Wanderer* (1820). The centenary of Wilde's death led to a spate of publications, exhibitions, and performances of his work and related to his work during the year 2000.

Wilhelm, Gale (1908–91). Lesbian US writer, born in Eugene, Oregon, the daughter of Ethel Gale Brewer and Wilson Price Wilhelm. Wilhelm was educated in Oregon, Ohio, and Washington. For most of her life she lived on the West Coast of America, in and around the San Francisco Bay Area. In 1935 she spent some time in New York City, working as an associate editor of *Literary America*. Following a long relationship with Helen Hope Rudolph Page, she settled with her second lover in Berkeley where they lived from 1948 until Wilhelm's death. Wilhelm had an independent income that enabled them to live without the necessity of having to earn a living. In the years prior

to Wilhelm's second relationship, between 1935 and 1945, Wilhelm published a number of poems, short stories, and six novels. *We Too Are Drifting* (1935) centres on the unhappy relationships a lesbian woodcut artist has with two women, one bisexual, the other young and 'innocent' but the object of her family's intervention. This novel is in many ways a period text, representing lesbianism as congenital and unhappy, and associating it with an artistic temperament. *No Letters for the Dead* (1936) is the story of a woman who supports herself through prostitution while her lover is in prison. Wilhelm's next novel, *Torchlight to Valhalla* (1938), was again lesbian in subject matter but, unlike her first one, had a happy outcome. Wilhelm's subsequent novels, *Bring Home the Bride* (1940), *Time between* (1943), and *Never Let Me Go* (1945) do not have any overt lesbian content. Following these, Wilhelm was not to write again though it is not quite clear why she abandoned writing.

Williams, Tennessee (1911–83). Born Thomas Lanier Williams in Mississippi to Edwina Dakin, a minister's daughter, and Cornelius Williams, a travelling salesman who called his son 'Miss Nancy', Williams was one of the greatest twentieth-century US playwrights. Williams's parents' marriage was not happy, and Williams sided with his mother. His deepest emotional attachment was to his sister Rose who was institutionalized by their mother in the 1930s and lobotomized after accusing their father of sexual abuse. Williams subsequently looked after his sister for the rest of his life, and for a long time found it difficult to forgive his mother this move. Williams was educated at the universities of Washington and Iowa, and in New York. Writing from his teenage years he began his career as a playwright in 1939 with *American Blues* (published 1948) and *Battle of Angels* (1940, published 1945, and revised in 1957 under the title *Orpheus Descend-*

ing). His play *The Glass Menagerie* (1944, published 1945), which is semi-autobiographical, featuring a frustrated southern belle mother and a crippled daughter, Laura, for whom the mother with the help of her son seeks to procure a 'gentleman caller', brought Williams his first success. His most famous play is *A Streetcar Named Desire* (1947) featuring Blanche DuBois, a character based on Williams's sister, whose desire for refinement is the object of ridicule of her brutally working-class brother-in-law Stanley Kowalski. Williams's passionate, highly sexually charged interrogation of certain types of masculinity and femininity in *Streetcar* opened this play for lesbian and gay interpretations. In recent years, *A Streetcar Named Desire* has been repeatedly appropriated by lesbian and gay theatre companies such as Bloolips and SPLIT BRITCHES. The latter's play *Belle Reprieve* (1991, published 1996) presents a butch–femme version of *Streetcar*. *Streetcar* brought Williams lasting international acclaim, especially after it was made into a Hollywood film featuring the then young Marlon Brando as Kowalski. Williams's dramas after *Streetcar* continued to be infused by a tense, sexually charged, melodramatic Southern atmosphere, full of frustrations and repressed passions. They included *The Rose Tattoo* (1950); the anti-naturalistic *Camino Real* (1953) in which the homosexual Baron de Charlus appears on stage; *Cat on a Hot Tin Roof* (1955), another play that was made into a highly successful Hollywood film; *Suddenly Last Summer* (1958), a play whose central character resembles Williams's sister Rose; *Sweet Bird of Youth* (1959); *The Night of the Iguana* (1962); and *Small Craft Warnings* (1970), which features an artist suffering from what one might describe as internalized homophobia, which he articulates in his monologues. Williams did not portray homosexuality in many of his plays though some have the quality of camp that allows homosex-

ual interpretations of his work for theatre. Homosexuality tends to feature as the unspoken and the not-lived in these plays. This is perhaps not surprising, given that he wrote most of them in the 1940s and 1950s, a period of intense homophobia in the USA. However, Williams also published short stories, memoirs, and a novella (*The Roman Spring of Mrs Stone*, 1950) and the first of these especially are more explicit about homosexuality. Williams himself did not come out until the publication of his *Memoirs* (1975). His *Collected Short Stories*, published two years after his death and including a preface he had written in the 1960s, are the most explicit of his writings about homosexuality, among them 'Hard Candy', 'The Mysteries of the Joy Rio', 'Open Arm', and 'Desire and the Black Masseur'. In his later years, Williams was a rather unhappy character whose life was marred by substance abuse. He died choking on the cap of a medicine bottle.

Wilson, Barbara (1950–). US novelist, publisher, and translator who grew up in Long Beach, California, and did not learn to read until she was seven years old. After college, in the late 1960s she travelled, teaching herself Spanish, German, and Norwegian. In the 1970s she worked for a time as an investigative journalist. In 1974 she moved permanently to Seattle. In 1976 she co-founded the Seal Press. In the 1980s Wilson – like Val MCDERMID, Katherine V. FORREST, Sarah DREHER, and other, often lesbian, female writers – first produced crime fiction based on a lesbian detective, Pam Nilsen. These novels include *Murder in the Collective* (1984), *Sisters of the Road* (1986), and *The Dog Collar Murders* (1989). In each of these Wilson takes up a contemporary socio-political issue ranging from racism to prostitution and sadomasochism in the lesbian community around which her narrative revolves. She has also published *Gaudi Afternoon* (1991), a crime novel featuring Reilly. Other works by Barbara

Wilson include the translated *Cora Sandel: Selected Short Stories* (1985) for which she received the Columbia Translation Prize, the novels *Ambitious Women* (1982) and *Cows and Horses* (1988), as well as two collections of short stories, *Thin Ice* and *Walking on the Moon* (1986).

Wilson, Elizabeth (1936–). British lesbian academic and writer, born in Devon who was educated at St Paul's Girls' School and at Oxford University where she studied English Literature, Wilson worked as a psychiatric social worker before becoming an academic. In 1973 she began teaching in Applied Social Studies at what was then North London Polytechnic and is now the University of North London. Wilson has had a long-term involvement with the women's movement and with lesbian and gay activism. Her partner is Angela Mason, the Executive Director of Stonewall, with whom she lives in North London. Together with Emma Healey, Mason co-edited a volume entitled *Stonewall 25: The Making of the Lesbian and Gay Community in Britain* (1994) to which Wilson contributed. Wilson herself has written many non-fiction texts including *Women in the Welfare State* (1977), *Only Halfway to Paradise* (1980), *Adorned in Dreams* (1985), *Hallucinations: Life in the Post-Modern City* (1988), and *The Sphinx in the City* (1991). Together with Juliet Ash she edited *Chic Thrills: A Fashion Reader* (1992). She has contributed regularly to the *Guardian* and *New Statesman and Society*. In 1982 she published *Mirror Writing: An Autobiography*, and she has also written a lesbian crime fiction novel, *The Lost Time Café* (1993).

Wilson, Lanford (1937–). Born in Lebanon, Missouri, to Violetta Tate Wilson and Ralph Eugene Wilson, gay American playwright Lanford Wilson had a somewhat unsettled childhood. His parents divorced when he was five years old, and

he moved with his mother to Springfield, Missouri, where she worked in a factory. After his mother's remarriage in Wilson's early teens, they moved to Ozark where Wilson went to high school, graduating in 1955. The following year he went to visit his father and step-family in San Diego, and for a time attended San Diego State before moving to Chicago, his base for six years. Then, in 1962, he moved to New York, where he became part of the avant-garde experimental theatre scene of Greenwich Village and had his plays produced at Caffe Cino and La Mama Experimental Theater. In 1969, together with Marshall Mason, Rob Thirkield, and Tanya Berezin, he founded the Circle Repertory Company with whom he has remained associated. Both his childhood in Missouri and his stay with his father informed his plays, the first manifesting itself in the Talley trilogy, the second in *Lemon Sky* (1970), which features Alan, trying to come to terms with his homosexuality as he seeks to get to know his estranged father. Wilson's early one-act play 'The Madness of Lady Bright' (1964) features a drag queen. *Balm in Gilead* (1965) also contained a number of gay characters. Wilson achieved success on Broadway with *The Gingham Dog* (1968), which centres on an inter-racial couple. The Talley trilogy, not written in chronological order, includes *Fifth of July* (1978), featuring the gay character Kenneth Talley trying to sell his home in Lebanon while his lover is working on a garden there, and *Talley's Folly* (1980), for which Wilson won the Pulitzer Prize in 1980. Other plays include *Burn This* (1987) and the one-act play *A Portrait of the Cosmos* (1987) in which a man accused of having murdered his gay lover is interrogated by an off-stage policeman.

Wilson, Sir Angus (1913–91). Born Angus Frank Johnstone-Wilson to a mother of South African descent and a Scottish father, the gay British writer Wilson, who had a rather oppressive childhood, was educated at Westminster and at Merton College, Oxford, where he gained an honours degree in History. In 1937 he started to work at the British Museum and, from 1942 until the end of the Second World War, he worked as a decoder at the Government Code and Cipher School. In 1946 he met Tony Garrett, the man who was to become his life-long companion and who nursed him in his final years when he had begun to suffer from dementia. After the Second World War Wilson continued to work at the British Museum where he became deputy superintendent of the Reading Room in 1949 and where he remained until 1955, resigning to devote his time to writing. Wilson's novels and short stories frequently feature homosexual characters. His first two collections of short stories, *The Wrong Set* (1949) and *Such Darling Dodos* (1950), were followed by a novel, *Hemlock and after* (1952), which centres on the attempts of a gay writer, Bernard Sands, to establish a writers' centre. Wilson's novel *Anglo-Saxon Attitudes* (1956) explored the issue of archaeological forgery and, like his previous novel, contained a middle-aged protagonist whose world and work is challenged by his mid-life experiences. Wilson soon became established as a satirist of English attitudes and snobbery. Following *A Bit off the Map* (1957), another collection of short stories, he published *The Middle Age of Mrs Eliot* (1958), a novel about a woman living with her younger gay brother and his companion who is trying to come to terms with her husband's death. Other novels include *The Old Men at the Zoo* (1961), *Late Call* (1964), *No Laughing Matter* (1967), a family saga which is partly autobiographical, *As If By Magic* (1973), and *Setting the World on Fire* (1980). In 1966 Wilson was appointed to a professorship at the University of East Anglia. He also held a variety of visiting professorships in the USA, and worked for the Arts Council of Great Britain and the Royal Society of Literature. In 1980

he was knighted for his services to literature. As well as his own fiction, Wilson produced studies of the writers Emile Zola (1950), Charles Dickens (1970), and Rudyard Kipling (1977). He also wrote an account of his own creative writing processes, *The Wild Garden* (1963), and a collection of critical writings, *Diversity and Depth in Fiction: Selected Critical Writings*, appeared in 1983.

Winckelmann, Johann Joachim (1717–68). Homosexual German art historian and scholar whose humble background as the son of a shoemaker did not prevent him from gaining the classical education that helped to establish him as the father of modern art history. In his writings Winckelmann celebrated Greek sculpture and the beauty of male nudes. Winckelmann attended the universities of Halle and Jena where he studied Theology, Medicine, Anatomy, and Physics. In 1742 he fell in love with a 14-year old pupil, Peter Lamprecht, with whom he subsequently lived until 1746. For a time Winckelmann was a schoolmaster in Seehausen, but from 1748 he worked as a librarian, first for a nobleman near Dresden, then for two cardinals in Italy where he lived for thirteen years following his conversion to Catholicism. Winckelmann's first work on Greek art, *Gedanken über die Nachahmungen der griechischen Werke in der Malerei und Bildhauerkunst* (*Thoughts on the Imitation of Greek Works in Painting and Sculpture*) was published in 1755, a year before he left for Italy. His major work, *Geschichte der Kunst des Altertums* (1764; *History of the Art of Antiquity*), was highly influential in suggesting that the political context in which art is created is central to its success. Winckelmann influenced writers such as Walter PATER and Johann Wolfgang von Goethe. The latter was one of the first to acknowledge Winckelmann's homosexuality. Winckelmann had a range of homosexual affairs and relationships throughout his life as his personal correspondence indicates. He was stabbed to death by a common thief.

Winsloe, Christa (1888–1944). Born in Darmstadt into a well-to-do family and educated at the strict Prussian Kaiserin-Augusta-Stift in Potsdam before being sent to a Swiss finishing school, Winsloe rebelled against her family's expectations. In 1909 she moved to Munich to study sculpture, and her sculptural work was as important to her as her writing. In 1913 she married a rich Hungarian, Lajos Hatvany, and lived on his estate until their divorce in 1924. During her marriage she wrote an unpublished novel, *Das schwarze Schaf* (*The Black Sheep*) about a girl who sees herself as a social outsider. After her divorce Winsloe went back to Munich where she resumed sculpting and continued to write. *Männer kehren Heim* (*Men Return Home*; date unknown) is a novella from this period, focusing on questions of sexual identity and gender roles. This theme also dominates her most famous work, which was based on her play *Ritter Nérestan* (*Nérestan the Knight*), first performed in Leipzig in 1930. The title was changed to *Gestern und heute* (*Yesterday and Today*) for its Berlin production and, in 1931, it was made into the film *Mädchen in Uniform* (*Girls in Uniform*), which is the title of the film script written by Christa Winsloe for this all-female production of a text that found its final form in the novel *Das Mädchen Manuela*, published in 1933 in Amsterdam, and a year later in Leipzig and Vienna where it was quickly banned by the Nazi regime. *Mädchen in Uniform*, which is probably the best-known title of this story, belongs to the genre of lesbian boarding-school fiction. Like many of these texts it centres on the tragic relationship between two female protagonists, in this instance a pupil and her teacher. Based on Winsloe's own boarding-school experiences, the story features Manuela von Meinhardis who falls in love with her teacher Fräulein von Bernburg. Following the performance of a school play in which Manuela, cross-dressed, plays the male lead, Manuela declares her love for her teacher but the teacher does not support her in the ensuing isolation from her fellow pupils and teachers that the headmistress imposes on Manuela, and Manuela commits suicide by jumping from a window. This tragic ending was suppressed in one film where the suicide is prevented by an intervention from Manuela's fellow pupils. However, as a narrative the story has much in common with similar fictions such as Rosemary MANNING's *The Chinese Garden* and Olivia's (see STRACHEY BUSSY, DOROTHY) *Olivia*, for example. Winsloe's own personal life, aided by her financial independence, changed once she had returned to Munich. She met the US journalist Dorothy Thompson in the early 1930s and the two embarked on a relationship, conducted both in Europe and in the USA, which lasted until 1935 when Winsloe returned to Europe as she could not find work in the USA and Thompson felt uneasy about living as a lesbian. Winsloe's 1935 novel, published only in English, *Life Begins*, centred autobiographically on a sculptress deciding to live openly as a lesbian with another woman. Following her last novel, *Passagiere* (1938; *Passengers*), Winsloe turned to writing film scripts. Now living in Paris, Winsloe was forced to move to the Côte d'Azur to flee from the Nazis. There she lived with her lover, the Swiss writer Simone Gentet. In 1944 the two women were shot dead in a wood near Cluny. Initially, it was suggested that they had been shot by members of the French Resistance Movement for collaborating with the Germans but it was later discovered that they had been the victims of common criminals.

Winterson, Jeanette (1959–). One of the best-known contemporary lesbian British writers, Winterson was born in Manchester and adopted by Constance and John William Winterson, Pentecostal evangelists. She rebelled against her upbringing in a small-town, evangelical atmosphere, leaving home at fifteen. While she supported herself through various jobs she attended Accrington College of Further Education, before eventually going to St Catherine's College, Oxford, from where she graduated in 1981. She then moved to London, working at the Roundhouse Theatre and in publishing. In 1985 *Boating for Beginners* appeared but it was with her other novel of the same year, *Oranges Are not the Only Fruit* that she achieved instant success and won the Whitbread Prize for a First Novel. This novel marked the beginning of her writing career, and established two of the characteristics that have become a hallmark of her work: the use of divergent stylistic devices that sometimes make her novels postmodern, and an interest in gender roles and sexual identities that in its play with ambiguity and uncertainty has rendered Winterson a writer of queer as well as of lesbian fiction. *Oranges Are not the Only Fruit* constitutes a kind of novel of development or *Bildungsroman* in which the autobiographically inflected heroine seeks to come to terms with her lesbian identity within a small-town evangelical community in which the males are largely sidelined and women are constructed as the driving force of religious zeal. Like Rita Mae BROWN's *Rubyfruit Jungle* this novel represents a lesbian-coming-to-identity tale by focusing on a rebellious and resilient central figure who in the end leaves behind her small-town community in order to assume a lesbian life elsewhere. *Oranges Are not the Only Fruit* was celebrated partly for its often highly comical presentation of small-town life but it was acclaimed even more because of its divergent style. Partly magic realist, the novel is divided into chapters that reflect the first seven books of the Old Testament. It also contains mythical and fairytale style narratives, offering alterna-

tive, interpretive discourses on the heroine's experiences, one of which, predictably, turns out to be with a girl who is only temporarily interested in another woman and then goes off to marry a local lad. In 1990 *Oranges Are not the Only Fruit* was made into a highly popular television series. Following on from this novel, Winterson went on to write *The Passion* (1987), which is set in the Napoleonic Wars and which begins to play more fully on queer identities and gender ambiguities than *Oranges* did. Winterson won the John Llewelyn Rhys Memorial Prize for best writer under thirty-five for this novel. In 1989 she published *Sexing the Cherry*, which begins in Restoration London with the characters of the Dog Woman and her son Jordan. This novel makes an interesting comparison to Rose Tremain's novel *Restoration* (1989) in which gender and the same period Winterson starts off with are also at stake. *Sexing the Cherry* won the E.M. FORSTER Award from the American Academy of Letters and Arts. *Written on the Body* (1992), which has a narrator whose gender is never revealed, is an erotic account of the narrator's passion for a terminally ill woman. This novel was followed by *Art and Lies* (1994) and *Gut Symmetries* (1997), the story of a triangular relationship between a man, his mistress, and the man's wife in which, eventually, the wife leaves the husband for his mistress. Winterson has also published *Art Objects: Essays on Ecstasy and Effrontery* (1995), and a volume of short stories, *The World and Other Places* (1998). A book on fitness for women, *Fit for the Future: The Guide for Women Who Want to Live Well*, appeared in 1986, and she has edited various collections of short stories, among them *Passion Fruit: Romantic Fiction with a Twist* (1986). Her fiction is marked by stylistic innovation and experimental representations of ambiguous identities. Together with her long-term partner, the academic Margaret (Peggy) Reynolds, Winterson lives in London and Gloucestershire where they have a farm.

Wittig, Monique (1935–). Born in the Haut-Rhin region of France, lesbian writer Monique Wittig went to Paris to study and worked in publishing. Her first novel, *L'Opoponax* (1964; translated as *The Opoponax*, 1966) won the Prix Médicis. This was followed by *Les Guérillères* (1969). In these early novels Wittig produced the lesbian feminist experimental form of writing which became her hallmark. During early 1970 Wittig became involved in the French feminist movement. She then wrote *Le Corps lesbien* (1973; translated as *The Lesbian Body*, 1975). In 1975 she met Sande Zeig. Zeig was studying mime and teaching karate in Paris; Wittig was one of her pupils. They became involved and went to Greece to write *Brouillon pour un dictionnaire des amantes* (1979; translated as *Lesbian Peoples: Materials for a Dictionary*, 1979). Both women were members of the International Lesbian Front created in Frankfurt in October 1974. In 1976 Wittig and Zeig went to the USA, to live in California. Wittig went on to write *Virgile, non* (1985; translated as *Across the Acheron*, 1987) and *Le Voyage sans fin* (1985; translated as *Constant Journey*. The latter is a play that Wittig co-directed with Zeig for the Théâtre du Rond-Point in France in 1985. While her experimental writing established Wittig as an innovative artist, her most powerful impact has been her essay, 'One is not Born a Woman' (1981), the title a quotation from Simone de BEAUVOIR's *The Second Sex* (1949), which was published in her collection of essays, *The Straight Mind and Other Essays* (1992). In this essay she famously proclaims a statement she had made at the 1978 annual MLA convention, namely that 'lesbians are not women'. Wittig's critique of heterosexuality and heterosexual institutions suggests, as does the work of some Italian feminists and in reference to Simone de Beauvoir's

pioneering ideas, that 'woman' is a construct within patriarchal culture and language, and as such already so heavily invested with heteropatriarchal meanings that the word cannot be applied to lesbians who by their sexuality refuse heteropatriarchy. Wittig's essay is part of a larger debate of how heteropatriarchy and women's oppression within it might be resisted. Her thinking is both radical and bears some affinity to the work of other radical lesbian thinkers such as Luce IRIGARAY and Marilyn FRYE. It refuses the notion of the 'lesbian continuum' opened up by Adrienne RICH and celebrated by some of the more moderate lesbian critics such as Lillian FADERMAN. Wittig, who has held various academic posts in the the USA, has also written short stories, critical pieces, and plays. The last include *L'Amant vert* (1967; *The Green Lover*), produced in Bolivia in 1969, and *Le Grand Cric-Jules, récreation, dialogue pour deux frères et la soeur*, a series of short plays commissioned by Radio Stuttgart.

Wolff, Charlotte (1897–1986). Lesbian German-Jewish writer, medical practitioner, psychiatrist, and cheirologist (reader of hands for the purposes of a medical diagnosis), Wolff was born as the second daughter into a well-to-do, middle-class family in Riesenburg, West Prussia. Her father was a corn merchant, her mother as was common in those days a housewife. The family moved to Danzig when Charlotte was thirteen years old and she attended grammar school there. She then went to Freiburg to study medicine, on the advice of her father who thought that medicine would provide Wolff with a livelihood. At Freiburg she took Philosophy under the philosophers E. Husserl and M. Heidegger as well as pursuing her medical degree. Wolff then attended several other universities in Germany including Tübingen and Berlin, where she gained her medical degree in 1928. She was then appointed to a hospital in Berlin but left Nazi Germany for Paris in 1933 and from there went to London in 1936, aided by Aldous and Maria Huxley. She was given a residence permit in 1938, and from 1952 was allowed to practise as a doctor again. A lesbian since childhood, though in the 1920s she had a brief period of doubt regarding her sexual identity, Wolff published poetry in 1924, mainly love poetry addressed to women, in the monthly magazine *Vers und Prosa* (*Verse and Prose*). Wolff devoted her professional life to writings on cheirology and to the exploration of sexual identities. These works include *The Human Hand* (1924), *A Psychology of Gesture* (1945), *The Hand in Psychological Diagnosis* (1952), *Love between Women* (1971), and *Bisexuality: A Study* (1977). Significantly she thought that male and female homosexuality were two distinct forms of sexual identity. From 1936 until her death Wolff lived in London. However, from the mid-1970s she began to make return visits to Berlin and she became a very influential figure in the German lesbian and in the German feminist movement, contributing to the autonomous summer universities set up in Berlin. In 1976 she published *An Older Love*, a lesbian novel in which the depiction of the lives of four women, two of them Jewish refugees in London, was in some respects autobiographically inflected. In her two volumes of memoirs, *On the Way to Myself* (1969), and in particular in *Hindsight* (1980), Wolff wrote freely about her lesbian relationships and her understanding of lesbianism.

Woods, Gregory (1953–). Born in Cairo, and brought up on the Gold Coast and in Ghana, this British gay poet and academic completed his doctorate at the University of East Anglia, Norwich, in 1983. He taught English at the University of Salerno in Italy between 1980 and 1984, returning to teach in the UK where he became Professor of Lesbian and Gay Studies at Nottingham Trent University, the first

person in the UK to have such a title, and one that was not achieved without controversy and the homophobic reactions to be expected in a country that enacted the infamous Section 28, forbidding, *inter alia*, the 'promotion' in education of homosexuality as an accepted way of living. Woods has been highly influential in recovering gay literature for the canon. His academic works include *Articulate Flesh: Male Homo-eroticism and Modern Poetry* (1987) and *A History of Gay Literature: A Male Tradition* (1997). A collection of poetry, *May I Say Nothing*, appeared in 1998, and a second collection, *The District Commissioner's Dream*, is due out in 2002.

Woolf, Virginia (1882–1941). Born Adeline Virginia Stephen at Hyde Park Gate, Woolf was the daughter of Julia Pattle Duckworth whose first marriage had ended with the death of her husband, leaving her with three children, and of Leslie Stephen, man of letters and editor of the *Dictionary of National Biography*. Woolf lived at Hyde Park Gate with her sister Vanessa and her brothers until 1904 when her father died. They then moved to Bloomsbury where they became the centre of the Bloomsbury Group, which began with Woolf's brother Thoby's meetings with artist friends in 1905. Woolf's teens and twenties were marked by the deaths of several of her closest relations including her mother in 1895, her half-sister Stella who had become a mother substitute in 1897, her father, and then in 1906 her brother Thoby. Woolf experienced mental breakdowns in the wake of two of these deaths, and these breakdowns remained with her throughout her life, marring her existence and finally leading to her suicide by walking into the river Ouse near her home at Rodmell, Sussex, when she was fifty-nine years old. Following Stella's death her sister Vanessa became Woolf's mother substitute. Woolf, who had been sexually molested by her half-brother Gerald Duckworth when a child, married Leonard Woolf, a penniless member of the Bloomsbury Group, in 1912 but throughout her life had strong emotional attachments to women, frequently older than herself and intellectually highly active. Among these was Vita SACKVILLE-WEST, the only woman with whom Woolf appears to have enjoyed a physical relationship as well as an emotional one. They began their relationship in 1922. It appears to have lasted until 1928 after which they remained friends but Woolf found it hard to cope with Sackville-West's other relationships with women. Their strong friendship continued until 1934. During the ten years of their friendship both women were highly productive as writers. Woolf is celebrated as one of the key figures of modernist writing. One specific interest for lesbian readers in her work is the repeated representation of intense emotional, possibly erotic, attachments between women, which she delineates in her work. Thus in her novel *Mrs Dalloway* (1925), the protagonist Clarissa Dalloway remembers her friend Sally Seton with whom she fell in love when they were girls. In *To the Lighthouse* (1927) Lily Briscoe is powerfully infatuated with Mrs Ramsay. The central character in *Orlando* (1928) is based on Vita Sackville-West, presenting a figure who changes from being a man to being a woman, living through four centuries, and enjoying relations with both women and men. In *A Room of One's Own* (1929), a text based on a series of lectures given at Newnham and at Girton College, Cambridge, Woolf pleaded powerfully for the need to represent women loving women. In *Between the Acts* (1941) Miss La Trobe is both an artist and a lesbian. Woolf's personal attachments to women, her representation of feminine consciousnesses, her repeated

engagement with questions of gender, identity, and sexual inequalities between women and men, as well as her writings on attachments between women have made her one of the leading literary figures of the lesbian canon. Her concern was, however, in part in keeping with her time, with women's intellectual rather than sexual or sensual emancipation. Thus she defended Radclyffe HALL's novel *The Well of Loneliness*, which was the object of an obscenity trial in 1928 in the name of freedom of speech rather than in terms of support for its representation of the lesbian as invert. Together with her husband she founded the Hogarth Press in 1917, a publishing house that became highly influential in publicizing the work of many leading modernists, including lesbian and gay writers such as Gertrude STEIN and Katherine MANSFIELD, and translations of the writings of the 'founder' of psychoanalysis, Sigmund Freud. Her other writings include the novels *The Voyage Out* (1915), *Night and Day* (1919), *Jacob's Room* (1922), *The Waves* (1931), *Flush* (1933), and *The Years* (1937). Her essays appeared in several collections including *The Common Reader* (1925). Some short stories were published as *The Haunted House* in 1943. Both her diaries and her letters have been published in several edited versions.

Wu Tsao (b. *c.* 1800–?). Chinese poet, the daughter of a merchant who herself apparently married a merchant. Wu Tsao wrote erotic poetry addressed to courtesans, and is considered one of the great Chinese lesbian poets. In her later life she led a secluded existence, becoming a Taoist priestess. Her poetry has been translated by Kenneth Rexroth and appears in a collection entitled *Women Poets of China* (1972).

Y

Yourcenar, Marguerite (1903–87). Born Marguerite Antoinette Jeanne Marie Ghislaine Cleenewerck de Crayencour to Franco-Belgian parents in Brussels, Yourcenar lost her mother in early infancy and was brought up by her wealthy and very much older father Michel with whom she travelled during her childhood. Educated privately, she showed an early aptitude for languages, learning English, Latin, Greek, and Italian. Her literary inclinations also manifested themselves from an early age. She chose the name Yourcenar, an anagram of her last name, in her teens during which time she had already published two books privately. Yourcenar kept her private life very much separate from her literary existence. In 1937 she met Grace Frick, an American academic, with whom she was to live until Frick's death from breast cancer in 1979. Yourcenar and Frick divided their life between the USA and France where Yourcenar was to become one of the greatest writers of the twentieth century. Much of Yourcenar's family inheritance was lost in the Wall Street crash of 1929 but her literary success with her novel *Alexis* in the same year allowed her to rely increasingly on her earnings from her publications. *Alexis* centres on a married man whose homosexuality, not mentioned as such in the novel, leads him to leave his family in order to assume a new identity in line with his sexuality. Whilst Yourcenar rarely portrayed lesbians, her works, in some respects rather like those of Mary RENAULT, presented male homosexual characters within various classical and historical settings and with great restraint regarding the expression of sexuality. From 1939 Yourcenar and Frick lived in the USA, initially in New York, and from 1950 at 'Petit Plaisance', a house at Mount Desert Island, off the coast of Maine, an area they had first visited in 1942. In 1959 Frick was diagnosed as suffering from breast cancer from which she eventually died. Yourcenar continued to live at 'Petit Plaisance' until her own death. Yourcenar published in a wide variety of genres, including poetry, fiction, drama, the essay, and autobiography. Her work was informed by an extensive knowledge of history and culture. Yourcenar's many works include *A Coin in Nine Hands* (1934; revised 1959), *La Nouvelle Eurydice* (1931; *The New Eurydice*), *Oriental Stories* (1938), *Coup de grâce* (1939), *Les Mémoires d'Hadrian* (1951; *Memoirs of Hadrian*, 1954), and *L'Œuvre au noir* (1968; *The Abyss*, 1976). In 1955 Yourcenar won the Page One Award of the Newspaper Guild of New York for *Memoirs of Hadrian* for which she also won the Prix Femina Vacaresco. This novel, a farewell letter by the Emperor Hadrian to his successor Marcus Aurelius, was one of Yourcenar's greatest literary successes. *The Abyss*, for which Yourcenar won the Prix Femina, was the object of a legal wrangle between the French publishing houses Gallimard and Plon in 1966, which ended with Yourcenar being awarded the choice of publisher. She chose Gallimard who then republished all her work. In 1969 Yourcenar was elected to the Royal Belgian Academy in 1969. In 1971 two volumes of Yourcenar's plays were published – for these she won the Prix Monaco in 1973. When the first volume of her grand genealogical autobiographical novel *The Labyrinth of the World* appeared in 1974, she won the Grand Prix des Lettres of the French Ministry of Culture (1975). This first volume entitled *Souvenirs Pieux* (*Dear Departed*) was followed by a second volume, *Archives du nord* (*Archives of the North*) in 1977, and a final volume, *Quoi? L'eternité* (*What? Eternity*), appeared posthumously in 1988. Yourcenar's greatest literary hour came in 1980 when, her French citizenship restored, she became the first woman to be elected to the *Académie française*.

Z

Zahle, Vilhelmine (1868–1940). Born in Copenhagen to Clara and Peter Christian Zahle, this Danish writer lost her mother when she was seven months old and was brought up by her maternal grandparents. Zahle wanted to be an actress and studied with Agnes Nyrop, an actress from the Royal Theatre of Copenhagen, to whom she was attracted. In 1890 she published *Vildsomme Veje* (*Pathless Ways*), which contained the story 'Ogsaa en Kærlighedshistorie' ('Also a Love Story'). This story centres on a young woman's emotional attachment to another woman, older than herself. This love is 'resolved' through both women's marriages. The story is one of the first in the Danish language to deal with same-sex love between women. In the year after its publication Zahle married Frederik Vilhelm Gjøl Korch. The marriage was not happy and in 1899 Zahle left her husband together with their daughter. She then earned her living as a journalist and private tutor before finally settling in Vejle, Jutland, where she worked as a teacher.

Zapata, Luis (1951–). Gay Mexican writer whose work centres on homosexual relationships, the position of the sexual and social outsider, and the tension between desire and reality. Born into an upper middle-class family in rural Chilpancingo, Zapata frequented the local cinema to escape that environment. The cinema, popular culture, and camp became a recurrent aspect of his writing. His novels include the acclaimed *Hasta en las mejores familias* (1975; *Even in the Best Families*), *Las aventuras, desaventuras y sueños de Adonis García, el vampiro de la colonia Roma* (1979; *Adonis García, a Picaresque Novel*) about a hustler in Mexico City, *De pétalos peremes* (1981; *Perennial Petals*), *Melodrama* (1983), *En jirones* (1985; *In Tatters*), *La hermana secreta de Angélica María* (1989; *The Secret Sister of Angélica María*), *¿Por qué mejor no nos vamos?* (1992; *Why Don't We Just Leave?*), and *La más fuerte pasión* (1995; *The Strongest Passion*). Zapata has also published two collections of short stories, *De Amor* (1983; *About Love*) and *Ese amor que hasta ayer nos quemaba* (1989; *That Love that Was Burning Us until Recently*). The dialogic nature of Zapata's writings, his explicit engagement with homosexuality, and his camp and often somewhat melodramatic narratives make Zapata one of the foremost contemporary gay Mexican writers.

Zaremba, Eve (1930–). Lesbian Canadian writer and activist who was born in Poland but left the country in 1940, initially for England where she attended school, and then for Canada to which she emigrated in 1952. In 1972 Zaremba published *Privilege of Sex: A Century of Canadian Women*. She is one of the first lesbian writers to produce a series of detective fictions based on a central lesbian detective figure, in her case that of Helen Karemos. Her first novel featuring that character was *A Reason to Kill* (1978). It was followed by *Work for a Million* (1987), *Beyond Hope* (1989), *Uneasy Lies* (1990), and *The Butterfly Effect* (1994). Zaremba has been a central figure in feminist lesbian activism in Toronto where she helped found the Women's Place in 1972, the Women's Credit Union in 1974, and the Lesbian Organization of Toronto in 1976. In 1978 she co-founded *Broadside*, a feminist newspaper.

Further reading

Austen, Roger (1977) *Playing the Game: The Homosexual Novel in America*, Indianapolis: Bobbs-Merrill.

Benstock, Shari (1986) *Women of the Left Bank: Paris 1900–1940*, Austin: University of Texas Press.

Bergman, David (1994) *The Violet Quill: The Emergence of Gay Writing After Stonewall*, New York: St Martin's Press.

—— (1991) *Gayiety Transfigured: Gay Self-representation in American Literature*, Madison: University of Wisconsin Press.

Clum, John M. (1992) *Acting Gay: Male Homosexuality in Modern Drama*, New York: Columbia University Press.

Curtin, Kaier (1987) *We Can Always Call Them Bulgarians*, Boston: Alyson.

Damon, Gene and Stuart, Lee (1967) *The Lesbian in Literature: A Bibliography*, San Francisco: Daughters of Bilitis.

D'arch-Smith, Timothy (1970) *Love in Earnest: Some Notes on the Lives and Writings of English 'Uranian' poets from 1889 to 1930*, London: Routledge.

Duberman, Martin, Vicinus, Martha and Chauncey, George, Jnr (eds) (1989) *Hidden from History: Reclaiming the Gay and Lesbian Past*, New York: New American Library.

Edelman, Lee (1994) *Homographesis: Essays in Gay Literary and Cultural Theory*, New York: Routledge.

Faderman, Lillian (1991) *Odd Girls Out and Twilight Lovers: A History of Lesbian Life in 20th-Century America*, New York: Columbia University Press.

—— (1981) *Surpassing the Love of Men: Romantic Friendship and Love between Women from the Renaissance to the Present*, New York: William Morrow & Co.

Foster, David William (1997) *Sexual Textualities: Essays on Queer-ing Latin American Writing*, Austin: University of Texas Press.

—— (1991) *Gay and Lesbian Themes in Latin American Writing*, Austin: University of Texas.

Foster, Jeannette H. (1956) *Sex Variant Women in Literature*, New York: Vantage Press.

Grahn, Judy (1984) *Another Mother Tongue: Gay Words, Gay Worlds*, Boston: Beacon Press.

Grier, Barbara (1981) *The Lesbian in Literature*, Tallahassee: Naiad Press.

—— (1976) *Lesbiana: Book Reviews from The Ladder*, Tallahassee: Naiad Press.

Griffin, Gabriele (1993) *Heavenly Love? Lesbian Images in 20th-Century Writing*, Manchester: Manchester University Press.

Halperin, David (1990) *One Hundred Years of Homosexuality and Other Essays on Greek Love*, New York: Routledge.

Hobby, Elaine and White, Chris (eds) (1991) *What Lesbians Do in Books*, London: Women's Press.

Hohmann, Joachim S. (ed.) (1979) *Der heimliche Sexus: homosexuelle Belletristik in Deutschland von 1900 bis Heute*, Frankfurt am Main: Förster.

Jay, Karla and Glasgow, Joanne (eds) (1990) *Lesbian Texts and Contexts*, New York: New York University Press.

Jones, Sonya (ed.) (1998) *Gay and Lesbian Literature since World War II: History and Memory*, Binghampton, New York: Harrington Park Press.

Jongh, Nicholas (1992) *Not in Front of the Audience: Homosexuality on Stage*, London: Routledge.

Koestenbaum, Wayne (1989) *Double Talk: The Erotics of Male Literary Collaboration*, New York: Routledge.

Levin, James (1991) *The Gay Novel in America*, New York: Garland.

Lilly, Mark (ed.) (1990) *Lesbian and Gay Writing: An Anthology of Critical Essays*, London: Macmillan.

Malinowski, Sharon and Brelin, Christa (eds) (1995) *The Gay and Lesbian Literary Companion*, Detroit: Visible Ink.

Marti, Madeleine (1992) *Hinterlegte Botschaften: die Darstellung lesbischer Frauen in der deutschsprachigen Literatur seit 1945*, Stuttgart: J.B. Metzler.

Martin, Robert K. (1979) *The Homosexual Tradition in American Poetry*, Austin: University of Texas Press.

Nelson, Emmanuel S. (ed.) (1993) *Contemporary Gay American Novelists: A Bio-bibliographical Critical Sourcebook*, Westport, CT: Greenwood Press.

Norton, Rictor (1992) *Mother Clap's Molly House: The Gay Subculture in England 1700–1830*, London: Gay Men's Press.

Picano, Felice (1980) *A True Likeness: Lesbian and Gay Writing Today*, New York: Sea Horse.

Popp, Wolfgang (1992) *Männerliebe: Homosexualität und Literatur*, Stuttgart: J.B. Metzler.

Reade, Brian (ed.) (1971) *Sexual Heretics: Male Homosexuality in English Literature from 1850 to 1900*, New York: Coward-McCann.

Rieder, Ines (1994) *Wer mit wem? Hundert Jahre lesbische Liebe*, Wien: Wiener Frauenverlag.

Roberts, J.R. (1981) *Black Lesbians: An Annotated Bibliography*, Tallahassee: Naiad Press.

Rule, Jane (1975) *Lesbian Images*, Trumansburg, New York: The Crossing Press.

Sedgwick, Eve Kosofsky (1993) *Tendencies*, Chapel Hill: University of North Carolina Press.

—— (1990) *Epistemology of the Closet*, Berkeley: University of California Press.

—— (1985) *Between Men: English Literature and Male Homosocial Desire*, New York: Columbia University Press.

Stambolian, George and Marks, Elaine (eds) (1979) *Homosexualities and French Literature*, Ithaca, New York: Cornell University Press.

Still, Judith and Worton, Michael (eds) (1993) *Textuality and Sexuality: Reading Theories and Practices*, Manchester: Manchester University Press.

Summers, Claude J. (ed.) (1995) *The Lesbian and Gay Literary Heritage: A Reader's Companion to the Writers and Their Works, from Antiquity to the Present*, London: Bloomsbury.

—— (ed.) (1992) *Homosexuality in Renaissance and Enlightenment England: Literary Representations in Historical Context*, New York: Haworth Press.

—— (1990) *Gay Fictions, Wilde to Stonewall: Studies in a Male Homosexual Literary Tradition*, New York: Continuum.

Woods, Gregory (1987) *Articulate Flesh: Male Homo-eroticism and Modern Poetry*, New Haven: Yale University Press.

Young, Ian (1975) *The Male Homosexual in Literature: A Bibliography*, Metuchen, New York: Scarecrow.

Zimmerman, Bonnie (1990) *The Safe Sea of Women: Lesbian Fiction 1969–1989*, Boston: Beacon Press.